UNITED

Born in London, Graham Betts attended his first game in 1965 and has seldom been absent since, family commitments notwithstanding. Aside from a number of football books he has also written extensively on music, an industry he has worked in for the last twenty or so years. He lives in Aston Clinton in Buckinghamshire with his wife and two children.

UNITED

DAY-TO-DAY LIFE AT OLD TRAFFORD

GRAHAM BETTS

MAINSTREAM
PUBLISHING

EDINBURGH AND LONDON

First published in Great Britain in 1998 by
MAINSTREAM PUBLISHING COMPANY (EDINBURGH) LTD
7 Albany Street
Edinburgh EH1 3UG

ISBN 1 84018 038 2

A catalogue record for this book is available from the British Library

Typeset in 9½ on 12pt Times
Printed and bound in Great Britain by Butler and Tanner Ltd, Frome

INTRODUCTION

Manchester United are probably the most popular club side in the world. Others in Italy and Spain may be more successful in terms of European trophies won, but none has the depth of support that United can muster. A Manchester United shirt (irrespective of how regularly they change them!) is recognised from the United States to the United Arab Emirates and just about everywhere in-between.

From humble beginnings as a works side formed by railway workers to unrivalled success in the FA Premier League, the United story has always been a mixture of highs and lows; almost going out of business at the turn of the century, the Munich disaster and relegation to the Second Division may well have been the depths of despair, but success in the European Cup, the European Cup-Winners' Cup and countless domestic trophies are indicative of a club that invariably bounces back.

Whilst countless United books before have tended to start with the club's humble beginnings and work their way through to the present day, this book tells the United story day by day and enables the reader to follow the Munich disaster, the run that led to the European Cup in 1968 and the ending of the championship-barren spell in 1993. There is also the ongoing story of George Best, perhaps the most talented footballer of his or any other generation but whose frequent disappearances are almost worth a volume of their own!

A book of this kind could not have been written without the invaluable help and assistance from numerous others, and I am therefore indebted to the following people for the part they have played in getting this project off the ground: John Thorne, Martin Peattie, Chris Wickens and John Skiller, all of whose lives seem bound up in the comings and goings at Old Trafford. Thanks also to Richard Lerman and Brian Watts for their encouragement along the way, and to Bill Campbell at Mainstream.

I would also like to thank my family, Caroline, Jo and Steven, who now find they are allowed into all of the rooms in the house.

The photographs in this book have been supplied by Wellard Huxley Promotions, Bob Bond and John Allen (proprietor of *The Football Card Collector* magazine).

JANUARY 1ST

1886   Harold Halse born in Stratford in East London. After a remarkable two seasons with Southend United, during which he scored 200 goals, Harold was snapped up by United for £350 in March 1908. Although he didn't score with the same regularity at Old Trafford, he was one of the most dangerous forwards of his age and would go on to score six goals in the FA Charity Shield match against Swindon. He won a League championship and FA Cup winners' medal whilst at United, and was sold to Aston Villa for £1,200 in 1912, adding a second FA Cup winners' medal at the end of his first season at Villa Park. His third appearance in the final came in 1915 when he was playing for Chelsea, although this time he had to settle for a runners-up medal. At the end of the First World War he returned to Chelsea, subsequently moving on to Charlton in 1921, retiring in 1923 and then scouting for the club for a further two years.

1892	Nottingham Forest	H	Football Alliance	1-1
1895	Port Vale	H	Second Division	3-0
1896	Grimsby Town	H	Second Division	3-2
1897	Newcastle United	A	Second Division	0-2
1898	Burton Swifts	H	Second Division	4-0
1900	Manchester City	A	Friendly	1-2
1901	Middlesbrough	A	Second Division	2-1
1902	Preston North End	H	Second Division	0-2
1907	Aston Villa	H	First Division	1-0

Four former Manchester City players, Jimmy Bannister, Herbert Burgess, Billy Meredith and Sandy Turnbull, made their League debuts for United. The previous year the Football Association had uncovered financial irregularities within the City club (in effect illegal payments to players) and had banned 17 players for seven months. All 17 were subsequently placed on the transfer list by City, with United swooping to take four of the best from their nearest rivals. Indeed, it was Meredith who centred for Turnbull to score the only goal of the game in front of 40,000 fans. The win, as stern a test as United could have faced, answered the main question on everyone's minds: the enforced layoff had done little to blunt the abilities of the four players. In an instant, United had acquired four players who would now make them a serious contender for the game's top honours.

1908	Bury	A	First Division	1-0
1909	Notts County	H	First Division	4-3
1910	Bradford City	A	First Division	2-0
1912	Woolwich Arsenal	H	First Division	2-0
1913	Bradford City	H	First Division	2-0
1914	West Bromwich Albion	H	First Division	1-0
1915	Bradford Park Avenue	H	First Division	1-2
1916	Stoke City	H	Lancashire Section Principal Tournament	1-2
1917	Manchester City	A	Friendly	0-0
1918	Manchester City	A	Friendly	2-0
1919	Manchester City	H	Friendly	2-0
1920	Liverpool	A	First Division	0-0
1921	Newcastle United	A	First Division	3-6
1923	Barnsley	H	Second Division	1-0
1925	Chelsea	H	Second Division	1-0
1927	Sheffield United	H	First Division	5-0
1929	Aston Villa	H	First Division	2-2
1931	Leeds United	H	First Division	0-0

1935	Southampton	H	Second Division	3-0
1936	Barnsley	A	Second Division	3-0
1937	Sunderland	H	First Division	2-1
1938	Newcastle United	A	Second Division	2-2
1944	Halifax Town	A	Football League North (Second Championship)	1-1
1948	Burnley	H	First Division	5-0

Charlie Mitten scored a brace of goals for the third consecutive game, although his achievement today was slightly overshadowed by Jack Rowley's hat-trick. Of the great United forward line of the era, Mitten was unlucky to be the only one not to have won international honours.

1949	Arsenal	H	First Division	2-0
1953	Derby County	H	First Division	1-0
1955	Blackpool	H	First Division	4-1
1957	Chelsea	H	First Division	3-0
1966	Liverpool	A	First Division	1-2
1972	West Ham United	A	First Division	0-3
1974	Queens Park Rangers	A	First Division	0-3
1977	Aston Villa	H	First Division	2-0
1983	Aston Villa	H	First Division	3-1
1985	Sheffield Wednesday	H	First Division	1-2
1986	Birmingham City	H	First Division	1-0
1987	Newcastle United	H	First Division	4-1
1988	Charlton Athletic	H	First Division	0-0
1989	Liverpool	H	First Division	3-1
1990	Queens Park Rangers	H	First Division	0-0
1991	Tottenham Hotspur	A	First Division	2-1

Spurs' midfielder Paul Gascoigne was sent off for the third time in his career. More crucially, he was the first player to be sent off during a live televised League match.

1992	Queens Park Rangers	H	First Division	1-4
1994	Leeds United	H	FA Premier League	0-0
1996	Tottenham Hotspur	A	FA Premier League	1-4

This was the first time United had conceded as many as four goals since the creation of the Premiership. Peter Schmeichel was injured during the pre-match warm-up and although he played in the first half was little more than a passenger as Spurs laid siege to the United goal. Peter was replaced at half-time with Spurs already 2-1 ahead, and two second-half goals saw United well beaten.

| 1997 | Aston Villa | H | FA Premier League | 0-0 |

JANUARY 2ND

| 1891 | Ardwick | A | Friendly | 1-1 |

The game was abandoned after fog descended upon the ground with the score still at 1-1.

1893	Ardwick	A	Friendly	5-3
1897	Nelson	H	FA Cup 4th Qualifying Round	3-0
1899	Burton Swifts	H	Second Division	2-2
1904	Bristol City	A	Second Division	1-1
1905	Bradford City	H	Second Division	7-0

A crowd of 10,000 saw United win their last home match during their run of 14 consecutive League wins, a League record. Both Arkesden and Roberts scored two apiece, with United's other goals being scored by Allan, Peddie, Robinson and an own goal.

1909	Preston North End	H	First Division	0-2
1911	Bradford City	H	First Division	1-0
1915	Manchester City	A	First Division	1-1

The largest crowd to watch United all season as 30,000 attended the local derby. United's goal was scored by Enoch West, one of nine he scored all season. At the end of the season, however, West would be banned from football!

1922	Sheffield United	A	First Division	0-3
1924	Coventry City	H	Second Division	1-2
1926	West Ham United	H	First Division	2-1
1932	Bradford Park Avenue	H	Second Division	0-2
1933	Plymouth Argyle	H	Second Division	4-0

Old Trafford's biggest crowd of the season; 30,257 witnessed the four-goal rout of Plymouth Argyle. Bill Ridding, who later managed Bolton Wanderers, grabbed two, whilst Chalmers and Spence scored one apiece.

1937	Derby County	H	First Division	2-2
1943	Chester	A	Football League North (Second Championship)	1-4
1954	Newcastle United	A	First Division	2-1

United's winning goal was a rare strike from Bill Foulkes, who shot from over 45 yards to net the second goal. United's other goal was scored by Jackie Blanchflower.

1960	Newcastle United	A	First Division	3-7

After this mauling United would probably be glad if they don't meet Newcastle for another six years! United's consolation efforts came from Albert Quixall (two goals) and Alex Dawson.

1971	Middlesbrough	H	FA Cup 3rd Round	0-0
1978	Birmingham City	H	First Division	1-2
1982	Watford	A	FA Cup 3rd Round	0-1
1984	Liverpool	A	First Division	1-1
1988	Watford	A	First Division	1-0
1989	Middlesbrough	A	First Division	0-1

JANUARY 3RD

1896 Bill Rawlings born in Andover. Although Bill made only 36 appearances for United during his 20 months with the club, he scored 19 goals to justify his reputation as a quality goalscorer. He began his professional career with Southampton in 1919 and transferred to United for £4,000 in 1928, moving on to Port Vale in November 1929, subsequently retiring in August 1930. In his career he scored 156 goals in 294 League appearances for his clubs.

1903	Gainsborough Trinity	H	Second Division	3-1
1905	Bolton Wanderers	A	Second Division	4-2

This was United's 14th consecutive win in the League, a run that had started the previous October with a 2-0 victory over Lincoln. But despite winning a further ten games during the season, United could only finish in third place and thus missed out on promotion to the First Division.

1914	Bolton Wanderers	A	First Division	1-6
1920	Chelsea	H	First Division	0-2
1925	Stoke City	H	Second Division	2-0
1931	Chelsea	H	First Division	1-0
1942	Bolton Wanderers	A	Football League Northern Section (Second Championship)	2-2
1948	Charlton Athletic	A	First Division	2-1
1953	Manchester City	H	First Division	1-1

1959	Blackpool	H	First Division	3-1
1970	Ipswich Town	A	FA Cup 3rd Round	1-0
1976	Oxford United	H	FA Cup 3rd Round	2-1
1977	Ipswich Town	A	First Division	1-2
1981	Brighton & Hove Albion	H	FA Cup 3rd Round	2-2
1983	West Bromwich Albion	H	First Division	0-0
1987	Southampton	A	First Division	1-1

1987 United defender Liam O'Brien was sent off after only 85 seconds, the quickest dismissal in the First Division.

| 1995 | Coventry City | H | FA Premier League | 2-0 |

JANUARY 4TH

1896	Leicester Fosse	A	Second Division	0-3
1902	Gainsborough Trinity	A	Second Division	1-1
1913	West Bromwich Albion	H	First Division	1-1
1930	Blackburn Rovers	A	First Division	4-5
1936	Bradford City	A	Second Division	0-1
1941	Blackburn Rovers	A	North Regional League	2-0
1947	Charlton Athletic	H	First Division	4-1

1951 Paddy Roche born in Dublin. After making the grade with Shelbourne he was transferred to United for a fee of £15,000 in October 1973 and made his League debut against Oxford United in February 1975. With stiff competition from first Alex Stepney and then Gary Bailey, first-team opportunities were limited, and after 53 first-team appearances he left for Brentford in 1982, later finishing his League career with Halifax Town. Won a total of seven caps for the Republic of Ireland.

1958	Workington Town	A	FA Cup 3rd Round	3-1
1964	Southampton	A	FA Cup 3rd Round	3-2
1969	Exeter City	A	FA Cup 3rd Round	3-1

1971 George Best missed the plane due to take him down to London for an appearance in front of the Disciplinary Committee, finally turning up 90 minutes late and getting fined £250 for slack time-keeping! Later that same week he missed the train to London and was promptly dropped by United from their team to face Chelsea!

1973 New York Cosmos announced they would like to sign George Best. According to his agent, George had expressed an interest in listening to the offer.

| 1975 | Walsall | H | FA Cup 3rd Round | 0-0 |
| 1994 | Liverpool | A | FA Premier League | 3-3 |

1994 United powered in to a seemingly unassailable 3-0 lead within 25 minutes, with the goals coming from Steve Bruce, Ryan Giggs and Dennis Irwin. Liverpool clawed their way back into one of the games of the season. It was later alleged, however, that this was one of the matches that Liverpool goalkeeper Bruce Grobbelaar had been paid to throw and that he stood to collect £125,000 if United won! Grobbelaar was later charged and subsequently acquitted over the allegations.

| 1998 | Chelsea | A | FA Cup 3rd Round | 5-3 |

1998 The FA Cup's match of the day pitted the holders, Chelsea, against the side who have won the trophy more times than any other, United. And whilst it had taken Chelsea 27 years to get their hands on the cup, their grip lasted barely 27 minutes as United took complete control. By the time United took their foot off the pedal they were 5-0 ahead, allowing Chelsea to score three goals which gave the final score line a respectability it didn't really deserve, such had been the superiority of United's performance.

JANUARY 5TH

1891	Stoke	H	Football Alliance	0-1
1895	Manchester City	H	Second Division	4-1
1901	Portsmouth	H	FA Cup Supplementary Round	3-0
1907	Notts County	A	First Division	0-3
1918	Southport Central	A	Lancashire Section Principal Tournament	0-3
1924	Bradford City	H	Second Division	3-0
1929	Manchester City	H	First Division	1-2

1932 Bill Foulkes born in St Helens. He joined Manchester United in August 1951, signing from Whiston Boys Club and made his first-team debut in 1952. By 1953 he was a regular and one of the renowned 'Busby Babes' who dominated English football during the mid-'50s. He won one cap for England, against Northern Ireland in 1955, and survived the Munich air disaster of 1958 (although the experience put him off flying for life), recovering sufficiently to captain United in their FA Cup final appearance that same year against Bolton. He won a winners' medal in the same competition in 1963 and, five years later, was centre-half in the side that finally won the European Cup at Wembley. Indeed it was Foulkes's goal in the second leg of the semi-final against Real Madrid that secured United's place in the final. Foulkes made 563 appearances for Manchester United (a record since overtaken by Bobby Charlton), scoring six goals. He retired in 1969.

1935	Sheffield United	H	Second Division	3-3
1946	Accrington Stanley	A	FA Cup 3rd Round 1st Leg	2-2

With League football still to resume following the cessation of hostilities in the Second World War, the Football Association decided that the early FA Cup rounds would be decided over two legs (this subsequently enabled Charlton Athletic to become one of the few clubs to have reached the FA Cup final despite losing an earlier match). A crowd of 9,968 crammed into Peel Park to see Stanley draw 2-2 with United.

1952	Stoke City	A	First Division	0-0
1957	Hartlepools United	A	FA Cup 3rd Round	4-3
1971	Middlesbrough	A	FA Cup 3rd Round Replay	1-2
1974	Plymouth Argyle	H	FA Cup 3rd Round	1-0
1980	Tottenham Hotspur	A	FA Cup 3rd Round	1-1
1985	AFC Bournemouth	H	FA Cup 3rd Round	3-0
1993	Bury	H	FA Cup 3rd Round	2-0
1997	Tottenham Hotspur	H	FA Cup 3rd Round	2-0

Irrespective of where either team lay in the League, there was still a magic about a United and Spurs cup-tie, and the reaction that greeted their pairing in the round when the draw was made meant that this would be another such occasion. As it was, Spurs were decimated by injuries, but United were in such sparkling form that even a full-strength opposition would have found it difficult to live with the rampant Reds. Goals from Cole and Cantona ensured passage into the fourth round.

JANUARY 6TH

1894	Everton	A	First Division	0-2
1900	Bolton Wanderers	H	Second Division	1-2
1906	Grimsby Town	H	Second Division	5-0
1912	Everton	A	First Division	0-4
1917	Burnley	H	Lancashire Section Principal Tournament	3-1
1923	Hull City	H	Second Division	3-2
1934	Lincoln City	A	Second Division	1-5

1940	Everton	A	War Regional League, Western Division	2-3

On the same day, Johnny Giles was born in Dublin. He began his career with Dublin City, Stella Maris and Home Farm before joining United in November 1957. He made his debut in the 5-1 defeat by Spurs in September 1959 and was a member of the side that won the FA Cup in 1963. That was to prove his Manchester swan song, for he was sold to Leeds United for £35,000 having made 98 League appearances for Manchester United. He went on to win a Second Division medal, two League championship medals, a further FA Cup winners' medal, a League Cup winners' tankard and two Fairs Cup winners' medals. His last match for the club was in their European Cup final defeat by Bayern Munich, and he subsequently joined West Bromwich Albion as player-manager. He wound down his playing career in Ireland, winning a Football Association of Ireland Cup winners' medal with Shamrock Rovers, and the United States before returning for a second spell in charge at the Hawthorns. He won 60 caps for the Republic of Ireland and was player-manager from 1973 until 1980.

1945	Huddersfield Town	H	Football League North (Second Championship)	1-0
1951	Oldham Athletic	H	FA Cup 3rd Round	4-1
1962	Bolton Wanderers	H	FA Cup 3rd Round	2-1
1968	West Ham United	H	First Division	3-1
1973	Arsenal	A	First Division	1-3
1982	Everton	H	First Division	1-1
1996	Sunderland	H	FA Cup 3rd Round	2-2

JANUARY 7TH

1893	Stoke	A	First Division	1-7

Newton Heath's first season in the Football League was not without its problems. Goalkeeper Jimmy Warner missed the train taking the team to their match at Stoke and the Heathens were forced to play with only ten men throughout. Three Heathens took it in turn to go in goal – Stewart, Fitzsimmons and Clements – but despite taking the lead through Coupar, Newton Heath finished the game well beaten. When the Newton Heath directors managed to speak to Warner and found out what had happened, they were not pleased, to say the least! In fact, Warner was suspended for the next two games by the club and made only two further appearances before being released and signing for Walsall Town Swifts.

1899	Manchester City	H	Friendly	2-0
1905	Bristol City	A	Second Division	1-1
1911	Nottingham Forest	H	First Division	4-2
1922	Cardiff City	H	FA Cup 1st Round	1-4
1928	Birmingham	H	First Division	1-1
1933	Southampton	H	Second Division	1-2
1939	West Bromwich Albion	A	FA Cup 3rd Round	0-0
1950	Weymouth	H	FA Cup 3rd Round	4-0
1956	Bristol Rovers	A	FA Cup 3rd Round	0-4
1961	Middlesbrough	H	FA Cup 3rd Round	3-0

1972 George Best went missing, having not been seen at United's training ground all week nor been in touch with the club throughout. He was therefore dropped for the next day's game at home to Wolverhampton Wanderers and told, assuming he could be contacted, to be in manager Frank O'Farrell's office on Monday morning.

1975	Walsall	A	FA Cup 3rd Round Replay	2-3 [aet]
1978	Carlisle United	A	FA Cup 3rd Round	1-1
1981	Brighton & Hove Albion	A	FA Cup 3rd Round Replay	2-0
1984	AFC Bournemouth	A	FA Cup 3rd Round	0-2

Despite finishing the season in fourth place in the League and reaching the semi-finals of the European Cup-Winners' Cup, the story of the 1983-84 season was undoubtedly the humiliating defeats in both domestic cup competitions by sides from the then Third Division: Oxford United in the Milk Cup and AFC Bournemouth in the FA Cup. A capacity crowd of 15,000 packed into Dean Court to see the holders slip out at the first hurdle thanks to goals from Graham and Thompson and thus ensure Bournemouth's presence in the fourth round for the first time in 24 years!

1989	Queens Park Rangers	H	FA Cup 3rd Round	0-0
1990	Nottingham Forest	A	FA Cup 3rd Round	1-0
1991	Queens Park Rangers	H	FA Cup 3rd Round	2-1

JANUARY 8TH

1884   Robert Beale born in Maidstone. Signed from Norwich City in 1912 for £275 he proved a reliable goalkeeper for United and was unfortunate that the First World War effectively cut across his career at Old Trafford. Although he helped out the reserves during the war, he signed for Gillingham in 1919 but still made the occasional appearance for the United reserve team, travelling up from his Maidstone home in 1921 to play at Southport. His son Walter also later signed for United but did not play for the first team. Robert died in Dymchurch on 5th October 1950.

1898	Woolwich Arsenal	A	Second Division	1-5
1910	Bury	A	First Division	1-1
1916	Burnley	A	Lancashire Section Principal Tournament	4-7

All four of United's goals in this war-time League match were scored by Travis.

1921	Liverpool	A	FA Cup 1st Round	1-1
1927	Reading	A	FA Cup 3rd Round	1-1
1938	Yeovil	H	FA Cup 3rd Round	3-0
1944	Stockport County	A	Football League North (Second Championship)	3-2

1947   Ted MacDougall born in Inverness. Following his goalscoring exploits for Bournemouth in the early 1970s, Ted cost United an initial fee of £200,000 in September 1972, then a record fee for a Third Division player. Unfortunately goals proved harder to come by in the First Division and barely five months later he was sold to West Ham. In 1978 United were ordered by the Law Courts to pay Bournemouth an additional £22,000 as part of a complicated clause in his initial contract that related to the number of goals he scored – he got five in eighteen appearances. By this time Ted was back at Bournemouth, having joined them on a free transfer from Southampton!

| 1949 | Bournemouth | H | FA Cup 3rd Round | 6-0 |

This was a historic occasion for Manchester United, for they played their first FA Cup tie at Old Trafford in ten years. With Old Trafford having been out of action following extensive bomb damage sustained during the Second World War, this was the first FA Cup tie at the ground since West Bromwich Albion's visit on 11th January 1939. Goals from Burke (two), Rowley (two), Pearson and Mitten ensured the holders progressed into the next round.

1955	Reading	A	FA Cup 3rd Round	1-1
1966	Sunderland	H	First Division	1-1
1972	Wolverhampton Wanderers	H	First Division	1-3
1977	Walsall	H	FA Cup 3rd Round	1-0
1983	West Ham United	H	FA Cup 3rd Round	2-0
1992	Leeds United	A	Rumbelows Cup 5th Round	3-1

JANUARY 9TH

1892	Bootle	A	Football Alliance	1-1
1897	Burton Swifts	H	Second Division	1-1

1902 Such were the financial problems being faced by Newton Heath, an application for a compulsory winding-up order was made against Newton Heath Football Club Company Limited. Interestingly, one of the creditors who brought the action, William Healey, was also president of the club, although the fact he was owed £242 17s 10d probably weighed heavier on his mind. Certainly, the local press thought he had been impatient in bringing the case in the first place. With little prospect of the club being able to meet their debts (which totalled over £2,000) and satisfy their creditors, the judge began bankruptcy proceedings, prompting the Football League to postpone their next fixture against Middlesbrough and the official receiver to close the ground.

1904	Port Vale	H	Second Division	2-0
1909	Middlesbrough	A	First Division	0-5
1915	Sheffield Wednesday	A	FA Cup 1st Round	0-1
1926	Port Vale	A	FA Cup 3rd Round	3-2
1932	Plymouth Argyle	A	FA Cup 3rd Round	1-4
1937	Manchester City	A	First Division	0-1
1943	Blackpool	A	Football League North (Second Championship)	1-1
1946	Accrington Stanley	H	FA Cup 3rd Round 2nd Leg	5-1
1954	Burnley	A	FA Cup 3rd Round	3-5

A flurry of goalscoring in the opening seven minutes saw United two down after only five minutes but claw back to draw level two minutes later! Burnley later took the lead again, only for United to equalise, before two final goals for Burnley saw them through to the next round.

1960	Derby County	A	FA Cup 3rd Round	4-2
1965	Chester	H	FA Cup 3rd Round	2-1
1971	Chelsea	A	First Division	2-1
1980	Tottenham Hotspur	H	FA Cup 3rd Round Replay	0-1 [aet]

In the very last minute of extra time, a goal by Spurs' Argentine midfielder Ossie Ardiles won the game for the visitors and ensured there would be no third meeting between the sides.

1986	Rochdale	H	FA Cup 3rd Round	2-0
1993	Tottenham Hotspur	H	FA Premier League	4-1
1994	Sheffield United	A	FA Cup 3rd Round	1-0
1995	Sheffield United	A	FA Cup 3rd Round	2-0

JANUARY 10TH

1891	Birmingham St George's	A	Football Alliance	1-6
1903	Burton United	A	Second Division	1-3
1914	Swindon Town	A	FA Cup 1st Round	0-1
1920	Port Vale	A	FA Cup 1st Round	1-0
1925	Sheffield Wednesday	A	FA Cup 1st Round	0-2
1931	Stoke City	A	FA Cup 3rd Round	3-3

A hat-trick from Tom Reid earned United a replay in this FA Cup tie, although the tie went to a second replay at Anfield before United triumphed 4-2.

1942	Oldham Athletic	H	Football League Northern Section (Second Championship)	1-1
1948	Aston Villa	A	FA Cup 3rd Round	6-4

One of the most exciting FA Cup ties United have ever played in saw Villa take the lead after only 13 seconds and United recover to lead 5-1 by half-time. Three goals from Villa in the second half led the home fans to believe their side might rescue the tie, but a sixth and final goal from Stan Pearson set United on the road that would lead to Wembley at the season's end.

| 1953 | Millwall | A | FA Cup 3rd Round | 1-0 |

1954   John Gidman born in Liverpool. He joined Liverpool straight from school but failed to make the grade and subsequently moved to Aston Villa. Whilst at Villa Park he won a League Cup winners' tankard and a solitary England cap before a £600,000 transfer took him to Everton in 1979. Two years later he made the opposite move as Mickey Thomas moved from Old Trafford to Goodison Park, and although his career at Manchester United was interrupted by injury, he was a member of the side that won the FA Cup in 1985. He later played for Manchester City and Stoke City before becoming assistant manager at Darlington.

| 1959 | Norwich City | A | FA Cup 3rd Round | 0-3 |
| 1970 | Arsenal | H | First Division | 2-1 |

1971   Manchester United suspended George Best for two weeks after he failed to make it to London in time for the match against Chelsea. Best later announced he was in the wrong and accepted the suspension.

1972   George Best turned up at Old Trafford to see Frank O'Farrell and was told to move out of his luxury home and back into digs where the club could keep an eye on him. Additionally, he was fined two weeks' wages and ordered to train morning and afternoon for at least the next week.

1976	Queens Park Rangers	H	First Division	2-1
1981	Brighton & Hove Albion	H	First Division	2-1
1987	Manchester City	H	FA Cup 3rd Round	1-0
1988	Ipswich Town	A	FA Cup 3rd Round	2-1

1991   Manchester United announced that they, like Tottenham Hotspur, were to float the club on the stock market and become a public company, despite reporting an overall loss for the last year of £2,863,677.

1995   One of the most contentious transfers of all time as Newcastle's Andy Cole was transferred to Premiership rivals Manchester United for a new British record transfer fee of £7 million. The fee was made up of £6 million in cash and Manchester United's Republic of Ireland international Keith Gillespie, valued at £1 million, making the opposite journey. Twenty-three-year-old Cole began his career at Arsenal, was transferred to Bristol City for £500,000 after only one appearance for the Gunners, and after plundering 20 goals for City in only 41 appearances (including eight goals in twelve games whilst on loan) moved to Newcastle for £1.75 million where his goalscoring record was phenomenal, including 34 League goals in one season. His transfer smashed the British record, which was set during the summer when Chris Sutton moved from Norwich City to Blackburn Rovers for £5 million. As fate would have it, Manchester United were due to play Newcastle at St James' Park this coming Saturday – both managers (Kevin Keegan and Alex Ferguson) agreed to omit Gillespie and Cole from their line-ups.

| 1998 | Tottenham Hotspur | H | FA Premier League | 2-0 |

JANUARY 11TH

| 1896 | Rotherham Town | H | Second Division | 3-0 |
| 1904 | Small Heath | N | FA Cup Intermediate Round 3rd Replay | 3-1 |

The most protracted FA Cup tie in United's history finally came to an end after four games and seven hours with a 3-1 win for United at Manchester City's Hyde Road ground. The goals that broke the deadlock were scored by Arkesden (two) and Grassam.

1908	Blackpool	H	FA Cup 1st Round	3-1
1913	Coventry City	H	FA Cup 1st Round	1-1
1919	Stockport County	A	Lancashire Section Principal Tournament	1-2

On the same day, Stan Pearson was born in Salford. He made his United debut in November 1937 against Chesterfield and was beginning to break into the side with greater regularity when the Football League was suspended indefinitely owing to the Second World War. Like many of his era he lost a considerable part of his career to the war, but scored a hat-trick in the 1948 FA Cup semi-final against Derby and one of United's four in the final against Blackpool to ensure their trophy win. He was also a member of the 1952 League championship winning side, but Matt Busby's later introduction of a succession of youngsters into the first team signalled the end of Stan's United career. He moved to Bury in 1954 and later played for Chester, subsequently becoming manager. Stan scored 128 League goals for United in only 315 appearances, a remarkable return, and also collected eight caps for England.

1930	Swindon Town	A	FA Cup 3rd Round	0-2
1936	Reading	A	FA Cup 3rd Round	3-1
1939	West Bromwich Albion	H	FA Cup 3rd Round Replay	1-5
1941	Blackburn Rovers	H	North Regional League	0-0
1947	Bradford Park Avenue	A	FA Cup 3rd Round	3-0

1957 Bryan Robson born in Chester-le-Street. A former England Youth international he signed with West Bromwich Albion as an apprentice and rose through the ranks to make his full League debut in 1974. After 197 League appearances for West Bromwich, during which time he had been capped for England at Under-21 and full level (13 caps) he was transferred to Manchester United for a then record fee of £1.5 million in 1981. Over the next 12 years he won just about every honour the game has to offer – three winners' medals in the FA Cup, a winners' medal in the European Cup-Winners' Cup, a total of 90 England caps and, during his final two years at Manchester United, winners' medals in the Premier League. He might have won another winners' medal in the FA Cup in 1994, but United manager Alex Ferguson preferred Brian McClair to the by-now 37-year-old Robson. Robson was given a free transfer at the end of the season and immediately appointed player-manager of Middlesbrough with a brief to revive football in the area, in much the same way Kevin Keegan had done a few miles further north at Newcastle, and return the club to the top flight, which he ultimately did. At the end of his first season in charge he guided them to the First Division championship and in 1997 took them to the finals of both the Coca-Cola and FA Cups, although they were subsequently beaten in both and relegated during the same season! They returned to the Coca-Cola-Cup final the following season but were once again beaten by Chelsea, who had won the FA Cup final clash in 1997 between the two sides! On a personal level he was awarded an OBE for his services to football.

1958	Leeds United	A	First Division	1-1
1964	Birmingham City	H	First Division	1-2
1969	Leeds United	A	First Division	1-2
1975	Sheffield Wednesday	H	Second Division	2-0
1978	Carlisle United	H	FA Cup 3rd Round Replay	4-2
1986	Oxford United	A	First Division	3-1
1989	Queens Park Rangers	A	FA Cup 3rd Round Replay	2-2 [aet]
1992	Everton	H	First Division	1-0

JANUARY 12TH

| 1895 | Rotherham Town | A | Second Division | 1-2 |
| 1898 | Burnley | H | Second Division | 0-0 |

1901	Burnley	H	Second Division	0-1
1907	Portsmouth	A	FA Cup 1st Round	2-2
1918	Southport Central	H	Lancashire Section Principal Tournament	0-0
1921	Liverpool	H	FA Cup 1st Round Replay	1-2
1924	Plymouth Argyle	H	FA Cup 1st Round	1-0
1927	Reading	H	FA Cup 3rd Round Replay	2-2
1929	Port Vale	A	FA Cup 3rd Round	3-0
1935	Bristol Rovers	A	FA Cup 3rd Round	3-1
1946	Grimsby Town	H	Football League North	3-0

All three United goals were scored by the prolific Jack Rowley. Although his exploits in the red shirt of United are well known to United's followers, what may not be so well known is that he was just as successful elsewhere whilst guesting for other clubs during the Second World War, including one game for Wolves where he scored eight times and another for Spurs that resulted in seven goals. Of course, at the end of the war he returned to United and continued terrorising Wolves, Spurs and everybody else's defence!

1952	Hull City	H	FA Cup 3rd Round	0-2
1955	Reading	H	FA Cup 3rd Round Replay	4-1

One of United's goals was scored by Jack Rowley, the last of the 208 League and Cup goals he scored for United during his career. He had scored his first goal for the club precisely 17 years and 39 days earlier.

1957	Newcastle United	H	First Division	6-1
1966	Leeds United	A	First Division	1-1
1974	West Ham United	A	First Division	1-2
1980	Middlesbrough	A	First Division	1-1

Immediately following the game at Ayresome Park a gate collapsed, killing two people and injuring several others.

1985	Coventry City	H	First Division	0-1
1991	Sunderland	H	First Division	3-0
1994	Portsmouth	H	Coca-Cola Cup 5th Round	2-2
1997	Tottenham Hotspur	A	FA Premier League	2-1

JANUARY 13TH

1894	Sheffield Wednesday	H	First Division	1-2
1900	Loughborough Town	A	Second Division	2-0
1906	Staple Hill	H	FA Cup 1st Round	7-2

Among the crowd of 7,560 at Clayton were politicians Winston Churchill and J.R. Clynes.

1912	Huddersfield Town	H	FA Cup 1st Round	3-1
1917	Blackpool	H	Lancashire Section Principal Tournament	3-2
1923	Bradford City	A	FA Cup 1st Round	1-1
1934	Portsmouth	H	FA Cup 3rd Round	1-1
1945	Huddersfield Town	A	Football League North (Second Championship)	2-2
1951	Tottenham Hotspur	H	First Division	2-1
1962	Blackpool	H	First Division	0-1
1973	Wolverhampton Wanderers	A	FA Cup 3rd Round	0-1

United were reduced to ten men when Tony Dunne, who had come on as a substitute for Brian Kidd, was sent off. Thereafter United faced an uphill struggle and eventually lost 1-0.

1984	Queens Park Rangers	A	First Division	1-1
1990	Derby County	H	First Division	1-2

| 1996 | Aston Villa | H | FA Premier League | 0-0 |

Gary and Phil Neville were both booked during the game, the first time a pair of brothers representing United had been cautioned in the same game.

JANUARY 14TH

1893	Nottingham Forest	H	First Division	1-3
1899	Glossop	H	Second Division	3-0
1905	Fulham	H	FA Cup Intermediate Round	2-2

With the Football League still being very much a northern domain, often the only opportunity clubs from the north had to test their skills against southern opposition came in the FA Cup. Fulham were members of the Southern League (then considerably stronger than it would appear, for Spurs had won the FA Cup in 1901 whilst still a Southern League club), although hovering in mid-table. Both United and Fulham took their fixture seriously enough to do a week's special training by the sea (the two clubs were billeted close to each other), but a crowd of only 16,000 were attracted by the tie. United missed an early penalty when Tom Arkesden shot wide and Fulham took the lead on the half-hour, although United were level by half-time thanks to Mackie. Early in the second half Arkesden atoned for his earlier miss by firing United ahead, but a later equaliser ensured the two teams would have to meet again at Craven Cottage.

1911	Blackpool	A	FA Cup 1st Round	2-1
1922	Newcastle United	H	First Division	0-1
1928	Brentford	H	FA Cup 3rd Round	7-1
1931	Stoke City	H	FA Cup 3rd Round Replay	0-0 [aet]
1933	Middlesbrough	H	FA Cup 3rd Round	1-4
1939	Grimsby Town	H	First Division	3-1
1950	Chelsea	H	First Division	1-0
1956	Sheffield United	H	First Division	3-1
1957	Red Star Belgrade	H	European Cup 3rd Round 1st Leg	2-1
1961	Tottenham Hotspur	H	First Division	2-0

Despite having to reshuffle the line-up following an injury to goalkeeper Harry Gregg that forced Alex Dawson into goal and Gregg into the forward line, United managed to defeat the side that would end the season with the first FA Cup and League double of the century. This was the only occasion Spurs failed to score all season. Harry Gregg quite enjoyed his foray out on field; he set up the second goal with a pass to Mark Pearson.

| 1967 | Tottenham Hotspur | H | First Division | 1-0 |
| 1969 | United had called a press conference at Old Trafford at which it was confidently | | | |

expected that a major new signing was about to be unveiled. Instead, Sir Matt Busby sat alongside club secretary Les Olive as the latter announced the former would be relinquishing his position of manager at the end of the season and assuming the role of general manager, although this would not give him any responsibilities for the team. It was a bombshell, but at the same time it was recognised that at the age of 58 and with 23 years service at Old Trafford, Sir Matt had earned a well-deserved rest.

| 1978 | Ipswich Town | A | First Division | 2-1 |
| 1989 | Millwall | H | First Division | 3-0 |

JANUARY 15TH

1898	Blackpool	H	Second Division	4-0
1906	Leeds City	H	Second Division	0-3
1910	Burnley	A	FA Cup 1st Round	0-2

1916	Preston North End	H	Lancashire Section Principal Tournament	4-0
1921	West Bromwich Albion	H	First Division	1-4
1927	Liverpool	H	First Division	0-1
1938	Luton Town	H	Second Division	4-2
1944	Stockport County	H	Football League North (Second Championship)	4-2
1962	Aston Villa	H	First Division	2-0
1966	Fulham	A	First Division	1-0
1972	Southampton	A	FA Cup 3rd Round	1-1

After all the problems he had suffered in recent weeks, George Best was finally able to put it all behind him and get on with what he did best – playing football. He turned in a superlative performance against Southampton and was indirectly responsible for the equalising goal: his dummy fooled the defence long enough for Bobby Charlton to fire home.

1975	Norwich City	H	League Cup Semi-Final 1st Leg	2-2
1977	Coventry City	H	First Division	2-0
1979	Chelsea	H	FA Cup 3rd Round	3-0
1983	Birmingham City	A	First Division	2-1
1992	Leeds United	A	FA Cup 3rd Round	1-0
1994	Tottenham Hotspur	A	FA Premier League	1-0
1995	Newcastle United	A	FA Premier League	1-1

JANUARY 16TH

| 1897 | Blackpool | H | FA Cup 5th Qualifying Round | 2-2 |
| 1901 | Billy Johnston born in Edinburgh. | | | |

Billy Johnston born in Edinburgh. Billy spent two spells at United, first joining them in October 1927 for £3,000 from Stockport County and was almost ever-present to the end of the season, although injuries caused him to miss much of 1928-29. He was transfer listed in June 1929 and joined Macclesfield, returning to United two years later and made a further 28 appearances. In all he played 77 times for the first team, scoring 27 goals.

1904	Glossop	H	Second Division	3-1
1907	Portsmouth	H	FA Cup 1st Round Replay	1-2
1909	Brighton & Hove Albion	H	FA Cup 1st Round	1-0
1913	Coventry City	A	FA Cup 1st Round Replay	2-1
1915	Bolton Wanderers	H	First Division	4-1
1926	Arsenal	A	First Division	2-3
1932	Swansea Town	A	Second Division	1-3
1937	Reading	H	FA Cup 3rd Round	1-0
1943	Blackpool	H	Football League North (Second Championship)	5-3
1954	Manchester City	H	First Division	1-1
1957	Athletico Bilbao	A	European Cup 2nd Round 1st Leg	3-5

After European competition had undergone a mid-winter shutdown, footballing hostilities were resumed in the European Cup. United began as though they were still in hibernation, allowing Athletico to take a commanding three-goal lead by half-time. Whatever was said by Matt Busby in the dressing-room at half-time obviously had the desired effect, for Tommy Taylor and Denis Viollet both netted to give United hope that they might draw level, but almost as quickly Bilbao restored their three-goal advantage with two further strikes. Bill Whelan scored another later goal for United to leave the final score 5-3; no one in the United camp doubted they could overturn their opponents in the second leg.

| 1960 | Birmingham City | H | First Division | 2-1 |
| 1961 | Tottenham Hotspur | H | First Division | 2-0 |

1965	Nottingham Forest	A	First Division	2-2
1971	Burnley	H	First Division	1-1
1988	Southampton	H	First Division	0-2
1991	Southampton	A	Rumbelows Cup 5th Round	1-1
1996	Sunderland	A	FA Cup 3rd Round Replay	2-1

Whilst United had never won at Roker Park in the FA Cup, Sunderland had never beaten United in any cup competition, so something was bound to give tonight. As it was, goals from Paul Scholes and Andy Cole ensured that United marched into the fourth round.

JANUARY 17TH

1885	Gorton AFC	A	Friendly	3-1
1891	Walsall Town Swifts	H	Football Alliance	3-3
1903	Bristol City	H	Second Division	1-2
1914	Chelsea	H	First Division	0-1
1920	Chelsea	A	First Division	0-1

1921 Charlie Mitten born in Rangoon, Burma. He joined United straight from school in 1936 but did not become a member of the professional ranks until 1945, following the end of the Second World War. He made his debut in United's first League match against Grimsby and quickly established himself as a permanent fixture in the team, making a total of 113 consecutive appearances by the end of the 1949-50 season. He had also collected an FA Cup winners' medal with United in 1948 against Blackpool. Then, in a sudden and unexpected move, he announced he was leaving United in order to try his luck in Colombia along with a number of other British players, all of whom were lured by the promise of wages considerably higher than those being earned under the maximum wage rule. Unfortunately, the expected riches never materialised and a year later Charlie was back at United, although the club immediately transfer listed him and duly sold him to Fulham. He subsequently moved on to Mansfield Town, where he finished his playing career, and later managed Newcastle United. His two sons were also on United's books for a while. But for his disappearance to Colombia, Charlie might well have gone on to collect international honours; as it was he was the only member of the 1948 Cup winning forward line not to win a full cap.

1923	Bradford City	H	FA Cup 1st Round Replay	2-0
1925	Coventry City	A	Second Division	0-1
1927	Reading	Villa Park	FA Cup 3rd Round 2nd Replay	1-2
1931	Newcastle United	A	First Division	3-4
1934	Portsmouth	A	FA Cup 3rd Round Replay	1-4
1942	Oldham Athletic	A	Football League Northern Section (Second Championship)	3-1

1945 Ian Storey-Moore born in Ipswich. Snapped up by Nottingham Forest straight from school, he scored 105 goals in 236 appearances for the City Ground club which in turn led to interest from other clubs. He spoke to Derby about joining them, signed a contract with the club and was duly paraded in front of the Derby fans as their latest signing. Unfortunately for Derby, the Forest secretary had reservations about letting Ian go to their nearest rivals and so did not sign the release forms, allowing United to come in with an offer. Ian subsequently signed for United for £200,000 and Derby were fined by the Football League over the matter! To make things worse, Ian then scored on his United debut! After 43 first-team games, during which he scored 12 goals, he suffered an ankle injury and aggravated it in United's gymnasium, resulting in his retirement from the game.

| 1948 | Arsenal | H | First Division | 1-1 |

With Old Trafford still suffering from bomb damage, Manchester United were playing their 'home' matches at Maine Road, the ground of their biggest rivals Manchester City. Today's visitors were League leaders (and eventual Champions) Arsenal and the match between the top two sides in England attracted not only the largest crowd of the day but a record for a League match played in this country – 83,260 to see a 1-1 draw.

1953	Portsmouth	H	First Division	1-0
1970	West Ham United	A	First Division	0-0
1976	Tottenham Hotspur	A	First Division	1-1

JANUARY 18TH

1890	Preston North End	A	FA Cup 1st Round	1-6
1902	Bristol City	A	Second Division	0-4

Newton Heath club officials had to undertake a house-to-house collection in order to raise sufficient money to buy rail tickets for the journey to Bristol! The club were already threatened with a winding-up order, their ground had been closed and their previous fixture, against Middlesbrough, postponed. Had the club been unable to fulfil today's fixture, the likelihood is that they would have been extinct within 24 hours. As it was, they lived on a hand-to-mouth basis for the next few months before finally resolving their financial problems.

1905	Fulham	A	FA Cup Intermediate Round Replay	0-0
1908	Sheffield United .	A	First Division	0-2
1913	Everton	A	First Division	1-4
1919	Stockport County	H	Lancashire Section Principal Tournament	0-2
1930	Middlesbrough	H	First Division	0-3
1936	Newcastle United	H	Second Division	3-1
1941	Bolton Wanderers	A	North Regional League	2-3
1947	Middlesbrough	A	First Division	4-2

1957 An astonishing crowd of 18,069 turned up at Wrexham for the Cheshire League match with Winsford United. As attractive a draw as Winsford are, the true reason for such a turnout was that Wrexham were shortly to meet another United, Manchester, in the FA Cup and tickets for this match went on sale today!

1958	Bolton Wanderers	H	First Division	7-2

Bobby Charlton scored the second League hat-trick of his career in this 7-2 demolition of Bolton. United's other goals were notched by Viollet (two), Edwards and Scanlon.

1964	West Bromwich Albion	A	First Division	4-1
1969	Sunderland	H	First Division	4-1
1975	Sunderland	A	Second Division	0-0
1986	Nottingham Forest	H	First Division	2-3
1992	Notts County	A	First Division	1-1
1993	Queens Park Rangers	A	FA Premier League	3-1
1997	Coventry City	A	FA Premier League	2-0

JANUARY 19TH

1885 Mickey Hamill born in Belfast. After sterling service for a number of Belfast clubs, Mickey was transferred to United in January 1911. After struggling to find his form in the forward line his career took off following a switch to half-back and he went on to make 59 appearances for the first team. After a dispute over a written guarantee of a benefit, he returned to Belfast in 1914 and rejected all offers from the United directors to settle the matter. He finally returned to Manchester in 1920, although he promptly signed for rivals City, and United collected £1,000 for their troubles! After a two-year spell playing in the United States he returned once again to Belfast to finish his career.

1901	Port Vale	A	Second Division	0-2
1907	Sheffield United	H	First Division	2-0
1918	Liverpool	A	Lancashire Section Principal Tournament	1-5
1924	Fulham	A	Second Division	1-3
1929	Leeds United	H	First Division	1-2
1931	Stoke City	Anfield	FA Cup 3rd Round 2nd Replay	4-2
1935	Barnsley	A	Second Division	2-0
1946	Grimsby Town	A	Football League North	0-1
1952	Manchester City	H	First Division	1-1
1957	Sheffield Wednesday	A	First Division	1-2
1972	Southampton	H	FA Cup 3rd Round Replay	4-1 [aet]

Once again George Best was the star of the show, scoring twice as United finally overcame strong opposition from Southampton after extra time. United's other goals were scored by Sadler and Aston and earned United the right to face Preston in the fourth round.

1974	Arsenal	H	First Division	1-1
1977	Bristol City	H	First Division	2-1
1983	Nottingham Forest	H	Milk Cup 5th Round	4-0
1991	Queens Park Rangers	A	First Division	1-1

1996   Manchester United paid £500,000 to Manchester City for goalkeeper Tony Coton, ostensibly as cover for Peter Schmeichel. In July the following year Tony moved on again to Sunderland for £350,000 without having made a first-team appearance at United.

1998	Southampton	A	FA Premier League	0-1

JANUARY 20TH

1897	Blackpool	A	FA Cup 5th Qualifying Round Replay	2-1
1900	Burton Swifts	H	Second Division	4-0
1906	Glossop	H	Second Division	5-2
1912	West Bromwich Albion	H	First Division	1-2
1917	Liverpool	A	Lancashire Section Principal Tournament	3-3
1923	Leeds United	H	Second Division	0-0
1934	Bolton Wanderers	A	Second Division	1-3
1940	Stoke City	H	War Regional League, Western Division	4-3
1951	Charlton Athletic	A	First Division	2-1
1962	Tottenham Hotspur	A	First Division	2-2
1965	Everton	H	Inter-Cities Fairs Cup 3rd Round 1st Leg	1-1

One of the few occasions in which English sides have met in European competition ended with a 1-1 draw, John Connolly getting United's goal.

1968	Sheffield Wednesday	H	First Division	4-2
1973	West Ham United	H	First Division	2-2
1988	Oxford United	A	Littlewoods Cup 5th Round	0-2

1994   Sir Matt Busby, perhaps the finest club manager of all time, died at Alexandra Hospital in Manchester at the age of 84. He was born at Bellshill, Lanarkshire on May 26th 1909 and joined Manchester City as a player in 1928. During his time with City he won an FA Cup winners' medal against Portsmouth in 1934, adequate compensation for the previous year's defeat against Everton, and was capped by Scotland once, in 1934 against Wales. He was transferred to Liverpool in 1936, but the Second World War cut short his playing career. He might have remained with Liverpool when the war was over, being offered a trainer's role at Anfield, but instead he chose to accept an offer from Manchester United in February 1945 to become their manager, taking up the post in October the same year. He arrived to take over a club with a bomb-damaged ground and few players, but set about the task of building a side around the mercurial talents of captain Johnny Carey and won the FA Cup in 1948 in one of the truly great finals against Blackpool. The same side was runners-up in the League for three consecutive seasons before finally lifting the title in 1951-52.

Despite this win Busby was already planning for the future, placing his faith in a youth scheme that became the envy of the football world. Players that won the FA Youth Cup for the first five years of its existence formed the backbone of a United side that won the Football League in 1955-56 by a clear 11 points and earned entry into the European Cup. Although they fell at the semi-final stage to Real Madrid, Busby said the only thing his team lacked was experience, and they were getting that. Back-to-back League titles ensured entry into the European Cup in season 1957-58 (they might have won the double the year before, for they reached the FA Cup final, but they came up against Aston Villa in general, and Roy McParland in particular, who, in the words of one newspaper report, 'was waiting to bag two goals and one goalkeeper'), where once again they reached the semi-final after a 3-3 draw in Belgrade against Red Star. On the way home the plane made a stopover at Munich and, on the third take-off attempt, crashed into a house at the end of the runway, killing seven players immediately (Byrne, Bent, Jones, Whelan, Colman, Pegg and Taylor). Duncan Edwards died two weeks later, and both Blanchflower and Berry suffered injuries that curtailed their playing careers. Busby was dreadfully injured; so badly in fact that the last rites were administered on three occasions. But he somehow pulled through and appeared at Wembley at the end of the season, where United's patched up team lost 2-0 to Bolton.

Busby built a third great side, although it took considerably longer to bear fruit; the FA Cup in 1963 (3-1 against Leicester City) was a stepping stone to League success in 1964-65 (on goal average) and again in 1966-67. United's European Cup exploits in 1965-66 had taken them to the semi-final stage once again; in 1967-68 they made it to the final (at last overcoming Real Madrid, with a goal from Munich veteran Bill Foulkes ensuring their passage) where they came up against Benfica at Wembley. A 4-1 victory after extra time gave Matt Busby the trophy he desired more than any other. After another tilt at the European Cup the following season (semi-finalists once again), Sir Matt Busby (he was knighted after the European Cup win, only the third soccer knight) became United's general manager in 1969. Although it has never been claimed he sought to influence the decisions of his successors, his presence did cast a shadow from which Wilf McGuinness and Frank O'Farrell in particular found it difficult to escape. Sir Matt continued to serve United through the '70s and '80s, first as a director and more recently as President, and there can have been no prouder man when United finally brought the League title back to Old Trafford in 1993. He continued to attend games right up until his death. There have been perhaps no more than half a dozen truly great managers in the British game – but Sir Matt Busby is undoubtedly one of them.

JANUARY 21ST

1893	Blackburn Rovers	A	FA Cup 1st Round	0-4
1899	Walsall	A	Second Division	0-2
1905	Glossop	H	Second Division	4-1
1911	Manchester City	A	First Division	1-1
1922	Sunderland	A	First Division	1-2
1928	Newcastle United	A	First Division	1-4
1933	Tottenham Hotspur	H	Second Division	2-1

1939	Stoke City	H	First Division	0-1
1950	Stoke City	A	First Division	1-3
1956	Preston North End	A	First Division	1-3
1961	Leicester City	A	First Division	0-6

1964 Danny Wallace born in London. One of three brothers who all played professional football (the other two being Rod and Ray) Danny began his career with Southampton and was sold to United in September 1989 for £1.3 million. Although he won an FA Cup winners' medal in 1990, the subsequent emergence of Ryan Giggs and the arrivals of Lee Sharpe and Andrei Kanchelskis restricted the first-team opportunities for Danny and he was sold to Birmingham City for £400,000 in October 1993.

| 1967 | Manchester City | A | First Division | 1-1 |

1975 Nicky Butt born in Manchester. He joined the club straight from school and progressed through the ranks and became a mainstay of the youth side, helping them win the FA Youth Cup in 1991-92 with a two-goal display in the first-leg win against Crystal Palace. He made his first-team debut in November 1992 against Oldham Athletic and following the subsequent departure of Paul Ince he became a permanent fixture in the United midfield. He has already collected two Premiership medals, an FA Cup winners' medal and two Charity Shields, including an action-packed appearance against Newcastle United in 1997 in which he scored with a superb header and later had to leave the field suffering from concussion. Has also represented England at Schoolboy, Youth, Under-21 and full levels.

1977 Phil Neville born in Bury. The younger brother of fellow United player Gary, Phil was a good all-round sportsman as a youngster, representing England Schoolboys at both football and cricket. Indeed, he was offered a professional contract with Lancashire as a cricketer but chose instead to concentrate on football and joined Manchester United. Captain of the Youth side that won the FA Youth Cup in 1994-95, he made his full League debut the same season. He became a first-team regular the following season and has since won two Premiership medals, an FA Cup winners' medal and an FA Charity Shield winners' medal. He has represented England at School, Youth, Under-21 and full levels, and in May 1996 against China he and brother Gary became the first brothers to represent England since the Charltons 23 years previously.

1978	Derby County	H	First Division	4-0
1984	Southampton	H	First Division	3-2
1989	West Ham United	A	First Division	3-1
1990	Norwich City	A	First Division	0-2

JANUARY 22ND

| 1898 | Manchester City | H | Lancashire Senior Cup 2nd Round | 1-0 |
| 1910 | Tottenham Hotspur | H | First Division | 5-0 |

This was the last League match played at United's Clayton ground, with the club shortly moving into the new custom-built ground at Old Trafford. A crowd of 7,000 saw this final game at Clayton. Shortly after United moved out of Clayton, the stands blew down!

1916	Stockport County	A	Lancashire Section Principal Tournament	1-3
1921	West Bromwich Albion	A	First Division	2-0
1927	Leeds United	A	First Division	3-2
1938	Barnsley	A	FA Cup 4th Round	2-2

Midway through the match Barnsley's Frank Bokas took a throw-in and lofted the ball into the penalty area towards the goal. With almost no one around him, United keeper Tom Breen did the unthinkable and played the ball as it entered the net, enabling Bokas to claim the honour of becoming the only player to have scored direct from a throw-in!

1944	Manchester City	H	Football League North (Second Championship)	1-3
1949	Manchester City	H	First Division	0-0
1955	Bolton Wanderers	H	First Division	1-1
1966	Derby County	A	FA Cup 3rd Round	5-2
1972	Chelsea	H	First Division	0-1
1975	Norwich City	A	League Cup Semi-Final 2nd Leg	0-1

With the first leg having finished in a 2-2 draw at Old Trafford, Norwich's single-goal win was enough to ensure a 3-2 aggregate win and an appearance at Wembley in the final.

1977	Birmingham City	A	First Division	3-2
1983	Nottingham Forest	H	First Division	2-0
1992	Aston Villa	H	First Division	1-0
1994	Everton	H	FA Premier League	1-0

A huge outpouring of emotion engulfed Old Trafford, with thousands laying scarves, flowers and messages outside the ground, in particular in front of the famous clock which records those who lost their lives at Munich, in tribute to the late Sir Matt Busby. A minute's silence was held at all football grounds around the country, with the most moving tribute coming at Old Trafford. A lone Scottish piper led the teams on to the pitch and all eyes then turned to the empty seat of club President Sir Matt Busby, which had been draped in a black ribbon. The two teams put in a performance to grace the occasion, with United winning 1-0 through a Ryan Giggs goal. It was also revealed that a worker from the undertaker's handling the burial had taken photographs of Sir Matt lying in his coffin and was attempting to sell them to the highest newspaper bidder. The police ultimately arrested and charged the 'snapper'.

| 1995 | Blackburn Rovers | H | FA Premier League | 1-0 |
| 1996 | West Ham United | A | FA Premier League | 1-0 |

JANUARY 23RD

| 1904 | Bradford City | A | Second Division | 3-3 |

On the same day, Harry Rowley was born in Bilston in Staffordshire. Signed by United from Shrewsbury Town in May 1928 for £100, he remained at United for three years before switching across Manchester to sign for City. Two years later he signed for Oldham and then returned to Old Trafford in December 1934 for £1,375, winning a Second Division championship medal in 1936. He left United in 1937 for non-League football.

1905	Fulham	N	FA Cup Intermediate Round 2nd Replay	0-1
1909	Manchester City	H	First Division	3-1
1915	Blackburn Rovers	A	First Division	3-3
1926	Manchester City	H	First Division	1-6

One of the most embarrassing defeats United have ever suffered at the hands of their nearest rivals, with a crowd of 48,657 witnessing the rout. United's consolation goal was scored by Rennox. Despite this and other heavy defeats during the course of the season (7-0 at Blackburn, 6-0 at Huddersfield and 5-0 at Liverpool), United still finished the season in ninth place in the First Division.

1932	Tottenham Hotspur	A	Second Division	1-4
1937	Sheffield Wednesday	A	First Division	0-1
1943	Everton	H	Football League North (Second Championship)	1-4
1954	Bolton Wanderers	H	First Division	1-5
1960	Tottenham Hotspur	A	First Division	1-2
1965	Stoke City	H	First Division	1-1

1969   Andre Kanchelskis born in Kirowgrad in the Soviet Union. He began his career with Dynamo Kiev and then Shakhtyor Donetsk before joining United on trial in March 1991. After successfully coming through he was offered a full contract and went on to win a League Cup winners' medal the following year. Despite also collecting Premiership medals in 1993 and 1994 and an FA Cup winners' medal in 1994, his appearances for United were often confined to coming on from the substitutes' bench. In August 1995, following a fallout with the manager, he was transferred to Everton for £5 million (a profit to United of £4.35 million). Although top scorer for the club in 1995-96, he subsequently moved on to Italian side Fiorentina for a fee of £8 million and then Glasgow Rangers.

1982	Stoke City	A	First Division	3-0
1989	Queens Park Rangers	H	FA Cup 3rd Round 2nd Replay	3-0
1991	Southampton	H	Rumbelows Cup 5th Round Replay	3-2
1993	Brighton & Hove Albion	H	FA Cup 4th Round	1-0

JANUARY 24TH

1891	Sheffield Wednesday	A	Football Alliance	2-1
1903	Glossop	A	Second Division	3-1
1914	Oldham Athletic	A	First Division	2-2
1920	West Bromwich Albion	A	First Division	1-2
1925	Oldham Athletic	H	Second Division	0-1
1931	Grimsby Town	A	FA Cup 4th Round	0-1
1948	Liverpool	H	FA Cup 4th Round	3-0

Although this was a 'home' FA Cup tie for United, Old Trafford was still not ready for use and so the tie was switched to Everton's Goodison Park ground, barely one mile from Liverpool's ground! A crowd of 74,000 saw United win 3-0.

1953	Bolton Wanderers	A	First Division	1-2
1955	Old Trafford was the venue when the FA Cup's most protracted tie was finally settled – Stoke City beat Bury 3-2 after 9 hours and 22 minutes of action.			
1970	Manchester City	H	FA Cup 4th Round	3-0
1973	Everton	H	First Division	0-0
1976	Peterborough United	H	FA Cup 4th Round	3-1
1981	Nottingham Forest	A	FA Cup 4th Round	0-1
1987	Arsenal	H	First Division	2-0
1988	Arsenal	A	First Division	1-1
1998	Walsall	H	FA Cup 4th Round	5-1

JANUARY 25TH

1890	Sunderland Albion	A	Football Alliance	0-2
1902	Blackpool	H	Second Division	0-1
1908	Chelsea	H	First Division	1-0
1913	Sheffield Wednesday	H	First Division	2-0
1919	Liverpool	A	Lancashire Section Principal Tournament	1-1
1930	Liverpool	A	First Division	0-1
1936	Stoke City	A	FA Cup 4th Round	0-0
1941	Bolton Wanderers	H	North Regional League	4-1
1947	Nottingham Forest	H	FA Cup 4th Round	0-2
1958	Ipswich Town	H	FA Cup 4th Round	2-0
1964	Bristol Rovers	H	FA Cup 4th Round	4-1
1969	Watford	H	FA Cup 4th Round	1-1
1986	Sunderland	A	FA Cup 4th Round	0-0

1995 Crystal Palace   A   FA Premier League   1-1
Eric Cantona was sent off for kicking out at Crystal Palace defender Richard Shaw during
Manchester United's 1-1 draw. As Cantona was making the walk back to the dressing-
room he reacted to the taunts of the fans and launched a two-footed martial arts style kick
at one, Matthew Simmons, then leaped to his feet in order to continue the attack with his
fists! United officials and players finally managed to haul him away from the fracas,
although team-mate Paul Ince was also implicated. Although both Ince and Cantona were
allowed to return to Manchester immediately after the match, the police said they
expected charges to follow, certainly against Cantona, as a result of serious allegations of
assault from a member of the public. The FA charged Cantona with bringing the game
into disrepute and gave him 14 days to prepare his defence, although they did not impose
any immediate ban. Although technically he was available for selection for the FA Cup
tie against Wrexham on Saturday, United said they would not name him in the team and
would announce any club punishment on the player on Friday at noon.
1997 Wimbledon   H   FA Cup 4th Round   1-1

JANUARY 26TH

1893 Notts County   A   First Division   0-4
1907 Bolton Wanderers   A   First Division   1-0
1918 Liverpool   H   Lancashire Section Principal Tournament   0-2
1924 Fulham   H   Second Division   0-0
1929 Bury   H   FA Cup 4th Round   0-1
1935 Nottingham Forest   A   FA Cup 3rd Round Replay   0-0
1938 Barnsley   H   FA Cup 4th Round Replay   1-0
1946 Preston North End   H   FA Cup 4th Round 1st Leg   1-0
1952 Tottenham Hotspur   H   First Division   2-0
The heirs to the League title beat the reigning League champions 2-0 thanks to goals
from Stan Pearson and an Alf Ramsey own goal in front of a crowd of 40,845.
1957 Wrexham   A   FA Cup 4th Round   5-0
1970 Leeds United   H   First Division   2-2
1974 Ipswich Town   H   FA Cup 4th Round   0-1
1985 Coventry City   H   FA Cup 4th Round   2-1
1991 Bolton Wanderers   H   FA Cup 4th Round   1-0
1994 Portsmouth   A   Coca-Cola Cup 5th Round Replay   1-0
1995 The police announced they had received a complaint regarding the behaviour of Eric
Cantona the night previously and that they would therefore investigate the incidents
involving Eric and team-mate Paul Ince. In addition the FA gave Cantona 14 days in
which to answer their charges.

JANUARY 27TH

1876 William Jackson born in Flint. A Welsh international forward by the time he joined
Newton Heath, William signed for the club in July 1899 from St Helens Recreation.
Over the next two seasons he made 64 appearances for the first team, scoring 14 goals,
a relatively low ration for a forward, and he was allowed to sign for Barrow in 1902.
He returned to Flint (with whom he had begun his career) in 1905 and died there on
25th March 1954.
1894 Middlesbrough   H   FA Cup 1st Round   4-0
1906 Stockport County   A   Second Division   1-0
1912 Sunderland   A   First Division   0-5
At the end of the 1910-11 season United had confirmed themselves as champions with
a 5-1 demolition of Sunderland at Old Trafford, but their defence of their title had

faltered and spluttered all season, with this 5-0 rout the third of four consecutive defeats. Not surprisingly, United finished the season in mid-table.

1917	Stockport County	H	Lancashire Section Principal Tournament	0-1
1923	Leeds United	A	Second Division	1-0
1934	Brentford	H	Second Division	1-3
1951	Leeds United	H	FA Cup 4th Round	4-0
1968	Tottenham Hotspur	H	FA Cup 3rd Round	2-2

Brian Kidd and Joe Kinnear of Spurs both received their marching orders in this fiercely fought FA Cup tie at Old Trafford.

1973	Coventry City	A	First Division	1-1
1982	West Ham United	H	First Division	1-0
1992	Southampton	A	FA Cup 4th Round	0-0
1993	Nottingham Forest	H	FA Premier League	2-0

1994 The funeral of Sir Matt Busby took place at Our Lady and St Johns Chuch in Chorlton-cum-Hardy with nearly 90 former United players in attendance. The funeral procession was watched by around 5,000 fans who lined the route and after two minutes' silence the body was taken to Southern Cemetery.

1995 Following his attack on a fan after being sent off at Selhurst Park two days ago Eric Cantona learned of his punishment from his club – Manchester United director Maurice Watkins announced the player was banned from the United first team for the rest of the season and had been fined the maximum sum allowable in his contract, £20,000. A short while after the press conference, United chairman/chief executive Martin Edwards claimed there was every likelihood Cantona would still be playing this season, albeit in the reserves. Later, FA chief executive Graham Kelly refuted this suggestion. Whilst generally welcoming the stand the club had taken against the player, he stated that it was unlikely he would play for the club before the FA hearing. On the strength of this, it appeared that Cantona would be banned for the rest of the season by the FA as well, except they couldn't tell him for nearly two weeks! At the same time, Crystal Palace announced that the fan involved in the fracas, Matthew Simmons, was to be banned from Selhurst Park for the rest of the season.

1996	Reading	A	FA Cup 4th Round	3-0

JANUARY 28TH

1899	Tottenham Hotspur	A	FA Cup 1st Round	1-1
1911	Everton	H	First Division	2-2
1922	Sunderland	H	First Division	3-1
1928	Bury	A	FA Cup 4th Round	1-1
1931	Sheffield Wednesday	H	First Division	4-1
1939	Chelsea	A	First Division	1-0
1950	Watford	A	FA Cup 4th Round	1-0
1961	Sheffield Wednesday	A	FA Cup 4th Round	1-1
1967	Stoke City	H	FA Cup 3rd Round	2-0
1978	West Bromwich Albion	H	FA Cup 4th Round	1-1

1980 Granada Television's *World in Action* investigated the activities of United chairman Louis Edwards, claiming United kept a secret cash fund in order to offer inducements to young players to join the club, that Edwards had been involved in irregular dealings relating to the purchase of club shares and had made a substantial profit on his way to obtaining a majority shareholding and that there were further irregularities involving cash and gifts for contracts for his meat firm. Although Edwards claimed he did not have a guilty conscience and that he was proud of what he had done for Manchester United, Sir Harold Thompson of the Football Association announced that there should be an FA investigation to look into the accusations.

1981	Sunderland	A	First Division	0-2
1989	Oxford United	H	FA Cup 4th Round	4-0
1990	Hereford United	A	FA Cup 4th Round	1-0
1995	Wrexham	H	FA Cup 4th Round	5-2

JANUARY 29TH

| 1898 | Walsall | H | FA Cup 1st Round | 1-0 |
| 1916 | Liverpool | H | Lancashire Section Principal Tournament | 1-1 |

1932 Tommy Taylor born in Barnsley. He joined Barnsley straight from school and turned professional in 1949. He made an almost immediate impression at Oakwell, scoring a phenomenal 26 goals in 44 League appearances before Matt Busby lured him to Old Trafford in March 1953 for a fee of £29,999, a figure deliberately £1 short so as not to burden the player with the tag of £30,000. At Old Trafford Tommy was converted from inside-forward to centre-forward and proved an immense success, netting 112 League goals in only 166 appearances. He also scored five FA Cup and 11 European goals during his time at Old Trafford. As well as winning two League championships with United, Tommy was capped for England on 19 occasions, appearing in the 1954 World Cup tournament and helping England qualify for the 1958 finals. Sadly, he lost his life in the Munich air crash that year, robbing both United and England of an exceptional goalscorer.

1936	Stoke City	H	FA Cup 4th Round Replay	0-2
1938	Stockport County	H	Second Division	3-1
1944	Manchester City	A	Football League North (Second Championship)	3-2
1949	Bradford Park Avenue	H	FA Cup 4th Round	1-1
1955	Manchester City	A	FA Cup 4th Round	0-2
1966	Sheffield Wednesday	A	First Division	0-0
1972	West Bromwich Albion	A	First Division	1-2
1977	Queens Park Rangers	H	FA Cup 4th Round	1-0
1983	Luton Town	A	FA Cup 4th Round	2-0
1986	Sunderland	H	FA Cup 4th Round Replay	3-0

1996 An FA inquiry found United guilty of poaching after Oldham Athletic had complained schoolboy David Brown was persuaded to sign for the Old Trafford club. United were fined £20,000 and ordered to pay costs for the inquiry.

| 1997 | Wimbledon | H | FA Premier League | 2-1 |

JANUARY 30TH

1892	Crewe Alexandra	H	Football Alliance	5-3
1897	Kettering	H	FA Cup 1st Round	5-1
1904	Woolwich Arsenal	H	Second Division	1-0
1909	Liverpool	A	First Division	1-3
1915	Notts County	H	First Division	2-2
1926	Tottenham Hotspur	A	FA Cup 4th Round	2-2
1932	Nottingham Forest	H	Second Division	3-2
1935	Nottingham Forest	H	FA Cup 4th Round	0-3
1937	Arsenal	A	FA Cup 4th Round	0-5
1943	Everton	A	Football League North (Second Championship)	5-0
1946	Preston North End	A	FA Cup 4th Round 2nd Leg	1-3

Despite having already beaten Preston 1-0 in the FA Cup, United were eliminated after Preston won the tie 3-2 on aggregate. This remains, of course, the only season in which the early rounds in the FA Cup have been subject to home and away legs.

1960	Liverpool	A	FA Cup 4th Round	3-1
1965	Stoke City	A	FA Cup 4th Round	0-0
1971	Huddersfield Town	A	First Division	2-1
1982	Swansea City	A	First Division	0-2
1988	Chelsea	H	FA Cup 4th Round	2-0
1993	Ipswich Town	A	FA Premier League	1-2
1994	Norwich City	A	FA Cup 4th Round	2-0

JANUARY 31ST

1903	Chesterfield	A	Second Division	0-2
1920	Aston Villa	H	FA Cup 2nd Round	1-2
1931	Grimsby Town	A	First Division	1-2
1933	Grimsby Town	A	Second Division	1-1
1942	Southport	A	Football League Northern Section (Second Championship)	3-1
1948	Sheffield United	A	First Division	1-2
1953	Walthamstow Avenue	H	FA Cup 4th Round	1-1

Unquestionably the shock of the round as Walthamstow, having already accounted for Stockport County in the third round, so nearly added the most prestigious League scalp of all to their belts: the League champions. A goal from Lewis spared United's blushes and ensured a replay for non-League Walthamstow.

1959	Newcastle United	H	First Division	4-4
1962	Arsenal	H	FA Cup 4th Round	1-0
1968	Tottenham Hotspur	A	FA Cup 3rd Round Replay	0-1 [aet]
1970	Derby County	H	First Division	1-0
1976	Birmingham City	H	First Division	3-1
1979	Fulham	A	FA Cup 4th Round	1-1
1981	Birmingham City	H	First Division	2-0
1987	Coventry City	H	FA Cup 4th Round	0-1
1998	Leicester City	H	FA Premier League	0-1

United's faltering continued right through the month of January as they finished with a home defeat by Leicester. Fortunately, the rest of the chasing pack were also tripping over themselves and so United's position at the top of the Premiership continued almost unchallenged.

FEBRUARY 1ST

1890	Ardwick	A	Friendly	3-0
1896	Kettering	H	FA Cup 1st Round	2-1
1899	Tottenham Hotspur	H	FA Cup 1st Round Replay	3-5

Despite having seemingly done the hard work in securing a draw at Tottenham and a hat-trick from William Bryant, United slid out of the cup 5-3.

1902	Stockport County	A	Second Division	0-1
1908	Chelsea	H	FA Cup 2nd Round	1-0
1913	Plymouth Argyle	A	FA Cup 2nd Round	2-0
1919	Liverpool	H	Lancashire Section Principal Tournament	0-1
1928	Bury	H	FA Cup 4th Round Replay	1-0
1930	West Ham United	H	First Division	4-2
1936	Southampton	H	Second Division	4-0
1947	Arsenal	A	First Division	2-6
1958	Arsenal	A	First Division	5-4

Although it was not apparent at the time, Manchester United's 'Busby Babes' played their last game on British soil, winning a thrilling match 5-4 at Highbury against Arsenal. A crowd of 63,578 were present to see Duncan Edwards, Tommy Taylor and Bobby Charlton power United into a 3-0 lead by half-time. Arsenal scored their first on the hour mark and then scored twice in two minutes through Jimmy Bloomfield to level the scores. Spurred once again into action, United restored their lead thanks to goals from Dennis Viollet and Tommy Taylor again, and although Tapscott reduced the lead to a single goal, United held on to win.

1961	Sheffield Wednesday	H	FA Cup 4th Round Replay	2-7
1964	Arsenal	H	First Division	3-1
1969	Ipswich Town	A	First Division	0-1
1975	Bristol City	H	Second Division	0-1
1978	West Bromwich Albion	A	FA Cup 4th Round Replay	2-3 [aet]
1992	Arsenal	A	First Division	1-1
1997	Southampton	H	FA Premier League	2-1

FEBRUARY 2ND

1895	Stoke	H	FA Cup 1st Round	2-3

1902 Sam Hopkinson born near Sheffield. After drifting in and out of League football Sam was signed by United in May 1929 and made his debut in January 1931, being introduced when the club had been all but relegated from the First Division. Although he made a number of appearances the following term in the Second Division, he was never a regular and was allowed to join Tranmere in May 1935.

1907	Newcastle United	A	First Division	0-5
1918	Stoke City	A	Lancashire Section Principal Tournament	1-5
1924	Huddersfield Town	H	FA Cup 2nd Round	0-3
1929	West Ham United	H	First Division	2-3
1935	Norwich City	A	Second Division	2-3
1938	Barnsley	A	Second Division	2-2
1946	Blackpool	H	Football League North	4-2
1957	Manchester City	A	First Division	4-2
1966	Benfica	H	European Cup 2nd Round 1st Leg	3-2

With Benfica unbeaten at home in European Cup competition for over four years, United needed to build a commanding lead if they were to survive the cauldron of the Stadium of Light and progress into the semi-finals. And, although United attacked from the off, it was the visitors who stunned the crowd into silence by taking the lead after half an hour after Augusto had headed home Eusebio's cross. By half-time, however, United had retrieved the initiative, equalising through David Herd and then taking the lead after Denis Law had converted Bobby Charlton's centre. A quarter of an hour into the second half Bill Foulkes scored one of his rare goals to inch United into a 3-1 lead and on the brink of the prospect of a famous victory. Unfortunately, Eusebio had other ideas, scoring once and coming mightily close on another two occasions to leave the final score at 3-2 in United's favour. Although it was a victory, there were those who felt a slender one-goal advantage would not be enough come the return leg.

1974	Coventry City	A	First Division	0-1
1980	Derby County	A	First Division	3-1
1985	West Bromwich Albion	H	First Division	2-0
1986	West Ham United	A	First Division	1-2

FEBRUARY 3RD

1894	Aston Villa	A	First Division	1-5

1896	Leicester Fosse	H	Second Division	2-0
1900	Sheffield Wednesday	H	Second Division	1-0

Newton Heath gave a debut to Gilbert Godsmark, who had just joined the club from Ashford FC. According to reports of the game, 'Godsmark proved a great success, he has any amount of dash and ability.' Unfortunately, after nine games he was called up as a reservist for the Boer War, ordered to report to the headquarters of the Army Service Corps in April 1900 and promptly shipped out to South Africa. Although Newton Heath retained his registration they were informed in February 1901 that Godsmark had been killed in action. It was later revealed that he had joined the club for an agreed fee of £40, half being payable immediately, the other half upon completion of a satisfactory trial period. As he had been shipped out to war before the period had been completed, the money had been withheld. Ashford FC then served a writ!

1906	Norwich City	H	FA Cup 2nd Round	3-0
1912	Coventry City	A	FA Cup 2nd Round	5-1
1917	Bury	A	Lancashire Section Principal Tournament	1-1
1923	Tottenham Hotspur	A	FA Cup 2nd Round	0-4
1926	Tottenham Hotspur	H	FA Cup 4th Round Replay	2-0
1934	Burnley	A	Second Division	4-1
1937	Preston North End	H	First Division	1-1
1945	Manchester City	H	Football League North (Second Championship)	1-3
1951	Middlesbrough	H	First Division	1-0
1962	Cardiff City	H	First Division	3-0
1965	Stoke City	H	FA Cup 4th Round Replay	1-0
1968	Tottenham Hotspur	A	First Division	2-1
1969	Watford	A	FA Cup 4th Round Replay	2-0
1979	Arsenal	H	First Division	0-2

1984   Twelve months after his failure to merge Reading and Oxford United, Robert Maxwell turned his attentions to another Football League club – Manchester United. The _Daily Mirror_, of which he was proprietor, revealed Maxwell's £10 million bid for United. Although the Edwards family, who controlled Manchester United, took the offer seriously enough to enter into discussions with Maxwell, the deal fell through ten days later because Maxwell would not increase his offer.

1990	Manchester City	H	First Division	1-1
1991	Liverpool	H	First Division	1-1
1996	Wimbledon	A	FA Premier League	4-2

Eric Cantona made his first appearance at Selhurst Park since his sending off against Crystal Palace a year previously. This time around he had more happy memories of the ground, scoring two of United's goals in the 4-2 win over Wimbledon. United's other goals were scored by Andy Cole and an own goal by Chris Perry.

FEBRUARY 4TH

1899	Port Vale	A	Second Division	0-1
1911	Aston Villa	H	FA Cup 2nd Round	2-1
1928	Tottenham Hotspur	A	First Division	0-4
1933	Oldham Athletic	H	Second Division	2-0
1939	Preston North End	H	First Division	1-1
1950	Burnley	H	First Division	3-2
1956	Burnley	H	First Division	2-0
1961	Aston Villa	H	First Division	1-1
1967	Burnley	A	First Division	1-1

1984	Norwich City	H	First Division	0-0
1995	Aston Villa	H	FA Premier League	1-0
1997	Wimbledon	A	FA Cup 4th Round Replay	0-1

In the final minutes and with United facing defeat, goalkeeper Peter Schmeichel appeared in the Wimbledon penalty area to try and lend his support to the attack. He had done this many times previously and even scored in a UEFA Cup tie, and his presence certainly unsettled the Wimbledon defence. Almost on the stroke of full-time he had the ball in the net and had appeared to have forced extra time, but unfortunately this effort was ruled out for offside and so ended United's reign as cup-holders.

FEBRUARY 5TH

1910	Preston North End	A	First Division	0-1
1916	Bury	A	Lancashire Section Principal Tournament	1-2
1921	Liverpool	H	First Division	1-1
1927	Burnley	A	First Division	0-1
1936	Tottenham Hotspur	A	Second Division	0-0
1938	Southampton	A	Second Division	3-3
1944	Bury	A	Football League North (Second Championship)	3-0

1946 David Sadler born in Yalding in Kent. Spotted by United whilst playing for Maidstone United, he was signed as an amateur in November 1962 and upgraded to the professional ranks in February 1963. Initially used as a forward, he won a medal from the FA Youth Cup winning side in 1964, but found greater first-team opportunities when converted to a defensive role. In this position he won a championship medal in 1967 and a European Cup winners' medal the following year, as well as four caps for England. After loan periods in the United States he left Old Trafford in November 1973 to link up with Bobby Charlton at Preston but was forced to retire owing to injury in May 1977.

| 1947 | Stoke City | H | First Division | 1-1 |
| 1949 | Bradford Park Avenue | A | FA Cup 4th Round Replay | 1-1 [aet] |

1952 Alex Forsyth born in Swinton in Lanarkshire. After a brief spell with Arsenal Alex joined Partick Thistle in 1968 and switched to Old Trafford in December 1972 for £100,000. After taking time to find his best form he was a member of the side that won the Second Division championship in 1975 and reached the FA Cup final the following year, but then lost his place to Jimmy Nicholl. After a spell on loan to Glasgow Rangers, he was sold to the Ibrox club and later played for Motherwell and Hamilton Academical.

| 1953 | Walthamstow Avenue | A | FA Cup 4th Round Replay | 5-2 |

Such was the interest generated by Walthamstow's draw at Old Trafford in the FA Cup, it was obvious that Avenue's own ground would be incapable of accommodating all of the spectators who wished to see the replay and so the decision was taken to move the tie to Arsenal's Highbury ground. A crowd of 49,119 turned up, all hoping to see the biggest cup upset since Walsall's win over Arsenal in the 1930s. In the event they were to be disappointed, for United made sure there was to be no giantkilling with a commanding performance. United's goals were scored by Jack Rowley (two), Byrne, Lewis and Pearson, setting up a fifth-round tie against Everton.

| 1955 | Huddersfield Town | A | First Division | 3-1 |
| 1958 | Red Star Belgrade | A | European Cup 3rd Round 2nd Leg | 3-3 |

Already 2-1 ahead from the first leg, United were quick to ensure Red Star faced an uphill struggle in their attempts to get back into the tie, taking the lead after only 90 seconds through Dennis Viollet. For the rest of the first half, expert defence and the ability to quickly counter-attack were United's chief weapons, and two goals from

Bobby Charlton meant United were 5-1 ahead on aggregate by half-time. It was only just enough, for Red Star came back with a vengeance in the second half and scored three times to level the game. The final three minutes, as Red Star pressed for another goal to level the aggregate scores, were breathtaking, but United held firm to ensure passage into the semi-finals. It was, many of the accompanying journalists reckoned, United's finest performance ever, but sadly it was to prove the last game for many, both writers and players, as the plane returning them all home again crashed at Munich.

| 1966 | Northampton Town | H | First Division | 6-2 |

1968 Lee Martin born in Hyde. Signed by United to professional forms in May 1986, he made his debut in August 1988. He remained with the club until January 1994 when he was transferred to Celtic, a tribunal later setting the fee at £350,000. He had made 83 full appearances and 25 as substitute during his time at Old Trafford, scoring two goals. One of those goals came in the 1990 FA Cup final replay and was the only goal of the game, enabling United to lift the cup for the seventh time in their history. In 1996 he signed for Bristol Rovers on a free transfer.

1972	Preston North End	A	FA Cup 4th Round	2-0
1977	Derby County	H	First Division	3-1
1983	Ipswich Town	A	First Division	1-1
1989	Tottenham Hotspur	H	First Division	1-0
1992	Southampton	H	FA Cup 4th Round Replay	2-2 [lost 4-2 on pens]

Manchester United became the first First Division club to be eliminated from the FA Cup via a penalty shoot-out – after their fourth-round replay with Southampton had ended 2-2 after extra time, penalty misses by Neil Webb and Ryan Giggs ensured it was United who were destined for the record books and the Saints for the fifth round.

| 1994 | Queens Park Rangers | A | FA Premier League | 3-2 |

FEBRUARY 6TH

1897	Loughborough Town	H	Second Division	6-0
1904	Notts County	A	FA Cup 1st Round	3-3
1909	Everton	H	FA Cup 2nd Round	1-0
1915	Sunderland	A	First Division	0-1
1924	Blackpool	A	Second Division	0-1
1926	Burnley	A	First Division	1-0
1932	Chesterfield	A	Second Division	3-1
1935	Port Vale	H	Second Division	2-1
1937	Arsenal	A	First Division	1-1
1943	Manchester City	A	Football League North (Second Championship)	0-0
1954	Preston North End	A	First Division	3-1
1957	Athletico Bilbao	H	European Cup 2nd Round 2nd Leg	3-0
			(played at Maine Road)	

1958 One of the worst tragedies to befall British sport as Manchester United's plane, returning from Belgrade, crashed on take-off at Munich, killing 23 people. The Elizabethan airliner had stopped off in Munich for refuelling on its way home from Belgrade. Snow was falling as the plane tried to take off, causing the pilot to abort the first two attempts. It is believed that on the fatal third attempt, at 3:04 p.m., the plane struck a house at the end of the runway and burst into flames. Killed immediately were United skipper Roger Byrne, players Eddie Colman, Liam Whelan, Tommy Taylor, David Pegg, Mark Jones and Geoff Bent, club secretary Walter Crickmer, coach Bert Whalley and trainer Tom Curry, two crew members, two other passengers and eight journalists, including former England goalkeeper Frank Swift, of the *News of the*

World. Matt Busby and Duncan Edwards were both reported to be close to death, with Busby giving most cause for concern having suffered a crushed chest. The injuries sustained by Johnny Berry and Jackie Blanchflower were such that neither played again.

1960	Manchester City	H	First Division	0-0
1965	Tottenham Hotspur	A	First Division	0-1
1971	Tottenham Hotspur	H	First Division	2-1
1982	Aston Villa	H	First Division	4-1
1988	Coventry City	H	First Division	1-0
1993	Sheffield United	H	FA Premier League	2-1

FEBRUARY 7TH

1914	Tottenham Hotspur	A	First Division	1-2
1920	Sunderland	A	First Division	0-3
1925	Clapton Orient	H	Second Division	4-2

Orient player Albert Pape had arrived at Old Trafford with everyone convinced he was to lead the visitors' forward line. But Pape had been in conversation with United officials since the previous day with a view to signing for Manchester United, a deal that was completed an hour or so before kick-off. The first the Orient players knew of his defection was when he joined the United players on their pitch inspection! To rub salt into the wound, Pape also scored in the game against his old club! But his career at Old Trafford never quite reached the same heights as those surrounding his initial arrival, and after only 18 games he left the club.

1931	Manchester City	H	First Division	1-3

Although Matt Busby would figure greatly in the history of Manchester football in the period after the Second World War, this was the only time he played in a derby match. His presence in the City half-back line enabled the visitors to quickly establish control, scoring through Eric Brook. Although Joe Spence equalised, City always looked the more likely to win the game, and late goals from Ernie Toseland and David Halliday settled the match.

1934	Jimmy Whitehouse died. Born in Birmingham in April 1873, Jimmy had joined

Newton Heath in September 1900 having previously served Grimsby for two spells and Aston Villa, being goalkeeper at the latter club when they had lifted the League and Cup double in 1897. He remained with the Heathens for almost three years before switching across the city to join Manchester City in February 1903, and he later played for Third Lanark, Hull and Southend before retiring.

1948	Charlton Athletic	H	FA Cup 5th Round	2-0

This FA Cup home tie was actually played at Huddersfield Town's Leeds Road ground as Manchester City, with whom United were sharing Maine Road, were also drawn at home in the cup to Preston.

1949	Bradford Park Avenue	H	FA Cup 4th Round 2nd Replay	5-0
1953	Aston Villa	H	First Division	3-1
1959	Tottenham Hotspur	A	First Division	3-1
1970	Northampton Town	A	FA Cup 5th Round	8-2

George Best was the hero of the day, scoring six of United's goals and seemingly beating Northampton on his own. The other two goals were both scored by Brian Kidd.

1976	Coventry City	A	First Division	1-1
1981	Leicester City	A	First Division	0-1
1984	Birmingham City	A	First Division	2-2
1987	Charlton Athletic	A	First Division	0-0

1998　Bolton Wanderers　　H　　FA Premier League　　1-1
The 40th anniversary of the Munich air disaster was acknowledged in this match against Bolton. The visitors were also a reminder of events 40 years ago, for United and Bolton met in the FA Cup final at the end of the season in 1957-58. All the survivors of the crash were presented to the crowd before the kick-off and a minute's silence was observed.

FEBRUARY 8TH

1890	Grimsby Town	A	Football Alliance	0-7
1896	Burton Swifts	A	Second Division	1-4
1908	Newcastle United	H	First Division	1-1
1913	Blackburn Rovers	A	First Division	0-0
1919	Southport Vulcans	A	Lancashire Section Principal Tournament	1-2

1929　Roger Byrne born in Manchester. Signed by United in March 1949, he began his career at inside-forward before finding his more favoured position at full-back. He made his League debut in 1951 and played sufficient games to collect his first League championship medal, but he had ended the season at outside-left. When he was selected in the same position the following season he put in a transfer request, but Matt Busby soon put him back in the team at full-back and he became one of the most accomplished players the game has seen. Capped for England in 33 consecutive games he captained United to two further League titles and the FA Cup final in 1957 and was sadly to lose his life in the Munich air crash when just two days short of his 29th birthday.

1930	Manchester City	A	First Division	1-0
1936	Port Vale	H	Second Division	7-2
1964	Leicester City	A	First Division	2-3
1969	Birmingham City	H	FA Cup 5th Round	6-2
1975	Oxford United	A	Second Division	0-1
1978	Bristol City	H	First Division	1-1
1992	Sheffield Wednesday	H	First Division	1-1
1993	Leeds United	A	FA Premier League	0-0

1995　More trouble for Eric Cantona – he failed to appear voluntarily before the police investigating last month's attack on a fan at Crystal Palace. He was believed to be on holiday in Antigua and therefore ran the risk of being arrested on his return. His United team-mate, Paul Ince, did appear and was questioned for two hours over his part in the night's events.

FEBRUARY 9TH

1901	Burnley	H	FA Cup 1st Round	0-0
1907	Stoke City	H	First Division	4-1
1918	Stoke City	H	Lancashire Section Principal Tournament	2-1
1921	Liverpool	A	First Division	0-2
1924	Blackpool	H	Second Division	0-0
1927	Newcastle United	H	First Division	3-1
1929	Newcastle United	A	First Division	0-5
1935	Swansea Town	A	Second Division	0-0
1946	Liverpool	H	Football League North	2-1
1952	Preston North End	A	First Division	2-1
1957	Arsenal	H	First Division	6-2
1965	Everton	A	Inter-Cities Fairs Cup 3rd Round 2nd Leg	2-1

With the two sides having drawn the first leg 1-1, United's 2-1 victory enabled them to progress into the next round with a 3-2 aggregate win. On the same day, Gordon Strachan was born in Edinburgh. Signed by Dundee straight from school, the diminutive midfielder soon impressed at Dens Park and was transferred to Aberdeen for £50,000 in 1977. Whilst with the club he won three Scottish Cups, a League championship and the European Cup-Winners' Cup as well as the Scottish Player of the Year in 1980. In August 1984 he was sold to United for £500,000 and collected an FA Cup winners' medal at the end of his first season at Old Trafford. In March 1989 he was surprisingly sold to Leeds United for £300,000 but proved to be still on top of his game, helping them win the Second Division championship in 1990 and the First Division in 1992, the latter at Manchester United's expense! He was released by Leeds on a free transfer in March 1995 and re-linked with Ron Atkinson, the manager who had signed him for Manchester United, at Coventry City. Initially player-coach, he subsequently became manager. He was awarded the OBE in 1993 for his services to football.

1974	Leeds United	H	First Division	0-2
1980	Wolverhampton Wanderers	H	First Division	0-1
1985	Newcastle United	A	First Division	1-1
1986	Liverpool	A	First Division	1-1

FEBRUARY 10TH

1894	Blackburn Rovers	H	FA Cup 2nd Round	0-0
1900	Lincoln City	A	Second Division	0-1
1904	Notts County	H	FA Cup 1st Round Replay	2-1
1906	Bradford City	A	Second Division	5-1

After the match, supporters of Bradford City attacked United full-back Bob Bonthron, having taken exception to his robust and uncompromising style of play. Several of the supporters were later charged over the incident. Bonthron had been born in Dundee in 1884 and had joined United in May 1903 from Dundee, and he remained a regular in the team until 1907 when he signed for Sunderland. He later played for Northampton Town, Birmingham and Leith Athletic.

1912	Sheffield Wednesday	A	First Division	0-3
1917	Stoke City	H	Lancashire Section Principal Tournament	4-2
1923	Notts County	A	Second Division	6-1
1934	Oldham Athletic	H	Second Division	2-3
1940	Manchester City	A	War Regional League, Western Division	0-1
1945	Manchester City	A	Football League North (Second Championship)	0-2

1948 Jimmy Rimmer born in Southport. Signed by United as an amateur in May 1963, he was upgraded to the professional ranks in May 1965. He was a member of the squad for the 1968 European Cup final, collecting a winners' medal even though he did not play, and was sold to Arsenal in 1974 for £40,000. Here he won an England cap, but the subsequent arrival of Pat Jennings as first choice goalkeeper prompted a move to Aston Villa in 1977. He won a League championship medal in 1981 and helped the club to the European Cup final the following season. Although he was forced to leave the field with an injury after only eight minutes, he once again collected a winners' medal. He finished his career with Swansea before turning to coaching.

1951	Arsenal	H	FA Cup 5th Round	1-0
1962	Manchester City	A	First Division	2-0
1970	Ipswich Town	A	First Division	1-0
1973	Wolverhampton Wanderers	H	First Division	2-1
1979	Manchester City	A	First Division	3-0
1988	Derby County	A	First Division	2-1

1990	Millwall	A	First Division	2-1
1991	Leeds United	H	Rumbelows Cup Semi-Final 1st Leg	2-1
1996	Blackburn Rovers	H	FA Premier League	1-0

FEBRUARY 11TH

1872   Willie Stewart born in Coupar Angus. Willie joined Newton Heath from Warwick County in 1889 and played and scored in the club's first Football Alliance fixture. He was still with the club when they achieved Football League status, and remained with the club until 1895 when he joined Luton Town. He later played for Millwall Athletic, Luton for a second spell, Thames Ironworks and Dundee where he finished his career. He died in Dundee in June 1945.

1893	Derby County	A	First Division	1-5
1902	Burnley	H	Second Division	2-0
1905	Lincoln City	A	Second Division	0-3
1911	Bristol City	H	First Division	3-1

1917   John Wassall born in Shrewsbury. Signed by United in February 1935 he finally broke into the side on a regular basis in 1938-39, a season in which United consolidated their position in the First Division. The outbreak of the Second World War meant all of John's best years as a player were lost during the hostilities, and by the time League football resumed John was released to sign for Stockport County.

1918   Enoch West's attempt to get his life ban by the FA overturned reached the Appeal Court where he was successful in getting a new trial ordered on the question of whether newspaper comments were defamatory but did not have the ban lifted. The new hearing was not heard for another 11 months and that too was unsuccessful on both counts – West was not libelled and his ban was not lifted.

1920	Oldham Athletic	H	First Division	1-1
1922	Huddersfield Town	H	First Division	1-1
1928	Leicester City	H	First Division	5-2
1933	Preston North End	A	Second Division	3-3
1939	Charlton Athletic	A	First Division	1-7
1950	Portsmouth	H	FA Cup 5th Round	3-3
1956	Luton Town	A	First Division	2-0
1961	Wolverhampton Wanderers	A	First Division	1-2
1967	Nottingham Forest	H	First Division	1-0
1978	Chelsea	A	First Division	2-2
1989	Sheffield Wednesday	A	First Division	2-0
1995	Manchester City	A	FA Premier League	3-0

FEBRUARY 12TH

1898	Liverpool	H	FA Cup 2nd Round	0-0
1910	Newcastle United	A	First Division	4-3
1916	Rochdale	A	Lancashire Section Principal Tournament	2-2
1921	Everton	H	First Division	1-2

United's goal was scored by winger Billy Meredith, who thus became United's oldest goalscorer at 48 years and 201 days.

1927	Cardiff City	H	First Division	1-1
1938	Brentford	A	FA Cup 5th Round	0-2
1944	Bury	H	Football League North (Second Championship)	3-3
1949	Yeovil	H	FA Cup 5th Round	8-0

Plucky Yeovil had accounted for First Division Sunderland in the fourth round, beating them 2-1 on their famous sloping pitch, and the subsequent pairing with United attracted considerable interest in Manchester, with a crowd of 81,565 gathering at Maine Road. Yeovil player-manager Alec Stock kept to his promise that his side would play football, but they were simply outclassed by United, Jack Rowley helping himself to a first-half hat-trick as United led 4-0 by half-time. There was no respite in the second half either, for another four goals saw off the non-League challenge for an 8-0 win for United. Rowley finished the match with five strikes to his credit, United's other goals being scored by Ronnie Burke with two and Charlie Mitten.

1955	Manchester City	H	First Division	0-5
1966	Rotherham United	H	FA Cup 4th Round	0-0
1972	Newcastle United	H	First Division	0-2
1977	Tottenham Hotspur	A	First Division	3-1
1979	Fulham	H	FA Cup 4th Round Replay	1-0
1984	Luton Town	A	First Division	5-0

FEBRUARY 13TH

1891 Teddy Partridge born in Lye in Worcestershire. After service in the First World War, Teddy signed with Ebbw Vale where his performances soon attracted the interest of bigger clubs. Signed by United in June 1920 for a £10 signing-on fee, he soon became a permanent fixture on the wing and went on to make 160 appearances for the first team. He joined Halifax in 1929 and finished his career with Crewe in 1931. He died in Manchester in 1973.

1897	Southampton	A	FA Cup 2nd Round	1-1
1901	Burnley	A	FA Cup 1st Round Replay	1-7
1904	Lincoln City	H	Second Division	2-0
1909	Sheffield United	A	First Division	0-0
1915	Sheffield Wednesday	H	First Division	2-0
1926	Leeds United	H	First Division	2-1
1929	Liverpool	A	First Division	3-2
1937	Brentford	H	First Division	1-3
1943	Manchester City	H	Football League North (Second Championship)	1-1
1954	Tottenham Hotspur	H	First Division	2-0
1960	Preston North End	H	First Division	1-1
1965	Burnley	H	First Division	3-2
1982	Wolverhampton Wanderers	A	First Division	1-0
1988	Chelsea	A	First Division	2-1
1994	Sheffield Wednesday	H	Coca-Cola Cup Semi-Final 1st Leg	1-0

FEBRUARY 14TH

1891	Crewe Alexandra	A	Football Alliance	1-0
1903	Blackpool	A	Second Division	0-2
1914	Burnley	H	First Division	0-1
1920	Sunderland	H	First Division	2-0
1925	Crystal Palace	A	Second Division	1-2
1931	West Ham United	H	First Division	1-0
1942	Sheffield United	A	Football League Northern Section (Second Championship)	2-0
1948	Preston North End	H	First Division	1-1
1953	Everton	A	FA Cup 5th Round	1-2
1970	Crystal Palace	H	First Division	1-1
1976	Leicester City	A	FA Cup 5th Round	2-1

United's twin assault on the League and FA Cup continued with a professional and polished performance at Filbert Street, goals from Gerry Daly and Lou Macari taking them into the sixth round at the expense of Leicester.

| 1987 | Watford | H | First Division | 3-1 |
| 1993 | Sheffield United | A | FA Cup 5th Round | 1-2 |

FEBRUARY 15TH

| 1890 | Nottingham Forest | A | Football Alliance | 3-1 |
| 1896 | Derby County | H | FA Cup 2nd Round | 1-1 |

The prospect of a visit from Derby County was one positively relished by Newton Heath; although the two teams were light years apart in terms of ability, a good crowd was almost guaranteed as soon as the draw had been made and this would provide considerable funds for the hard-up club. In the event 20,000 attended, filling the Heathens' coffers with some £500. Derby arrived with a veritable reputation; and with a team that boasted such internationals as Jack Robinson, England's goalkeeper, and John Goodall and Steve Bloomer leading the front line. It was the Derby forwards who started the game at a ferocious pace, shooting from long distance and forcing Ridgway in the Newton goal into making a number of fine saves, although there was little he could do to prevent Bloomer from putting the visitors ahead following a skirmish in the goalmouth area. There were many who were convinced that once Derby had got ahead Newton would simply collapse, but to their credit the Heathens refused to give up the fight and were rewarded in the second half when Kennedy managed to meet a Peters centre and squared the score. Indeed, they might have gone on to even greater heights, for they had a goal disallowed thereafter and certainly finished the stronger side. All told, however, a draw against Derby (who would finish the season as runners-up in the League) was an extremely creditable result.

1902	Glossop	H	Second Division	1-0
1908	Blackburn Rovers	H	First Division	1-2
1913	Derby County	H	First Division	4-0
1919	Southport Vulcans	H	Lancashire Section Principal Tournament	1-3
1930	Grimsby Town	A	First Division	2-2
1941	Everton	H	League War Cup	2-2
1950	Portsmouth	A	FA Cup 5th Round Replay	3-1

1958 United had been due to play Sheffield Wednesday in the fifth round of the FA Cup, but in the aftermath of the Munich air disaster this match was postponed until the following Wednesday.

1964	Barnsley	A	FA Cup 5th Round	4-0
1966	Rotherham United	A	FA Cup 4th Round Replay	1-0 [aet]
1969	Wolverhampton Wanderers	A	First Division	2-2
1975	Hull City	H	Second Division	2-0
1983	Arsenal	A	Milk Cup Semi-Final 1st Leg	4-2
1985	Blackburn Rovers	A	FA Cup 5th Round	2-0
1998	Barnsley	H	FA Cup 5th Round	1-1

FEBRUARY 16TH

1898	Liverpool	A	FA Cup 2nd Round Replay	1-2
1901	Gainsborough Trinity	H	Second Division	0-0
1907	Blackburn Rovers	A	First Division	4-2
1918	Bury	H	Lancashire Section Principal Tournament	0-0
1924	Derby County	A	Second Division	0-3
1929	Burnley	H	First Division	1-0
1946	Liverpool	A	Football League North	5-0

United attacked Liverpool right from the off, forcing a corner and scoring direct from the resulting kick all before a minute had passed! Wrigglesworth scored that first goal, with Hanlon and Rowley adding two apiece to complete the rout.

1952	Derby County	A	First Division	3-0
1957	Everton	H	FA Cup 5th Round	1-0
1959	Manchester City	H	First Division	4-1
1974	Derby County	A	First Division	2-2
1977	Liverpool	H	First Division	0-0
1980	Stoke City	A	First Division	1-1

FEBRUARY 17TH

1886 Arthur Whalley born in Rainford in Lancashire. Arthur cost United £50 when they signed him from Blackpool in June 1909, the fee reflecting both his inexperience (he had played only five games for Blackpool) and the fact he was expected to be cover for the regular centre-half. He did rather better than expected, being able to slot into any of the three half-back positions and did well enough to earn a League championship medal in 1911. He was a regular in the side in 1912-13 but sustained a serious knee injury which restricted his appearances prior to the First World War. He was wounded during the war whilst on service in the army at Passchendale but recovered and was back at United when League football resumed in 1919. He might have remained at United for longer but for the board's refusal to guarantee him a benefit in 1920, and he was transferred to Southend for £1,000 in September 1920. He later played for Charlton and Millwall before becoming trainer and coach at Barrow. He died in Manchester on 23rd November 1952.

1894	Blackburn Rovers	A	FA Cup 2nd Round Replay	1-5
1897	Southampton	H	FA Cup 2nd Round Replay	3-1
1900	Small Heath	H	Second Division	3-2
1906	West Bromwich Albion	H	Second Division	0-0
1912	Bury	H	First Division	0-0
1917	Southport Central	A	Lancashire Section Principal Tournament	1-0
1923	Derby County	H	Second Division	0-0
1932	Burnley	H	Second Division	5-1
1938	Sheffield United	A	Second Division	2-1
1945	Bury	H	Football League North (Second Championship)	2-0
1951	Wolverhampton Wanderers	H	First Division	2-1

1958 An official Memorial Service for the victims of the Munich air disaster was held in the church of St Martin-in-the-Fields in London, where the lesson was read by FA chairman Arthur Drewry and the address was given by the Lord Bishop of Chester.

1962	Sheffield Wednesday	A	FA Cup 5th Round	2-0
1968	Burnley	A	First Division	1-2
1973	Ipswich Town	A	First Division	1-4
1981	Tottenham Hotspur	H	First Division	0-0

FEBRUARY 18TH

1899	Loughborough Town	A	Second Division	1-0
1905	Licester Fosse	H	Second Division	4-1
1911	Newcastle United	A	First Division	1-0
1922	Birmingham City	A	First Division	1-0
1928	Birmingham	H	FA Cup 5th Round	1-0
1939	Blackpool	A	First Division	5-3
1950	Sunderland	A	First Division	2-2

| 1953 | Sunderland | A | First Division | 2-2 |

United arrived at Roker Park without a recognised goalkeeper, Wood, Allen and Crompton all being unavailable, and so Johnny Carey was forced to play in goal! He did remarkably well too, pulling off a string of saves as United battled for a point. Johnny Carey appeared in every position for United bar one; he was never selected at outside-left.

1956	Wolverhampton Wanderers	A	First Division	2-0
1957	Charlton Athletic	A	First Division	5-1
1961	Bolton Wanderers	H	First Division	3-1
1967	Norwich City	H	FA Cup 4th Round	1-2

1975 Gary Neville born in Bury. Signed by United as an apprentice in 1991, he was upgraded to the professional ranks in January 1993 and made his debut in May 1994. Since then he has helped the club win two Premiership titles and one FA Cup, as well as collecting over 20 caps for England. He and his younger brother Phil became the first brothers to be capped for England in the same side since the celebrated Charltons.

1976	Liverpool	H	First Division	0-0
1984	Wolverhampton Wanderers	A	First Division	1-1
1989	AFC Bournemouth	A	FA Cup 5th Round	1-1
1990	Newcastle United	A	FA Cup 5th Round	3-2
1991	Norwich City	A	FA Cup 5th Round	1-2
1996	Manchester City	H	FA Cup 5th Round	2-1
1998	Aston Villa	A	FA Premier League	2-0

FEBRUARY 19TH

| 1896 | Derby County | A | FA Cup 2nd Round Replay | 1-5 |

The heroics performed by Newton Heath in the first match between the two sides the previous Saturday could not be repeated, for Derby virtually romped home to win the tie 5-1, Newton's consolation effort coming from Donaldson. But the Heathens did have one or two problems to contend with during the game, losing goalkeeper Ridgway for a while after he had broken a finger and Carlin, also injured, so that for a time they were down to nine men.

| 1901 | New Brighton | A | Second Division | 0-2 |
| 1910 | Liverpool | H | First Division | 3-4 |

United's first game at their brand new ground at Old Trafford. United had announced their intention to vacate their ground at Bank Street in Clayton in 1908, with the plans for the new stadium being first revealed in March 1909, shortly before United played in the FA Cup final. The original plans, drawn up by Archibald Leitch, were for an impressive ground capable of holding 100,000 spectators. The new site, close to the Lancashire Cricket Ground, was purchased with a £60,000 grant from the club's chairman John Henry Davies (by comparison Bank Street was sold to the Manchester Corporation for a mere £5,500), but as construction work added a further £30,000 to the bill, the plans were modified to accommodate a meagre 60,000! Even so, the amenities for the players were superb – a billiard room, massage rooms, gymnasium, laundry and plunge bath. Those for the spectators were no less impressive: 13,000 under cover, with prices of 6d for admission to the terraces; 1s, 1s 6d, and 2s to the covered stand; and 5s for a reserved seat in the centre of the stand (where attendants directed patrons to their tip-up seats!). A crowd of over 50,000 attended the opening game (which had been due to have been the fixture against Spurs but work was not quite complete), with at least 5,000 gaining free admission when the gates were opened as the turnstile operators were unable to cope with the queues of people. The honour of scoring the first goal at Old Trafford fell to Sandy Turnbull, but thereafter

Liverpool ignored the script and ran out 4-3 winners.

1916	Blackpool	H	Lancashire Section Principal Tournament	1-1
1927	Aston Villa	A	First Division	0-2
1938	Tottenham Hotspur	H	Second Division	0-1

1939   Pat Crerand born in Glasgow. Pat began his career with Celtic in 1957, but by the time he moved to United six years later he had won little of note. He cost United £56,000 in February 1963, and had sufficient time to establish a place in the side that won the FA Cup in May of that year. He also won two League championships and European Cup medals before he retired from playing in 1971. He then moved on to United's coaching staff and later had a spell in charge at Northampton Town.

| 1944 | Oldham Athletic | H | Football League North (Second Championship) | 3-2 |

1945   Although Germany and her allies had yet to capitulate in Europe and Japan showed no sign of wilting, victory in both theatres of war was certain and thoughts had already begun to turn to the resumption of normality. United had already decided that they would need the services of a full-time manager and had approached a player who was at that time on the books of Liverpool. Although he had been offered a five-year contract at Anfield to become assistant to manager George Kay, the player was ultimately swayed by the strength of argument at Manchester United. The club had no ground, having suffered extensive bomb damage during the war, and were forced to share with their nearest rivals. Many of the players who had been signed prior to 1939 were unlikely or unable to resume their careers, and the club was in genuine financial hardship. Still, Company Sergeant-Major Instructor Matthew Busby agreed to become the new manager of Manchester United.

| 1949 | Aston Villa | A | First Division | 1-2 |
| 1958 | Sheffield Wednesday | H | FA Cup 5th Round | 3-0 |

Old Trafford has witnessed many emotional occasions, but few could ever hope to match this particular game. It was United's first match since the Munich air disaster, and such was United's turmoil that Jimmy Murphy, who had taken charge of the club whilst Matt Busby lay fighting for his life, had had to sign players just to appear in this game – Ernie Taylor arrived from Blackpool and Stan Crowther from Aston Villa. Crowther actually signed for the club a little over an hour before the kick-off tonight, and even though he had already appeared for Villa in the FA Cup that season, he received special dispensation from the FA to play in the game. The United team line-up in the programme was left blank; there was no way of knowing who was available and who wasn't. The programme promised 'United will go on'; a crowd of 59,848 and goals from Shay Brennan (two) and Alex Dawson made it a winning start for Murphy's braves.

1964	Bolton Wanderers	H	First Division	5-0
1966	Stoke City	A	First Division	2-2
1972	Leeds United	A	First Division	1-5
1977	Newcastle United	H	First Division	3-1
1983	Derby County	A	FA Cup 5th Round	1-0
1995	Leeds United	H	FA Cup 5th Round	3-1
1997	Arsenal	A	FA Premier League	2-1

FEBRUARY 20TH

1885   George Wall born in Boldon Colliery near Sunderland. George began his professional career with Barnsley in 1903 before a fee of £175 brought him to United in April 1906. With George operating on the left wing and Billy Meredith on the right, United were one of the most potent attacking forces of the day. He helped United win two League championships (1908 and 1911) and the FA Cup (1909) as well as representing

England, winning a total of seven caps during his career. But for the First World War George might well have helped United to further honours, but in 1919, soon after his demobilisation from the Black Watch regiment, he was sold to Oldham for £200. He later played for Hamilton Academical and Rochdale and by the time of his retirement from professional football had appeared in more than 500 League matches. Upon retiring he worked on the Manchester docks and died in Manchester in 1962.

1892	Sheffield Wednesday	H	Football Alliance	1-1
1897	Leicester Fosse	H	Second Division	2-1
1904	Sheffield Wednesday	A	FA Cup 2nd Round	0-6
1909	Blackburn Rovers	H	FA Cup 3rd Round	6-1
1915	West Bromwich Albion	A	First Division	0-0
1921	Sunderland	H	First Division	3-0
1926	Sunderland	A	FA Cup 5th Round	3-3
1932	Preston North End	A	Second Division	0-0
1937	Portsmouth	H	First Division	0-1
1943	Crewe Alexandra	H	Football League North (Second Championship)	7-0
1954	Burnley	A	First Division	0-2
1960	Sheffield Wednesday	H	FA Cup 5th Round	0-1
1965	Burnley	H	FA Cup 5th Round	2-1
1971	Southampton	H	First Division	5-1
1979	Colchester United	A	FA Cup 5th Round	1-0
1982	Arsenal	H	First Division	0-0
1988	Arsenal	A	FA Cup 5th Round	1-2
1993	Southampton	H	FA Premier League	2-1
1994	Wimbledon	A	FA Cup 5th Round	3-0

FEBRUARY 21ST

1891	Sheffield Wednesday	H	Football Alliance	1-1
1903	Everton	A	FA Cup 2nd Round	1-3
1914	Middlesbrough	A	First Division	1-3
1920	Arsenal	A	First Division	3-0
1923	Notts County	H	Second Division	1-1
1931	Arsenal	A	First Division	1-4
1934	Preston North End	A	Second Division	2-3

1940 Alex Dawson born in Aberdeen. Alex signed for United in March 1957 and helped the club retain their League title in the final three games of the season. He became a regular after the Munich air crash and played in the 1958 Cup final, only moving on following the signing of David Herd, joining Preston in October 1961. He later played for Bury and Brighton before finishing his career in the non-League game.

1942	Preston North End	H	Football League Northern Section (Second Championship)	0-2
1948	Stoke City	A	First Division	2-0
1953	Wolverhampton Wanderers	H	First Division	0-3

1958 After a valiant two-week battle, Duncan Edwards died as a result of the injuries he sustained in the Munich air disaster. His kidneys, crushed in the crash, had caused his circulation to fail.

1959	Wolverhampton Wanderers	H	First Division	2-1
1970	Middlesbrough	A	FA Cup 6th Round	1-1
1973	Fiorentina	H	Anglo-Italian Tournament Group One	1-1
1976	Aston Villa	A	First Division	1-2
1981	Manchester City	A	First Division	0-1

1987	Chelsea	A	First Division	1-1
1996	Everton	H	FA Premier League	2-0
1998	Derby County	H	FA Premier League	2-0

FEBRUARY 22ND

1902	Doncaster Rovers	A	Second Division	0-4
1908	Aston Villa	A	FA Cup 3rd Round	2-0
1913	Oldham Athletic	A	FA Cup 3rd Round	0-0
1919	Burnley	A	Lancashire Section Principal Tournament	2-4
1930	Portsmouth	H	First Division	3-0
1933	Burnley	H	Second Division	2-1
1936	Sheffield United	A	Second Division	1-1
1941	Everton	A	League War Cup	1-2
1947	Blackpool	H	First Division	3-0
1958	Nottingham Forest	H	First Division	1-1

Three members of the Red Star team travelled overland from Belgrade to attend the special service held at Old Trafford before the start of the match with Nottingham Forest in honour of the dead of Munich. The Red Star players brought with them gifts to replace those destroyed in the crash. United's biggest post-war crowd, 66,124 saw Alex Dawson score their goal.

1964	Blackburn Rovers	A	First Division	3-1
1975	Aston Villa	A	Second Division	0-2
1986	West Bromwich Albion	H	First Division	3-0
1989	AFC Bournemouth	H	FA Cup 5th Round Replay	1-0
1992	Crystal Palace	H	First Division	2-0
1995	Norwich City	A	FA Premier League	2-0
1997	Chelsea	A	FA Premier League	1-1

FEBRUARY 23RD

| 1907 | Preston North End | H | First Division | 3-0 |
| 1918 | Bury | A | Lancashire Section Principal Tournament | 2-1 |

1919 Johnny Carey born in Dublin. He joined United in November 1936 and made his debut for the club in September the following year, although he was frequently in competition with Stan Pearson for selection. At the end of the Second World War Johnny returned to United and captained the side to the FA Cup in 1948. Named Footballer of the Year in 1949, he also won a title medal in 1952. He retired in 1953 and was asked to remain at United in a coaching capacity but instead chose to become manager of Blackburn Rovers. He later had spells as manager at Everton, Leyton Orient and Nottingham Forest before returning to Blackburn.

1924	Derby County	H	Second Division	0-0
1925	Sheffield Wednesday	A	Second Division	1-1
1929	Cardiff City	A	First Division	2-2
1935	Oldham Athletic	A	Second Division	1-0
1938	West Ham United	H	Second Division	4-0
1946	Bury	A	Football League North	1-1
1952	Manchester City	H	Friendly	4-2
1955	Wolverhampton Wanderers	H	First Division	2-4
1957	Blackpool	H	First Division	0-2
1963	Blackpool	H	First Division	1-1
1971	Everton	A	First Division	0-1
1974	Wolverhampton Wanderers	H	First Division	0-0

| 1980 | Bristol City | H | First Division | 4-0 |
| 1983 | Arsenal | H | Milk Cup Semi-Final 2nd Leg | 2-1 |

With United having already won the first leg 4-2 at Highbury, they were favourites to progress into the final for the first time since the competition began as the League Cup in 1960. Goals from Steve Coppell and Kevin Moran ensured an aggregate win of 6-3 and a place at Wembley against Liverpool.

| 1985 | Arsenal | A | First Division | 1-0 |
| 1988 | Tottenham Hotspur | A | First Division | 1-1 |

FEBRUARY 24TH

1873 George Perrins born in Birmingham. Signed by Newton Heath just before they joined the Football League, George was a regular in the side at half-back for three seasons until a loss of form in 1895-96, although he did make two appearances as an emergency goalkeeper. He left Clayton in the close season to join Luton Town, later playing for Chatham and Stockport County.

| 1900 | New Brighton Tower | A | Second Division | 4-1 |
| 1906 | Aston Villa | H | FA Cup 3rd Round | 5-1 |

One of the most impressive performances by United in their early days was this 5-1 rout of Aston Villa. Villa arrived at Clayton with a pedigree second to none: five times League champions (1894, 1896, 1897, 1899 and 1900), four times FA Cup winners (1887, 1895, 1897 and 1905) and only the second side to have won the coveted League and Cup double, a feat they achieved in 1897. They were also the current FA Cup holders, having won the trophy in fine style against Newcastle United the previous season. By comparison, United were still a Second Division club, although they would end the season in second place and therefore promoted. Villa did not take their task lightly, spending a week on the North Wales coast preparing for the tie, and a crowd of 40,000 paying then record receipts of £1,460 were drawn to the attraction, with the gates being closed 45 minutes before kick-off and thousands milling around outside unable to gain admittance. On a dull day with a light drizzle (conditions that would ultimately suit United rather than Villa) United started the better side, opening the scoring after only ten minutes. It took Villa some time to get the measure of their opponents, equalising not long after United had gone ahead but then being pressed back for much of the rest of the half. By half-time United had inched ahead again, and in the second half, as the pitch cut up even more, Villa visibly tired and United added three further goals. United's scorers were John Picken with a hat-trick and Charlie Sagar grabbing the other two, but there were many other heroes in the United team that day, not least John Peddie.

1912	Reading	A	FA Cup 3rd Round	1-1
1917	Blackburn Rovers	H	Lancashire Section Principal Tournament	1-0
1926	Sunderland	H	FA Cup 5th Round Replay	2-1
1934	Bradford Park Avenue	H	Second Division	0-4
1940	Chester	H	War Regional League, Western Division	5-1

On the same day, Denis Law was born in Aberdeen. Signed by Bill Shankly as a junior for Huddersfield Town, he developed into one of the most dangerous forwards in the game. Transferred to Manchester City in March 1960, he once scored six goals in a cup-tie at Luton before the game was abandoned. He also scored in the replay, although Luton won 3-1. He spent a season in Italy with Torino before returning to Manchester with City's chief rivals, Manchester United. In 11 years with United he helped the club to two League titles and the FA Cup, but was injured and lying in hospital when United lifted the European Cup. He wound down his career at Manchester City and indeed scored the goal which effectively sent United down to the

Second Division. A distraught Law retired immediately after. He scored a record 30 goals for Scotland in 55 appearances and after retiring became a broadcaster.

1945	Bury	A	Football League North (Second Championship)	1-3
1951	Birmingham City	A	FA Cup 6th Round	0-1
1960	Leicester City	A	First Division	1-3
1962	West Bromwich Albion	H	First Division	4-1
1965	Sunderland	A	First Division	0-1
1968	Arsenal	A	First Division	2-0
1979	Aston Villa	H	First Division	1-1
1990	Chelsea	A	First Division	0-1
1991	Leeds United	A	Rumbelows Cup Semi-Final 2nd Leg	1-0

With United having won the first leg 2-1 the tie was delicately poised for the second leg, but a Lee Sharpe goal eased some of the pressure on United. Thereafter they held Leeds at bay and booked their place in the final with a 3-1 aggregate win.

1995 Manchester United star Eric Cantona was banned by the FA for seven months and fined £20,000 for the incident arising following his sending off at Crystal Palace last month. The ban, in addition to the ban imposed by his club, meant he would not be able to play for the club before September 30th 1995. In view of the fact that Cantona also faced police action over the alleged assault, the FA ban was seen to be lenient.

FEBRUARY 25TH

| 1899 | Small Heath | H | Second Division | 2-0 |
| 1901 | Walsall | A | Second Division | 1-1 |

Vince Hayes made his debut for Newton Heath and although it was to be his only appearance in the season he went on to play over 120 games in two spells with the club. Signed from local football, Vince, born in Manchester in 1879, did not enjoy the best of luck during his first sojourn with the Heathens, for he broke his leg twice and was transferred to Brentford in May 1907. He returned to United 12 months later and had the good fortune to remain injury-free and win an FA Cup winners' medal against Bristol City. In November 1910 he was on his way again, this time to Bradford, and he later coached the Norwegian national side for the Stockholm Olympic Games. The game against Walsall was also notable for the appearance of Jimmy Whitehouse in the forward line, for he was more normally found in goal! He laid on the goal for Billy Morgan too.

1905	Barnsley	A	Second Division	0-0
1911	West Ham United	A	FA Cup 3rd Round	1-2
1920	West Bromwich Albion	H	First Division	1-2
1922	Birmingham City	H	First Division	1-1
1928	Cardiff City	A	First Division	0-2
1939	Derby County	H	First Division	1-1
1950	Charlton Athletic	A	First Division	2-1
1956	Aston Villa	H	First Division	1-0
1961	Nottingham Forest	A	First Division	2-3
1967	Blackpool	H	First Division	4-0
1970	Middlesbrough	H	FA Cup 6th Round Replay	2-1
1976	Derby County	H	First Division	1-1
1978	Liverpool	A	First Division	1-3
1984	Sunderland	H	First Division	2-1
1989	Norwich City	A	First Division	1-2
1994	West Ham United	A	FA Premier League	2-2
1995	Everton	A	FA Premier League	0-1

1996 Bolton Wanderers   A   FA Premier League   6-0
In their first match at Burnden Park for 19 years, United registered their biggest away win in the FA Premier League with a 6-0 win over Bolton.
1998 Barnsley   A   FA Cup 5th Round Replay   2-3

FEBRUARY 26TH

1889	Ardwick	H	Friendly	3-2
1898	Woolwich Arsenal	H	Second Division	5-1
1910	Aston Villa	A	First Division	1-7
1913	Oldham Athletic	H	FA Cup 3rd Round Replay	1-2
1916	Southport Central	A	Lancashire Section Principal Tournament	0-5
1927	Bolton Wanderers	H	First Division	0-0
1938	Blackburn Rovers	H	Second Division	2-1
1944	Oldham Athletic	A	Football League North (Second Championship)	1-1
1949	Hull City	A	FA Cup 6th Round	1-0
1951	Sheffield Wednesday	A	First Division	4-0
1955	Cardiff City	A	First Division	0-3
1964	Sporting Club Lisbon	H	European Cup-Winners' Cup 3rd Round 1st Leg	4-1
1966	Burnley	H	First Division	4-2
1969	Rapid Vienna	H	European Cup 3rd Round 1st Leg	3-0
1972	Middlesbrough	H	FA Cup 5th Round	0-0

1973 Ole Gunnar Solskjaar born in Norway. Ole joined United from FC Molde in July 1996 for £1.5 million and was expected to spend some considerable time in the reserves before breaking into the first team, but during his first season at Old Trafford he helped the club win the League championship by finishing top goalscorer with 18 goals.
1977 Southampton   A   FA Cup 5th Round   2-2
1980 Manchester United chairman Louis Edwards died of a heart attack. Following recent allegations of financial irregularities, exposed by the Granada TV programme *World in Action*, Edwards had been the subject of a police and joint FA and Football League Committee investigation.

1983	Liverpool	H	First Division	1-1
1991	Sheffield United	A	First Division	1-2
1992	Chelsea	H	First Division	1-1

FEBRUARY 27TH

1892	Small Heath	A	Football Alliance	2-3
1897	Derby County	A	FA Cup 3rd Round	0-2
1900	Manchester City	H	Friendly	1-0

1901 With Newton Heath still severely short of cash, it was decided to host a bazaar in order to raise £1,000 for the purposes of acquiring new players to try and improve the club's position in the League. The bazaar, formally opened at the St James's Hall by Sir James Ferguson, the Conservative MP for Manchester North East, was to remain open for four days, with visitors being able to view exhibits from around the world. Unfortunately, the bazaar was not the success the club had hoped for, with little in the way of profit being realised once expenses had been taken into account. However, the event did lead to salvation in a most unlikely way. Club captain Harry Stafford was the owner of a St Bernard's dog which he loaned to the bazaar, and the dog roamed the hall with a collection tin around its neck! One evening the dog escaped and was later found on the streets by a pub landlord. He showed the dog to the owner of the Manchester Brewery Company, John Henry Davies, who took an immediate fancy to it and bought it from the landlord. Later, feeling guilty, he decided to trace the rightful owner and found himself in conversation with Harry Stafford. When Stafford explained how the dog had come to be wandering the streets and the perilous financial position of Newton Heath, Davies made a contribution to the club and also offered further help in the future. As can be seen elsewhere in this book, Harry Stafford and John Henry Davies were as important in establishing the name and reputation of Manchester United in the first few years of the century as Matt Busby was in the immediate aftermath of the Second World War.

1903	Liverpool	H	FA Cup 1st Round	2-1
1909	Nottingham Forest	A	First Division	0-2
1915	Everton	H	First Division	1-2
1922	Huddersfield Town	A	First Division	1-1
1926	Tottenham Hotspur	A	First Division	1-0
1932	Barnsley	H	Second Division	3-0
1937	Chelsea	A	First Division	2-4
1943	Crewe Alexandra	A	Football League North (Second Championship)	3-2

On the same day, Jimmy Nicholson was born in Belfast. Spotted by United at the age of 15, he became a professional in February 1960 and made his debut in August the same year. Widely acclaimed as one of United's best young prospects in many a year, he was soon capped by Northern Ireland, but just as he broke through on the international stage, so his club career began to falter. Competition from the likes of Nobby Stiles subsequently led to him being sold to Huddersfield Town for £8,000 in December 1964, and he went on to make over 300 appearances for their first team. He later played for Bury before going into the non-League game.

1954	Sunderland	A	First Division	2-0
1960	Blackpool	A	First Division	6-0
1965	Wolverhampton Wanderers	H	First Division	3-0
1971	Newcastle United	H	First Division	1-0

Although United won 1-0 thanks to a goal from Brian Kidd, of far greater concern was a knife thrown from the crowd on to the pitch during the game. The Football League immediately promised an enquiry into the incident.

1980	Bolton Wanderers	H	First Division	2-0
1982	Manchester City	H	First Division	1-1
1993	Middlesbrough	H	FA Premier League	3-0

FEBRUARY 28TH

| 1891 | Ardwick | A | Friendly | 3-1 |

1901 Harry Thomas born in Swansea. Signed by United from Porth FC in April 1922, Harry was given a tough baptism in a United side already doomed to relegation from the First Division. He did not become a regular in the side until 1925-26, and helped United reclaim their First Division status and reach the FA Cup semi-final. Although he made 135 appearances for United's first team in his eight years with the club, his lack of goals probably restricted him from making more appearances, although he did win a cap for Wales. He left United for Merthyr Town in October 1930, finishing his career with Abercarn.

1903	Doncaster Rovers	A	Second Division	2-2
1914	Newcastle United	H	First Division	2-2
1920	Arsenal	H	First Division	0-1
1925	Wolverhampton Wanderers	H	Second Division	3-0

1932 Noel Cantwell born in Cork in Ireland. He joined West Ham in September 1952 and stayed with the club for eight years before a £29,500 transfer took him to United. He later became captain and led the club to the 1963 FA Cup final success and was still captain in 1967. He had begun taking an interest in coaching and was considered by many to be Matt Busby's successor, but in October 1967 he became manager at Coventry. He later took over at Peterborough United before moving to America in 1977, although he returned to Peterborough in 1986.

1942	Preston North End	A	Football League Northern Section	
			(Second Championship)	3-1
1948	Preston North End	H	FA Cup 6th Round	4-2
1953	Stoke City	A	First Division	1-3

1956 Jimmy Nicholl born in Hamilton in Ontario, Canada. His family moved to Belfast whilst Jimmy was at an early age and he was spotted by United whilst playing schools football. He was signed as an amateur in November 1971 and became a professional in March 1974. After battling with Alex Forsyth, Jimmy made the right-back berth his own in 1976-77 and subsequently appeared in two FA Cup finals, collecting a winners' medal in 1977 and a runners-up medal in 1979. The subsequent arrival of new manager Ron Atkinson and the purchase of John Gidman cost him his place in the team and after a loan spell with Sunderland he was sold to Toronto Blizzard in Canada for £250,000 in April 1983. He was later to play for West Bromwich Albion and Glasgow Rangers before moving into management and coaching.

1959	Arsenal	A	First Division	2-3
1962	Wolverhampton Wanderers	A	First Division	2-2
1968	Gornik Zabrze	H	European Cup 3rd Round 1st Leg	2-0
1970	Stoke City	A	First Division	2-2
1976	West Ham United	H	First Division	4-0
1979	Queens Park Rangers	H	First Division	2-0
1981	Leeds United	H	First Division	0-1
1987	Everton	H	First Division	0-0
1998	Chelsea	A	FA Premier League	1-1

FEBRUARY 29TH

| 1896 | Burton Wanderers | H | Second Division | 1-2 |

Having recently sold William Douglas to Derby and with Joe Ridgeway having broken a finger, the Heathens were without a regular goalkeeper. For this match they selected George Perrins, more normally found at half-back, as an emergency goalkeeper, although the move was not a success.

1908	Birmingham	H	First Division	1-0
1912	Reading	H	FA Cup 3rd Round Replay	3-0
1936	Blackpool	H	Second Division	3-2
1964	Sunderland	H	FA Cup 6th Round	3-3
1972	Middlesbrough	A	FA Cup 5th Round Replay	3-0
1992	Coventry City	A	First Division	0-0

MARCH 1ST

1890	Crewe Alexandra	H	Football Alliance	1-2
1902	Lincoln City	H	Second Division	0-0
1913	Middlesbrough	H	First Division	2-3
1919	Burnley	H	Lancashire Section Principal Tournament	4-0
1924	Nelson	A	Second Division	2-0

A crowd of only 2,750 saw United win thanks to goals from Fred Kennedy and Joe Spence. This was the lowest crowd to have watched United in a competitive game since the First World War.

| 1930 | Bolton Wanderers | A | First Division | 1-4 |
| 1941 | Chesterfield | A | North Regional League | 1-1 |

1947	Sunderland	A	First Division	1-1
1952	Aston Villa	H	First Division	1-1
1958	West Bromwich Albion	A	FA Cup 6th Round	2-2
1969	Everton	A	FA Cup 6th Round	0-1
1975	Cardiff City	H	Second Division	4-0
1978	Leeds United	H	First Division	0-1
1980	Ipswich Town	A	First Division	0-6
1986	Southampton	A	First Division	0-1
1997	Coventry City	H	FA Premier League	3-1

MARCH 2ND

| 1895 | Burton Wanderers | H | Second Division | 1-1 |
| 1897 | Darwen | H | Second Division | 3-1 |

Billy Morgan made his debut for Newton Heath. He joined the Heathens from local football in January 1897 and was a regular in the side until his departure for Bolton in March 1903, although he left Burnden Park after only a few months and joined Watford. He later played for Leicester Fosse and New Brompton before returning nearer home to play for Newton Heath Athletic.

1901	Burton Swifts	H	Second Division	1-1
1907	Birmingham	A	First Division	1-1
1912	Notts County	H	First Division	2-0
1918	Oldham Athletic	H	Lancashire Section Principal Tournament	2-1
1929	Birmingham	A	First Division	1-1
1935	Newcastle United	H	Second Division	0-1
1946	Bury	H	Football League North	1-1
1957	Bournemouth	A	FA Cup 6th Round	2-1
1959	Blackburn Rovers	A	First Division	3-1
1963	Blackburn Rovers	A	First Division	2-2
1968	Chelsea	H	First Division	1-3
1974	Sheffield United	A	First Division	1-0
1983	Stoke City	A	First Division	0-1
1985	Everton	H	First Division	1-1
1991	Everton	H	First Division	0-2
1994	Sheffield Wednesday	A	Coca-Cola Cup Semi-Final 2nd Leg	4-1

Two goals from Mark Hughes and single strikes from Brian McClair and Ryan Giggs enabled United to progress into the final with a 5-1 aggregate win.

MARCH 3RD

1894	Sunderland	H	First Division	2-4
1900	Grimsby Town	H	Second Division	1-0
1906	Hull City	H	Second Division	5-0
1917	Manchester City	A	Lancashire Section Principal Tournament	0-1
1923	Southampton	H	Second Division	1-2
1927	Hugh McLenahan was signed from Stockport County, the fee being three freezers full of ice cream!			
1928	Blackburn Rovers	A	FA Cup 6th Round	0-2
1934	Bury	H	Second Division	2-1
1945	Oldham Athletic	H	Football League North (Second Championship)	3-2
1951	Arsenal	H	First Division	3-1
1956	Chelsea	A	First Division	4-2
1962	Birmingham City	A	First Division	1-1

1967	Arsenal	A	First Division	1-1

Whilst 63,363 watched the game at Highbury, a further 28,423 were at Old Trafford watching the same match on closed-circuit television. This was the first time such a scheme had been utilised and it was not without its teething problems, for one of the seven screens on to which the pictures were being projected blew down midway through the game.

1973	West Bromwich Albion	H	First Division	2-1
1979	Bristol City	A	First Division	2-1
1984	Aston Villa	A	First Division	3-0
1990	Luton Town	H	First Division	4-1

MARCH 4TH

1882	West Gorton	A	Friendly	1-2
1893	Sunderland	H	First Division	0-5
1899	Grimsby Town	A	Second Division	0-3
1905	West Bromwich Albion	H	Second Division	2-0
1911	Middlesbrough	A	First Division	2-2
1916	Everton	H	Lancashire Section Subsidiary (Southern) Tournament	0-2
1933	Millwall	A	Second Division	0-2
1939	Sunderland	A	First Division	2-5
1944	Wrexham	A	Football League North (Second Championship)	4-1
1950	Chelsea	A	FA Cup 6th Round	0-2
1961	Manchester City	A	First Division	3-1
1963	Huddersfield Town	H	FA Cup 3rd Round	5-0
1964	Sunderland	A	FA Cup 6th Round Replay	2-2 [aet]
1972	Tottenham Hotspur	A	First Division	0-2
1978	Middlesbrough	H	First Division	0-0
1992	Middlesbrough	A	Rumbelows Cup Semi-Final 1st Leg	0-0
1995	Ipswich Town	H	FA Premier League	9-0

Manchester United shattered the Premier League goalscoring record with a 9-0 whipping of Ipswich Town at Old Trafford. At the same time, record transfer buy Andy Cole grabbed five goals to become the first player to score as many in a Premier League match. It was also Manchester United's biggest League win since 1892, when they beat Wolves 10-1.

1996	Newcastle United	A	FA Premier League	1-0
1998	Monaco	A	European Cup Quarter-Final 1st Leg	0-0

United struggled to come to terms with the pitch at Monaco (the ground is actually on top of a car park!) and were somewhat negative in their approach to the game. This was to have severe consequences in the second leg, for had United scored an away goal they might have progressed further in the competition.

MARCH 5TH

1892	Walsall Town Swifts	H	Football Alliance	5-0
1910	Sheffield United	H	First Division	1-0
1914	Preston North End	A	First Division	2-4
1921	Sunderland	A	First Division	3-2
1927	Bury	H	First Division	1-2
1932	Notts County	A	Second Division	2-1
1938	Sheffield Wednesday	A	Second Division	3-1
1949	Charlton Athletic	A	First Division	3-2

1953   Matt Busby paid £29,999 to Barnsley to take Tommy Taylor to Old Trafford. The fee was widely quoted as being £30,000, a then record, but Busby did not want to burden Taylor with the tag of being the first £30,000 player and so paid a pound less. According to legend, the extra pound was given to a tea-lady!

1955	Burnley	H	First Division	1-0
1958	West Bromwich Albion	H	FA Cup 6th Round Replay	1-0
1960	Wolverhampton Wanderers	H	First Division	0-2
1966	Wolverhampton Wanderers	A	FA Cup 5th Round	4-2
1969	Rapid Vienna	A	European Cup 3rd Round 2nd Leg	0-0

Having already won the first leg 3-0 at Old Trafford, United's progress into the next round and their grip on the European Cup, of which they were holders, were never likely to be troubled, but they still put in a superb defensive display to keep the Austrians at bay.

1977	Manchester City	H	First Division	3-1
1983	Manchester City	A	First Division	2-1
1986	West Ham United	A	FA Cup 5th Round	1-1
1988	Norwich City	A	First Division	0-1
1994	Chelsea	H	FA Premier League	0-1
1997	FC Porto	H	European Cup Quarter-Final 1st Leg	4-0

A superb display of counter-attacking football had the crowd at Old Trafford enthralled, as United powered their way into a 4-0 first-leg lead thanks to goals from David May, Eric Cantona, Ryan Giggs and Andy Cole.

MARCH 6TH

| 1893 | Aston Villa | A | First Division | 0-2 |
| 1909 | Burnley | A | FA Cup 4th Round | 0-1 |

There were just 18 minutes to go when a severe snowstorm forced the referee, Herbert Bamlett, to abandon the game with United 1-0 down. United won the replayed match on their way to winning the cup that season, and Herbert Bamlett later became manager of United!

1920	Everton	H	First Division	1-0
1926	Fulham	A	FA Cup 6th Round	2-1
1937	Stoke City	H	First Division	2-1
1943	Manchester City	H	Football League North (Second Championship)	0-1
1948	Sunderland	H	First Division	3-1

1949   Martin Buchan born in Aberdeen. Signed by Aberdeen to professional forms in 1966, he was captain by the age of 20 and guided them to victory in the 1970 Scottish Cup final. He cost United £125,000 in March 1972 and was a regular feature of the side for the next 11 years, giving the club exceptional service. He won a Second Division championship medal in 1975 and appeared in three FA Cup finals, collecting a winners' medal in 1977. After a series of injuries he was given a free transfer in 1983 and joined Oldham Athletic, although he retired through injury in October 1984. He later had a brief spell as manager of Burnley.

1954	Wolverhampton Wanderers	H	First Division	1-0
1957	Everton	A	First Division	2-1
1971	West Bromwich Albion	A	First Division	3-4
1976	Wolverhampton Wanderers	H	FA Cup 6th Round	1-1
1982	Birmingham City	A	First Division	1-0
1985	Videoton	H	UEFA Cup 4th Round 1st Leg	1-0
1991	Montpellier	H	European Cup-Winners' Cup 3rd Round 1st Leg	1-1
1993	Liverpool	A	FA Premier League	2-1

MARCH 7TH

1891	Small Heath	A	Football Alliance	1-2
1896	Rotherham Town	A	Second Division	3-2
1898	Burnley	A	Second Division	3-6
1903	Lincoln City	H	Second Division	1-2

Harry Stafford made his last appearance for the club. He had joined Newton Heath from Crewe in 1895 and soon became the club captain. In all he made 200 appearances for the club, scoring just one goal, but his contribution to the club exceeded anything he did on the field, for he was invariably at the centre of any fund-raising activities, organised door-to-door collections when the club had insufficient funds to pay for train journeys to away fixtures and often handed back his own wages in order that the other players were paid their full amounts (and which also helped him maintain his amateur status). In 1902 he had galvanised the support of John Henry Davies and others and helped rescue the club from bankruptcy. When he retired as a player, Stafford's loyalty was rewarded with a place on the board, a position he retained until 1911 when ill-health led him to move overseas. In gratitude United gave him £50, a measly sum in comparison to the efforts he had put in on their behalf. Indeed, in the report of the public meeting in March 1902, the *Manchester Evening News* finished its coverage with the following testimonial. 'The Newton Heath officials are indeed fortunate in having such a player as Stafford. Ever since he joined the team he has been a tireless worker in its interests, both on and off the field, and it is questionable if any club ever possessed such a thorough sportsman. By the winding-up proceedings he lost considerably, but fortunately for him he has been in a position for some time to play football for the love of the game, and if the efforts which he is now making are accepted in the proper spirit, there is a chance of the team being placed on a better footing than it has been before.'

1908	Fulham	A	FA Cup 4th Round	1-2
1925	Fulham	A	Second Division	0-1
1928	Huddersfield Town	H	First Division	0-0
1931	Birmingham	A	First Division	0-0

1933 Jackie Blanchflower born in Belfast. The younger brother of Danny, Jackie was signed by United as an amateur in May 1949 and became a professional in March 1950. He established himself as a regular in the side in 1953-54 but subsequently lost out to John Doherty, although he did win a championship medal in 1955-56. He lost his place the following season and did not qualify for a League medal, although he did appear in the FA Cup final that year and played as an emergency goalkeeper following the injury to Ray Wood. He survived the Munich air crash but the injuries he sustained were so severe that he was not able to play again, and his contract was cancelled in June 1959.

1936	West Ham United	A	Second Division	2-1
1953	Preston North End	H	First Division	5-2
1959	Everton	H	First Division	2-1
1964	West Ham United	A	First Division	2-0
1981	Southampton	A	First Division	0-1
1984	Barcelona	A	European Cup-Winners' Cup 3rd Round 1st Leg	0-2
1987	Manchester City	H	First Division	2-0
1995	Wimbledon	A	FA Premier League	1-0
1998	Sheffield Wednesday	A	FA Premier League	0-2

MARCH 8TH

1897 Jack Wilson born in Leadgate. Jack began his professional career with Newcastle

United in 1919 but broke both his legs and was allowed to drift back into the non-League game with Leadgate United as player-manager. He returned to League football with Durham City in 1922 but after only eight games moved on to Stockport County. Whilst at Edgeley Park he was converted from inside-forward to half-back and did well enough for United to pay £500 for him in September 1926. He enjoyed a six-year spell at Old Trafford, making over 140 appearances for the first team until being released at the end of the 1931-32 season, in which the club had been unsuccessful in securing promotion into the First Division. He then joined Bristol City for one season.

1902	West Bromwich Albion	A	Second Division	0-4
1913	Notts County	A	First Division	2-1
1919	Stoke City	A	Lancashire Section Principal Tournament	2-1
1924	Nelson	H	Second Division	0-1
1930	Aston Villa	H	First Division	2-3
1941	Bury	H	North Regional League	7-3

Three days after this game Old Trafford was hit by bombs dropped by the German Luftwaffe and was unable to host another game for eight years. United went out in good fashion, with both Johnny Carey and Jack Rowley scoring hat-tricks in this game, United's other goal coming from John Smith.

1947	Aston Villa	H	First Division	2-1
1950	Aston Villa	H	First Division	7-0
1952	Sunderland	A	First Division	2-1
1958	West Bromwich Albion	H	First Division	0-4
1969	Manchester City	H	First Division	0-1
1972	Everton	H	First Division	0-0
1975	Bolton Wanderers	A	Second Division	1-0
1977	Southampton	H	FA Cup 5th Round Replay	2-1
1997	Sunderland	A	FA Premier League	1-2

MARCH 9TH

1875   Charlie Richards born in Burton-upon-Trent. Charlie made only eight appearances in United's League side and scored one goal, but as that goal came in the first Football League match as Manchester United, a 1-0 win over Gainsborough Trinity in 1902, his place in the club's history is assured. Before joining United in 1902 he had played for Notts County, Nottingham Forest (with whom he won an FA Cup winners' medal in 1898), Grimsby Town and Leicester Fosse, and in March 1903 he signed for Doncaster Rovers.

1895   Walsall   H   Second Division   14-0

This result should, of course, be Newton Heath's (and Manchester United's) record win, but the match was later declared null and void. Walsall had arrived at the Bank Street ground in Clayton, taken one look at the pitch and immediately lodged a protest with the referee, Mr Jeffries, complaining that the pitch was not even suitable for schoolboys to play on. True, there was little grass, an awful lot of mud and far too much sand, making the conditions extremely heavy, but it has also to be said that Walsall arrived for the fixture third from bottom in the Second Division and one wonders whether their apprehension had more to do with their League status rather than genuine fears over the state of the pitch. Apart from adding more sand on to the worst of the mud, there was little Newton Heath could do, and so the game kicked off as expected. True to form, Newton Heath played like a side second from top, whilst their visitors played like one at the other end of the table, although by half-time the score was still a respectable 3-0. It was in the second half, to the delight of the 4,000 or so spectators, that the Heathens ran riot, adding a further 11 goals without reply.

Richard Smith led the charge, scoring six goals, with Cassidy adding four. Unfortunately, after the game the referee echoed the complaints made by Walsall over the state of the pitch and the Football League decided that the match should be declared void and a replay staged later in the season. In an instant, Newton Heath had their record win wiped off the books.

1903	Woolwich Arsenal	H	Second Division	3-0
1904	Blackpool	A	Second Division	1-2
1912	Blackburn Rovers	H	FA Cup 4th Round	1-1
1918	Oldham Athletic	A	Lancashire Section Principal Tournament	0-2
1921	Everton	A	First Division	0-2
1929	Huddersfield Town	H	First Division	1-0
1935	West Ham United	A	Second Division	0-0
1940	Crewe Alexandra	A	War Regional League, Western Division	4-1
1946	Blackburn Rovers	H	Football League North	6-2
1957	Aston Villa	H	First Division	1-1
1963	Tottenham Hotspur	H	First Division	0-2
1964	Sunderland	Leeds Road		
		FA Cup 6th Round 2nd Replay		5-1

United had come in for some considerable criticism over their inability to beat Second Division Sunderland in the FA Cup tie, but a blistering spell of five goals in 15 minutes drove them on to a semi-final place. They could even afford the luxury of allowing Sunderland to take the lead, just as they had done in their previous encounters.

1966	Benfica	A	European Cup 2nd Round 2nd Leg	5-1

This was the match that was effectively the making of the George Best legend. It was not just the two goals he scored, vital though they were to ensuring United progressed in the competition, nor was it the equally vital goals he created for others on the night. It was that he managed to eclipse the European Footballer of the Year, on his own ground and in front of his own supporters. Indeed, the evening began with Eusebio being handed his statuette with 90,000 Portuguese fans roaring their approval, but it took 19-year-old George only six minutes to stun them into silence, rising above everyone to head home the first. He added a second six minutes later, racing through to hit a low shot into the net. Four minutes later Best turned provider to set up John Connelly and the tie was effectively over. Although Benfica got a consolation goal (an own goal through Shay Brennan), United got two more from Pat Crerand and Bobby Charlton and had two further efforts disallowed. It was undoubtedly United's finest ever performance in Europe and perhaps George Best's finest in a United shirt. The Portuguese papers the next morning obviously thought so, hailing him 'El Beatle'.

1976	Wolverhampton Wanderers	A	FA Cup 6th Round Replay	3-2 [aet]
1985	West Ham United	H	FA Cup 6th Round	4-2
1986	West Ham United	H	FA Cup 5th Round Replay	0-2
1991	Chelsea	A	First Division	2-3
1993	Oldham Athletic	A	FA Premier League	0-1

MARCH 10TH

1894	Sheffield United	H	First Division	0-2

1896 George Sapsford born in Manchester. Signed by United as an amateur in April 1919 and as a professional in May 1920, he had made his first-team debut in April the same year. His two years on United's books were spent alternating between the first and second teams and in May 1922 he was sold to Preston for £2,500. He joined Southport in September 1925 where he finished his career in 1927. He later became a publican and died on 17th October 1970.

1899   Following an investigation two players were placed on the transfer list and a third
       suspended by the club. A later report in the *Athletic News* stated: 'During the week the
       directors of Newton Heath have been forced to take strong measures with some of
       their players. Boyd, who seems to be a most capricious individual, has been placed on
       the transfer list, and so has Cunningham. I suppose we have heard the last of these
       players, as far as Newton Heath are concerned, and it is as well. If men who are paid
       good wages don't think it worth their while to keep themselves in condition they are
       better out of any team.' The implication, therefore, was that the players had been
       drinking, although the third player, Gillespie, apparently apologised to the club and
       was forgiven. However, he did leave the club during the 1900 close season.

1900	Woolwich Arsenal	A	Second Division	1-2
1906	Woolwich Arsenal	H	FA Cup 4th Round	2-3
1909	Burnley	A	FA Cup 4th Round	3-2

This was in fact a replay of the match that was abandoned after 72 minutes four days
previously. Goals from Harold Halse and two from Jimmy Turnbull were enough to
take United into the next round.

1917	Everton	H	Lancashire Section Principal Tournament	0-2
1923	Manchester City	A	Friendly	0-5
1926	Liverpool	H	First Division	3-3
1928	West Ham United	H	First Division	1-1

This match was also played as a benefit for Teddy Partridge, with the player being
guaranteed a payment of £650 in recognition of his eight years of loyal service to the
club. A crowd of 21,577 saw a 1-1 draw.

1934	Hull City	A	Second Division	1-4
1945	Halifax Town	A	Football League North (Second Championship)	0-1
1951	Portsmouth	A	First Division	0-0
1956	Cardiff City	H	First Division	1-1
1962	Preston North End	A	FA Cup 6th Round	0-0
1965	Wolverhampton Wanderers	A	FA Cup 6th Round	5-3
1969	Everton	A	First Division	0-0
1973	Birmingham City	A	First Division	1-3
1979	Tottenham Hotspur	A	FA Cup 6th Round	1-1
1984	Leicester City	H	First Division	2-0

MARCH 11TH

1905	Burnley	A	Second Division	0-2
1911	Preston North End	H	First Division	5-0
1916	Oldham Athletic	A	Lancashire Section Subsidiary (Southern) Tournament	0-1
1922	Arsenal	H	First Division	1-0
1933	Port Vale	H	Second Division	1-1
1939	Aston Villa	H	First Division	1-1

1941   During the evening the German air force, the Luftwaffe, paid Trafford Park a visit,
       intent on bombing the industrial estate which was producing arms for Britain's war
       effort. Some of the incendiary bombs hit Old Trafford itself, virtually destroying the
       main stand and a section of terracing and scorching the pitch. Owing to censorship,
       little or nothing was said in the media about the extent of the damage, but in the cold
       light of day it was obvious that there would be no football played there for some
       considerable time. Thankfully, Manchester City immediately offered use of their
       facilities, and so Maine Road would play host to United until 1949.

| 1944 | Wrexham | H | Football League North (Second Championship) | 2-2 |

1950	Middlesbrough	A	First Division	3-2
1961	Newcastle United	A	First Division	1-1
1963	Aston Villa	H	FA Cup 4th Round	1-0
1967	Newcastle United	A	First Division	0-0
1972	Huddersfield Town	H	First Division	2-0
1978	Newcastle United	A	First Division	2-2
1990	Sheffield United	A	FA Cup 6th Round	1-0
1992	Middlesbrough	H	Rumbelows Cup Semi-Final 2nd Leg	2-1

With the first leg having finished goalless the tie was evenly poised and Middlesbrough were not overawed by the Old Trafford crowd, managing to take the game into extra time. There, a goal from Ryan Giggs was enough to book a return trip to Wembley in what was still the only domestic trophy to have eluded United's grasp, the League Cup. Lee Sharpe had earlier scored United's other goal.

1996	Southampton	H	FA Cup 6th Round	2-0
1998	West Ham United	A	FA Premier League	1-1

MARCH 12TH

1894	Blackburn Rovers	H	First Division	5-1
1904	Burnley	H	Second Division	3-1
1910	Woolwich Arsenal	A	First Division	0-0
1921	Bradford City	H	First Division	1-1
1927	Birmingham	A	First Division	0-4
1930	Arsenal	A	First Division	2-4
1932	Plymouth Argyle	H	Second Division	2-1
1938	Fulham	H	Second Division	1-0
1949	Stoke City	H	First Division	3-0
1960	Manchester City	A	Friendly	3-1
1966	Chelsea	A	First Division	0-2
1977	Leeds United	H	First Division	1-0
1980	Everton	H	First Division	0-0
1983	Everton	H	FA Cup 6th Round	1-0
1985	Tottenham Hotspur	A	First Division	2-1
1988	Sheffield Wednesday	H	First Division	4-1
1989	Aston Villa	A	First Division	0-0
1994	Charlton Athletic	H	FA Cup 6th Round	3-1

Shortly before half-time Peter Schmeichel came racing out of his goal to deal with a Charlton counter-attack. Unfortunately he was outside the penalty area when he attempted to block a shot with his hands and was subsequently sent off, and the resulting one-match suspension was sufficient to deprive him of a place in the Rumbelows Cup final. Forced to reshuffle, Alex Ferguson pulled off Paul Parker and sent Les Sealey into goal, and an early goal in the second half from Mark Hughes eased some of the pressure on United. Andrei Kanchelskis added two further goals before Charlton scored a late consolation.

1995	Queens Park Rangers	H	FA Cup 6th Round	2-0

MARCH 13TH

1897	Darwen	A	Second Division	2-0
1901	Barnsley	H	Second Division	1-0
1909	Chelsea	A	First Division	1-1
1915	Bradford City	H	First Division	1-0
1920	Everton	A	First Division	0-0

1926	Huddersfield Town	A	First Division	0-5
1937	Charlton Athletic	A	First Division	0-3
1943	Manchester City	A	Football League North (Second Championship)	0-2
1948	Derby County	Hillsborough		
			FA Cup Semi-Final	3-1
1954	Aston Villa	A	First Division	2-2
1965	Chelsea	H	First Division	4-0
1968	Gornik Zabrze	A	European Cup 3rd Round 2nd Leg	0-1

Despite a hostile atmosphere generated by a crowd of 105,000 United held their nerve throughout. Having lost the first leg 2-0, Gornik were always expected to take the game to United in an attempt to overturn the deficit, but despite pulling back one goal were superbly marshalled by the United defence. A 2-1 aggregate win was to be rewarded with a semi-final clash against one of the greatest names in European football: Real Madrid.

1971	Nottingham Forest	H	First Division	2-0
1974	Manchester City	A	First Division	0-0

Both Lou Macari of United and Mike Doyle of City were sent off by referee Clive Thomas, although both initially refused to accept the decision. So if the two guilty players wouldn't walk, the referee decided everyone should: he picked up the ball and took the two teams off the field, to the amazement of the 51,331 crowd! Eventually play was resumed with ten men apiece and the game was completed without further incident. Afterwards Thomas said, 'I had no option but to pick up the ball, walk off the field of play and call off the two teams.'

1976	Leeds United	H	First Division	3-2
1991	Southampton	A	First Division	1-1

MARCH 14TH

1891	Birmingham St George's	H	Football Alliance	1-3
1896	Grimsby Town	A	Second Division	2-4
1908	Sunderland	H	First Division	3-0
1912	Blackburn Rovers	A	FA Cup 4th Round Replay	2-4
1914	Aston Villa	H	First Division	0-6
1923	Derby County	A	Second Division	1-1
1925	Portsmouth	H	Second Division	2-0

United gave a debut first-team appearance to Clatworthy Rennox. His unusual Christian name led him to be known as Charlie throughout his career, which began at Clapton Orient in July 1921. He was signed by United in March 1925 and made 68 appearances before he was released in July 1927, subsequently signing for Grimsby.

1928	Everton	H	First Division	1-0
1936	Swansea Town	H	Second Division	3-0
1953	Burnley	A	First Division	1-2
1959	West Bromwich Albion	A	First Division	3-1
1962	Preston North End	H	FA Cup 6th Round Replay	2-1
1964	West Ham United	Hillsborough		
			FA Cup Semi-Final	1-3
1970	Leeds United	Hillsborough		
			FA Cup Semi-Final	0-0
1979	Tottenham Hotspur	H	FA Cup 6th Round Replay	2-0
1981	Aston Villa	A	First Division	3-3
1987	Luton Town	A	First Division	1-2
1990	Everton	H	First Division	0-0

1992	Sheffield United	A	First Division	2-1
1993	Aston Villa	H	FA Premier League	1-1
1998	Arsenal	H	FA Premier League	0-1

The battle between the top two sides in the Premiership was switched to an 11.15 a.m. kick-off in order to accommodate live television coverage, and after a tentative start the two sides did not disappoint. United led the table by nine points at kick-off time, although Arsenal had three games in hand, but for much of the game both teams seemed to have settled for a point apiece. Both had penalty appeals turned down, Arsenal perhaps more harshly, and it was Arsenal who carved out the game's better chances. Ten minutes from time Marc Overmars scored the only goal of the game and United were stirred from their slumbers. With two minutes remaining Peter Schmeichel ventured up field for a corner, as he had done on previous occasions when United were chasing an equaliser. This time his presence did not have the desired effect and as Arsenal broke away through Bergkamp, Schmeichel stretched out for a tackle, only to tear his hamstring muscle. United therefore lost the game, allowing Arsenal back into the title race, but lost their giant goalkeeper at a vital stage of the season – he would be out of action for at least a month.

MARCH 15TH

1890	Small Heath	A	Football Alliance	1-1
1902	Woolwich Arsenal	H	Second Division	0-1
1909	Sunderland	H	First Division	2-2
1911	Tottenham Hotspur	H	First Division	3-2
1913	Sunderland	H	First Division	1-3
1919	Stoke City	H	Lancashire Section Principal Tournament	3-1

1920 Billy Meredith became the oldest international to play for one of the Home Countries when he was selected for Wales in their match against England at Highbury. He was 45 years and 229 days old.

1924	Hull City	H	Second Division	1-1
1930	Derby County	A	First Division	1-1
1947	Derby County	A	First Division	3-4

On the same day, former United player Neil McBain became the oldest player to have appeared in the Football League. A spate of injuries had left New Brighton, where he was manager, without a goalkeeper, and so McBain turned out in goal in the clash at Hartlepools United in an emergency. He was 51 years and 120 days old at the time and New Brighton lost 3-0.

1950	Liverpool	H	First Division	0-0
1952	Wolverhampton Wanderers	H	First Division	2-0
1958	Burnley	A	First Division	0-3
1965	Fulham	H	First Division	4-1
1969	Chelsea	A	First Division	2-3
1975	Norwich City	H	Second Division	1-1
1978	Manchester City	H	First Division	2-2
1980	Brighton & Hove Albion	A	First Division	0-0
1985	West Ham United	A	First Division	2-2
1986	Queens Park Rangers	A	First Division	0-1
1995	Tottenham Hotspur	H	FA Premier League	0-0
1997	Sheffield Wednesday	H	FA Premier League	2-0

MARCH 16TH

1901	Woolwich Arsenal	H	Second Division	1-0

1907	Woolwich Arsenal	A	First Division	0-4
1912	Preston North End	A	First Division	0-0
1918	Stockport County	H	Lancashire Section Principal Tournament	2-0
1929	Bolton Wanderers	A	First Division	1-1
1931	Portsmouth	H	First Division	0-1
1935	Blackpool	H	Second Division	3-2
1940	Liverpool	H	War Regional League, Western Division	1-0
1946	Blackburn Rovers	A	Football League North	3-1

1949 Alan Gowling born in Stockport. Alan joined United as an amateur in 1965 and became a professional in August 1967, making his debut in March the following year. Although he seldom let anyone down when selected – once scoring four goals in a match – he struggled to command a regular place and was sold to Huddersfield in 1972 for £65,000. He later played for Newcastle and Bolton before finishing his career with Preston.

1957	Wolverhampton Wanderers	A	First Division	1-1
1963	Chelsea	H	FA Cup 5th Round	2-1
1968	Coventry City	A	First Division	0-2
1974	Birmingham City	A	First Division	0-1
1991	Nottingham Forest	A	First Division	1-1
1994	Sheffield Wednesday	H	FA Premier League	5-0
1996	Queens Park Rangers	A	FA Premier League	1-1

MARCH 17TH

1894	Derby County	H	First Division	2-6
1900	Barnsley	H	Second Division	3-0
1902	Chesterfield	A	Second Division	0-3
1906	Chesterfield	H	Second Division	4-1
1917	Rochdale	A	Lancashire Section Principal Tournament	0-2
1923	Bradford City	A	Second Division	1-1

Frank Mann made his United debut. Born in Newark in March 1891, he began his professional career with Aston Villa in 1911, later moving to Huddersfield and helping them win the FA Cup in 1922. He joined United in March 1923 for £1,750, even though he was 32 years of age. His experience proved invaluable at United, helping the side to win promotion in 1924-25 and he went on to complete nearly 200 appearances for the first team. He left United in August 1930 and went into non-League football.

1926	Bolton Wanderers	A	First Division	1-3
1928	Portsmouth	A	First Division	0-1
1934	Fulham	H	Second Division	1-0

Jack Griffiths made his debut for United at full-back. Jack was born in Staffordshire and had spent three years with Wolves before moving to Bolton. Unable to break into the Wolves side and troubled by injuries at Burnden Park, he was to become a regular with United and went to make 176 appearances for the first team, scoring one goal. The outbreak of the Second World War brought his United career to an end, although he did guest for a number of clubs during the war.

1945	Halifax Town	H	Football League North (Second Championship)	3-0
1948	Grimsby Town	A	First Division	1-1
1951	Everton	H	First Division	3-0
1956	Arsenal	A	First Division	1-1
1962	Bolton Wanderers	A	First Division	0-1
1970	Burnley	H	First Division	3-3

1973	Newcastle United	H	First Division	2-1
1976	Norwich City	A	First Division	1-1
1982	Coventry City	H	First Division	0-1
1984	Arsenal	H	First Division	4-0

MARCH 18TH

1896 Burton Wanderers A Second Division 1-5

Injuries and transfers had left the Heathens without a recognised goalkeeper and so half-back George Perrins was pressed into emergency service. At half-time, with the Heathens having already conceded four goals, Perrins was put out on the field and Walter Cartwright took over.

1899 New Brighton Tower H Second Division 1-2

A crowd of 20,000 gathered to see whether Newton Heath could make a final push towards promotion, but instead witnessed an erratic performance from the referee, who chose to ignore his linesmen on at least one crucial decision and made several other bizarre rulings. At the end of the game, 'a crowd of hot-headed youths got round him and jeered and booed him,' reported the *Athletic News*. Fortunately for him, club officials and several policemen were on hand to ensure there was no serious trouble, although the incident was not viewed with much pleasure by the newspaper, even if they were prepared to admit that the crowd had been provoked by the referee's dubious handling of the game. As the Heathens finished the season in fourth place, the two points lost here were not ultimately vital.

1902 A public meeting at the New Islington Hall in Ancoats was held to discuss the continued financial problems confronting Newton Heath. Bankruptcy proceedings were already under way, the club's Clayton ground had been closed by the receiver and the reserve side was suffering a nomadic existence, playing at different venues each week. Club secretary James West advised the meeting that since the proceedings were instigated the club had receipts of £402 and had incurred no further debts, although there was the players' wage bill of £181 10s 6d still to be paid. Club captain Harry Stafford then rose and asked how much the club would need in order to solve all of its problems. When told the sum of £2,000, he immediately replied, 'I know of five men who will each give two hundred pounds.' When asked who these men might be, he gave their names as 'A Mr Davies of Salford [John Henry Davies, whom Stafford had met thanks to his dog!], Mr Brown of Denton, Mr Deakin of Manchester, Mr Taylor of Sale and myself.' The investment was on condition that the five men named would take control of the club, and the public meeting was adjourned so that the club's directors could discuss in private the handing over of the club to this consortium. By the time the meeting ended, John Henry Davies was the new president of Newton Heath Football Club.

1905	Grimsby Town	H	Second Division	2-1
1911	Notts County	A	First Division	0-1
1916	Liverpool	H	Lancashire Section Subsidiary (Southern) Tournament	0-0
1922	Blackburn Rovers	H	First Division	0-1
1933	Notts County	A	Second Division	0-1
1939	Wolverhampton Wanderers	A	First Division	0-3
1944	Birmingham City	A	Football League North (Second Championship)	1-3
1950	Blackpool	H	First Division	1-2
1961	Arsenal	H	First Division	1-1
1963	West Ham United	A	First Division	1-3
1964	Sporting Club Lisbon	A	European Cup-Winners' Cup 3rd Round 2nd Leg	0-5

With United protecting a 4-1 lead from the first leg, it was widely expected that the club would advance into the semi-final. But with West Ham having just knocked them out of the FA Cup at the semi-final stage, United's minds weren't on their game in the second leg in Lisbon. Sporting Lisbon scored five goals within an hour, and although United woke up a bit in the last half-hour, they were unable to score and so slid out of the competition. Matt Busby was furious after the game, berating his side for a lame performance and threatening to make wholesale changes by the time of the next match. As it was United finished the season empty-handed, for they also finished runners-up in the League.

1967	Leicester City	H	First Division	5-2
1972	Stoke City	H	FA Cup 6th Round	1-1
1978	West Bromwich Albion	H	First Division	1-1
1981	Nottingham Forest	H	First Division	1-1
1989	Nottingham Forest	H	FA Cup 6th Round	0-1
1990	Liverpool	H	First Division	1-2
1992	Nottingham Forest	A	First Division	0-1
1998	Monaco	H	European Cup Quarter-Final 2nd Leg	1-1

Having gone out at the semi-final stage of the competition last year, there were high hopes that United might go at least one better and reach the European Cup final for the first time since 1968. Hopes had been raised against Monaco after the first leg of the quarter-final had finished goalless, although in truth United might have come away from the principality with a vital away goal had they shown a little more endeavour. It still meant Monaco had to score if they were to progress and after only five minutes David Trezeguet unleashed an unstoppable drive, clocked at 98 mph, past goalkeeper Raimond Van Der Gouw, giving the visitors a dream start. United were now forced to take the game to Monaco, but despite a succession of chances arrived at half-time still seeking an equaliser. That came early in the second half when Ole Solksjaer stroked home inside the six-yard area when United might have had a penalty. That set up a final charge for the winning goal, but Monaco's defence held firm, particularly the goalkeeper, and United went out on away goals.

MARCH 19TH

| 1892 | Nottingham Forest | A | Football Alliance | 0-3 |
| 1898 | Darwen | A | Second Division | 3-2 |

1900 Charlie Radford born in Walsall. Charlie was spotted by United whilst playing centre-forward for Walsall and signed with the Old Trafford club in May 1920. Unfortunately, United were well served by centre-forwards at this time and so Charlie was tried out at full-back, more to give him a game than anything else, but he did so well in this position he was soon in the first team and a permanent fixture. Sadly, he was killed in July 1924 in a motorcycle accident in Wolverhampton whilst at the peak of his career.

1904	Preston North End	A	Second Division	1-1
1910	Bolton Wanderers	H	First Division	5-0
1921	Bradford City	A	First Division	1-1
1927	West Ham United	H	First Division	0-3
1932	Leeds United	A	Second Division	4-1
1938	Plymouth Argyle	A	Second Division	1-1
1949	Birmingham City	A	First Division	0-1
1955	Everton	H	First Division	1-2
1960	Nottingham Forest	H	First Division	3-1
1966	Arsenal	H	First Division	2-1

1969	Queens Park Rangers	H	First Division	8-1

United were in scintillating form at Old Trafford, with Willie Morgan scoring the only hat-trick of his United career. The other goals were scored by George Best (two), John Aston, Brian Kidd and Nobby Stiles in front of a crowd of 36,638.

1977	Aston Villa	H	FA Cup 6th Round	2-1
1983	Brighton & Hove Albion	H	First Division	1-1
1986	Luton Town	H	First Division	2-0
1988	Nottingham Forest	A	First Division	0-0
1991	Montpellier	A	European Cup-Winners' Cup 3rd Round 2nd Leg	2-0
1994	Swindon Town	A	FA Premier League	2-2
1995	Liverpool	A	FA Premier League	0-2
1997	FC Porto	A	European Cup Quarter-Final 2nd Leg	0-0

MARCH 20TH

1897	Burton Wanderers	A	Second Division	2-1
1901	Leicester Fosse	H	Second Division	2-3
1909	Blackburn Rovers	H	First Division	0-3
1915	Burnley	A	First Division	0-3
1920	Bradford City	H	First Division	0-0
1926	Everton	H	First Division	0-0
1937	Grimsby Town	H	First Division	1-1
1943	Bury	H	Football League North (Second Championship)	4-1
1948	Wolverhampton Wanderers	H	First Division	3-2
1954	Huddersfield Town	H	First Division	3-1

1961 Jesper Olsen born in Fakse in Denmark. He began his professional career with Ajax of Amsterdam, signing for the Dutch giants in 1982. After helping Ajax win a number of domestic honours he was sold to United for a reported £700,000 in July 1984, arriving with a glowing reputation. By the end of his first season he had helped the club win the FA Cup, but inconsistent performances were to dog him throughout his stay at Old Trafford. In November 1988 he was sold to Bordeaux in France for £400,000, later playing for Caen.

1962	Nottingham Forest	A	First Division	0-1
1965	Sheffield Wednesday	A	First Division	0-1
1971	Stoke City	A	First Division	2-1
1976	Newcastle United	A	First Division	4-3
1979	Coventry City	A	First Division	3-4
1982	Notts County	A	First Division	3-1
1985	Videoton	A	UEFA Cup 4th Round 2nd Leg	0-1

(lost 5-4 on pens)

Videoton were the surprise package of the UEFA Cup in 1984-85, reaching the final before being beaten by Real Madrid. United had won the first leg at Old Trafford 1-0, but a similar scoreline in Hungary took the game into extra time. With no further goals being scored the game was decided by a penalty shoot-out, Videoton scoring all five of theirs to ensure their progress into the next round.

1993	Manchester City	A	FA Premier League	1-1
1996	Arsenal	H	FA Premier League	1-0

MARCH 21ST

1877 Jack Peddie born in Glasgow. He began his career in amateur football in Scotland before signing with Third Lanark in June 1895, moving to England with Newcastle in 1897. He joined United for the first time in June 1902, playing in their first game as

Manchester United, but after only one season joined Plymouth Argyle, finishing top scorer at Home Park in season 1903-04. He returned to United in May 1904 and spent a further three years at Old Trafford before returning to Scotland to play for Hearts. He later emigrated to America where he died in Detroit in October 1928.

1898	Luton Town	A	Second Division	2-2
1903	Leicester Fosse	H	Second Division	5-1
1908	Woolwich Arsenal	A	First Division	0-1
1913	Woolwich Arsenal	H	First Division	2-0
1923	Bradford City	H	Second Division	1-1
1925	Hull City	A	Second Division	1-0
1931	Blackpool	A	First Division	1-5
1936	Leicester City	A	Second Division	1-1
1942	Sheffield United	H	Football League Northern Section (Second Championship)	2-2
1959	Leeds United	H	First Division	4-0
1964	Tottenham Hotspur	A	First Division	3-2

1968 Gary Walsh born in Wigan. Signed by United straight from school, he broke into the team as first-choice goalkeeper in 1986-87 and looked more than capable of holding the spot for the next ten years or so until two head injuries the following season found him facing stiff competition from Chris Turner. The subsequent arrivals of Jim Leighton, Les Sealey and Peter Schmeichel over the next couple of years meant much jostling for places, and after loan spells with Airdrieonians and Oldham, Gary was sold to Middlesbrough for £500,000 in 1995.

1970	Chelsea	A	First Division	1-2
1973	Lazio Roma	A	Anglo-Italian Tournament Group One	0-0
1981	Ipswich Town	H	First Division	2-1
1984	Barcelona	H	European Cup-Winners' Cup 3rd Round 2nd Leg	3-0

This was one of United's finest performances in Europe, overcoming a 2-0 deficit from the first leg and beating a Barcelona side that could boast the likes of Maradona and Schuster in their line-up. Bryan Robson proved inspirational throughout, leading by example in the first half when he opened the scoring and in the second when he grabbed the second. Frank Stapleton put United ahead on aggregate a minute later and they held out for a superb victory, with the crowd swarming on to the pitch at the end to hail their hero Robson.

1987	Sheffield Wednesday	A	First Division	0-1
1990	Sheffield Wednesday	A	First Division	0-1
1992	Wimbledon	H	First Division	0-0

MARCH 22ND

1890	Long Eaton Rovers	A	Football Alliance	3-1
1897	Woolwich Arsenal	H	Second Division	1-1
1902	Barnsley	A	Second Division	2-3
1913	Aston Villa	H	First Division	4-0
1919	Bury	A	Lancashire Section Principal Tournament	2-0
1924	Hull City	A	Second Division	1-1
1941	Oldham Athletic	A	North Regional League	1-0
1947	Everton	H	First Division	3-0
1948	Aston Villa	A	First Division	1-0
1952	Huddersfield Town	A	First Division	2-3
1958	Fulham	Villa Park	FA Cup Semi-Final	2-2

The emotional wave that was carrying United to Wembley after the Munich air crash nearly suffered a setback in the semi-final at Villa Park before two goals from Bobby Charlton ensured a replay at Highbury.

1965	Blackpool	H	First Division	2-0
1969	Sheffield Wednesday	H	First Division	1-0
1972	Stoke City	A	FA Cup 6th Round Replay	1-2 [aet]
1975	Nottingham Forest	A	Second Division	1-0
1980	Manchester City	H	First Division	1-0

The 100th League meeting with Manchester City was won thanks to a single strike from Mickey Thomas in front of a crowd of 56,387.

1983	West Ham United	H	First Division	2-1
1986	Manchester City	H	First Division	2-2
1994	Arsenal	A	FA Premier League	2-2

Eric Cantona was sent off for the second consecutive game, although the incident which led to his dismissal at Highbury even had the Arsenal players protesting his innocence.

| 1995 | Arsenal | H | FA Premier League | 3-0 |
| 1997 | Everton | A | FA Premier League | 2-0 |

MARCH 23RD

1894	Stoke	H	First Division	6-2
1895	Grimsby Town	H	Second Division	2-0
1896	Port Vale	A	Second Division	0-3
1901	Blackpool	A	Second Division	2-1
1903	Stockport County	H	Second Division	0-0

1909 Hugh McLenahan born in Manchester. Hugh began his career as an amateur with Stockport County in February 1927, transferring to United three months later. The fee was later believed to have been a freezer full of ice cream! Introduced to the side immediately, he suffered a broken leg at the beginning of the 1927-28 season and was out for over a year, although he subsequently recovered and made a total of 116 appearances for the first team. He was transferred to Notts County in December 1936, finishing his career at the outbreak of the Second World War.

1912	Liverpool	H	First Division	1-1
1918	Stockport County	A	Lancashire Section Principal Tournament	1-2
1929	Sheffield Wednesday	H	First Division	2-1
1935	Bury	A	Second Division	1-0
1940	Port Vale	A	War Regional League, Western Division	3-1
1946	Bradford Park Avenue	A	Football League North	1-2
1951	Derby County	H	First Division	2-0
1957	Birmingham City	Hillsborough	FA Cup Semi-Final	2-0

United kept on track to complete the first double of the century thanks to a 2-0 win over Birmingham City at Hillsborough. Birmingham were beaten finalists the previous year and were looking to go one better this season, but goals from Johnny Berry and Bobby Charlton ended City's run. Now only Aston Villa, the last team to have won the double, stood between United and the record.

1963	Ipswich Town	H	First Division	0-1
1964	Chelsea	H	First Division	1-1
1968	Nottingham Forest	H	First Division	3-0
1970	Leeds United	Villa Park	FA Cup Semi-Final Replay	0-0 [aet]
1974	Tottenham Hotspur	H	First Division	0-1
1977	West Bromwich Albion	H	First Division	2-2

| 1985 | Aston Villa | H | First Division | 4-0 |
| 1991 | Luton Town | H | First Division | 4-1 |

1995 Eric Cantona was sentenced to two weeks in prison for assaulting Crystal Palace fan Matthew Simmons in January. The sentence, dished out at Croydon Magistrates Court, was tougher than expected, and the same bench refused to consider an appeal. Cantona's lawyers were successful in getting their client bail, however, and another court released him pending an appeal, which would be heard the following Friday. Earlier, fellow Manchester United player Paul Ince had had his case – for which he had pleaded not guilty – adjourned. Cantona, meanwhile, had joined celebrated company, for in the last few years Tony Adams, Jan Molby, Terry Fenwick, George Best and Dennis Wise had all been imprisoned.

MARCH 24TH

1894	Bolton Wanderers	H	First Division	2-2
1900	Leicester Fosse	A	Second Division	0-2
1906	Port Vale	A	Second Division	0-1
1917	Bolton Wanderers	H	Lancashire Section Principal Tournament	6-3
1934	Southampton	A	Second Division	0-1
1945	Burnley	A	Football League North (Second Championship)	3-2
1951	Burnley	A	First Division	2-1
1956	Bolton Wanderers	H	First Division	1-0

1961 Peter Davenport born in Birkenhead. Signed by Nottingham Forest in 1982, he was viewed as a promising striker at the City Ground and was signed by United for £375,000 in 1986 to replace Mark Hughes. Unfortunately, he had as much initial luck at United as previous Forest import Garry Birtles and his confidence took a battering. Although he rediscovered his form and goalscoring prowess, the return of Hughes prompted a move to Middlesbrough for Peter in 1988. He later played for Sunderland before moving to Scotland to play for Airdrieonians.

1962	Sheffield Wednesday	H	First Division	1-1
1969	Stoke City	H	First Division	1-1
1973	Tottenham Hotspur	A	First Division	1-1
1979	Leeds United	H	First Division	4-1

Andy Ritchie became United's youngest scorer of a post-war League hat-trick with his three strikes in the match against Leeds United. He was 18 years and 118 days old. United's other goal was scored by Mickey Thomas.

1990	Southampton	A	First Division	2-0
1993	Arsenal	H	FA Premier League	0-0
1996	Tottenham Hotspur	H	FA Premier League	1-0

MARCH 25TH

1899	Lincoln City	A	Second Division	0-2
1905	Blackpool	A	Second Division	1-0
1907	Sunderland	H	First Division	2-0
1908	Liverpool	A	First Division	4-7
1910	Bristol City	H	First Division	2-1
1911	Oldham Athletic	H	First Division	0-0
1913	Bradford City	A	First Division	0-1
1916	Manchester City	H	Lancashire Section Subsidiary (Southern) Tournament	0-2
1921	Burnley	A	First Division	0-1
1922	Blackburn Rovers	A	First Division	0-3

1931	Leicester City	H	First Division	0-0
1932	Charlton Athletic	H	Second Division	0-2
1933	Bury	H	Second Division	1-3

1940 Nobby Lawton born in Newton Heath. Nobby joined United from school, signing amateur forms in 1956 and being upgraded to the professional ranks in April 1958. He made his debut for the club in April 1960 and broke into the side on a regular basis in 1961-62, although he lost his place the following season and with United having just bought Pat Crerand he was allowed to leave. He went on to Preston and was part of the side that reached the 1964 FA Cup final, losing to West Ham at Wembley. He later played for Brighton and Lincoln before injury forced him to retire at the age of 32 in July 1972.

1944	Birmingham City	H	Football League North (Second Championship)	1-1
1950	Huddersfield Town	A	First Division	1-3
1953	Tottenham Hotspur	H	First Division	3-2
1957	Bolton Wanderers	H	First Division	0-2

Old Trafford's floodlights were switched on for the first time at a League match and attracted United's biggest crowd of the season, 60,862.

1961	Sheffield Wednesday	A	First Division	1-5
1967	Liverpool	A	First Division	0-0
1972	Crystal Palace	H	First Division	4-0
1977	Manchester City	A	Glyn Pardoe Testimonial	2-4
1978	Leicester City	A	First Division	3-2
1989	Luton Town	H	First Division	2-0

MARCH 26TH

1892	Grimsby Town	H	Football Alliance	3-3
1894	Blackburn Rovers	A	First Division	0-4
1904	Grimsby Town	H	Second Division	2-0
1910	Chelsea	A	First Division	1-1
1921	Huddersfield Town	A	First Division	2-5
1927	Sheffield Wednesday	A	First Division	0-2
1932	Oldham Athletic	H	Second Division	5-1
1937	Everton	H	First Division	2-1
1938	Chesterfield	H	Second Division	2-1
1948	Bolton Wanderers	H	First Division	0-2
1949	Wolverhampton Wanderers	Hillsborough		
			FA Cup Semi-Final	1-1

United's grip on the cup won at Wembley the previous season was already in the process of being loosened, but a Charlie Mitten goal enabled them to force a replay with Wolves at Hillsborough. A crowd of 62,250 were in attendance.

1951	Derby County	A	First Division	4-2
1955	Preston North End	A	First Division	2-0
1958	Fulham	Highbury	FA Cup Semi-Final Replay	5-3

A hat-trick from Alex Dawson helped United on their way to the FA Cup final, but Fulham battled them all the way in a compelling semi-final replay. Dawson's three goals made him the youngest hat-trick hero for United since the war, at the age of 18 years and 33 days, and additional goals from Shay Brennan and Bobby Charlton took United into the final to face Bolton.

1960	Fulham	A	First Division	5-0
1966	Preston North End	A	FA Cup 6th Round	1-1
1970	Leeds United	Burnden Park		
			FA Cup Semi-Final 2nd Replay	0-1

1973   George Best announced he was willing to play football again, but only for Northern Ireland and not for Manchester United. Whilst the Irish FA were interested, United stated that Best's suspension was registered with FIFA and he could not therefore play for anybody without the club's permission.

1983   Liverpool   Wembley Milk Cup Final   1-2 [aet]
United's first appearance in the Milk Cup final (the competition had previously been the League Cup) seemed to be heading for glory when Norman Whiteside shot United into the lead and himself into the record books as the youngest ever scorer in the final after only 12 minutes. But United, already depleted by the absence of Bryan Robson, John Gidman and Martin Buchan, suffered a further loss when Kevin Moran was forced to limp out of the game, being replaced by Lou Macari. Then Gordon McQueen pulled a hamstring and it seemed as though everything was conspiring against United, although they held out gamely until the 75th minute when Liverpool equalised. Extra time was one-way traffic as Liverpool took advantage of their patched up opponents, and Whelan scored the winner for the men from Anfield. United had a chance of forcing a replay right near the end, however, when McQueen, pushed up front because of his injury, broke through only to be brought crashing to the ground by Grobbelaar, who was lucky to remain on the field after the challenge.

1988   West Ham United   H   First Division   3-1

MARCH 27TH

1893   Ardwick   H   Friendly   3-2
1897   Notts County   H   Second Division   1-1
1909   Newcastle United   Bramall Lane
                                       FA Cup Semi-Final   1-0
United's first ever appearance in the FA Cup semi-final could not have given them stiffer opposition; Newcastle United were the cup-holders and also heading the League as they pursued an elusive double. With Manchester United having already accepted that their chances of the League had disappeared, they could concentrate on the FA Cup, whilst Newcastle played like a side finding the twin assault too much to bear. A single goal from Harold Halse was enough to put Manchester United through to their first final, which would be at Crystal Palace (not the current League ground at Selhurst Park) against Bristol City.

1915   Tottenham Hotspur   A   First Division   1-1
1920   Bradford City   A   First Division   1-2
1926   Manchester City   Bramall Lane
                                       FA Cup Semi-Final   0-3
This was only the second FA Cup meeting between the two Manchester rivals, but the stakes were considerably greater than they were on that previous occasion, for Wembley was now in view. The turning point in the match came in the 14th minute when City were awarded a highly disputed goal. Tommy Browell rose to meet a George Hicks corner and the ball certainly beat Alf Steward in goal, but United were to claim that the ball never crossed the line and that Browell had used his arms to gain an advantage. The referee, standing only three yards from the action, ruled that Browell's challenge had been legal and that the ball had crossed the line for a goal. The seeming injustice caused some United heads to drop, and when Frank Barson was spoken to by the referee following his flooring of Sam Cowan, all the fight seemed to visibly drain from United. Browell grabbed his second of the match on 75 minutes and Frank Roberts added a third to complete the scoring.

1935   Burnley   H   Second Division   3-4

1937	Liverpool	A	First Division	0-2
1943	Bury	A	Football League North (Second Championship)	5-3
1946	Blackpool	A	Football League North	5-1
1948	Huddersfield Town	A	First Division	2-0
1954	Arsenal	A	First Division	1-3
1959	Portsmouth	H	First Division	6-1
1964	Fulham	A	First Division	2-2
1965	Leeds United	Hillsborough		
			FA Cup Semi-Final	0-0

In view of the fact that the game ended goalless, it would be fair to say that both teams lived to fight another day, but in view of the events at Hillsborough, when all they seemed to do was fight, it is not the most apt description. Although matches between United and Leeds were usually (and remain) tight and tense affairs, there was little excuse for the ill-tempered display that was witnessed by 65,000 fans. Two players were booked, but there can have been few complaints if five had been dismissed, and the referee came in for considerable criticism for his failure to take effective control.

1967	Fulham	A	First Division	2-2
1968	Manchester City	H	First Division	1-3
1976	Middlesbrough	H	First Division	3-0
1978	Everton	H	First Division	1-2
1979	Middlesbrough	A	First Division	2-2
1982	Sunderland	H	First Division	0-0
1989	Nottingham Forest	A	First Division	0-2
1994	Aston Villa	Wembley Coca-Cola Cup Final		1-3

Aston Villa joined Liverpool and Nottingham Forest as four-times winners of the League Cup (in its various guises) with a 3-1 victory over Manchester United at Wembley. After taking a 2-0 lead through Dalian Atkinson and Dean Saunders, Villa allowed United to get back into the match with a goal seven minutes from the end but, as Villa relieved the pressure on themselves with an attack in the last minute, United's Russian winger Andrei Kanchelskis handled a goal-bound shot on the line and became the first player dismissed in a League Cup final at Wembley (a United player was also the first to be dismissed in the FA Cup final at Wembley). Dean Saunders netted the resulting penalty to finish the scoring.

MARCH 28TH

1891	Darwen	A	Football Alliance	1-2
1902	Burnley	A	Second Division	0-1
1904	Stockport County	A	Second Division	3-0
1908	Sheffield Wednesday	H	First Division	4-1

It took Harold Halse all of 30 seconds to score for United on his debut, the first of 50 goals he was to score for the club in first-team matches.

1910	Bristol City	A	First Division	1-2
1921	Burnley	H	First Division	0-3
1925	Blackpool	H	Second Division	0-0
1928	Derby County	A	First Division	0-5
1931	Sheffield United	H	First Division	1-2
1932	Charlton Athletic	A	Second Division	0-1
1936	Norwich City	H	Second Division	2-1
1942	Southport	H	Football League Northern Section (Second Championship)	4-2
1953	Sheffield Wednesday	A	First Division	0-0

1959	Burnley	A	First Division	2-4
1964	Wolverhampton Wanderers	H	First Division	2-2
1967	Fulham	H	First Division	2-1
1970	Manchester City	H	First Division	1-2
1975	Bristol Rovers	A	Second Division	1-1
1981	Everton	A	First Division	1-0
1987	Nottingham Forest	H	First Division	2-0
1988	Tottenham Hotspur	A	Danny Thomas Benefit	3-2

Tottenham's Danny Thomas was an England full-back whose career was brought to an untimely end following a rash tackle in a League match against QPR the previous season. The Spurs side on the night featured guest appearances by Liverpool's Kenny Dalglish and John Barnes, although even they could not help to stop United, who won 3-2.

1992	Queens Park Rangers	A	First Division	0-0
1998	Wimbledon	A	FA Premier League	2-0

MARCH 29TH

1890	Darwen	H	Football Alliance	2-1
1898	Loughborough Town	H	Second Division	5-1
1902	Leicester Fosse	H	Second Division	2-0
1906	Leicester City	A	Second Division	5-2
1913	Liverpool	A	First Division	2-0
1918	Manchester City	A	Lancashire Section Subsidiary Tournament	0-3
1919	Bury	H	Lancashire Section Principal Tournament	5-1

Joe Spence scored four of United's goals in the 5-1 demolition of Bury, the other coming from Wilf Woodcock. Although the First World War was now over, fans had still to accept that this regional football was anything more than a pale imitation of proper Football League fare, and a crowd of 19,000 was in attendance.

1924	Stoke City	H	Second Division	2-2
1929	Bury	A	First Division	3-1

By mid-February United looked certain to be relegated from the First Division. A run of 16 matches without a win, during which only four points were collected, had left them firmly rooted at the bottom of the table. The subsequent arrival of Tom Reid from Liverpool changed United's fortunes, for in the last 17 games of the season he scored 14 goals as United were beaten only three times. More importantly, they won ten and drew four of those games to finish the season in 12th place, a quite respectable position given their status in February. Tom scored two of United's goals in this match, the other coming from Harry Thomas.

1930	Burnley	A	First Division	0-4
1937	Everton	A	First Division	3-2
1939	Everton	H	First Division	0-2
1941	Blackpool	A	North Regional League	0-2
1947	Huddersfield Town	A	First Division	2-2
1948	Bolton Wanderers	A	First Division	1-0
1958	Sheffield Wednesday	A	First Division	0-1
1969	West Ham United	A	First Division	0-0
1975	York City	H	Second Division	2-1
1978	Aston Villa	H	First Division	1-1
1980	Crystal Palace	A	First Division	2-0
1986	Birmingham City	A	First Division	1-1

1889   Jack Mew born in Sunderland. Signed by United as an amateur in July 1912, he was upgraded to the professional ranks in September the same year. Although he made his League debut in March 1913, the First World War cut right across his playing career and the bulk of his appearances were made when League football resumed in 1919. He remained at United until September 1926 when he joined Barrow, by which time he had made 199 appearances for the first team, won an England cap and received two benefits from the club. He later coached overseas and died in 1963.

1895	Woolwich Arsenal	A	Second Division	2-3
1901	Stockport County	H	Second Division	3-1
1903	Preston North End	H	Second Division	0-1
1907	Bury	A	First Division	2-1
1912	Aston Villa	A	First Division	0-6

United were already injury-ravaged when they turned up at Villa Park, being without regular goalkeeper Hugh Edmonds and several other key players. Additional injuries sustained by Tony Donnelly and Dick Duckworth inside the opening 15 minutes left United facing an uphill struggle and they crashed to their biggest defeat of the season.

1918	Stoke City	H	Lancashire Section Subsidiary Tournament	2-1
1923	South Shields	H	Second Division	3-0
1929	Derby County	A	First Division	1-6
1934	West Ham United	H	Second Division	0-1
1935	Hull City	H	Second Division	3-0
1940	Tranmere Rovers	H	War Regional League, Western Division	6-1
1946	Bradford Park Avenue	H	Football League North	4-0
1956	Newcastle United	H	First Division	5-2
1957	Leeds United	A	First Division	2-1
1959	Portsmouth	A	First Division	3-1
1960	Sheffield Wednesday	A	First Division	2-4
1963	Coventry City	A	FA Cup 6th Round	3-1
1964	Fulham	H	First Division	3-0
1966	Preston North End	H	FA Cup 6th Round Replay	3-1
1968	Stoke City	A	First Division	4-2
1970	Coventry City	H	First Division	1-1

1972   Karel Poborsky born in Czechoslovakia. A series of exceptional performances for his country during the 1996 European Championships held in England prompted a £3.5 million transfer from Slavia Prague in August 1996. Affectionately known as 'The Express Train' this exciting winger delighted many with his wing play, not least his manager, who said, 'He's got great feet and vision and is also very tenacious. He will give me the variety on the right wing because he's a different type of player from the likes of David Beckham and Terry Cooke.' So it proved, for although Karel spent various spells on the substitutes bench during his first season in the Premier League, he did help United win the title at the end of it.

1974	Chelsea	A	First Division	3-1
1991	Norwich City	A	First Division	3-0
1994	Liverpool	H	FA Premier League	1-0

1886   Enoch West born in Hucknall Torkard in Nottinghamshire. Known throughout his career as Knocker, Enoch began his career with Sheffield United in 1903 but failed to make the grade and drifted into non-League football with his hometown club. Nottingham Forest offered him a return to League action in June 1905 and this time he made amends, scoring 100 goals for the club in League and cup matches in just 183 appearances. Indeed, he was one of three players who scored hat-tricks in Forest's 12-0 win over Darwen in 1909. In June 1910 he was signed by United as replacement for Jimmy Turnbull and helped his new club with the First Division championship at the end of his first season, scoring 19 goals to finish as top goalscorer for the club. He missed the opening month of the following campaign owing to suspension but still headed the club's goalscoring lists with 17, in a season in which United disappointingly slipped to 13th place. Worse was to follow, for in 1914-15, the last season before League football was suspended owing to the First World War, United looked in real danger of being relegated, only escaping at the very last thanks to a 1-0 win over Aston Villa. Already an investigation was taking place into the circumstances surrounding the match against Liverpool on 2nd April, which United had won 2-0; an abundance of bets on the exact score had alarmed the bookmakers and they in turn had asked the Football Association to investigate. When they reported their findings, eight players, including Enoch West, were banned from the game for life for fixing the match. Although the bans on all the other seven were lifted immediately after the war in recognition of the effort each player had made during the war, Enoch West's was not. For this Enoch must shoulder the blame, for whilst the other seven players had accepted the original decision of the FA, he had not, launching an appeal and then a libel case against the *Athletic News*, the paper which had first questioned the events of the match, both of which he subsequently lost. The FA did finally lift his ban in 1945, but by this time he was both too old and too bitter towards the game to have any interest in returning in any capacity.

1893	Stoke	H	First Division	1-0
1894	Stoke	A	First Division	1-3
1900	Luton Town	H	Second Division	5-0
1906	Barnsley	H	Second Division	5-1
1909	Aston Villa	H	First Division	0-2
1913	Tottenham Hotspur	A	First Division	1-1
1917	Stoke City	A	Lancashire Section Subsidiary Tournament	1-2
1923	Blackpool	A	Second Division	2-1
1928	Aston Villa	A	First Division	1-3
1934	Blackpool	H	Second Division	2-0
1945	Burnley	H	Football League North (Second Championship)	4-0
1951	Chelsea	H	First Division	4-1
1956	Huddersfield Town	A	First Division	2-0
1958	Aston Villa	A	First Division	2-3
1961	Blackpool	A	First Division	0-2
1962	Tottenham Hotspur	Hillsborough		
			FA Cup Semi-Final	1-3
1965	Leeds United	City Ground, Nottingham		
			FA Cup Semi-Final Replay	0-1
1969	Nottingham Forest	A	First Division	1-0
1970	Nottingham Forest	A	First Division	2-1
1973	Southampton	A	First Division	2-0
1975	Oldham Athletic	H	Second Division	3-2
1979	Liverpool	Maine Road		
			FA Cup Semi-Final	2-2
1984	West Bromwich Albion	A	First Division	0-2
1985	Liverpool	A	First Division	1-0
1986	Everton	H	First Division	0-0

1990	Coventry City	H	First Division	3-0
1992	Norwich City	A	First Division	3-1

1995 Eric Cantona was saved from the ignominy of prison as his two-week gaol sentence was commuted to 120 hours of community service. The United star, sentenced last week at Croydon Magistrates Court, won his appeal at Croydon Crown Court and would now pass on some of his footballing skills to youngsters in Manchester. At a hastily convened press conference later, Cantona's only comment on the judgement was, 'When the seagulls are following a trawler it is because they think the sardines are going to be thrown into the sea.'

1996 Chelsea   Villa Park FA Cup Semi-Final   2-1

United kept on course for a second historic double with a 2-1 semi-final victory over Chelsea at Villa Park. Those seeking omens pointed to the fact that United had beaten Chelsea in the final in 1994, when they last achieved the double, so their semi-final win was all the more poignant for that. Goals from Andy Cole and David Beckham left only Liverpool at Wembley standing in their way.

APRIL 1ST

1893	Preston North End	H	First Division	2-1
1897	Lincoln City	A	Second Division	3-1
1899	Woolwich Arsenal	H	Second Division	2-2

Billy Griffiths made his debut as centre-half for Newton Heath. He was signed from a local works team and fitted in remarkably well into a higher grade of football and went on to make 175 appearances for the first team, scoring 30 goals. Indeed, in season 1903-04 he was joint top goalscorer with 11 goals, a remarkable tally for a centre-half. His United career came to an end in 1905, but he had been granted a benefit match two years previously. The reserve team fixture against Manchester City realised some £150.

1904 Chesterfield   A   Second Division   2-0

Walter Cartwright made the last of his 257 appearances for the club. He had joined in June 1895 from Crewe and played for the club during its most difficult period, with little to show in the way of medals for his ten years of service. At times money at the club was so short he would have to pay his own rail fare to matches, and it was reported that his benefit game was not the financial success that had been hoped for. The club were in receivership at the time and Walter received only just over four pence in every pound that was collected. His benefit therefore amounted to the equivalent of £1.30 which he spent on a night out in Crewe!

1905	Doncaster Rovers	H	Second Division	6-0
1907	Liverpool	A	First Division	1-0
1911	Liverpool	H	First Division	2-0
1916	Stockport County	A	Lancashire Section Subsidiary (Southern) Tournament	3-5
1918	Manchester City	H	Lancashire Section Subsidiary Tournament	2-0
1922	Bolton Wanderers	H	First Division	0-1
1929	Bury	H	First Division	1-0
1933	Fulham	A	Second Division	1-3

1935 Billy Whelan born in Dublin. Spotted by United whilst playing for Home Farm, Billy was signed by the club in May 1953 and made his debut in the club's colours in the FA Youth Cup final against Wolves that month. He made his first-team debut in 1955 but was not a regular until 1956-57, for although he won a League championship medal in 1955-56, he also qualified for a medal for helping the reserve team win the Central League! He collected a second League championship medal in 1957 and also appeared in the FA Cup final, but by the following season he and Bobby Charlton were both vying for the role of inside-right. Billy did not play in the European Cup tie against Red Star Belgrade but was part of the squad that travelled to Yugoslavia and was one of the players who lost their lives when the plane crashed at Munich.

1936	Fulham	A	Second Division	2-2
1939	Huddersfield Town	A	First Division	1-1
1944	Bolton Wanderers	A	Football League North (Second Championship)	0-3
1950	Everton	H	First Division	1-1

1954 Gordon Hill born in Sunbury-on-Thames. He began his career with Millwall in 1973 and soon established a reputation of being a tricky winger, with United paying £70,000 in November 1975, with a further £10,000 payable in the event he won full England honours – which he did within six months. At United he linked with Steve Coppell and helped the club to successive FA Cup finals in 1976 and 1977, and although he was substituted in both finals, he collected a winners' medal in 1977 as United overcame Liverpool. A disagreement with the management at Old Trafford prompted a reunion with Tommy Docherty at Derby for £250,000 in 1978. He did not settle at the Baseball Ground and in November 1979 was sold to QPR for £175,000, the buying manager being Tommy Docherty for the third time! In 1981 he went to play in America and later in Europe before returning home for non-League football.

1961	Fulham	H	First Division	3-1
1963	Fulham	H	First Division	0-2
1967	West Ham United	H	First Division	3-0
1972	Coventry City	A	First Division	3-2
1978	Arsenal	A	First Division	1-3

APRIL 2ND

1892	Lincoln City	A	Football Alliance	6-1
1898	Grimsby Town	A	Second Division	3-1

Grimsby were awarded three penalties during the match, with the Heathens goalkeeper Frank Barrett saving two of them. Indeed, he had a superb game throughout as Newton Heath won 3-1.

1904	Leicester Fosse	A	Second Division	1-0
1910	Blackburn Rovers	H	First Division	2-0
1915	Liverpool	H	First Division	2-0

United were battling against relegation whilst Liverpool were safe in mid-table; this was a match United had to win and which they did 2-0. A couple of days later a letter appeared in the *Athletic News* asking the football authorities to look more closely into the game, which was said to have been the most impassionate in football history; the crowd were booing the players, particularly those from Liverpool for their lack of effort throughout, and even more so after United missed a penalty. The letter, most probably written by a disgruntled bookmaker (the bookies had taken a rush of bets on United upsetting the form book and beating Liverpool 2-0) did indeed alert the authorities, who questioned just about everyone connected with this match and then, over a year later, announced the result to have been fixed. Life suspensions from the game were handed to a number of players who took part, although most were lifted immediately after the First World War in recognition of the service given by the players to the war effort. The one exception was Enoch West, who, as well as losing a libel case against the *Athletic News*, did not have his suspension lifted until 1945, when he was 62 – a suspension of over 30 years. The result of this game was allowed to stand and had several repercussions when football resumed after the war: the two points United collected were enough to lift them above Chelsea in the League and out of a relegation spot; when the League was extended immediately after the war, Chelsea were allowed to keep their place in the First Division because the United v Liverpool match had been fixed. Spurs, who would have finished bottom regardless, were voted out in preference to Arsenal, who finished fifth in the Second Division, the only club, therefore, not to have earned their place in the First Division. One participant in the United v. Liverpool match was Billy Meredith, who had earlier been embroiled in a similar match-rigging claim whilst playing for Manchester City.

1920	Bradford Park Avenue	H	First Division	0-1
1921	Huddersfield Town	H	First Division	2-0
1923	South Shields	A	Second Division	0-0
1926	Notts County	A	First Division	3-0
1927	Leicester City	H	First Division	1-0

Whilst the team were winning a vital match in their battle against relegation thanks to a goal from Spence, the club were announcing the name of their new manager: Herbert Bamlett. He joined United from Middlesbrough and had also been in charge at Oldham Athletic and Wigan Borough, although he had begun his career as a referee. Indeed, he had officiated at the 1915 FA Cup final and was also known to United; in 1909 he had called off a tie between Burnley and United with 18 minutes left and with Burnley winning 1-0 – and United won the replayed match! Bamlett's time at Old Trafford, however, showed he had little of the same authority off the pitch as he had previously displayed on it, and following relegation in 1931 he was sacked.

1932	Bury	A	Second Division	0-0
1934	West Ham United	A	Second Division	1-2
1938	Aston Villa	A	Second Division	0-3
1945	Blackpool	A	Football League North (Second Championship)	1-4
1949	Wolverhampton Wanderers	Goodison Park	FA Cup Semi-Final Replay	0-1
1955	Sheffield United	H	First Division	5-0

On the same day as United were beating Sheffield United 5-0, Duncan Edwards was collecting the first of his 18 caps for England when selected against Scotland, a match which England won 7-2. Edwards was England's youngest international player this century, being 18 years and 183 days old, an honour he held until 1998 when Michael Owen of Liverpool was even younger when picking up his first cap.

1956	Newcastle United	A	First Division	0-0
1960	Bolton Wanderers	H	First Division	2-0
1969	West Bromwich Albion	H	First Division	2-1
1977	Norwich City	A	First Division	1-2
1980	Nottingham Forest	A	First Division	0-2
1983	Coventry City	H	First Division	3-0
1988	Derby County	H	First Division	4-1
1989	Arsenal	H	First Division	1-1
1991	Wimbledon	H	First Division	2-1
1994	Blackburn Rovers	A	FA Premier League	0-2
1995	Leeds United	H	FA Premier League	0-0

APRIL 3RD

| 1895 | Walsall | H | Second Division | 9-0 |

With Newton Heath's 14-0 win over Walsall on March 9th having been declared null and void by the Football League owing to the state of the pitch at Bank Street, the two teams were forced into a replay. This time round Walsall were without three key players and the weather was far more pleasant, although Newton Heath's groundstaff (assuming there were any!) had done little other than add more sand to the problem spots. By half-time it appeared that Walsall were faring better than the first time around, being only one goal behind, but, as they had done the first time the two sides had met, collapsed in the second half. Eight goals flew into the net, a figure that might have been considerably higher were it not for some superb goalkeeping and woeful misses by the Heathen forward line. As it was, Newton Heath had to be content with a 9-0 victory in which Cassidy, Donaldson, Smith and Peters scored two apiece and Clarkin completed the rout.

| 1896 | Darwen | H | Second Division | 4-0 |

One of Newton Heath's great characters Harry Stafford made his debut for the club. Born in Crewe in 1869, Harry joined the Heathens from Crewe in March 1896 and was soon established as captain. On the field Harry made exactly 200 appearances for the first team in competitive matches, scoring just one goal (an FA Cup tie against Portsmouth in 1901) but proving an inspirational captain who could often turn a game purely by his ability to lift his team-mates. His involvement in United's history off the field is equally vital, for it is doubtful whether there would have been a United at all but for the efforts of Harry Stafford. When the club could not afford train fares for the team to travel to away games, it was usually Harry who conducted door-to-door collections in order that the required money could be found. He invariably went without wages or expenses, found the club a ground to play on when Clayton was closed by the official receiver and, quite fortuitously, introduced John Davies to the club. His initial meeting with John Davies came about after Davies found Harry's St Bernard dog, which had last been seen wandering around a hall where the Heathens were holding a fund-raising bazaar with a collection tin around its neck! The involvement of John Davies as benefactor and Harry's own donation of £500 enabled the wound-up Newton Heath to re-emerge as Manchester United in 1902. Harry was reinstated as an amateur in that year and later served United as a director of the club until illness forced him to leave in 1911. He later emigrated to Australia and then Canada, where he owned a large hotel.

1897	Woolwich Arsenal	A	Second Division	2-0
1899	Blackpool	A	Second Division	1-0
1909	Sheffield Wednesday	A	First Division	0-2
1915	Newcastle United	A	First Division	0-2
1920	Bolton Wanderers	H	First Division	1-1
1926	Bury	H	First Division	0-1
1931	Liverpool	A	First Division	1-1
1937	Leeds United	H	First Division	0-0
1943	Crewe Alexandra	H	Football League North (Second Championship)	4-1
1948	Derby County	H	First Division	1-0
1953	Charlton Athletic	A	First Division	2-2
1954	Cardiff City	H	First Division	2-3
1961	Blackpool	H	First Division	2-0
1965	Blackburn Rovers	A	First Division	5-0
1971	West Ham United	A	First Division	1-2
1972	Liverpool	H	First Division	0-3
1974	Burnley	H	First Division	3-3
1976	Derby County	Hillsborough	FA Cup Semi-Final	2-0
1982	Leeds United	A	First Division	0-0
1985	Leicester City	H	First Division	2-1

APRIL 4TH

1893	Sunderland	A	First Division	0-6
1896	Loughborough Town	H	Second Division	2-0
1899	Barnsley	A	Second Division	2-0
1903	Burnley	H	Second Division	4-0

1904 United's Bank Street ground in Clayton played host to the fixture between the English League and their Scottish counterparts. A crowd estimated at 40,000 turned up (although only half of these had been anticipated), making this one of the largest crowds to have gathered at Bank Street. The English League won 2-1 with Steve Bloomer netting the winner.

1908	Bristol City	A	First Division	1-1
1914	Derby County	A	First Division	2-4
1925	Derby County	A	Second Division	0-1
1931	Sunderland	A	First Division	2-1
1936	Doncaster Rovers	A	Second Division	0-0
1942	Blackburn Rovers	A	Football League Northern Section (Second Championship)	2-1
1953	Cardiff City	H	First Division	1-4

Duncan Edwards made his debut for United at the age of 16 years and 182 days. He had yet to sign professional forms with the club!

1958	Sunderland	H	First Division	2-2
1959	Bolton Wanderers	H	First Division	3-0
1962	Leicester City	A	First Division	3-4
1964	Liverpool	A	First Division	0-3

On the same day, Paul Parker was born in London. He began his career with Fulham, making his debut in 1981. He was sold to QPR in the same deal that took Dean Coney to Loftus Road and was soon not only a regular in the QPR side but involved in the England set-up as well. A £1.7 million transfer took him to United in August 1991, where he won two Premiership titles and an FA Cup winners' medal as well as adding further to his tally of England caps. He was released on a free transfer in August 1996 and promptly signed for Derby, later joining Sheffield United, Fulham and Chelsea.

1970	Newcastle United	A	First Division	1-5
1972	Sheffield United	A	First Division	1-1
1973	Bari	H	Anglo-Italian Tournament Group One	3-1
1979	Liverpool	Goodison Park	FA Cup Semi-Final Replay	1-0
1981	Crystal Palace	H	First Division	1-0
1983	Sunderland	A	First Division	0-0
1987	Oxford United	H	First Division	3-2
1988	Liverpool	A	First Division	3-3
1994	Oldham Athletic	H	FA Premier League	3-2

APRIL 5TH

1890	Nottingham Forest	H	Football Alliance	0-1
1901	Lincoln City	A	Second Division	0-2
1904	Barnsley	A	Second Division	2-0
1912	Woolwich Arsenal	A	First Division	1-2
1913	Bolton Wanderers	H	First Division	2-1
1915	Bradford Park Avenue	A	First Division	0-5
1919	Port Vale	A	Lancashire Section Subsidiary Tournament	3-1
1922	Arsenal	A	First Division	1-3

1924	Stoke City	A	Second Division	0-3
1926	Notts County	H	First Division	0-1
1930	Sunderland	H	First Division	2-1
1933	Bradford Park Avenue	A	Second Division	3-1
1941	Blackpool	H	North Regional League	2-3

Following the bomb damage sustained by Old Trafford on 11th March, this was United's first 'home' match at their new temporary home of Maine Road. Crowd restrictions, as well as the unfamiliar surroundings, probably contributed to an attendance of only 4,000.

1947	Wolverhampton Wanderers	H	First Division	3-1
1952	Portsmouth	A	First Division	0-1
1958	Preston North End	H	First Division	0-0
1969	Nottingham Forest	H	First Division	3-1
1975	Southampton	A	Second Division	1-0

United clinched the Second Division championship with a goal from Lou Macari, even though there were still three games left to play.

1977	Everton	A	First Division	2-1
1980	Liverpool	H	First Division	2-1
1986	Coventry City	A	First Division	3-1
1993	Norwich City	A	FA Premier League	3-1
1997	Derby County	H	FA Premier League	2-3

APRIL 6TH

1883 Charlie Roberts born in Darlington. A more detailed biography can be found under 7th August 1939, the date of his death.

1895	Newcastle United	H	Second Division	5-1
1896	Port Vale	H	Second Division	2-1
1901	Small Heath	A	Second Division	0-1
1907	Manchester City	H	First Division	1-1
1910	Everton	H	First Division	3-2
1912	Newcastle United	H	First Division	0-2
1915	Oldham Athletic	A	First Division	0-1
1917	Port Vale	A	Lancashire Section Principal Tournament	0-3
1918	Stoke City	A	Lancashire Section Subsidiary Tournament	0-0
1920	Bradford Park Avenue	A	First Division	4-1
1928	Bolton Wanderers	A	First Division	2-3
1929	Sunderland	H	First Division	3-0
1931	Liverpool	H	First Division	4-1
1935	Nottingham Forest	A	Second Division	2-2

1938 Fred Erentz died in Denton. The elder brother of Harry, who also played for Newton Heath (although he found greater fame at Spurs), Fred was born in Dundee in 1870 and joined the Heathens in June 1892. He was paid £2 10s a week, although he almost walked out when he learned he would not be paid during the summer months. He stayed and went on to make over 300 appearances for the first team until his retirement in 1902, brought about by a knee injury.

1940	Stockport County	H	War Regional League, Western Division	6-1
1942	Blackburn Rovers	H	Football League Northern Section (Second Championship)	3-1
1946	Manchester City	H	Football League North	1-4
1949	Huddersfield Town	A	First Division	1-2
1953	Charlton Athletic	H	First Division	3-2

| 1957 | Tottenham Hotspur | H | First Division | 0-0 |

1960   Colin Gibson born in Bridport. Although Colin had been an amateur with Portsmouth he signed with Aston Villa as an apprentice in 1976 and was upgraded to the professional ranks in July 1978. Although he won a League championship medal with Villa, he was injured when they won the European Cup, and in November 1985 was signed by United for £275,000. A knee injury sustained in 1988 resulted in almost two years of operations and attempted comebacks, and in December 1990 he was sold to Leicester for £100,000. He was given a free transfer in 1994.

1964	Aston Villa	H	First Division	1-0
1966	Aston Villa	A	First Division	1-1
1968	Liverpool	H	First Division	1-2
1974	Norwich City	A	First Division	2-0
1985	Stoke City	H	First Division	5-0
1991	Aston Villa	A	First Division	1-1
1996	Manchester City	A	FA Premier League	3-2
1998	Blackburn Rovers	A	FA Premier League	3-1

APRIL 7TH

| 1890 | Small Heath | H | Football Alliance | 9-1 |

The first occasion in which brothers have both scored for Newton Heath in a League match came in this Football Alliance game. Elder brother Jack Doughty scored twice and Roger once in the 9-1 win. The Heathens' other goals were scored by Willie Stewart, who got a hat-trick, T. Craig, Alf Farman and E. Wilson.

1894	Nottingham Forest	A	First Division	0-2
1900	Port Vale	A	Second Division	0-1
1902	Middlesbrough	H	Second Division	1-2
1906	Clapton Orient	A	Second Division	1-0
1917	Manchester City	H	Lancashire Section Subsidiary Tournament	5-1
1923	Blackpool	H	Second Division	1-0
1928	Burnley	H	First Division	4-3
1934	Bradford City	A	Second Division	1-1
1939	Leeds United	H	First Division	0-0
1945	Stoke City	H	Football League North (Second Championship)	6-1
1947	Leeds United	H	First Division	3-1
1948	Manchester City	H	First Division	1-1
1950	Birmingham City	H	First Division	0-2
1951	Stoke City	A	First Division	0-2
1956	Blackpool	H	First Division	2-1

Ever since United had first headed the League table in October there had been a feeling that this would be the Busby Babes' year, and by April only Blackpool still stood between them and the League title. A crowd of 62,277, then a post-war record at Old Trafford, poured into the ground to witness the title being won, although there was one noticeable absentee: Matt Busby was in Scotland attending a funeral. Goals from Berry and Taylor confirmed United's victory, and they wound up the season 11 points ahead of Blackpool.

1958	Sunderland	A	First Division	2-1
1962	Ipswich Town	H	First Division	5-0
1973	Norwich City	H	First Division	1-0
1979	Norwich City	A	First Division	2-2
1980	Bolton Wanderers	A	First Division	3-1
1982	Liverpool	H	First Division	0-1

| 1984 | Birmingham City | H | First Division | 1-0 |
| 1992 | Manchester City | H | First Division | 1-1 |

APRIL 8TH

1893	Accrington	H	First Division	3-3
1898	Gainsborough Trinity	H	Second Division	1-0
1899	Luton Town	A	Second Division	1-0
1905	Gainsborough Trinity	A	Second Division	0-0
1908	Everton	A	First Division	3-1
1911	Bury	A	First Division	3-0
1916	Everton	A	Lancashire Section Subsidiary (Southern) Tournament	1-3

1920 Harry McShane born in Holytown in Lanarkshire. Having begun his career with Blackburn in 1937 the subsequent outbreak of the Second World War meant many of his best playing years were wasted, but when League football resumed in 1946 he joined Huddersfield, later signing for Bolton, before moving to United in September 1950. A cartilage injury in November 1951, at a time when he was a regular in the side, sidelined him for a considerable time and he was sold to Oldham for £750 in February 1954. After finishing his playing career in non-League football, Harry, whose son Ian is the well-known actor, returned to Old Trafford and was the PA announcer at the stadium.

1922	Bolton Wanderers	A	First Division	0-1
1933	Chesterfield	H	Second Division	2-1
1939	Portsmouth	H	First Division	1-1
1944	Bolton Wanderers	H	Football League North (Second Championship)	3-2
1947	Leeds United	A	First Division	2-0
1950	Wolverhampton Wanderers	A	First Division	1-1
1955	Sunderland	A	First Division	3-4

1957 United's youth team suffered their first ever defeat in the FA Youth Cup since the competition was introduced in 1952. Having won the trophy in each of the first four seasons, they were beaten 3-2 at Old Trafford in the semi-final second leg. Fortunately, they had already won the first leg at The Dell 5-1 and so moved into the final with a 7-4 aggregate victory.

1961	West Bromwich Albion	A	First Division	1-1
1969	Coventry City	A	First Division	1-2
1970	West Bromwich Albion	H	First Division	7-0
1972	Leicester City	A	First Division	0-2
1978	Queens Park Rangers	H	First Division	3-1
1989	Millwall	A	First Division	0-0
1990	Oldham Athletic	Maine Road	FA Cup Semi-Final	3-3

One of the most exciting FA Cup semi-finals in recent years ended all square and the clubs facing a replay before the winners could take their place at Wembley against Crystal Palace. Oldham took a shock lead after only five minutes, then goals from Bryan Robson and Neil Webb (his only FA Cup goal for United) looked to have won the tie for United, but Marshall equalised to take the game into extra time. Danny Wallace restored United's lead but a final goal from Palmer ensured a replay.

| 1996 | Coventry City | H | FA Premier League | 1-0 |

APRIL 9TH

| 1892 | Birmingham St George's | H | Football Alliance | 3-0 |

1894	Ardwick	A	Friendly	2-1
1898	Small Heath	H	Second Division	3-1
1901	Barnsley	A	Second Division	2-6

On the same day, Ernie Hine was born in Smithy Cross near Barnsley. By the time Ernie arrived at United in February 1933 he had a fearsome reputation as a striker and had represented England. Sadly, his luck and form deserted him at Old Trafford, and in 53 appearances he was to find the net only 12 times. In December 1934 he was sold to Barnsley for his second spell with the club. He died in Huddersfield in 1974.

1904	Blackpool	H	Second Division	3-1
1909	Bristol City	H	First Division	0-1
1910	Nottingham Forest	A	First Division	0-2
1912	Tottenham Hotspur	A	First Division	1-1
1917	Port Vale	H	Lancashire Section Subsidiary Tournament	5-1
1921	Middlesbrough	A	First Division	4-2
1927	Everton	A	First Division	0-0
1928	Bolton Wanderers	H	First Division	2-1
1932	Port Vale	H	Second Division	2-0
1938	Norwich City	H	Second Division	0-0
1949	Chelsea	H	First Division	1-1
1955	Leicester City	A	First Division	0-1
1960	Luton Town	A	First Division	3-2
1963	Aston Villa	A	First Division	2-1
1966	Leicester City	H	First Division	1-2

1969 Ever since Sir Matt Busby's shock announcement of his decision to quit at the end of the season, there had been mounting speculation as to who would take over the role of manager. Today the club unveiled his successor: Wilf McGuinness, who was appointed chief coach so as to prepare him for taking over following Sir Matt's departure.

1977	Stoke City	H	First Division	3-0
1983	Southampton	H	First Division	1-1
1985	Sheffield Wednesday	A	First Division	0-1
1986	Chelsea	H	First Division	1-2
1995	Crystal Palace	Villa Park FA Cup Semi-Final		2-2

An hour and a half before the semi-final clash, over 100 fans of both sides were involved in a large-scale fight outside a public house in Walsall. Bottles and bricks were thrown, one brick hitting a Palace fan on the head. He fell in front of a coach, and subsequently died from multiple injuries. Five other fans were seriously injured. It was believed the trouble stemmed from the January League clash between the two sides, which saw United ace Eric Cantona sent off and then launching a two-footed attack on a Palace fan. The game itself passed almost without incident, ending in a 2-2 draw.

| 1997 | Borussia Dortmund | A | European Cup Semi-Final 1st Leg | 0-1 |

APRIL 10TH

1891 Frank Barson born in Sheffield. A legendary character within the game, Frank joined United from Aston Villa in 1922. He had already collected an FA Cup winners' medal whilst at Villa, but it was the FA Cup semi-final in 1926 for which he is best remembered: an alleged foul on Manchester City's Sam Cowan left the City player unconscious, and although the referee had not seen the incident and took no action, the FA later banned Frank for two months. He also spent six months banned whilst at Watford! He left United on a free transfer in 1928 after helping the club attain its First

Division status. Indeed, in 1925 Frank was promised a pub if he helped the club win promotion. When they did he was given the keys to a hotel in Ardwick Green, but got so fed up with the flattery being handed out by his customers on the first day he handed the keys to the head waiter and telegraphed his wife to stop the delivery of their furniture! He died in Birmingham on 13th September 1968.

1893	Ardwick	H	Friendly	2-1
1897	Loughborough Town	A	Second Division	0-2
1903	Manchester City	A	Second Division	2-0
1907	Sheffield Wednesday	H	First Division	5-0
1909	Everton	H	First Division	2-2
1914	Sunderland	A	First Division	0-2
1915	Middlesbrough	H	First Division	2-2
1920	Bolton Wanderers	A	First Division	5-3
1925	Stockport County	H	Second Division	2-1
1926	Blackburn Rovers	A	First Division	0-7

This remains United's biggest defeat, a scoreline that was later equalled in 7-0 reverses against Aston Villa and Wolves.

1936	Burnley	A	Second Division	2-2
1937	Birmingham City	A	First Division	2-2
1939	Leeds United	A	First Division	1-3
1943	Crewe Alexandra	A	Football League North (Second Championship)	6-0
1944	Manchester City	A	Football League North (Second Championship)	1-4
1948	Everton	A	First Division	0-2
1950	Birmingham City	A	First Division	0-0
1954	Blackpool	A	First Division	0-2
1962	Blackburn Rovers	A	First Division	0-3
1967	Sheffield Wednesday	A	First Division	2-2
1970	Watford		Highbury FA Cup 3rd/4th-Place Play-Off	2-0

An extremely short-lived concept was the introduction of a third- and fourth-place play-off match between the two beaten semi-finalists, to be played on a neutral ground the night before the main event, the FA Cup final. United had been beaten in the semi-final by Leeds United, Watford by Chelsea, and in the match to decide third place, current form and League status served United well, for two goals from Brian Kidd won the game. A crowd of only 15,105 saw the game, and after a further play-off the following year the idea was dropped.

1971	Derby County	H	First Division	1-2
1976	Ipswich Town	A	First Division	0-3
1982	Everton	A	First Division	3-3
1991	Legia Warsaw	A	European Cup-Winners' Cup Semi-Final 1st Leg	3-1
1993	Sheffield Wednesday	H	FA Premier League	2-1
1994	Oldham Athletic		Wembley FA Cup Semi-Final	1-1

United's quest for the FA Cup and League double came closest to coming off the rails in the semi-final clash at Wembley against Oldham, the second time the clubs had met at this stage in four years. The first 90 minutes had finished goalless and extra time looked to be heading the same way when Pointon gave Oldham the lead in the second minute of the second period of extra time. United were forced on to the attack thereafter, and with virtually the last kick of the game, a spectacular volley from Mark Hughes levelled the game. The United and Oldham semi-final would require a second game, just as it had done four years previously.

| 1998 | Liverpool | H | FA Premier League | 1-1 |

APRIL 11TH

Year	Opponent	H/A	Competition	Score
1891	Sunderland Albion	A	Football Alliance	1-2
1896	Lincoln City	A	Second Division	0-2
1903	Preston North End	A	Second Division	1-3
1908	Notts County	H	First Division	0-1
1914	Manchester City	H	First Division	0-1
1923	Southampton	A	Second Division	0-0
1925	South Shields	H	Second Division	1-0
1931	Blackburn Rovers	H	First Division	0-1
1936	Bradford Park Avenue	H	Second Division	4-0
1942	Wolverhampton Wanderers	H	Football League Northern Section (Second Championship)	5-4

1951 Jim Holton born in Lesmahagow in Lanarkshire. Jim was signed by United from Shrewsbury for £80,000 in January 1973 and quickly established himself as a favourite with the crowd, who chanted, 'Six foot two, eyes of blue, big Jim Holton's after you . . .' – even though he was only 6' 1" and his eyes were brown! He broke his leg midway through United's Second Division championship season of 1974-75 and then suffered another break during his comeback game for the reserves. This effectively finished his career at Old Trafford and he was sold to Sunderland for £40,000 in October 1976. He later played for Coventry and Sheffield Wednesday and died in 1993 at the premature age of 42 years.

Year	Opponent	H/A	Competition	Score
1952	Burnley	A	First Division	1-1
1953	Newcastle United	A	First Division	2-1
1955	Sunderland	H	First Division	2-2
1957	Real Madrid	A	European Cup Semi-Final 1st Leg	1-3

The European Cup semi-final draw which pitted United against Real Madrid took United back to Spain to face the holders. Real's team of all talents was legendary, including such players as Alfredo Di Stefano and Raymond Kopa, and would later be improved by the addition of Ferenc Puskas. According to Matt Busby, the only thing his side lacked was experience, and that was why they had entered Europe in the first place. In front of 135,000 enthusiastic fans at the Bernabeau Stadium, Real's experience proved a little too much for United, and the home side finished 3-1 winners. There were those who claimed that some of the tactics employed by Real had been questionable, but Busby remained confident that his side could overturn the deficit in the second leg.

Year	Opponent	H/A	Competition	Score
1959	Luton Town	A	First Division	0-0
1973	Crystal Palace	H	First Division	2-0
1977	Sunderland	A	First Division	1-2
1979	Bolton Wanderers	H	First Division	1-2
1981	Coventry City	A	First Division	2-0
1984	Juventus	H	European Cup-Winners' Cup Semi-Final 1st Leg	1-1

Whilst Juventus could boast a line-up that featured Michel Platini, Paolo Rossi and Dino Zoff, seasoned internationals who had won the game's top honours, United, by comparison, were badly hit by injuries and had lost almost their entire midfield, with Bryan Robson, Ray Wilkins and Arnold Muhren all unavailable. Just as he had done in the previous round against Barcelona, Graeme Hogg had the misfortune to put through his own net to give Juventus the lead. Alan Davies later equalised, but United's inability to secure a lead for the second leg, plus Juventus's priceless away goal, meant the initiative had now passed to the Italian club.

Year	Opponent	Venue	Competition	Score
1990	Oldham Athletic	Maine Road	FA Cup Semi-Final Replay	2-1

Goals from Brian McClair and Mark Robins booked United's place in the FA Cup final for the first time since 1985 in this semi-final replay. Their opponents at Wembley would be Crystal Palace, who had beaten Liverpool in their semi-final.

APRIL 12TH

1895	Bury	H	Second Division	2-2
1899	Luton Town	H	Second Division	5-0
1904	Grimsby Town	A	Second Division	1-3
1909	Bristol City	A	First Division	0-0
1913	Sheffield United	A	First Division	1-2
1919	Port Vale	H	Lancashire Section Subsidiary Tournament	2-1
1924	Crystal Palace	H	Second Division	5-1
1941	Everton	A	North Regional League	2-1
1947	Brentford	A	First Division	0-0
1952	Liverpool	H	First Division	4-0
1958	Tottenham Hotspur	A	First Division	0-1
1961	Burnley	H	First Division	6-0
1965	Leicester City	H	First Division	1-0
1968	Fulham	A	First Division	4-0
1969	Newcastle United	A	First Division	0-2
1971	Wolverhampton Wanderers	H	First Division	1-0
1972	Manchester City	H	First Division	1-3
1975	Fulham	H	Second Division	1-0
1980	Tottenham Hotspur	H	First Division	4-1
1982	West Bromwich Albion	H	First Division	1-0
1988	Luton Town	H	First Division	3-0
1992	Nottingham Forest	Wembley	Rumbelows Cup final	1-0

A single strike from Brian McClair finally enabled United to get their hands on the one piece of domestic silverware to have eluded them during their history, the Rumbelows (or League) Cup. After defeats at the final stage in 1983 and 1991, it was third time lucky for the men from Old Trafford, although the cup was seen as little more than an hors d'oeuvre for the main course that season, the League title.

1993	Coventry City	A	FA Premier League	1-0
1995	Crystal Palace	Villa Park	FA Cup Semi-Final Replay	2-0

Manchester United and Crystal Palace replayed their FA Cup semi-final at Villa Park (despite appeals from Palace to delay the game as a mark of respect) following the death of a Palace fan before the first clash on Sunday. Many Palace fans heeded their club's appeal to boycott the game, with only 17,987 attending the semi-final – over 7,000 fewer than the lowest post-war semi-final of 1988 (when Luton met Wimbledon). Whilst there was little, if any, trouble off the pitch, tempers got somewhat frayed on it, with United's Roy Keane being sent off for stamping on an opponent and Palace's Darren Patterson following him down the tunnel for pushing him. United won the game 2-0 (both goals coming from Steve Bruce, who had been suspended from the first game!) to reach their 13th FA Cup final, a new record.

1997	Blackburn Rovers	A	FA Premier League	3-2

APRIL 13TH

1895	Newcastle United	A	Second Division	0-3
1900	Leicester Fosse	H	Second Division	3-2
1901	Grimsby Town	H	Second Division	1-0
1903	Doncaster Rovers	H	Second Division	4-0

| 1906 | Chelsea | A | Second Division | 1-1 |

This was a match vital to both club's promotion aspirations: United were in second place whilst Chelsea were third, with Bristol City leading the field. A crowd of 60,000, then the largest crowd United had ever played before, crammed into Stamford Bridge to witness the action. The point gained here thanks to Charlie Sagar's goal virtually assured United of at least second spot, for by the end of the season they held a nine-point advantage over The Pensioners.

1907	Middlesbrough	A	First Division	0-2
1909	Notts County	A	First Division	1-0
1912	Sheffield United	A	First Division	1-6
1914	West Bromwich Albion	A	First Division	1-2
1918	Port Vale	H	Lancashire Section Subsidiary Tournament	2-0
1925	Chelsea	A	Second Division	0-0
1929	Blackburn Rovers	A	First Division	3-0
1935	Brentford	H	Second Division	0-0
1936	Burnley	H	Second Division	4-0
1946	Manchester City	A	Football League North	3-1
1957	Luton Town	A	First Division	2-0
1963	Liverpool	A	First Division	0-1
1964	Sheffield United	H	First Division	2-1
1966	Partizan Belgrade	A	European Cup Semi-Final 1st Leg	0-2
1968	Southampton	A	First Division	2-2
1970	Tottenham Hotspur	A	First Division	1-2
1971	Coventry City	A	First Division	1-2

George Best was wanted by Queens Park Rangers, with chairman Jim Gregory and manager Gordon Jago discussing a possible transfer in meetings with Sir Matt Busby and other United directors in Manchester.

1974	Newcastle United	H	First Division	1-0
1985	Liverpool	Goodison Park		
			FA Cup Semi-Final	2-2 [aet]
1986	Sheffield Wednesday	H	First Division	0-2
1994	Oldham Athletic	Maine Road		
			FA Cup Semi-Final Replay	4-1
1996	Southampton	A	FA Premier League	1-3

By half-time United were already three goals down, and Alex Ferguson ordered his team to change their grey kit for a blue one when they emerged for the second half. After the game he claimed that his players had been unable to see their team-mates against the crowd in the grey kit and he had thereafter instructed them to change! Two days later, United announced the grey kit was being withdrawn.

APRIL 14TH

1890	Grimsby Town	H	Football Alliance	0-1
1894	Preston North End	H	First Division	1-3
1900	Walsall	H	Second Division	5-0
1906	Burnley	H	Second Division	1-0

1910 Stanley Gallimore born in Bucklow Hill in Cheshire. Signed by United as an amateur in September 1929 he became a full professional two months later. He made his debut for the club in 1930 and was fairly regular in the side until injured in 1932-33. He was released on a free transfer at the end of the season but went into hospital of his own accord and underwent a cartilage operation. In January 1934 he returned to United and asked to join in for training and did well enough to earn a new contract. He was released a second time at the end of the season, although he had played his part in ensuring the club retained their Second Division status, and went into non-League football.

1917	Stoke City	H	Lancashire Section Subsidiary Tournament	1-0
1923	Leicester City	A	Second Division	1-0
1926	Newcastle United	A	First Division	1-4
1928	Bury	A	First Division	3-4
1930	Sheffield Wednesday	H	First Division	2-2
1933	Nottingham Forest	A	Second Division	2-3
1934	Port Vale	H	Second Division	2-0
1941	Manchester City	A	North Regional League	7-1
1945	Stoke City	A	Football League North (Second Championship)	4-1
1951	West Bromwich Albion	H	First Division	3-0
1952	Burnley	H	First Division	6-1
1956	Sunderland	A	First Division	2-2
1962	Burnley	A	First Division	3-1
1973	Stoke City	A	First Division	2-2
1979	Liverpool	A	First Division	0-2
1981	Liverpool	A	First Division	1-0
1984	Notts County	A	First Division	0-1
1987	West Ham United	A	First Division	0-0
1990	Queens Park Rangers	A	First Division	2-1

APRIL 15TH

1895	Bury	A	Second Division	1-2
1899	Leicester Fosse	H	Second Division	2-2
1905	Burton United	H	Second Division	5-0
1911	Sheffield United	H	First Division	1-1
1914	Liverpool	A	First Division	2-1
1916	Oldham Athletic	H	Lancashire Section Subsidiary (Southern) Tournament	3-0
1922	Oldham Athletic	H	First Division	0-3
1927	Derby County	H	First Division	2-2
1933	Bradford City	A	Second Division	2-1

1934 David Herd born in Hamilton in Lanarkshire, although he was brought up in Manchester. He was signed by Stockport County in 1949 and when he made his debut in 1951 was in the same line-up as his father Alec! David was sold to Arsenal for £10,000 in 1954 and remained at Highbury for seven years before a £35,000 switch to United in July 1961. By this time he was an accomplished forward with a good goalscoring record, a reputation he further enhanced at Old Trafford. He scored 144 goals in 262 appearances, including two in the 1963 FA Cup final, and won two League championship medals, although missed out on the European Cup success having broken his leg the previous season. In 1968 he moved on to Stoke and later had a brief spell in Ireland before managing Lincoln City.

1938	Burnley	A	Second Division	0-1
1939	Arsenal	A	First Division	1-2
1944	Burnley	H	Football League North (Second Championship)	9-0
1949	Bolton Wanderers	A	First Division	1-0
1950	Portsmouth	H	First Division	0-2
1960	West Ham United	A	First Division	1-2
1961	Birmingham City	H	First Division	4-1

1963	Leicester City	H	First Division	2-2
1968	Fulham	H	First Division	4-0
1970	Sheffield Wednesday	H	First Division	2-2
1972	Southampton	H	First Division	3-2
1974	Everton	H	First Division	3-0
1978	Norwich City	A	First Division	3-1
1989	Derby County	H	First Division	0-2
1995	Leicester City	A	FA Premier League	4-0

APRIL 16TH

1898	Loughborough Town	A	Second Division	0-0
1904	Gainsborough Trinity	A	Second Division	1-0
1906	Gainsborough Trinity	H	Second Division	2-0
1910	Sunderland	H	First Division	2-0
1921	Middlesbrough	H	First Division	0-1
1927	Blackburn Rovers	H	First Division	2-0
1932	Millwall	A	Second Division	1-1
1938	Swansea Town	A	Second Division	2-2
1949	Burnley	A	First Division	2-0
1954	Charlton Athletic	H	First Division	2-0
1955	West Bromwich Albion	H	First Division	3-0
1958	Portsmouth	A	First Division	3-3
1960	Blackburn Rovers	H	First Division	1-0
1962	Arsenal	H	First Division	2-3
1963	Leicester City	A	First Division	3-4
1966	Sheffield United	A	First Division	1-3
1977	Leicester City	H	First Division	1-1
1979	Coventry City	H	First Division	0-0
1983	Arsenal	Villa Park	FA Cup Semi-Final	2-1

A resurgent Arsenal took the lead through Tony Woodcock ten minutes before half-time and had certainly had the best of an entertaining first half. Five minutes after the interval, Bryan Robson, returning after injury, equalised for United to set the game up for the last 40 minutes, and a little over 20 minutes from the end, Norman Whiteside scored to capture the victory. United survived a number of late scares as Arsenal pressed for an equaliser, but could not find a way through United's defence. United would meet Brighton, already doomed to relegation from the First Division, in the final at Wembley.

1986	Newcastle United	A	First Division	4-2
1991	Derby County	H	First Division	3-1
1992	Southampton	H	First Division	1-0
1994	Wimbledon	A	FA Premier League	0-1

APRIL 17TH

1900	Walsall	A	Second Division	0-0
1908	Nottingham Forest	A	First Division	0-2
1909	Leicester Fosse	A	First Division	2-3
1911	Sheffield Wednesday	A	First Division	0-0
1912	Middlesbrough	A	First Division	0-3
1915	Sheffield United	A	First Division	1-3
1920	Blackburn Rovers	H	First Division	1-1
1922	Sheffield United	H	First Division	3-2

1926 Old Trafford played host to the England v Scotland full international, the last occasion when this match between the two great rivals has been held at an English ground other than Wembley. Scotland won the game 1-0 thanks to a goal from Alan Jackson.

1933	Nottingham Forest	H	Second Division	2-1
1937	Middlesbrough	H	First Division	2-1
1943	Oldham Athletic	H	Football League North (Second Championship)	3-0
1948	Chelsea	H	First Division	5-0
1954	Portsmouth	H	First Division	2-0
1965	Leeds United	A	First Division	1-0
1971	Crystal Palace	A	First Division	5-3
1976	Everton	H	First Division	2-1
1982	Tottenham Hotspur	H	First Division	2-0
1984	Watford	A	First Division	0-0
1985	Liverpool	Maine Road		
		FA Cup Semi-Final Replay		2-1

Liverpool were destined to finish the season as runners-up in the League and European Cup and beaten semi-finalists in the FA Cup. Once their hopes of a treble had disappeared with this defeat, the onus switched to their neighbours and rivals Everton, who would go on to win the League and European Cup-Winners' Cup before facing United in the FA Cup final. Liverpool had taken the lead thanks to a Paul McGrath own goal six minutes before half-time, but United, inspired by Bryan Robson, were in no mood to let the game slip. It was Robson who levelled the scores shortly after the interval, and a Mark Hughes goal on the hour booked United's place in the final.

1990	Aston Villa	H	First Division	2-0
1993	Chelsea	H	FA Premier League	3-0
1995	Chelsea	H	FA Premier League	0-0
1996	Leeds United	H	FA Premier League	1-0

APRIL 18TH

1903	Port Vale	H	Second Division	2-1
1908	Manchester City	A	First Division	0-0
1914	Bradford City	A	First Division	1-1
1919	Manchester City	A	Lancashire Section Subsidiary Tournament	0-3
1924	Clapton Orient	A	Second Division	0-1
1925	Bradford City	A	Second Division	1-0
1927	Derby County	A	First Division	2-2
1930	Huddersfield Town	H	First Division	1-0
1931	Derby County	A	First Division	1-6
1936	Nottingham Forest	A	Second Division	1-1
1938	Burnley	H	Second Division	4-0
1942	Wolverhampton Wanderers	A	Football League Northern Section (Second Championship)	0-2
1949	Bolton Wanderers	H	First Division	3-0
1951	Manchester City	A	Lancashire Senior Cup Semi-Final	0-0
1953	West Bromwich Albion	H	First Division	2-2
1955	Newcastle United	A	First Division	0-2

1958 Seventy-one days after the crash that had decimated his team, Matt Busby arrived home in Manchester. Although it was still uncertain as to when he might be sufficiently well enough to take up the reins at Old Trafford again, he promised to be at Wembley when United took on Bolton in the FA Cup final the following month.

1959	Birmingham City	H	First Division	1-0

1960	West Ham United	H	First Division	5-3
1964	Stoke City	A	First Division	1-3
1967	Southampton	H	First Division	3-0
1973	Leeds United	A	First Division	1-0
1979	Nottingham Forest	A	First Division	1-1
1981	West Bromwich Albion	H	First Division	2-1
1987	Newcastle United	A	First Division	1-2
1992	Luton Town	A	First Division	1-1
1998	Newcastle United	H	FA Premier League	1-1

If the title was to remain at Old Trafford for a third consecutive season then three points were an absolute must in this clash with Newcastle, but despite dominating for large periods of the game, two points went missing. There were other problems for United to contend with, including Peter Schmeichel pulling a hamstring during the warm-up which required a substitution midway through the first half, and Ole Gunnar Ssolskjaar becoming the first United player to be dismissed all season following a professional foul on Robert Lee. Although David Beckham scored his first goal at Old Trafford since the beginning of the season, Arsenal were to go back on top following their 5-0 win over Wimbledon.

APRIL 19TH

1890	Birmingham St George's	H	Football Alliance	2-1
1897	Burnley	A	Test Match	0-2
1902	Port Vale	A	Second Division	1-1
1913	Newcastle United	H	First Division	3-0
1915	Chelsea	A	First Division	3-1
1919	Stoke City	H	Lancashire Section Subsidiary Tournament	0-1
1924	Crystal Palace	A	Second Division	1-1
1926	Birmingham	A	First Division	1-2
1930	Everton	H	First Division	3-3
1941	Chester	A	North Regional League	6-4
1946	Newcastle United	A	Football League North	1-0
1947	Blackburn Rovers	H	First Division	4-0
1952	Blackpool	A	First Division	2-2
1954	Charlton Athletic	A	First Division	0-1
1957	Burnley	A	First Division	3-1
1958	Birmingham City	H	First Division	0-2

Whilst United were taking on Birmingham City in a First Division match, Bobby Charlton made his first England appearance in the 4-0 win over Scotland at Hampden Park and scored the first of his 49 goals. On the same day, Billy Meredith died in Manchester at the age of 84 years. A detailed biography can be found under his birthdate of 30th July 1874.

1965	Birmingham City	A	First Division	4-2
1969	Burnley	H	First Division	2-0
1971	Liverpool	H	First Division	0-2
1975	Notts County	A	Second Division	2-2
1976	Burnley	A	First Division	1-0
1977	Queens Park Rangers	A	First Division	0-4
1980	Norwich City	A	First Division	2-0
1983	Everton	A	First Division	0-2
1986	Tottenham Hotspur	A	First Division	0-0
1997	Liverpool	A	FA Premier League	3-1

APRIL 20TH

1895	Notts County	H	Second Division	3-3
1903	Small Heath	A	Second Division	1-2
1908	Aston Villa	H	First Division	1-2
1912	Oldham Athletic	H	First Division	3-1
1918	Port Vale	A	Lancashire Section Subsidiary Tournament	0-3
1929	Arsenal	H	First Division	4-1
1935	Fulham	A	Second Division	1-3
1940	Manchester City	H	League War Cup 1st Round 1st Leg	0-1
1946	Sheffield Wednesday	H	Football League North	4-0
1953	Liverpool	H	First Division	3-1
1957	Sunderland	H	First Division	4-0

United secured their fifth League title with this 4-0 hammering of Sunderland, although the destination of the trophy had not been in any doubt since January. Goals from Bill Whelan (two), Duncan Edwards and Tommy Taylor made it certain United retained the title and set up another assault on Europe the following season. They finished the campaign eight points ahead of Spurs and Preston.

1963	Sheffield United	H	First Division	1-1
1966	Partizan Belgrade	H	European Cup Semi-Final 2nd Leg	1-0

United's quest for the European Cup fell at the semi-final stage for the third time, although they pushed their Yugoslavian opponents mighty close at the end. With United already two goals behind from the first leg, it would have required a remarkable comeback if United were to make the final. A crowd of 62,500 obviously thought United were capable of pulling off the impossible and willed them from the first whistle to the last, but it took until the 73rd minute before United could find the net, Nobby Stiles narrowing the deficit to one goal. The final 15 minutes or so were among the most frantic ever witnessed at Old Trafford, but that elusive goal would not come and United would have to wait for another two years before realising their dream.

1968	Sheffield United	H	First Division	1-0
1974	Southampton	A	First Division	1-1
1982	Ipswich Town	A	First Division	1-2
1987	Liverpool	H	First Division	1-0
1992	Nottingham Forest	H	First Division	1-2
1996				

Eric Cantona's rehabilitation into the English game following his lengthy suspension over events at Selhurst Park the previous January was confirmed when he won the coveted Footballer of the Year award from the Football Writers Association. Previous United winners of the trophy were Johnny Carey (1949), Bobby Charlton (1966) and George Best (1968).

APRIL 21ST

1890	Walsall Town Swifts	H	Football Alliance	2-1
1897	Burnley	H	Test Match	2-0
1900	Middlesbrough	A	Second Division	0-2
1902	Burton United	H	Second Division	3-1
1905	Chesterfield	A	Second Division	0-2
1906	Leeds City	A	Second Division	3-1

Although there was still an extremely small mathematical chance that they might slip up, this was effectively the game with which United confirmed their promotional future. Goals from Allan, Peddie and Wombwell ensured the points.

1916	Stockport County	H	Lancashire Section Subsidiary (Southern) Tournament	3-2

1917	Manchester City	A	Lancashire Section Subsidiary Tournament	1-0
1919	Manchester City	H	Lancashire Section Subsidiary Tournament	2-4
1923	Leicester City	H	Second Division	0-2
1924	Clapton Orient	H	Second Division	2-2
1926	Sunderland	H	First Division	5-1
1928	Sheffield United	H	First Division	2-3
1934	Notts County	A	Second Division	0-0
1937	Sunderland	A	First Division	1-1
1945	Doncaster Rovers	A	Football League North (Second Championship)	2-1
1949	Sunderland	H	First Division	1-2
1951	Newcastle United	A	First Division	2-0
1952	Chelsea	H	First Division	3-0
1956	Portsmouth	H	First Division	1-0
1958	Wolverhampton Wanderers	H	First Division	0-4
1962	Everton	H	First Division	1-1
1973	Manchester City	H	First Division	0-0
1976	Stoke City	H	First Division	0-1
1979	Tottenham Hotspur	A	First Division	1-1
1984	Coventry City	H	First Division	4-1
1985	Luton Town	A	First Division	1-2
1990	Tottenham Hotspur	A	First Division	1-2
1991	Sheffield Wednesday	Wembley	Rumbelows Cup final	0-1

With United having already got one foot into the final of the European Cup-Winners' Cup there was a distinct hope that a unique double might be achieved. United were the undoubted favourites going into the game, their crown as the cup kings yet to be dislodged, but Second Division Sheffield Wednesday were keen to give their supporters something to cheer about after the ignominy of relegation the previous year. So it proved, a single strike from John Sheridan enough to give Wednesday their first honour since the FA Cup in 1935.

| 1993 | Crystal Palace | A | FA Premier League | 2-0 |

APRIL 22ND

| 1893 | Small Heath | Stoke | Test Match | 1-1 |

Newton Heath's first season of Football League action had been a baptism of fire: out of 30 games played they had managed only six victories (although one of these was a 10-1 win over Wolves, a result that is still United's record League win) and had finished the season bottom of 16 clubs. Fortunately, the Football League had not yet introduced automatic promotion and relegation between their two divisions, meaning the Heathens had a chance to save themselves. They were pitched against Small Heath, who had topped the Second Division and were widely expected to beat Newton Heath over the two games, having lost only three times all season and scored 90 goals in the process. Small Heath tore straight into the attack, pinning Newton back in their own half during the opening exchanges, but without being able to find a way through to goal. Instead, it was the Heathens who scored first, catching Small Heath by surprise when Farman was on hand to meet a Cassidy cross. As expected this stirred Small Heath into even more vigorous action, but by half-time the Heathens were still holding out. Concerted pressure by Small Heath was sure to bring about a result eventually and shortly after play had resumed for the second half, Wheldon equalised with a great shot. Although both sides carved out a number of chances in the time that remained, there was no further score. This threw the Football League into a dilemma, for at the time they had not considered the prospect of the game ending all-square, but eventually they announced that there should be a replay, which duly took place the following Thursday.

| 1899 | Darwen | A | Second Division | 1-1 |

1904 Whilst at least one half of Manchester had their attentions concentrated on the FA Cup (City were appearing in the final the following day), United were acquiring one of the most important players in their history, as Charlie Roberts was transferred from Grimsby for £400. Signed by Ernest Mangnall after only one season with Grimsby, Charlie Roberts became an influential member of the team, rising to club captain and an inspiration both on and off the field. Indeed, Italian coach Vittorio Pozzo modelled his 1934 World Cup-winning team on Roberts's style, having witnessed first hand Charlie playing at Clayton. Whilst Roberts was considered influential by United, to the Football Association he was confrontational: he insisted on playing in short shorts when FA rules dictated that shorts should cover the knees, was a pioneer and later chairman of the Players' Union, and later helped in the formation of Outcasts FC, a team formed by rebels from the Players' Union. Such actions ensured the lasting hostility of the FA, with Roberts only collecting three caps for England when his abilities dictated he should have won considerably more. Nicknamed 'The Ghost in Boots' during his time with United, he left for Oldham in 1913 and retired as a player during the First World War, later being appointed manager at Oldham in July 1921. He resigned 18 months later, citing he could not stand the strain of watching as his reason.

1905	Liverpool	A	Second Division	0-4
1907	Everton	H	First Division	3-0
1908	Bolton Wanderers	A	First Division	2-2
1911	Aston Villa	A	First Division	2-4

Aston Villa and United had been neck and neck in the race for the League all season, although as Easter approached United held the upper hand: four points clear and with only six games to play, the title would surely go to Old Trafford. United won their next two matches to maintain their grip at the top, but then the nerves began to appear. Successive draws (against Sheffield United and Sheffield Wednesday), coupled with Villa's relentless pursuit, saw the gap down to a single point. The crunch game was Villa versus United on the penultimate Saturday of the season. The importance of the game was reflected by the attendance, 55,000 packing into Villa Park to witness a match that was little more than an ill-tempered battle from the first whistle to the last. United's chances were not helped by having Enoch West sent off, and despite two goals from Harold Halse, Villa's four in reply put them on top of the table for the first time since November, a point ahead of United and with one game left to play.

1914	Sheffield United	H	First Division	2-1
1916	Liverpool	A	Lancashire Section Subsidiary (Southern) Tournament	1-7
1922	Oldham Athletic	A	First Division	1-1
1925	Southampton	H	Second Division	1-1
1930	Huddersfield Town	A	First Division	2-2
1933	West Ham United	H	Second Division	1-2
1935	Southampton	A	Second Division	0-1
1939	Brentford	H	First Division	3-0
1944	Burnley	A	Football League North (Second Championship)	3-3
1946	Newcastle United	H	Football League North	4-1
1950	Newcastle United	A	First Division	1-2

Jack Warner made his last appearance for United and in so doing became the oldest player to have appeared for the club since the Second World War. He was 38 years old at the time. The player he replaced in the team for this match was Jeff Whitefoot, who the previous week had just become United's youngest player since the war at the age of only 16!

1957	Burnley	H	First Division	2-0

With United shortly to play a European Cup semi-final against Real Madrid in three days time, Matt Busby rested eight of his first team and brought in reserves. Goals from Dawson and Webster saw United win 2-0.

1961	Preston North End	A	First Division	4-2
1963	Wolverhampton Wanderers	H	First Division	2-1
1967	Sunderland	A	First Division	0-0
1972	Nottingham Forest	A	First Division	0-0
1978	West Ham United	H	First Division	3-0
1989	Charlton Athletic	A	First Division	0-1
1992	West Ham United	A	First Division	0-1

APRIL 23RD

1898	Darwen	H	Second Division	3-2
1902	Chesterfield	H	Second Division	2-0
1904	Burton United	H	Second Division	2-0
1910	Everton	A	First Division	3-3
1921	Blackburn Rovers	A	First Division	0-2
1927	Huddersfield Town	A	First Division	0-0
1932	Bradford City	H	Second Division	1-0
1938	Bradford Park Avenue	H	Second Division	3-1
1949	Preston North End	H	First Division	2-2
1955	Arsenal	A	First Division	3-2
1958	Newcastle United	H	First Division	1-1
1960	Arsenal	A	First Division	2-5
1962	Sheffield United	H	First Division	0-1
1966	Everton	Burnden Park	FA Cup Semi-Final	0-1
1969	AC Milan	A	European Cup Semi-Final 1st Leg	0-2

United's grip on the European Cup won so impressively the previous season was loosened before an hour's play in the first leg of the semi-final, for AC Milan had scored twice and looked capable of adding more. United defended resolutely thereafter to prevent further goals, despite losing John Fitzpatrick, who was sent off for a foul on Kurt Hamrin.

1973	Sheffield United	H	First Division	1-2
1974	Everton	A	First Division	0-1
1977	Leeds United	Hillsborough	FA Cup Semi-Final	2-1
1980	Aston Villa	H	First Division	2-1
1983	Watford	H	First Division	2-0
1994	Manchester City	H	FA Premier League	2-0
1997	Borussia Dortmund	H	European Cup Semi-Final 2nd Leg	0-1

With United seeking to overturn a 1-0 defeat from the first leg it was vital that there was an early goal in the second leg at Old Trafford. There was too, but it came from Borussia Dortmund's Ricken and took them into an unassailable 2-0 aggregate lead, with United now needing three goals if they were to progress into the final. Resolute defending by the Germans, undoubtedly the surprise package of the European Cup this season, ensured United never got close, and Borussia Dortmund went into the final to meet Juventus.

APRIL 24TH

1897	Sunderland	H	Test Match	1-1
1899	Manchester City	H	Healey Cup Final	1-2
1905	Blackpool	H	Second Division	3-1
1909	Bristol City	Crystal Palace		
		FA Cup Final		1-0

Ever since United had beaten Newcastle in the semi-final, Cup final fever had gripped at least one half of Manchester. Whilst the fans were booking their places on the excursions being organised (a day return on the trains was available at 11s), manager Ernest Mangnall had decided to take the team away for a week's preparation. The United entourage were booked into the Royal Forest Hotel, enjoying a few rounds of golf, some light training and being entertained by music hall comedian George Robey. Robey had once been a player on United's books but had found greater fame (and fortune!) as a comedian. He was also a member of the club and presented the team with a new set of shirts for the final; as the two strips would have clashed, United were instructed to change and instead played in white shirts with a red V on the front. After a light lunch at the Great Eastern Hotel United journeyed to Crystal Palace, arriving shortly before 2 p.m. The only doubt within the side concerned Sandy Turnbull, who was nursing a knee injury, but with Charlie Roberts backing his selection, Turnbull took his place in the team. Bristol City, meanwhile, had already lost a number of key players through injury and they thus started the game as underdogs. Not for the last time the final itself was not the showpiece everyone had hoped for, with Billy Meredith the main difference between the stalemate that threatened. It was Sandy Turnbull who scored the only goal of the game, reacting quicker than anyone else after a shot from Harold Halse had struck the crossbar. If the game was a disappointment to the 71,401 crowd, then the result was anything but to the United fans in attendance. In successive seasons they had now won the League and FA Cup; surely further honours lay waiting for their team.

1915   With the Crystal Palace ground having already been requisitioned owing to the First World War, Old Trafford was chosen to stage the FA Cup final between Sheffield United and Chelsea. In what later became known as the 'Khaki Cup Final' owing to the abundance of soldiers in the crowd of 49,557, United won 3-0.

1920	Blackburn Rovers	A	First Division	0-5
1937	West Bromwich Albion	A	First Division	0-1

Defeat at the Hawthorns condemned United to an immediate return to the Second Division, two points away from safety.

1943	Oldham Athletic	A	Football League North (Second Championship)	1-3
1948	Blackpool	Wembley	FA Cup Final	4-2

Whilst the FA Cup final at Wembley often promises much, seldom does it live up to its billing. There are one or two exceptions, and this clash with Blackpool, complete with Stanley Matthews and Stan Mortensen, is widely regarded as one of the best ever seen. United had been in sparkling form throughout the season, finishing second in the League behind Arsenal (without ever having had much chance of catching them) and gliding through the early rounds of the FA Cup. At Wembley they and Blackpool produced a sparkling match of attacking football. Blackpool took the lead from the penalty spot after only 12 minutes, although the foul by Chilton on Mortensen was probably outside the area. Jack Rowley then pounced to level the score after a mix-up between the Blackpool goalkeeper and a defender, but barely seven minutes later United were behind once again through Mortensen. After the break it became obvious that United needed to stop Matthews, who was supplying most of the crosses for Mortensen, and skipper Johnny Carey marshalled his defenders superbly to cut out any further threats to the United goal. Up front, Rowley and Pearson began to get the better of their markers and in a 15-minute spell took control of the game. Jack Rowley brought United level for a second time with a header from Morris's free-kick. Pearson then put United ahead for the first time in the game and seven minutes from time Anderson put the result beyond doubt with a centre that went in off Kelly. Johnny Carey duly collected the cup, 39 years to the day since United had last won the trophy.

1954	Sheffield United	A	First Division	3-1
1962	Sheffield United	A	First Division	3-2
1965	Liverpool	H	First Division	3-0
1968	Real Madrid	H	European Cup Semi-Final 1st Leg	1-0

This was the fourth time United had reached the semi-final stage of the European Cup and 63,000 fans jammed themselves into Old Trafford to see their heroes come face to face with Real Madrid. Although United battled well throughout, all they had to show for the endeavours at the end of 90 minutes was a single goal from George Best. The slenderest of leads was not much to take to Spain, but they had managed to prevent Real from scoring a priceless away goal.

1971	Ipswich Town	H	First Division	3-2
1976	Leicester City	A	First Division	1-2
1982	Brighton & Hove Albion	A	First Division	1-0
1985	Southampton	H	First Division	0-0
1991	Legia Warsaw	H	European Cup-Winners' Cup Semi-Final 2nd Leg	1-1

United may not have been able to give their fans a victory to savour, but they were able to reach their second European final with a 4-2 aggregate win over their Polish opponents. Lee Sharpe scored United's goal.

APRIL 25TH

1903	Barnsley	A	Second Division	0-0
1904	Bolton Wanderers	A	Second Division	0-0
1906	Lincoln City	A	Second Division	3-2
1908	Preston North End	H	First Division	2-1

United had begun the season in blistering form, losing only twice by the turn of the year and being so far ahead of the field to have virtually sown up the title. There was the prospect of setting an abundance of records to keep the side on their toes, but inexplicably they went off the boil, losing seven times, including a 7-4 mauling at Anfield at the hands of Liverpool. In the end, whilst they did manage to overcome Newcastle's haul of 51 points, the championship win owed as much to the chasing pack falling over themselves as it did to United's superiority. Victory over Preston, which enabled United to register 52 points during the season, came courtesy of goals from Halse and a Rodway own goal, an unspectacular end to the season. The fans also thought so, for only 8,000 bothered to attend this fixture when 50,000 had witnessed the clash with Newcastle. United finally finished the season nine points ahead of both Aston Villa and Manchester City, with captain Charlie Roberts collecting the famous League trophy on behalf of the club.

| 1914 | Blackburn Rovers | H | First Division | 0-0 |
| 1925 | Port Vale | H | Second Division | 4-0 |

United virtually guaranteed their return to the First Division with a convincing 4-0 win over Port Vale, leaving only Derby County with a slight mathematical chance of still overtaking them.

1928	Sunderland	H	First Division	2-1
1936	Bury	H	Second Division	2-1
1942	Oldham Athletic	H	Football League Northern Section (Second Championship)	5-1

| 1953 | Middlesbrough | A | First Division | 0-5 |
| 1957 | Real Madrid | H | European Cup Semi-Final 2nd Leg | 2-2 |

United could not have wished for more glorious opponents to play against in their first European Cup match at Old Trafford, the floodlights having now been installed. Although United started 3-1 behind they were confident that a crowd of 65,000, closer to the pitch than the Spaniards would normally be used to, could produce an intimidating atmosphere to unsettle Real Madrid. It didn't quite work out like that, for Kopa and Mateos put Real 2-0 ahead by half-time and United must have known there and then that the first challenge on Europe was over. Goals from Whelan and Bobby Charlton enabled United to finish the evening level but 3-5 down on aggregate, although they had spent most of the second half encamped in their opponents' half and attacking almost at will. The European Cup may have gone, but the League champions had retained their title and still had the FA Cup final to come.

1959	Leicester City	A	First Division	1-2
1964	Nottingham Forest	H	First Division	3-1
1966	Everton	A	First Division	0-0
1972	Arsenal	A	First Division	0-3
1978	Bristol City	A	First Division	1-0
1979	Norwich City	H	First Division	1-0
1981	Norwich City	H	First Division	1-0
1984	Juventus	A	European Cup-Winners' Cup Semi-Final 2nd Leg	1-2

With the first leg at Old Trafford having finished a goal apiece, United were always likely to face an uphill struggle, despite the return of Ray Wilkins to the side. Juventus took an early lead, the signal for their fans in the 64,655 crowd to light their firecrackers and start celebrating, but United still had a sting in the tail. Norman Whiteside came off the bench to fire home an equaliser and set up the prospect of extra time and possibly penalties to decide the tie, but in the dying seconds Paolo Rossi hit the winner to send them into the final. United had put up a brave fight, but it was not to be their year in the Cup-Winners' Cup.

| 1987 | Queens Park Rangers | A | First Division | 1-1 |

APRIL 26TH

| 1890 | Sheffield Wednesday | H | Football Alliance | 1-2 |
| 1897 | Sunderland | A | Test Match | 0-2 |

By 1897 the Test Match system of 'first past the post' had been replaced by a mini League system; the two promotion candidates would meet the two relegation candidates home and away and the top two teams at the end of the four-game League would start the next season in the First Division. By the time Newton Heath travelled to face Sunderland in the final match of the series, the situation had become clear: Notts County (the other promotion candidate) were top with four points, Newton Heath and Burnley both had three points, and Sunderland had two points. This meant Newton had only to win to ensure First Division football the following season, although depending on how the other game finished even a draw might be enough. Sunderland simply had to win this game; any other result would relegate them. A crowd of 6,000 turned out to see the action, with Sunderland tearing into their opponents right from the off, such was their desperation. They scored after only 15 minutes and kept up the pace, but somehow the Newton goal held out until ten minutes before the end of the game when a second goal was added. The 2-0 win confirmed Sunderland would remain in the First Division and condemned Newton Heath to remain in the Second Division.

1902   The *Manchester Evening News* announced that Newton Heath had officially changed its name to Manchester United Football Club. The new name had first been proposed at the public meeting in March, although there had been little support for this change. However, since John Henry Davies had taken control of the club, the need to distance the new regime from that of the old had been paramount, and one of the things the club had decided to change was the name. One of the points that dictated this change was the number of times teams had turned up at the club's Clayton ground late, as the *Manchester Evening News* explained: 'Visiting teams and supporters have many times been led astray by the name of the club and have journeyed either by car or train to Newton Heath only to find that they were miles away from the home of the club.' Both Manchester Central and Manchester Celtic had been considered for the club's new name, but following a suggestion from Louis Rocca, Manchester United was duly adopted.

1911   Old Trafford got its first glimpse of the new FA Cup trophy after the replay between Bradford City and Newcastle United was staged in front of a crowd of 58,000. A single strike by Spiers took the cup, manufactured in Bradford by Thomas Fattorini & Sons, back to Bradford!

1913	Oldham Athletic	A	First Division	0-0
1915	Aston Villa	H	First Division	1-0
1919	Stoke City	A	Lancashire Section Subsidiary Tournament	2-4
1920	Notts County	H	First Division	0-0
1924	Sheffield Wednesday	H	Second Division	2-0
1930	Leeds United	A	First Division	1-3
1941	Liverpool	A	North Regional League	1-2
1947	Portsmouth	A	First Division	1-0
1952	Arsenal	H	First Division	6-1

One of the closest finishes to the First Division in many years saw League leaders Manchester United entertaining the second-placed club Arsenal on the last day of the season. Arsenal, two points behind United, had to win by seven goals to lift the title – but they lost 6-1! The defeat was so severe they were also pipped for the runners-up spot – that went to last season's champions Spurs. In truth, of course, United had been building towards their third title ever since League football had resumed in 1946, having been runners-up in the League no fewer than four times since then. A hat-trick from Jack Rowley, two from Stan Pearson and one from Roger Byrne ensured the title was back at Old Trafford.

1955	Charlton Athletic	A	First Division	1-1
1958	Chelsea	A	First Division	1-2
1965	Arsenal	H	First Division	3-1

United clinched their first title since the Busby Babes' success of 1957 with an emphatic 3-1 win over Arsenal. Denis Law grabbed two of the goals that made sure, even though he finished the game injured. With Leeds managing no more than a draw at Birmingham, United were confirmed as champions and would therefore get another crack at the European Cup.

1975	Blackpool	H	Second Division	4-0
1977	Middlesbrough	A	First Division	0-3
1980	Coventry City	H	First Division	2-1
1986	Leicester City	H	First Division	4-0
1992	Liverpool	A	First Division	0-2

APRIL 27TH

1893	Small Heath	Bramall Lane	
		Test Match Replay	5-2

If Small Heath had gone into the first Test Match meeting with Newton Heath as favourites, based entirely on their form during the season, then the odds had switched somewhat by the time the two teams lined up for their replay. Newton Heath's fine performance in that first match was only partly responsible, for the Heathens considered Sheffield to be a lucky city for them. A crowd of 6,000 gathered to watch the replay, with Small Heath taking an early lead which should have settled their nerves. Instead it was Newton Heath, playing for their First Division lives, who responded the better, taking whatever luck went their way and equalising from the penalty spot through Farman. Evenly balanced as they went into the second half, Small Heath again took the lead, but it was to be short-lived as Cassidy equalised almost immediately. The second equaliser almost drained the spirit from Small Heath, for they started to look weary and tired. The Heathens, however, rose to the occasion, adding goals from Coupar and a further two from Farman to win by the surprise margin of 5-2 and maintain their First Division status.

1895	Stoke	Burslem	Test Match	0-3
1898	Manchester City	H	Healey Cup Final	2-4
1901	Chesterfield	H	Second Division	1-0
1908	Queens Park Rangers	Stamford Bridge		
			FA Charity Shield	1-1

Although there had been Charity Shield matches since 1898, these had invariably been between a top professional and amateur side of the day. When the Football Association took over organisation of the event, they decreed that the game should be between the Football League champions and their Southern League counterparts. Thus this match between United and QPR was the first FA Charity Shield ever played. A crowd of 6,000 saw United, reluctant to take part in the game in the first place, struggle to match their opponents, and only a fine solo effort from Billy Meredith enabled them to leave the pitch level with QPR. The FA duly announced there would be a replay on August 29th.

1909	Woolwich Arsenal	H	First Division	1-4

Three days previously United had been victorious in the FA Cup final. After the game they had enjoyed an evening at the Alhambra Theatre in the company of George Robey, at whose home they had then spent Sunday. After sightseeing in London on Monday they had caught the train from St Pancras back to Manchester on Tuesday morning, finally arriving at Central Station, Manchester at 3.30 p.m. Thousands of spectators had turned out to welcome home the conquering heroes, lining the route to the Town Hall and straining for a glimpse of the famous cup itself. The journey seemed to take an age as more and more fans followed the horse-drawn carriages around the city. At the Town Hall the Mayor gave an address and added his voice to the congratulations that were being issued. Then it was back into the carriages for the final journey of the day – to Bank Street in Clayton, where the team were due to play the last League match of the season. Not surprisingly, United were in little state to offer much more than token opposition to Woolwich Arsenal, ending up on the wrong end of a 4-1 beating. But the 30,000 crowd were not interested in the two League points on offer; they were more concerned with seeing the cup being paraded around the ground. After the game chairman John Henry Davies took the cup into the Arsenal dressing-room, emptied a bottle of champagne into it and invited the Arsenal players to drink to the health of Manchester United.

1912	Bolton Wanderers	A	First Division	1-1
1917				

1917 Tommmy Breen born in Belfast. He began his career as a forward for Drogheda United but had to take over in goal in an emergency and did so well he was retained in that position! Indeed, he subsequently replaced Elisha Scott in the Northern Ireland side. Signed by United in 1936 from Belfast Celtic, he was a regular until replaced by Jack Breedon and at the outbreak of the Second World War returned to Belfast Celtic. He later played for Linfield, Shamrock Rovers, Newry Town and Glentoran.

1921 Billy McGlen born in Bedlington. Signed by United as an amateur in 1946 he was upgraded to the professional ranks in May of the same year and made his debut two months later. Although seldom a regular in the side Billy made over 120 appearances for the United side, usually at half-back although he was adaptable enough to have also played at outside-left and full-back. He was sold to Lincoln City for £8,000 in 1952, later serving that club as trainer.

1928 Les Olive born in Salford. Although Les made only two appearances for the United first team, both as emergency goalkeeper when Ray Wood, Jack Crompton and Reg Allen were injured, he has served United in one capacity or another since his signing in 1942. He was appointed assistant secretary in 1955, taking over as secretary following the death of Walter Crickmer in the Munich air crash. He retired from this position in 1988 but was subsequently appointed to the board of directors.

1929	Everton	A	First Division	4-2
1935	Bradford Park Avenue	H	Second Division	2-0
1940	Manchester City	A	League War Cup 1st Round 2nd Leg	2-0
1946	Sheffield Wednesday	A	Football League North	0-1
1949	Everton	A	First Division	0-2
1957	Cardiff City	A	First Division	3-2
1963	Southampton	Villa Park	FA Cup Semi-Final	1-0
1966	Blackpool	H	First Division	2-1
1968	West Bromwich Albion	A	First Division	3-6

1973 George Best resumed training with Manchester United, four months after announcing his 'retirement'.

1974 Manchester City   H   First Division   0-1
The Manchester derby had an extra bite to it, for United were battling against relegation to the Second Division. With 85 minutes gone and the score still delicately poised at 0-0, ex-United star Denis Law back-heeled the ball into the United net to give City the lead. The pitch was invaded by thousands of United fans and the match was abandoned, with the score being allowed to stand. It was the last goal Denis Law scored in first-class football, but even if he had scored for United instead of against them, they still wouldn't have avoided relegation. (Ironically, in 1963 Denis Law was playing for Manchester United against Manchester City in a relegation battle and won a penalty that sent City down!)

1985	Sunderland	H	First Division	2-2
1994	Leeds United	A	FA Premier League	2-0

APRIL 28TH

1894 Liverpool   Ewood Park
                          Test Match   0-2
Once again Newton Heath finished bottom of the First Division, and again they won only six of their 30 matches. This time the Test Match system pitched them against Liverpool, a team who had only been in existence for two seasons but who had topped the Second Division without losing a single game. They didn't look likely to lose this one either, scoring through McLean and McQueen by half-time and holding on to their lead without ever being really troubled. Thus, when League football resumed in September, Liverpool would take their place among the elite in the First Division and Newton Heath were condemned to the Second Division.

| 1900 | Chesterfield | H | Second Division | 2-1 |
| 1906 | Burton United | H | Second Division | 6-0 |

Having already clinched promotion back into the First Division, United finished the 1905-06 season in cavalier fashion with a 6-0 thrashing of the second bottom club Burton United. The contrasting fortunes of the two clubs after this game could not be greater: United used promotion as a springboard that would ultimately see both the League championship and FA Cup come to rest in the boardroom, whilst Burton United disappeared into oblivion after one more season. At the end of the game the pitch was invaded by delirious fans, who carried the team off on their shoulders. Chairman John Henry Davies and Secretary Ernest Mangnall (in effect the manager) addressed the crowd and promised this was only the beginning of United's rise. It was not to be a false promise either.

1917	Port Vale	A	Lancashire Section Subsidiary Tournament	2-5
1923	Barnsley	A	Second Division	2-2
1926	Cardiff City	H	First Division	1-0
1928	Arsenal	A	First Division	1-0
1934	Swansea Town	H	Second Division	1-1
1945	Doncaster Rovers	H	Football League North (Second Championship)	3-1
1946				

Billy Porter died in Ashton-under-Lyme. Born in Fleetwood in July 1905 Billy began his League career with Oldham, joining them in May 1926 and spent nearly ten years with the club before his switch to Old Trafford in January 1935. He won a medal in the Second Division championship side of 1935-36 and he managed 65 appearances for the first team before the outbreak of the Second World War, although he continued to guest for the club throughout the hostilities. In 1944 he left to take up the position of player-manager at Hyde United, a position he held until his sudden death.

1948	Blackpool	A	First Division	0-1
1951	Huddersfield Town	H	First Division	6-0
1953				

Brian Greenhoff born in Barnsley. The younger brother of Jimmy, who also played for United, Brian joined the club as an apprentice in August 1968 and was upgraded to the professional ranks in June 1970. Whilst with the club he won a Second Division championship medal, an FA Cup winners' medal and two runners-up medals in the same competition, although he had been a non-playing substitute in the final against Arsenal in 1979. In August 1979 he was sold to Leeds for £350,000 and later rejoined his brother at Rochdale.

1954	Manchester City	A	Friendly	2-3
1962	Fulham	A	First Division	0-2
1965	Aston Villa	A	First Division	1-2

The title had already been won two days previously with a 3-1 win over Arsenal, Leeds's inability to get more than a point from their clash with Birmingham City confirming United as champions. Had a win been required in this fixture no doubt United would have raised their game, but as it was a 2-1 defeat left United on top by the slenderest of margins. Both Manchester United and Leeds had won 26 and drawn nine of their 42 games, but United boasted a goal average of 89:39 compared with Leeds's 83:52.

| 1973 | Chelsea | A | First Division | 0-1 |

Bobby Charlton bowed out of the game he had graced for so long at Stamford Bridge, making the last of his 606 League appearances for United. Both teams had formed a guard of honour as he strode out on to the pitch for the last time and Chelsea made a presentation to him in recognition of his feat. There was to be no fairy tale ending, however, as Chelsea won 1-0. Ironically, down at Southampton, brother Jack was playing his last League game for Leeds United as they lost 3-1.

1979	Derby County	H	First Division	0-0
1984	West Ham United	H	First Division	0-0
1996	Nottingham Forest	H	FA Premier League	5-0
1998	Crystal Palace	A	FA Premier League	3-0

APRIL 29TH

1893	Ardwick	A	Friendly	0-3
1909	Bradford City	A	First Division	0-1
1911	Sunderland	H	First Division	5-1

Villa's 4-2 win over United the previous week had been enough to put them on top of the table, one point ahead of United, as the teams prepared for their final matches of a long and gruelling season. United undoubtedly had the tougher closing game, for Sunderland, at one time potential champions themselves, were third in the table, whilst Villa travelled to Anfield to take on a Liverpool side languishing in mid-table. The mathematics were simple enough to work out: Villa, the defending champions, needed only a point to claim their seventh title; United had to win and pray for a Liverpool win to notch their second title. Whilst the United players still believed they had a chance, the fans did not, for only 10,000 bothered to see the match against Sunderland. The players' belief never wavered, not even when Sunderland took the lead, for, inspired by the legendary Billy Meredith, they merely rolled up their sleeves and tried that bit harder. Turnbull headed an equaliser from a Meredith cross, West converted another Meredith centre and Halse added a third soon after. United headed off for the dressing-room at half-time and heard the news they had longed for: Liverpool were two up against Villa. Fortified by this, United raised their game even higher for the second half, adding further goals from Halse (from yet another Meredith cross) and a Wilton own goal, who turned into his own net from a corner from who else but Meredith. The final whistle came as a relief to Sunderland and they headed off to the dressing-room. The United players, once they had congratulated each other on their performance that day, could do little else but wait agonisingly for the news from Anfield and remained on the pitch. Billy Meredith, the star of the day, chewed on his customary toothpick as though his life depended upon it. Then a cheer went up from a section of the ground and began spreading around the stadium as each man told his next door neighbour what he had just heard: Liverpool had beaten Villa 3-1 and United were champions! If the final few matches had seen United falter, then their performances over the season had been worthy of champions.

1912	Blackburn Rovers	H	First Division	3-1
1916	Manchester City	A	Lancashire Section Subsidiary (Southern) Tournament	1-2
1922	Cardiff City	H	First Division	1-1
1933	Lincoln City	A	Second Division	2-3
1936	Bury	A	Second Division	3-2

Having made a slow start to the season, suffering seven defeats by the turn of the year, United had shifted into promotion-winning form and now stood on the verge of returning to the First Division. Three points from their final two games (with Hull City still to be visited) would also confirm them as Second Division champions. United were in irresistible form in the opening 30 minutes, powering into a three-goal lead before easing up. That almost cost them dear, for Bury grabbed two goals back and set up a final 15-minute charge that must have been heart-stopping for all the United fans in the crowd. Their heroes held on to win and at the end of the game, United's fans invaded the pitch and chaired their men off towards the dressing-rooms. Three days later they got the other point needed at Hull to clinch the title.

1939	Bolton Wanderers	A	First Division	0-0
1944	Oldham Athletic	H	Football League North (Second Championship)	0-0
1950	Fulham	H	First Division	3-0

1956 Kevin Moran born in Dublin. After playing Gaelic football locally he took up association football and was spotted by United playing for Pegasus, a college team. He signed with United in February 1978 and broke into the side in April 1979, finally becoming a regular during the 1980-81 season. He won FA Cup medals in 1983 and 1985, although he had the misfortune to become the first player to be sent off in a Wembley FA Cup final in 1985 and for some time his medal was withheld. It was finally presented without fanfare some two weeks after the final. He left United in August 1988 and played in Spain, subsequently returning to England with Blackburn in 1990.

1957	West Bromwich Albion	H	First Division	1-1
1961	Cardiff City	H	First Division	3-3
1967	Aston Villa	H	First Division	3-1

1970 Old Trafford, Manchester played host to the first FA Cup final replay since the final moved to Wembley. Chelsea came from behind (just as they did in the first game) to beat Leeds United 2-1 after extra time and lift the Cup for the first time in their history.

1972	Stoke City	H	First Division	3-0
1974	Stoke City	A	First Division	0-1
1978	Wolverhampton Wanderers	A	First Division	1-2
1989	Coventry City	H	First Division	0-1

APRIL 30TH

1897	Manchester City	A	Manchester & Salford Cup Final	5-2
1904	Leicester Fosse	H	Second Division	5-2
1910	Middlesbrough	H	First Division	4-1

All four United goals were scored by Jack Picken, the first time Old Trafford had seen a player score a hat-trick in a League match for United. A crowd of 10,000 were in attendance at the last League match of the season.

1919	Blackpool	H	Lancashire Section Principal Tournament	5-1
1921	Blackburn Rovers	H	First Division	0-1
1927	Sunderland	H	First Division	0-0
1932	Bristol City	A	Second Division	1-2
1938	West Ham United	A	Second Division	0-1
1949	Newcastle United	A	First Division	1-0

1954 Gerry Daly born in Dublin. Signed by United for £20,000 from Bohemians in 1973, he was an integral part of the side that won the Second Division championship in 1975 and reached the FA Cup the following season. He might have gone on to be a pivotal part in their later success but for the deterioration of his relationship with Tommy Docherty, who sold him to Derby for £175,000. Six months later Docherty followed him to the Baseball Ground and the two maintained an uneasy truce, although Docherty had departed by the time Gerry was sold to Coventry for £310,000 in 1980. He later played for Birmingham City, Shrewsbury Town, Stoke City and Doncaster Rovers before moving to non-League Telford in 1989.

1955	Chelsea	H	First Division	2-1
1960	Everton	H	First Division	5-0
1966	West Ham United	A	First Division	2-3
1977	Queens Park Rangers	H	First Division	1-0
1979	Southampton	A	First Division	1-1

1981 United announced they had sacked manager Dave Sexton and his assistant Tommy

Cavanagh, stating, 'The team's performance has failed to live up to the high standards of football entertainment expected of Manchester United.' United had just finished the season with seven straight wins, although a final League position of eighth was deemed unacceptable.

1983	Norwich City	A	First Division	1-1
1988	Queens Park Rangers	H	First Division	2-1
1990	Wimbledon	H	First Division	0-0

MAY 1ST

1920	Notts County	A	First Division	2-0
1926	West Bromwich Albion	H	First Division	3-2
1943	Sheffield United	H	Football League North (Second Championship)	2-0
1946	Manchester City	H	Lancashire Senior Cup Semi-Final	3-0
1948	Blackburn Rovers	H	First Division	4-1
1963	Sheffield Wednesday	H	First Division	1-3
1971	Blackpool	A	First Division	1-1
1976	Southampton	Wembley	FA Cup Final	0-1

A faltering run-in to the League campaign had denied United of the title; from being certainties with six games to go, they had lost three and slipped to third place. Although there was still the FA Cup to provide some cheer, few could appreciate just how demoralising that run-in had been. Southampton, on the other hand, had sauntered through a season in the Second Division, rarely challenging the promotion candidates, but containing sufficient fire-power from Mike Channon and Peter Osgood to threaten United. So it proved, although the winning goal came from Bobby Stokes, one of the unsung heroes rather than big-money names, as United looked jaded throughout. Docherty promised his side at the end they would be back next year, though whether this was bravado remained to be seen.

1982	Southampton	H	First Division	1-0
1994	Ipswich Town	A	FA Premier League	2-1
1995	Coventry City	A	FA Premier League	3-2

MAY 2ND

1921	Derby County	A	First Division	1-1
1925	Barnsley	A	Second Division	0-0

A 4-0 win over Port Vale in their previous match had virtually guaranteed United the second promotion spot in the Second Division; only a defeat at Barnsley and a massive Derby win at home to Blackpool could prevent them returning to the First Division. As it was, Derby failed to get a win of any kind, drawing 2-2, so United's draw at Barnsley was largely academic; they were back in the top flight.

1931	Middlesbrough	H	First Division	4-4

United finished their sorry season bottom of the table, with only seven wins achieved and with the fans all but having deserted them, for only 3,969 attended the fixture with Middlesbrough.

1936	Hull City	A	Second Division	1-1
1942	Oldham Athletic	A	Football League Northern Section (Second Championship)	2-1
1949	Middlesbrough	H	First Division	1-0
1973	Verona	A	Anglo-Italian Tournament Group One	4-1

1975 David Beckham born in London. Although David trained with Spurs as a youngster, he was signed by United as a trainee in January 1993 after helping the youth side win the FA Youth Cup in 1992. Loaned to Preston in February 1995, he broke into the

United first team in 1994-95 and was soon established as a regular in the side. He helped the club win the Premier League in 1996 and 1997 and the FA Cup in 1996, and has also broken into the England side. He was named PFA Young Footballer of the Year in 1997.

1983	Arsenal	A	First Division	0-3
1987	Wimbledon	H	First Division	0-1
1988	Oxford United	A	First Division	2-0
1989	Wimbledon	H	First Division	1-0
1990	Nottingham Forest	A	First Division	0-4
1992	Tottenham Hotspur	H	First Division	3-1

1993   Alex Ferguson became the first manager to lead sides to the championship in both Scotland (with Aberdeen) and England (with Manchester United) courtesy of Oldham Athletic's 1-0 win at Aston Villa. It was United's first championship since 1967 and Ferguson was told of his success whilst out on a golf course.

MAY 3RD

1917   Sandy Turnbull was killed in action in France during the First World War. Sandy had joined United in 1906 from Manchester City, where he was serving a suspension imposed by the Football Association over illegal payments made to 17 players by the club. United's hijacking of four of City's players before they could be auctioned is covered elsewhere; suffice to say Turnbull had an immediate impact at United, scoring the winning goal on his debut. He also scored the winning goal when United won the FA Cup in 1909, and continued to live up to the nickname bestowed on him during his City days: 'Turnbull The Terrible'. He also won two League titles whilst at United, and ended up with a career record of 90 League goals in 229 games, and 10 goals from 25 Cup appearances. His career at Old Trafford was brought to an end by a life ban as a result of a match-fixing and betting scandal that engulfed the club, but, like many other players, Sandy Turnbull answered the call to arms when the First World War broke out and sadly lost his life fighting for his country.

1919   Reg Allen born in London. Reg began his League career with QPR, signing for them in 1938 and joined United in June 1950 when he took over from Jack Crompton in goal. He won a championship medal in 1951-52 and left United for non-League football with Altrincham in 1953.

1924	Sheffield Wednesday	A	Second Division	0-2
1930	Sheffield United	H	First Division	1-5
1941	Liverpool	H	North Regional League	1-1
1947	Liverpool	A	First Division	0-1

After one of the worst winters on record had decimated the League programme, fixtures were still being completed by mid-June! United had been involved in a four-horse race for the title with Liverpool, Wolves and Stoke City, but United's crunch match came four matches from the end with a visit to Anfield. A single goal was enough to give Liverpool the upper hand, but they were not to be crowned champions until 14th June when Stoke's surprising defeat by Sheffield United ended the season. United finished in second place, the first of three consecutive seasons that finished with them as runners-up.

1958   Bolton Wanderers   Wembley FA Cup Final   0-2

United had reached the FA Cup final, having been willed to do so by the entire country following the Munich air disaster, but at Wembley their luck ran out as for the second year in succession, as a questionable piece of refereeing effectively cost them the game. Matt Busby had returned home to England and was able to take a seat on the bench for the game, although it was Jimmy Murphy who had picked the side and the tactics. It all began to go wrong in the third minute when Nat Lofthouse put Bolton ahead, a lead they didn't look likely to surrender even though United battled gamely. In the tenth minute of the second half, however, came the incident that put the match beyond United. Goalkeeper Harry Gregg leaped to collect a high ball only to be bundled, together with the ball, into the net by Lofthouse. The referee gave a goal, an astonishing decision even then when goalkeepers were afforded little protection, and with United short on experience they ran out of ideas, leaving Bolton 2-0 winners.

1972	Manchester City	A	Alan Oakes Testimonial	3-1
1977	Liverpool	A	First Division	0-1
1980	Leeds United	A	First Division	0-2
1986	Watford	A	First Division	1-1
1993	Blackburn Rovers	H	FA Premier League	3-1

There have been many better games, more resounding wins and perhaps even more important games than this end-of-season clash, but since this was the game that confirmed Manchester United as champions, after a wait of some 26 years, it will live long in the memory of their followers. In truth, of course, the title was already won; Oldham's surprise 1-0 win at Villa Park 24 hours previously had removed the final obstacle to United. But manager Alex Ferguson was keen to serve notice that United intended dominating English club football for the rest of the decade and that nothing less than victory in the final two games of the season would be good enough. There were plenty of sore heads among the United faithful when their team took to the field on this occasion, and judging by their first half performance, perhaps even one or two among the players, for Blackburn were showing they had every intention of gatecrashing the party. In the end, goals from Ryan Giggs, Paul Ince and Gary Pallister (his first of the season) gave United a deserved victory. Blackburn's role in the event may have been as understudy, but two years on they too took centre stage, winning the title and pushing United into second place. That was still in the future, however, for after receiving the trophy the party began in earnest.

1997	Leicester City	A	FA Premier League	2-2
1998	Leeds United	H	FA Premier League	3-0

Arsenal's 4-0 win over Everton 24 hours earlier had confirmed them as the new Premiership champions, and so United's 3-0 win over Leeds was largely academic. However, with the runners-up also qualifying for the European Champions League the following season, it was vital that United finished the season on a high. Goals from Ryan Giggs, Dennis Irwin (from the penalty spot) and David Beckham ensured victory in front of a crowd of 55,167.

MAY 4TH

1929	Portsmouth	H	First Division	0-0
1935	Plymouth Argyle	A	Second Division	2-0
1940	Blackburn Rovers	A	League War Cup 2nd Round 1st Leg	2-1
1946	Stoke City	H	Football League North	2-1
1949	Sheffield United	H	First Division	3-2
1957	Aston Villa	Wembley	FA Cup Final	1-2

In the 60 years since Aston Villa had won the League and Cup double, there had been several occasions when the feat might have been repeated. That it hadn't, not even by the great Huddersfield side of the 1920s and Arsenal a decade on, left many to conclude that it was unlikely to be done this century, whilst others claimed the only reason it hadn't been achieved was because no one had been good enough. In 1957 United were undoubtedly good enough; they had retained their League title by eight clear points and had reached the semi-final of the European Cup, where defeat by holders Real Madrid had been no disgrace. The only team who now stood between them and the double were . . . Aston Villa! United were favourites to win the Cup, for whilst they had held on to their League championship, Villa had been meandering in mid-table for most of the season. But all the efforts of a 42-match League campaign and five straight wins to Wembley were undone in the sixth minute: Villa winger Peter McParland charged into United goalkeeper Ray Wood and fractured his cheekbone, thereby putting him out of the game. It was a reckless challenge that totally unsettled United, for it meant Jackie Blanchflower had to take over in goal, Duncan Edwards move to centre-half and United battle on with only ten men, even though Wood re-appeared briefly to run up and down the right wing. McParland, however, recovered from the injuries he sustained in the challenge sufficiently well enough to score both goals for Villa (one of these was strongly disputed for offside) and put them in the driving seat. A late goal by Tommy Taylor gave United some hope, but although Wood returned to goal and United played with the style that had brought them so much success in the final, Villa held on. The reports after were scathing about the manner of Villa's win, with one claiming McParland had bagged two goals and one goalkeeper, although United would undoubtedly be back for another attempt at the double.

1958   Even though United had failed in their bid to win the FA Cup against Bolton the previous day, thousands lined the streets of Manchester to welcome home their side. Indeed, so many turned out that the only thing missing was the cup; such processions are normally reserved for winning teams.

1963	Burnley	A	First Division	1-0
1966	West Bromwich Albion	A	First Division	3-3
1968	Newcastle United	H	First Division	6-0
1976	Manchester City	H	First Division	2-0
1985	Norwich City	A	First Division	1-0
1991	Manchester City	H	First Division	1-0
1994	Southampton	H	FA Premier League	2-0

MAY 5TH

1928   Liverpool   H   First Division   6-1

The final League table produced at the end of the 1927-28 season was little short of a mathematical freak: on the last day of the season any one of six teams still stood the chance of being relegated, and after the games were played, only four points had separated the bottom 13 clubs! United's victory was enough to pull them out of the relegation trap door; the emphatic win lifted them into 18th place, level on points with six other clubs! The two clubs who went down, Spurs and Middlesbrough, did so with the highest points totals ever amassed by clubs relegated, but such feats counted for nothing at the end of the day; they went down and United stayed up!

1934   Millwall   A   Second Division   2-0

Outside cup finals and League championship deciders, of which there have been many during Manchester United's long and illustrious career, the most important match they played was undoubtedly the closing game of the 1933-34 season. United had struggled all season and by the last game of the season were occupying the second relegation spot. Lincoln, in bottom place, were already down, so the final place was between United, Swansea and, irony upon irony, Millwall. Defeat or a draw would see United relegated into the Third Division for the first time in their history, and they were facing a Millwall side that were renowned fighters at their own Den ground. The opening play favoured Millwall, who tore into their opponents with a frenzy, but United's defence held firm and slowly United began to get a grip on the game, allowing the wing pairing of Manley and Cape to gain control, although with barely 20 minutes gone Ernie Hine was left a virtual passenger after being injured. It was Manley who both began and finished the move that led to United's opening goal after eight minutes, sending Cape away along the wing and racing into the box to net the return. As important as that first goal was, there was still the need to prevent Millwall from equalising. Two minutes into the second half Cape extended the lead with a powerful shot, and although that ended the scoring, there were still plenty of heart-stopping moments before United could emerge triumphant, sending Millwall into the Third Division as a result.

1945	Chesterfield	H	Football League North (Second Championship)	1-1
1951	Blackpool	A	First Division	1-1
1971	Manchester City	A	First Division	4-3
1979	West Bromwich Albion	A	First Division	0-1
1982	Nottingham Forest	A	First Division	1-0
1984	Everton	A	First Division	1-1
1990	Charlton Athletic	H	First Division	1-0
1996	Middlesbrough	A	FA Premier League	3-0

By January 1996 the title seemed destined for a different United; Newcastle had opened up a 12-point lead at the top of the table and would not be caught, so everyone imagined. But Manchester United had kept plugging away, whittling down the lead slowly but surely, hitting top form at just the right time in the season and taking over on the home stretch. That set up another tight finish, although United's destiny was in their own hands, for if they won at Middlesbrough, nothing Newcastle could do at home to Spurs could prevent them lifting the trophy. What made the final match all the more poignant was the identity of Middlesbrough's manager – none other than Bryan Robson. Inspired by Eric Cantona, United made sure of top spot, with Newcastle's draw too little and too late to stop another title and another tilt at the European Cup for the men from Old Trafford. It meant Alex Ferguson had become the first man to guide a Scottish club to three League titles and then repeat that success in England, and the FA Cup also beckoned.

| 1997 | Middlesbrough | H | FA Premier League | 3-3 |

MAY 6TH

1916	Manchester City	A	Friendly	2-2
1922	Cardiff City	A	First Division	1-3
1933	Swansea Town	H	Second Division	1-1

1937 Shay Brennan born in Manchester. Signed by United as a professional in 1955, he made his debut in the FA Cup tie against Sheffield Wednesday in 1958, the first game after the Munich disaster. He missed out on the cup final that year and was displaced from the side shortly before the 1963 cup final, but did play in the European Cup final of 1968 and two League championship winning sides. He also won 19 caps for the Republic of Ireland and left United in 1970 to become player-manager of Waterford.

1939	Liverpool	H	First Division	2-0
1940	New Brighton	H	War Regional League, Western Division	6-0
1944	Oldham Athletic	A	Football League North (Second Championship)	3-1
1963	Arsenal	H	First Division	2-3
1967	West Ham United	A	First Division	6-1

United had been challenging for the title since the start of the season, heading the table at the turn of the year by two points from Liverpool. The Anfield men briefly led in February but were quickly caught by those from Old Trafford, who moved up a gear to stay one step ahead of the chasing pack thereafter. By the penultimate game of the season, the challenge to United had been effectively evaporated, with only

Nottingham Forest and Spurs still in with a mathematical shout of overhauling them. Those shouts were reduced to silence by United's most accomplished performance of the season, a 6-1 win at West Ham that confirmed them as champions, with various sections of the media reckoning that the first 30 minutes, during which United powered into a three-goal lead, was one of the finest displays witnessed since the war.

1985	Nottingham Forest	H	First Division	2-0
1987	Coventry City	A	First Division	1-1
1989	Southampton	A	First Division	1-2
1991	Arsenal	A	First Division	1-3

MAY 7TH

| 1921 | Derby County | H | First Division | 3-0 |

Billy Meredith made his last League appearance for United in the final game of the season. He had joined United in 1906 from rivals Manchester City and had gone on to make 332 appearances in the first team. However, during the First World War he had guested for City and when League football resumed in 1919 had asked United if they would transfer him to his old club. United initially refused, but then changed their minds and demanded a transfer fee. This angered Meredith and he refused to move, claiming that players should not be sold to the highest bidder, and so he remained a United player for a further two seasons, making only 21 appearances during that time. In July 1921 United relented and allowed Meredith to return to City as player-coach, where he continued as a player until he was 50 years of age.

1927	West Bromwich Albion	A	First Division	2-2
1932	Southampton	A	Second Division	1-1
1938	Bury	H	Second Division	2-0

After an uneasy opening to the 1937-38 season, United had settled down to the task at hand, winning promotion once again. They had timed their run to perfection, for by the time Easter was out of the way, all that was left to conclude was which one of three clubs would be accompanying Aston Villa. On the penultimate Saturday of the season, all three – Sheffield United, Manchester United and Coventry City – lost, but whilst Sheffield United had completed their programme and could do little but sit and wait, United and City both had one game to play. United, two points behind their Sheffield rivals and level with City, had to win, which, thanks to goals from McKay and Smith, they did at home to Bury in front of 53,604 fans. Coventry could only draw 1-1 at Stockport, County's equaliser coming in the last minute thanks to a disputed penalty. United therefore won promotion on goal average, but it was close.

1949	Portsmouth	H	First Division	3-2
1951	Manchester City	H	Lancashire Senior Cup Semi-Final Replay	2-1
1965				

Norman Whiteside born in Belfast. Spotted by United whilst playing schools football in Belfast, he was signed by United as an apprentice in June 1981 and made his League debut in May 1982, scoring in the match against Brighton. That summer he was one of the stars of the Northern Ireland side that played in the World Cup finals in Spain, and his assured performances in midfield belied his tender years. His appearance made him the youngest player to have played in the World Cup finals, beating the previous record held by Pele. The following season, on club duty, he continued to break records: the youngest player to have scored in a League Cup final (which he did against Liverpool), the youngest player to score in an FA Cup final (against Brighton), and the first player to score in the finals of both major cup competitions in the same season. Two years later he scored the winner in the FA Cup final against Everton to deprive them of a treble. A string of injuries in 1988-89 was followed by a £750,000 move to Everton in August 1989, but his time at Goodison

Park was blighted as he struggled to overcome a knee injury, and in June 1991 he announced his retirement. After a brief spell as assistant manager at Northwich Victoria, he resigned in order to concentrate on physiotherapy.

1966	Blackburn Rovers	A	First Division	4-1
1977	Bristol City	A	First Division	1-1
1979	Wolverhampton Wanderers	H	First Division	3-2
1983	Swansea City	H	First Division	2-1
1984	Ipswich Town	H	First Division	1-2
1988	Portsmouth	H	First Division	4-1
1995	Sheffield Wednesday	H	FA Premier League	1-0

MAY 8TH

| 1943 | Liverpool | A | Lancashire Cup Final 1st Leg | 3-1 |

1956 United played a friendly match against Helsingborg with centre-half Jackie Blanchflower spending the entire 90 minutes in goal!

| 1958 | AC Milan | H | European Cup Semi-Final 1st Leg | 2-1 |

Five days after going down to Bolton at Wembley, United put their disappointment behind them with a 2-1 win over AC Milan in the European Cup semi-final at Old Trafford. A crowd of 44,880 saw a penalty by Tommy Taylor and Dennis Viollett score the goals that gave United the slenderest of leads to take to Milan for the second leg six days later.

1982	West Ham United	A	First Division	1-1
1988	Manchester City	H	Arthur Albiston Testimonial	0-2
1989	Queens Park Rangers	A	First Division	2-3
1994	Coventry City	H	FA Premier League	0-0

Bryan Robson made his last competitive appearance for United having already been told he was being released on a free transfer at the end of the season. There was something to celebrate however, for the Premiership trophy was paraded around the ground at the end of the game.

| 1997 | Newcastle United | H | FA Premier League | 0-0 |

MAY 9TH

| 1942 | Blackburn Rovers | A | Football League Northern Section (Second Championship) | 1-1 |

1953 United won the FA Youth Cup in its inaugural season following a 2-2 draw against Wolves. They had already won the first leg 7-1 and so won the trophy 9-3 on aggregate. United went on to win the cup for the first five seasons, a record run of wins that has not been equalled, let alone beaten, since.

1966	Aston Villa	H	First Division	6-1
1983	Luton Town	H	First Division	3-0
1987	Aston Villa	H	First Division	2-1
1988	Wimbledon	H	First Division	2-1
1993	Wimbledon	A	FA Premier League	2-1

MAY 10TH

1915 The Football Association investigation into allegations regarding the match between United and Liverpool, played on April 2nd and which resulted in a 2-0 win for United, began in Manchester. The investigation would take some months to complete once all the players had been interviewed and the circumstances looked into. The result of the commission would be announced in December.

| 1941 | Bury | A | North Regional League | 1-5 |

1947	Preston North End	A	First Division	1-1
1963	Birmingham City	A	First Division	1-2
1977	Stoke City	A	First Division	3-3
1989	Everton	H	First Division	1-2
1995	Southampton	H	FA Premier League	2-1
1998	Barnsley	A	FA Premier League	2-0

Barnsley may well have finished the season relegated back into the First Division after just one year in the top flight, and United missed out on the championship to Arsenal, but the game was still treated as something of a celebration. Barnsley placed eight bottles of champagne and a letter of thanks to Alex Ferguson in the United dressing-room, a wonderful gesture fully appreciated by the United contingent. They, in return, netted goals from Andy Cole and Teddy Sheringham to grab all three points!

MAY 11TH

1940	Blackburn Rovers	A	League War Cup 2nd Round 2nd Leg	1-3
1968	Sunderland	H	First Division	1-2

The title race of 1967-68 had been between four clubs for much of the season: reigning champions United, their close rivals Manchester City, and perennial challengers Liverpool and Leeds. By the time of the last game, that challenge was down to the two Manchester clubs, although United's slip against West Bromwich Albion two weeks previously (they had lost 6-3) had handed the initiative to City. If United were to retain their crown and dreams of a double (they had the second leg of the European Cup semi-final still to come), they had to beat Sunderland and pray City got less than full points from their clash at Newcastle. As it was, nerves got the better of United and Sunderland were able to slide into a two-goal lead, which George Best reduced just before half-time. United pressed hard for an equaliser in the second half with no joy, and the news that City had won 4-3 meant the League trophy would not be staying at Old Trafford but crossing the city to Maine Road. There was still the European Cup to come, however.

1983	Tottenham Hotspur	A	First Division	0-2
1985	Queens Park Rangers	A	First Division	3-1
1991	Crystal Palace	A	First Division	0-3
1996	Liverpool		Wembley FA Cup Final	1-0

Six teams had won the double since the formation of the Football League in 1888: Preston, Aston Villa, Spurs, Arsenal, Liverpool and Manchester United. No one had done it twice, although the last four clubs could all make convincing claims that they had come close. United had the disappointment of the previous season – when they had finished runners-up in both competitions – out of their system and were now in sight of a second double. Just as there had been only one goal in the FA Cup final the previous year, so one goal settled this one, with Eric Cantona striking home in the 86th minute to win the cup for a record ninth time and a second double.

1997	West Ham United	H	FA Premier League	2-0

For the fourth time in five years the Old Trafford faithful were to witness the parading of the Premiership trophy around the ground, with West Ham being despatched in cavalier fashion as the champions strengthened their grip on the title.

MAY 12TH

1929 Don Gibson born in Manchester. Signed by United as an amateur in November 1946, he became a full professional in August 1947. He made his debut in March 1950 and won a championship medal in 1952, although he lost his place later that season following a reshuffle in the team. He was sold to Sheffield Wednesday for £8,000 in 1955 and later played for Leyton Orient.

1945   Chesterfield   A   Football League North (Second Championship)   1-0
1951   Foreign opposition visited Old Trafford for the first time as United played host to Red Star Belgrade in a Festival of Britain friendly. The game ended in a 1-1 draw thanks to a late penalty by Jack Rowley.
1965   Racing Strasbourg   A   Inter-Cities 4th Round 1st Leg   5-0
1979   Arsenal   Wembley FA Cup Final   2-3
It would have been little consolation but United played their part in what was one of the most enthralling cup finals for many a year. Indeed, it was United's spirited fightback that had lifted this final from the ordinary to heart-stopping. Arsenal had roared into a 2-0 lead which they held until the 86th minute without looking too troubled. Then Gordon McQueen stuck out a leg to send the ball past Pat Jennings, although Arsenal fans were still convinced they were going to win. Sammy McIlroy collected the ball with some 90 seconds left and jinked his way into the penalty area before stroking home an equaliser. With delirium engulfing the United fans, Liam Brady sent Graham Rix down the left and a deep cross found Alan Sunderland free to fire home an unbelievable winner. It was an astonishing finish that broke United's hearts.

1982   West Bromwich Albion A   First Division   3-0
1984   Tottenham Hotspur   A   First Division   1-1
1990   Crystal Palace   Wembley FA Cup Final   3-3
By 1990 patience with manager Alex Ferguson had begun to wear a bit thin, for United still seemed to be some considerable way off producing a championship winning side and a cup victory was therefore important to appease the disgruntled customers. At Wembley United started as slight favourites, but in overcoming Liverpool in the semi-final Crystal Palace had shown they were more than capable of springing a few surprises. They sprang one on United too, taking an early lead, although Bryan Robson soon levelled the score with a thundering header. Mark Hughes put United ahead in the second half, but the arrival of Ian Wright from the Palace bench soon evened the score and forced extra time. Wright added his second to seemingly take the cup to South London, but Mark Hughes was once again on hand to set up a replay. Jim Leighton in the United goal came in for some criticism over his performance, but Ferguson would not make a public announcement over his plans for the replay.

MAY 13TH

1940   Wrexham   A   War Regional League, Western Division   2-3
1967   Stoke City   H   First Division   0-0
Prior to the start of the game the League Championship trophy was handed to the United team for the seventh time in their history, but surprisingly it would take a further 26 years before the title would be back at Old Trafford. Interestingly, the trophy remained in Manchester for two years, for Manchester City were to take the title the following year.
1985   Watford   A   First Division   1-5
1989   Newcastle United   H   First Division   2-0
1994   Alex Ferguson was confirmed as Manager of the Year in recognition of United having won the FA Premier League for the second consecutive season.

MAY 14TH

1901   Frank McPherson born in Barrow-in-Furness. Frank began his playing career with Barrow in 1921, shortly before the club joined the new Third Division North. After starring in their debut season he was signed by United in May 1922, making his

League debut in August 1923 at outside-left, later switching to centre-forward. He netted 52 goals for the first team during his six years at Old Trafford, signing for Watford in September 1928 after a brief spell with Manchester Central. After three years with Reading he returned to Watford for four years and finished his career with Barrow. He died on 5th March 1953.

| 1958 | AC Milan | A | European Cup Semi-Final 2nd Leg | 0-4 |

Whilst United's pre-Munich side might have stood a chance of overcoming Milan and making it to the final, the patched-up troops that were sent out for the second leg looked as though they had been through a long and emotional season. In the end United suffered their heaviest defeat in the European Cup, a result that would not be equalled until Barcelona won by a similar scoreline in 1994.

1977	Arsenal	H	First Division	3-2
1983	Notts County	A	First Division	2-3
1994	Chelsea	Wembley	FA Cup Final	4-0

Having safely secured the title in 1994, attention could now turn to the other half of the domestic double, the FA Cup. For once, luck, which had been missing in the 1950s, seemed to be on their side as they survived a scare in the semi-final before finally overcoming Oldham after a replay. Although by virtue of their title win they were acknowledged as the best side in the country, they were facing a resurgent Chelsea team who had proven to be something of a bogey side for United in recent years. Indeed, United's first two defeats during the season had both been inflicted by Chelsea! On Wembley's lush and spacious turf, both teams began hesitantly, not wishing to give too much away to their opponents. If anything Chelsea, whose search for a major trophy had stretched over 20 years, had the better of the opening half, fashioning a number of lively attacks. Slowly but surely, however, Manchester United got the better of Chelsea and finally took the lead on the hour thanks to a penalty scored by Eric Cantona. He added another penalty seven minutes later, and the fight seemed to visibly drain from Chelsea. The final score of 4-0 (Hughes and McClair added later goals) may well have flattered United, but few would deny they thoroughly deserved to complete the double.

| 1995 | West Ham United | A | FA Premier League | 1-1 |

Having won the double the previous season United were seemingly headed for a repeat performance. Going into the last match of the season they were second in the table but in sight of Blackburn, who faced a difficult match at Liverpool, whilst United could repeat their success of 1967 with victory at West Ham. With an ear on events at Anfield and eyes on the developments at Upton Park, it was as close a finish to the season as anyone could remember. When news came through of a late Liverpool winner, the pressure to fire a winner against West Ham became greater, but despite several late scares that goal proved elusive. Blackburn may have won the title, but United had ran them close.

MAY 15TH

1943	Liverpool	H	Lancashire Cup Final 2nd Leg	3-3
1963	Manchester City	A	First Division	1-1
1968	Real Madrid	A	European Cup Semi-Final 2nd Leg	3-3

It did not matter if Real Madrid were no longer the same magical side they had been in the late 1950s, nor that they no longer dominated European football. They were still a magical name, and they still stood between United and a longed-for appearance in the European Cup final. Although United had won the first leg 1-0, over 125,000 Spaniards were convinced Real Madrid would overcome them and sweep into the final. After 40 minutes they could have been forgiven for thinking they had done so, for Pirri had levelled the aggregate score and Gento had put them ahead. Real scored twice more before half-time, although one was an own goal, to leave the half-time score 3-1 in their favour. Matt Busby delivered what was probably his finest team talk during the ten-minute break, for it inspired United in the second half, and only some resilient Real defending prevented an avalanche of goals. With 20 minutes to go United finally got a breakthrough, David Sadler sidefooting home, and eight minutes later Best sent over a cross that Bill Foulkes, one of the survivors from the Munich air disaster, headed home for the equaliser to put United into the final at last.

1969　AC Milan　　　　　　　H　　　European Cup Semi-Final 2nd Leg　　　　1-0
United failed to overcome a two-goal deficit from the first leg, but they went mightily close; already one up on the night, a Pat Crerand chip provoked a mad scramble in the goalmouth and the ball looked to have crossed the line. Although the referee ignored United's appeals, television footage later revealed that the ball had indeed crossed the line for an equaliser. Further problems for United came with the throwing of missiles from the Stretford End which knocked the Milan goalkeeper unconscious.

1982　Stoke City　　　　　　　H　　　First Division　　　　　　　　　　　2-0
1991　Barcelona　　　　　　Rotterdam European Cup-Winners' Cup Final　　　2-1
Any triumph in Europe is one to be savoured, but this was extra special. It enabled Alex Ferguson to make history as the first man to manage English and Scottish sides to European honours, it gave English football its pride back after five years in the wilderness following the Heysel stadium disaster, it gave United's followers yet more silverware to gloat over, and it was a personal triumph for Mark Hughes. Hughes had endured a living nightmare during his time with Barcelona, and so to score the two goals which captured the cup was the perfect revenge. Over 25,000 fans travelled over to Rotterdam to watch the game, behaving in exemplary fashion during their time in the Dutch city and raising the roof in support of their team on the night. A late consolation from Ronald Koeman could do nothing to dampen the spirits.

1994　The new chart produced by the CIN (the Chart Information Network) placed 'Come On You Reds' at number one in the Top 40. This was the first time a club record had reached the number one position, and the single held on to the top spot for two weeks on its way to earning a silver disc for sales in excess of 200,000 copies. The actual date of the chart is 21st May, but this refers to the cover date of the industry magazine *Music Week*, not the date the chart was compiled.

MAY 16TH

1906　United manager Ernest Mangnall pulled off the transfer coup of the century in luring Manchester City player Billy Meredith to the club. Meredith had joined City in 1894 and helped them win the FA Cup in 1904. In August 1905 he had been suspended by the Football Association over allegations that he had tried to bribe an Aston Villa player to throw a game, and when the FA had investigated these claims they had found further irregularities at City, including illegal payments to players – the maximum wage had been fixed at £4 per week, but many of City's team were receiving £6 or £7 each. A furious FA dismissed five of the club's directors and forbade 17 of the players from ever appearing for the club again, which meant that City would have to dismantle their cup-winning side immediately. Mangnall was a more than interested observer in developments across the city and began secret negotiations with Meredith to secure his services. In his favour was the fact that Meredith, who had a number of business interests in the city, would prefer to remain in Manchester. Negotiations were completed swiftly, even though Meredith was still banned from playing until 31st December 1906. Despite all he had achieved for Manchester City during his time with the club, City were privately glad to see the back of him, for during his ban the club had had to report him to the FA for trying to claim wages from them. Meredith was in many ways the original George Best: skilful, rebellious and extremely popular with the fans even if the club seldom shared the same view. He later tried to obtain wages from the City club because he said they had been the instigators of the attempted bribery of Aston Villa, allegations the club were quick to refute. Having landed Meredith, Mangnall moved into action once again. Manchester City had planned an auction for the coming November at which the 17 players would be sold to the highest bidder, but Mangnall was not prepared to wait for the price to be forced up. Instead, he entered into direct negotiations with the players he wanted, Herbert Burgess, Sandy Turnbull and Jimmy Bannister and got agreements with all that they would join Manchester United. Other clubs, in particular Everton, were furious at what they saw as underhand dealings by United, but a protest to the FA fell on deaf ears and all three became United players, even if they were not able to play until 31st December.

1942	Blackburn Rovers	H	Football League Northern Section	
			(Second Championship)	0-1
1977	West Ham United	A	First Division	2-4
1979	Chelsea	H	First Division	1-1
1984	Nottingham Forest	A	First Division	0-2

MAY 17TH

1941	Burnley	H	North Regional League	1-0
1947	Portsmouth	H	First Division	3-0
1969	Leicester City	H	First Division	3-2
1990	Crystal Palace	Wembley	FA Cup Final Replay	1-0

If the majority of the action surrounding the first clash had taken place on the pitch, then for the replay the reverse was true. Alex Ferguson sensationally dropped Leighton from the United team, putting Les Sealey, on loan from Luton, in his place in goal, and Sealey responded to the challenge well, diving bravely and handling soundly throughout. The only goal of the game came from Lee Martin, only his second for the club but surely his most vital, for it won United a match they seldom looked likely to lose. At the end of the game Sealey thoughtfully offered his winning medal to the distraught Leighton.

MAY 18TH

| 1940 | New Brighton | A | War Regional League, Western Division | 0-6 |

1942 Nobby Stiles born in Manchester. He joined United as a junior in 1959 and made the first of 312 appearances for the Reds in 1960. Something of a slow developer, he wasn't firmly established in the side until the departure of Johnny Giles to Leeds, but thereafter he made the wing-half berth his own, winning two League championship medals and a European Cup winners' medal. A tough-tackling defender, he was awarded his first England cap in 1965 and by the time the World Cup came around was an established member of the England team. His performances in the opening group games led to calls for his exclusion from the team, but Ramsey stuck by him and was rewarded with performances from the quarter-final onwards that were little short of commanding. He won 28 caps for England. In May 1971 he joined Middlesbrough and then wound down his career with Preston in 1973, retiring as a player in 1974 and moving into management with varying degrees of success.

| 1963 | Leyton Orient | H | First Division | 3-1 |
| 1985 | Everton | Wembley | FA Cup Final | 1-0 [aet] |

Just as United had shattered Liverpool's dream of a treble in 1977, so they now deflated the other half of Merseyside eight years on. Everton were already League champions and holders of the European Cup-Winners' Cup and began the brighter of the two teams, adrenalin driving them towards a third trophy. But United weathered the storm and fought back and a much more even battle ensued during the second half. Then came the incident that is still talked about even now. Peter Reid was charging through the midfield when he was upended by Kevin Moran. It was a clumsy rather than malicious challenge, as Reid was one of the first to point out, but the referee decided it was of sufficient severity to warrant a sending off. Despite United's protestations, Moran left the field and his team with only ten men. Everton might have taken the initiative at that point, but their exertions in Rotterdam during the week had tired them far more than they had realised. In the second half of extra time, with a replay looking the likeliest outcome, Norman Whiteside scored one of his special goals to win the cup and medals for United. Moran was prevented from collecting his on the day; indeed it seemed for at least two weeks or so that he wouldn't be getting one at all, but following representations from United he did in fact get a winners' medal.

1997   Eric Cantona shocked the football world with his announcement he was retiring with immediate effect. In six seasons in English football he had won five League championship medals (one with Leeds and four with Manchester United) as well as a host of medals from other competitions, but at the age of 31 he felt it was time to bow out of the game at the top. His decision wiped £8.7 million off the club's share price when announced!

MAY 19TH

| 1945 | Bolton Wanderers | A | Football League North (Second Championship) | 0-1 |
| 1965 | Racing Strasbourg | H | Inter-Cities Fairs Cup 4th Round 2nd Leg | 0-0 |

As United had won the first leg in Strasbourg 5-0, their fans were hoping for an avalanche of goals in the second leg. A crowd of 34,188 were to be disappointed, however, as Strasbourg shut up shop in a desperate attempt to salvage some pride in the second leg. For their part, having already done the hard part of qualifying, United were already beginning to show signs of fatigue as a long season stretched onwards. They had won the League title and reached the FA Cup semi-finals during the season and already faced the prospect of playing into June.

| 1966 | Leeds United | H | First Division | 1-1 |

MAY 20TH

| 1889 | Ardwick | A | Friendly | 1-2 |
| 1963 | Nottingham Forest | A | First Division | 2-3 |

1970   Bobby Charlton scored his 49th and last goal for England in the World Cup warm-up match in Bogota against Colombia as England won 4-0.

| 1991 | Tottenham Hotspur | H | First Division | 1-1 |

There was a carnival atmosphere all around Old Trafford as both United and their visitors had something to celebrate. Five days previously United had won the European Cup-Winners' Cup in Rotterdam, whilst Spurs had replaced United as winners of the FA Cup on the Saturday. The respective captains, Bryan Robson and Gary Mabbutt, paraded both trophies to an enthralled and excited crowd of 44,595 before the match which, not surprisingly, was played with as much passion as a testimonial. It had been a long and hard season for both clubs; their reward was that they would both be representing England in the following season's European Cup-Winners' Cup.

| 1995 | Everton | | Wembley FA Cup Final | 0-1 |

The previous Saturday United had woken up at the weekend with the double still firmly in their sights. However, a draw at West Ham on the Sunday, even though

Blackburn had lost at Liverpool, had wrenched the League title from their grasp, and six days later the FA Cup was gone too. The exertions of the season, which had also included Europe, proved too much, and a Paul Rideout goal won the cup for Everton. It was United's 13th appearance in the FA Cup final, a new record, but that was all they had to show for the season.

MAY 21ST

1977   Liverpool   Wembley   FA Cup Final   2-1
Liverpool were the heavy favourites; already crowned League champions, they were going for an unprecedented treble with the European Cup to come in five days' time. They also looked much the better side on the day, but United defended well when it was required and rode their luck up the other end too. All three goals came in a five-minute spell in the second half: Stuart Pearson shot under Ray Clemence for United, Case equalised, and then the ball cannoned off Jimmy Greenhoff for the winner. Everyone connected with United celebrated at the end, none more so than the brothers Brian and Jimmy Greenhoff and manager Tommy Docherty. A few weeks later, Docherty's world was to turn upside down.

1983   Brighton & Hove Albion   Wembley   FA Cup Final   2-2 [aet]
At half-time it seemed as though history was repeating itself. Just as they had been in 1976, United were favourites but had struggled to contain a lively Brighton side already relegated. Brighton held a 1-0 lead at the break, but United emerged fired up and soon equalised through Frank Stapleton and later took the lead thanks to Ray Wilkins. With their experience United should have managed to contain Brighton, but with just minutes remaining they forced extra time. Although there were no further goals, right at the death Brighton had a glorious chance to steal the trophy, but Gordon Smith's shot was saved by Gary Bailey and the third consecutive replay was needed in the FA Cup final.

MAY 22ND

1946   George Best born in Belfast. The most talented and yet infuriating player of the last 30 years, he at times found success difficult to handle. He made his debut for Manchester United at the age of 17 and after barely 15 League games was selected by Northern Ireland, winning the first of 37 caps in 1964 against Wales. Whilst with Manchester United Best won a League championship medal and played a monumental part in getting United to the European Cup final against Benfica at Wembley, where he scored the goal in extra time which restored United's lead. Benfica had played the game totally afraid of what Best could do to them – his performance in Lisbon a couple of years earlier had earned him the nickname 'El Beatle' from the local press. The change of manager at Manchester United following Matt Busby's retirement was the beginning of the end for Best, for he began disappearing, not bothering to turn up for training or sometimes even matches, and spent more and more time with a succession of women. In his own words, he went 'missing' – Miss America, Miss World . . . ! He announced his 'retirement' in January 1974 having made 466 appearances for the club, but in later years turned out for Los Angeles Aztecs, Fulham, Dunstable, Cork Celtic, Bournemouth, Hibernian, Motherwell and Stockport County. Perhaps if he had remained at United and concentrated on his football instead of outside interests he might have helped Northern Ireland reach the finals of a major tournament long before they finally did in 1982, by which time Best's day had passed and he never did get to grace the world stage. A confessed alcoholic, Best now makes a living on the after-dinner circuit in tandem with Rodney Marsh (although even here he is prone to failing to turn up).

MAY 23RD

1884   Jimmy Turnbull born in East Plain in Bannockburn. Signed by United from Leyton FC in May 1907, he was quickly linked with his namesake Sandy Turnbull and helped the club win the League championship at the end of his first season at Old Trafford. The following season he added an FA Cup winners' medal and might have won more had he remained with the club. As it was he and United were unable to agree terms in the close season of 1910 and United signed Enoch West as replacement, allowing Jimmy to sign for Bradford in September 1910. After a spell at Chelsea Jimmy returned to United in September 1914 for a one-month trial and did well enough for United to consider signing him full-time, but Chelsea's insistence on a £300 fee at a time when football was likely to be halted owing to the First World War was considered 'too much in the present crisis'.

1942   Manchester City   A   Football League Northern Section
                                            (Second Championship)   3-1

1953   Johnny Carey announced his retirement as a player even though United had been keen for him to continue. He had announced internally after the final game of the season that he intended quitting but United had made several attempts to try and get him to change his mind, even offering him a position with the coaching staff. Instead Johnny would go on to become manager at Blackburn Rovers before serving Everton, Leyton Orient and Nottingham Forest in the same capacity.

MAY 24TH

1908   Ferencvaros   A   Friendly   7-0
        Si Torna Klub
        This was United's second match against Ferencvaros during their post-season tour of Europe, although the atmosphere during and after the match was anything but friendly. United had already built up a healthy lead despite the poor refereeing throughout by a local official. Midway through the match Thomson, a reserve centre-half, was penalised for a foul, a decision which he disagreed with. He remonstrated with the referee, grabbing hold of his arm as he tried to explain what had happened. The referee, who spoke no English (and Thomson was not fluent in Hungarian either!), assumed from the gesture that he was about to be hit and set about protecting himself! In an instant players from both sides had rushed to the incident and once tempers were cooled, three United players, including Thomson, were ordered from the field. All three refused to leave, further fuelling the hostility of the 11,000 crowd that were in attendance. Interpreters were called for and after 15 minutes of heated discussion the game was allowed to restart with United maintaining their full complement of players. They finally finished the game 7-0 victors. As United left the field stones and rocks were hurled at the players, some were spat at and it looked as though the players might be attacked. The Hungarian police drew their swords and cleared a way through the hostile crowd for the United players to get safely to the changing-rooms. After the team had changed and boarded the bus that was to take them back to their hotel in Budapest, a crowd of 5,000 jeered them on their way and another group lay waiting a couple of miles on the route to ambush the bus with stones and other missiles. Again the police had to draw swords and charge into the mob, making countless arrests in order that the bus could continue its journey. The two teams were due to attend a banquet that evening, which did go ahead. United accepted the profuse apologies of the Hungarian authorities and played the incident down, promising to return to Budapest the following year to show there were no hard feelings. Once safely back in England, however, Ernest Mangnall vowed never to return to Hungary again!

1966   Eric Cantona born in Paris in France. After a distinguished career in France, Eric first came to the notice of English football following his transfer to Leeds United in February 1992 for £900,000. Nine months later, with a championship medal in his pocket, he was sensationally transferred to Manchester United for £1,200,000 and turned United from a nearly team to champions. He collected a further four title medals whilst at United as well as two winners' medals in the FA Cup, scoring in both finals. At the end of the 1996-97 season he announced his immediate retirement from the game, although aged only 31.

MAY 25TH

1940   Stoke City   A   War Regional League, Western Division   2-3
1963   Leicester City   Wembley   FA Cup Final   3-1
After the disappointments of 1957 and 1958, United managed to win the FA Cup for only the third time in their history. For once United were the underdogs for the clash against Leicester; United had finished the League season fourth from bottom in the First Division, their opponents fourth from top. Leicester had also finished runners-up in the FA Cup two years previously, so there were many on their side with experience of the big day, whilst United were unrecognisable from the side that had lost in 1958. As it was Leicester were the team that froze on the day, with even Gordon Banks making a number of mistakes. After surviving a scare when Cantwell almost turned into his own goal, United began to take control. Denis Law gave United the lead just before half an hour had passed, and just before the hour mark David Herd increased the lead after Banks had been unable to stop a Charlton shot. Leicester got back into the game briefly through Keyworth, but a final goal from Herd, after another Banks error, gave United the cup.

MAY 26TH

1909   Matt Busby born in Lanarkshire. He made his name as a player with Manchester City and Liverpool and after the Second World War was appointed manager of Manchester United, turning them into one of the most famous names in world football. A more detailed biography can be found on January 20th.
1932   Ian Greaves born in Shaw near Oldham. Although utlimately became better known for his managerial skills, particularly in the lower divisions, he had been a player on United's books in May 1953, joining the club from Buxton United. He appeared in the closing 14 games of the 1955-56 season, replacing the injured Bill Foulkes, and in the 1958 FA Cup final. He left United for Lincoln in 1960. His first managerial position was with Huddersfield in 1968.
1945   Bolton Wanderers   H   Football League North (Second Championship)   2-2
1947   Sheffield United   H   First Division   6-2
1982   Jimmy Rimmer collected his second European Cup medal; having been on the bench for United in 1968 when they beat Benfica, he was Aston Villa's goalkeeper for their clash with Bayern Munich, but an injury after only eight minutes forced him off the field! Nigel Spink took over and helped Villa win 1-0.
1983   Brighton & Hove Albion Wembley   FA Cup Final Replay   4-0
With Sir Matt Busby sitting in the stands on his 74th birthday, United gave him the perfect present with a victory in the FA Cup. The final score was the highest margin of victory for 80 years or so, though it could have been much worse for Brighton as United attacked at will. Bryan Robson started the rout in the 25th minute, Norman Whiteside then became the youngest FA Cup final goalscorer four minutes later, and Robson added a third two minutes before half-time. Whether United eased off in the second half will never be known, but the only additional goal was a penalty strike from Dutchman Arnold Muhren after Robson had been wrestled to the ground. Robson

might have taken the penalty himself for his hat-trick, but probably felt that lifting the cup as captain was sufficient compensation.

MAY 27TH

1971　Lee Sharpe born in Halesowen. After an unsuccessful stint with Birmingham City, Lee was taken on by Torquay United and quickly developed into a fine winger, prompting the attentions of bigger clubs. A fee of £185,000 took him to United in June 1988 and he helped the club with two FA Cups, three Premiership titles, the League Cup and the European Cup-Winners' Cup. In August 1996 he was sold to Leeds United for £4.5 million, where injuries have restricted his first-team opportunities.

MAY 28TH

1956　By virtue of their League Championship win United were invited to participate in the following season's European Cup. Although the Football League and Football Association would try to block United competing, Matt Busby was adamant that United would enter the competition as England's first representatives.

MAY 29TH

1949　Brian Kidd born in Manchester. Signed by United as an apprentice in August 1964, he was upgraded to the professional ranks in June 1966. He made his competitive debut in the FA Charity Shield in 1967 and held his place for the next seven years, helping United win the European Cup at the end of his first season and scoring one of the goals in the final. He joined Arsenal in 1974 for £110,000 and later had similar big money moves to Manchester City, Everton and Bolton before winding down his playing career in the United States. Upon returning to England he moved on to coaching and management and is currently assistant to Alex Ferguson.

1968　Benfica　　　　　　　　Wembley　European Cup Final　　　　　　　4-1 [aet]
Although United had at last managed to make the European Cup final after three previous semi-final disappointments, only winning the trophy would provide the perfect memorial to those who had perished in the Munich disaster of some ten years previously. Only winning the trophy would satisfy manager Matt Busby, his team and the hordes of United's followers who swamped Wembley for the final. Standing in their way were equally seasoned European Cup campaigners Benfica, with several of the hugely successful Portuguese national side in their line-up, including the incomparable Eusebio, Torres and Simoes. The first half was largely uninspiring as both teams tentatively probed and tested without ever seriously threatening either goal. The tempo picked up in the second half, as was expected given what was at stake, and United made the first breakthrough when Bobby Charlton netted a glancing header from Sadler's cross. As the half wore on that goal looked enough to have won the trophy for United, but with barely ten minutes left Graca hit an equaliser that deflated United for a vital five minutes. Indeed, Eusebio might have scored a winner with only four minutes left on the clock but, in wanting to score the perfect goal rather than a simple tap in, allowed a chance to go begging. Having been given a reprieve, United set about their business, at last, in extra time, netting three goals from George Best, Brian Kidd (celebrating his 19th birthday) and a second from Bobby Charlton. When the final whistle blew and United's ultimate dream became reality, there were two abiding memories of the game that will remain forever: during the heat of the battle Eusebio, perhaps one of the finest sportsmen to have graced the game, took time out from his labours to shake Alex Stepney's hand in recognition of a fine save; and the scenes at the very end when Matt Busby, Bobby Charlton and Bill Foulkes, the three survivors from the Munich disaster, embraced each other in joyful celebration.

MAY 30TH

1985 In the aftermath of the Heysel Stadium disaster, in which 39 people lost their lives the previous day, the Belgian FA announced an immediate ban on British clubs (they initially made no distinction between English and British) playing in the country. This was seen as the first step on the way to a European ban on English clubs competing in the three cups the following season, which affected United, Liverpool, Everton, Spurs, Norwich City and Southampton.

MAY 31ST

1965 Ferencvaros   H   Inter-Cities Fairs Cup Semi-Final 1st Leg   3-2
The fact that United's fans thought the competition to be something of a second-class affair was reflected in a crowd figure of only 39,902 attending the first leg of the semi-final clash against the Hungarians. United lost Pat Crerand midway through the action after he was sent off and fell behind to a goal from Novak. Denis Law equalised from the penalty spot after his header had been handled on the line, and David Herd scored twice in the second half to seemingly put United on their way to the final. But a late goal from Rakosi as United's ten men tired visibly seemed to give the Hungarians hope of overturning the deficit.

1998 Glenn Hoddle announced his squad of 22 for the forthcoming World Cup in France and there was both joy and despair for United's players. In the squad were Teddy Sheringham, Paul Scholes, Gary Neville and David Beckham, but out were Nicky Butt and Phil Neville. The news of Butt and Neville's omission was overshadowed by the fact that Paul Gascoigne was one of those discarded, but for the Neville brothers in particular, it was a bittersweet moment.

JUNE 1ST

1926 Johnny Berry born in Aldershot. Spotted whilst playing in the Army, he was recommended to Birmingham City and signed as a professional in September 1944, gaining a regular place in the first team soon after. In August 1951 he was signed by Matt Busby as a replacement for Jimmy Delaney at right wing and proved to be worth every penny of the £15,000 fee he cost. He won three League championship medals with United (1952, 1956 and 1957) and appeared in the 1957 FA Cup final. Unfortunately, the injuries he sustained in the Munich air disaster ended his career in February 1958 and he later opened a sports goods business.

1940 Everton   H   War Regional League, Western Division   0-3
United's line-up featured some of the most illustrious names in the game appearing as guests, including Stanley Matthews, Peter Doherty and Raich Carter, but even they could not prevent Everton from winning 3-0.

1955 Jack Hacking died in Accrington. Jack was born in Blackburn on 22nd December 1897 and had joined United in March 1934 when nearing the end of his long and illustrious career. He made 34 appearances in goal for United (including the vital match at Millwall in 1934-35) before moving on to become player-manager at Accrington Stanley in 1935. In May 1949 he became manager of Barrow, a position he held until his death.

1969 Wilf McGuinness assumed his position as chief coach of United, in effect becoming the new manager in all but title. A year later he was officially given the title of manager.

JUNE 2ND

1894 Clarence Hilditch born in Hartford in Cheshire. Known throughout the game as 'Lal', he had signed for United in January 1916 and was appointed player-manager in October 1926, holding the position until the end of the season in April 1927. He then resumed his career as a player and finally retired in 1932. He made over 300 appearances for the club during his long association with them, but sadly won no medals, although he did represent England in a Victory International in 1919 and played for the Football League. At the end of his playing career he coached United's Colts team.

1951   Arnold Muhren born in Vollendam in Holland. After starring in Holland for Ajax of Amsterdam and FC Twente Enschede, Arnold was brought to England by Ipswich Town and helped them win the 1981 UEFA Cup. The following year he joined United and helped them win the FA Cup in 1983, scoring a penalty in the replay as United won 4-0. An injury in March 1984 came at a crucial time for United, and his influence was sadly missed during the rest of the campaign. Thereafter he struggled to command a regular place and was released in 1985, going home to sign for Ajax for a second time. Even though he was now 34 years old, he still had much to offer, as a European Cup winners' medal in 1987 and a European Championship medal in 1988 would testify.

1978   Ernest Vincent died in Bircotes, near Worksop. Born in County Durham on 28th October 1907, he began his professional career with Southport in July 1930 and cost United £1,000 when they signed him in February 1932. He remained at Old Trafford for a little over three years before signing for QPR in June 1935, and he finished his career with Doncaster Rovers.

JUNE 3RD

1898   Charlie Moore born in Cheslyn Bay in Staffordshire. Charlie signed for United in May 1919 from non-League football and made his debut in August of that year. He was a regular in the side until a serious ankle injury forced him to retire in 1921, with United paying out on an insurance policy. A year later he turned up at Old Trafford, apparently fit again, and asked for a trial for the reserves. He passed this and was soon back in the first team, going on to make over 300 appearances for United in the League and proving himself to be one of the most consistent right-backs of the era. He retired a second time, this time for good, in 1931.

1935   James Brown signed from Burnley. United had previously had a player with the same name on their books, but this James had begun his career in the coal industry before chancing his luck as a footballer. Signed by Burnley in May 1927, he made over 200 League appearances for the club before switching to Old Trafford for £1,000. He won a Second Division championship medal at the end of his first season and made over 100 appearances for the club before moving on to Bradford Park Avenue in 1939. He retired as a player during the Second World War.

JUNE 4TH

1949   Lou Macari born in Edinburgh. Signed by Celtic in July 1966, he spent seven years at Celtic Park, winning numerous domestic honours, before United paid £200,000 to bring him south of the border in January 1973. Although he took time to adjust to the differences between the two styles of football, he soon became a favourite with the crowd and added to his tally of medals, winning a Second Division championship medal in 1975 and an FA Cup winners' medal in 1977, as well as two runners-up medals in the same competition and a runners-up medal in the League Cup. In July 1984 he took over as player-manager at Swindon, later holding managerial posts at West Ham, Birmingham City, Stoke and Celtic.

1983   Tottenham Hotspur   Swaziland   Royal Swazi Hotel Tournament   2-1

JUNE 5TH

1985   Frank Hodges died in Southport. Frank was born in Birmingham on 26th January 1891 and joined United in August 1919, having previously played for Birmingham.

Although he had a good first season with United, he was unable to agree financial terms with the club during the close season and was placed on the transfer list, subsequently joining Wigan Borough in June 1921. He finished his League career with Crewe before playing for non-League Winsford.

JUNE 6TH

1965   Ferencvaros   A   Inter-Cities Fairs Cup Semi-Final 2nd Leg   0-1
A single goal for Ferencvaros was enough to tie the aggregate score at 3-3. In the days before away goals counted double, this meant a third, decisive meeting between the two sides, with the toss of a coin deciding the venue. United lost this and would have to return to Hungary in ten days' time for the play-off.

JUNE 7TH

1989   George Roughton died in Southampton. Born in Manchester on 11th December 1909, George signed for Huddersfield Town in October 1928 as an amateur and became a professional a month later, even though he continued to live in Manchester. He remained at Huddersfield for almost eight years before returning 'home', signing for United in September 1936 as a replacement for Billy Porter. But for the Second World War he would undoubtedly have made more than the 92 appearances he managed for the first team, but he did help the club reclaim their First Division status in 1938. After guesting for Huddersfield during the war he was appointed player-manager at Exeter City in 1945, and he became manager at Southampton in March 1952. Ill-health and a heart by-pass operation forced his retirement in September 1955, and he severed all links with the game.

JUNE 8TH

1870   James McNaught born in Dumbarton. James was signed by Newton Heath in February 1893 for the likelihood the club made the Test series of matches, although he dislocated his elbow in a friendly in March and was unable to take his place in the side until September 1893. When he settled in he proved a worthwhile acquisition by the club and made over 160 appearances for the first team before his surprising move to Spurs in May 1898. There he was a member of the team that won the Southern League but he missed out on the FA Cup final in 1901 owing to injury. He left Spurs for Maidstone in 1907 and retired in 1909.

1898   Ernie Goldthorpe born in Middleton. Ernie arrived at Old Trafford in 1922 having already given good service to Spurs, Bradford City in two spells and Leeds United. He made an impact at United, scoring 15 League goals in only 27 outings, but a dislocated collarbone in a collision with the goalkeeper in a match against Blackpool in 1923 limited his opportunities and he was released to join Rotherham in October 1925.

1971   United announced the appointment of Frank O'Farrell as manager of the club in succession to Sir Matt Busby. Sir Matt had taken control of United for a second time in December 1971 when the board had felt compelled to replace Wilf McGuinness, although this was only seen as a temporary measure until a proper replacement could be found. After a day of discussions with O'Farrell and the Leicester City board, where O'Farrell was currently manager, it was agreed he would be coming to Old Trafford and would take up his new job on 1st July. Sir Matt Busby would be relinquishing his responsibilities and taking a seat on the United board.

JUNE 9TH

1965   Harold Hardman died in Sale in Cheshire. Born in Manchester on 4th April 1882, Harold spent his entire playing career as an amateur, but was still good enough to have collected an FA Cup winners' medal with Everton in 1906, made four appearances for the full England team and won an Olympic Gold medal in the 1908 Games in London, where the English amateurs overcame their Danish counterparts 2-0. He had two spells at United as a player but made only four first-team appearances, but he served the club for over 50 years as a director and was chairman of the club from 1951 to 1965. He also served on the Football Association, Lancashire FA and the Central League, and was widely regarded as one of the finest administrators the game has ever seen.

1996   Old Trafford staged the European Championship group match between Germany and the Czech Republic, with Germany winning 2-0.

JUNE 10TH

1945   Tommy Baldwin born in Gateshead. Tommy, better known for his eight years with Chelsea, spent a month on loan to United as cover for the injured Stuart Pearson in January 1975, making two appearances for the first team.

1957   Peter Barnes born in Manchester. Peter began his career with local rivals Manchester City but arrived on loan at United in May 1984 from Leeds United. He signed for £50,000 in July 1985 from Coventry, but after starring in the early games of 1985-86 he lost his place and was sold to Manchester City for £30,000. He finished his playing career in Ireland.

1966   David Platt born in Chadderton. Although he signed for United straight from school, he was released on a free transfer to Crewe without having made a single appearance for the first team. He later moved to Aston Villa and broke into the England side, proof of 'the one that got away' as far as United were concerned.

1969   Ronny Johnsen born in Norway. Signed by United for £1.2 million in July 1996, he is equally at home in central defence or midfield, and after making his debut as a replacement for the injured Nicky Butt he soon slotted into a place in the centre of defence. He won a championship medal at the end of his first season at Old Trafford and looks an excellent prospect for a good few years to come.

1994   Bobby Charlton was knighted in the Birthday Honours list, becoming the fourth footballer thus honoured, following Sir Stanley Matthews, Sir Alf Ramsey and Sir Matt Busby.

JUNE 11TH

1916   Dick Pegg died in Leicester. Dick was born in Leicester in 1878 and had first come to prominence whilst playing for Leicester Fosse as an amateur in 1895. He then played for Loughborough Town, Kettering, Reading and Preston before signing with United in June 1902, remaining at Clayton for two years. He scored the first hat-trick registered by a United player in a League match (against Bradford City on 26th September 1903) but struggled to hold his place in the side the following season and was released to sign for Fulham in 1904. He later played for Barnsley, where injury ended his career in 1906. At the time of his death he was a publican in his home town.

1931   Ray Wood born in County Durham. Ray was signed by Newcastle United as an amateur but turned professional with Darlington in September 1949. After only 12 games for the Shakers he was sold to United for £5,000 in December 1949, going straight into the first team and proving himself a safe and reliable goalkeeper. Initially he battled with Jack Crompton and Reg Allen for the role of first choice, but by 1953-54 he had won the position by rights. He won League championship medals in 1956 and 1957 and might have collected a winners' medal in the 1957 FA Cup final but for an early collision with Aston Villa's Peter McParland which effectively put him out of the match. He spent some considerable time on the wing before returning to goal for the final ten minutes, but the disruption effectively cost United their chance of the double. He survived the Munich air crash but once he had recovered from his injuries was unable to dislodge Harry Gregg from goal, and in December 1958 he was sold to Huddersfield Town for £1,500. He went on to make over 200 appearances for Huddersfield and finished his playing career with Bradford City and Barnsley. He then moved into coaching and has coached all over the world.

1983   Tottenham Hotspur   Swaziland   Royal Swazi Hotel Tournament   0-2

JUNE 12TH

1885   Dick Holden born in Middleton. After starring for a number of local sides, Dick was on the verge of signing with Bury when United made a late bid for him in May 1904, signing him initially as an amateur and then as a professional in September of the same year. He won a League championship medal in 1908 but was injured for the following season's FA Cup success, and although he recovered for the 1910-11 season and appeared to be at the peak of his form, he suffered another breakdown and so missed out on a second championship medal. He remained with United until May 1914 and was later reported to have joined the RAF.

1987   United signed Celtic striker Brian McClair, although the fee would be decided by a tribunal as the two clubs were unable to agree. Celtic were asking £2 million, considerably more than United were prepared to pay. In the event, McClair cost United £850,000.

JUNE 13TH

1995   United refused permission for Steve Bruce to talk to Derby County, where he was wanted as player-manager. Although he left United almost a year later, the decision was not without its compensation, for Steve collected his third League title medal, although he was absent from the side that also won the FA Cup that season.

JUNE 14TH

1952   Tottenham Hotspur   Toronto   Friendly   0-5
1970   Bobby Charlton made his 106th and final appearance for England in the World Cup quarter-final against West Germany in Leon in Mexico. Although Bobby had a quiet game, his very presence had shackled Franz Beckenbauer into a defensive role as England stormed into a 2-0 lead. Bobby was replaced by Manchester City's Colin Bell, but with Beckenbauer now able to operate in a freer role, West Germany fought back to win the match 3-2 and eliminate the world champions.

JUNE 15TH

1933   Mark Jones born in Barnsley. First spotted whilst playing for Barnsley Schoolboys, Mark was signed by United on amateur forms in June 1948 and upgraded to the professional ranks in July 1950. That same year he made his League debut but did not establish himself as a regular in the side until 1954-55. Although he won two League championship medals at United he missed out on the 1957 FA Cup final, having lost his place to Jackie Blanchflower, but he was surely destined for future greatness when he lost his life in the Munich air crash in 1958. He was 24 years old.

1952   Tottenham Hotspur   New York   Friendly   1-7
        Twenty-four hours earlier Spurs had beaten United 5-0 in an exhibition match in Toronto, even though United were the reigning League champions. The two sides had travelled together for the second fixture in New York, which took place at the Yankee Stadium, more normally used for baseball. Indeed, prior to the start, captains Johnny

Carey and Ronnie Burgess laid a wreath in front of the memorials to Babe Ruth and Lou Gehrig and the two sides lined up in silent tribute. The British Consul kicked the game off and both sides turned in an exceptional performance, with Spurs winning 7-1 despite United having taken the lead!

1959   Alan Brazil born in Glasgow. After starring for Ipswich in their UEFA Cup success in 1981 and earning a number of Scottish caps, Alan earned the first big-money move of his career when he was signed by Spurs in March 1983 for £450,000. His time at Spurs was not a success, and a further move to Old Trafford for £625,000 in June 1984 also failed to revive his career. He was transferred to Coventry as part of the deal that brought Terry Gibson to United, but after only six months at Highfield Road he moved on again to QPR. There a back injury forced his retirement from League football in January 1987.

1989   Alex Ferguson completed the signings of Neil Webb from Nottingham Forest and Mike Phelan from Norwich City. Webb would ultimately cost £1.5 million, the figure being decided by a tribunal, whilst Phelan cost half that sum at £750,000.

1996   A bomb explosion in the centre of Manchester put the European Championship match between Germany and Russia, due to be played at Old Trafford the following day, in jeopardy, although with security extremely tight in and around the city the match did go ahead.

JUNE 16TH

1965   Ferencvaros   A   Inter-Cities Fairs Cup Semi-Final Play-off   1-2
United at last reached the end of a long and exhausting season with a 2-1 defeat by Ferencvaros in the Inter-Cities Cup semi-final play-off. Tired United held their Hungarian opponents at bay for nearly an hour, but then Ferencvaros went into a 2-0 lead and the game was effectively over as a contest. John Connelly scored a late consolation for the League champions.

1982   United captain Bryan Robson scored the fastest goal in the history of the World Cup, netting after only 27 seconds in the England v. France clash in Bilbao. England went on to win 3-1.

1996   Old Trafford staged the European Championship group match between Germany and Russia, with the Germans winning 3-0.

JUNE 17TH

1915   Billy Fielding born in Broadhurst. Billy had begun his career with Cardiff and signed for United from Bolton in January 1947. He let in six goals in his first League match and his career at Old Trafford barely recovered, for he retired at the end of the 1947-48 season having made just seven appearances for United.

1964   Graeme Hogg born in Aberdeen. Although he represented Aberdeen at schoolboy level, Graeme was signed as an apprentice by United in July 1980 and upgraded to the professional ranks in June 1982. He made his debut in the FA Cup tie at Bournemouth in 1984 and became a regular in the defence until injured the following season, missing out on the FA Cup victory over Everton. Restricted first-team opportunities thereafter prompted a move to Portsmouth in 1988 before he returned to Scotland with Hearts in 1991.

1982   Norman Whiteside, who had made just two League appearances for Manchester United, became the youngest player to compete in the final stages of the World Cup when he played for Northern Ireland against Yugoslavia. He was just 17 years and 41 days old.

JUNE 18TH

1996 Gary Neville was one of England's heroes in an emphatic 4-1 win over Holland in the final European Championship group match at Wembley. England's goals were shared by Alan Shearer and Teddy Sheringham, the latter later becoming a United player, whilst the England side also included former player Paul Ince.

JUNE 19TH

1946 Jimmy Greenhoff born in Barnsley. The brother of fellow United star Brian, Jimmy joined United from Stoke in 1976 for £120,000. He had begun his career with Leeds United, and later played for Birmingham City before switching to Stoke City. He was credited with scoring United's winner in the 1977 FA Cup final, although it was more a case of him being struck by Lou Macari's shot. He left United for Crewe in 1980 and later moved on to coaching.

1996 Old Trafford staged the European Championship group match between Italy and Germany which finished a goalless draw, thus eliminating the Italians from the competition.

JUNE 20TH

1933 Warren Bradley born in Hyde. Signed by United from Bishop Aukland in February 1958, along with Bob Hardisty and Derek Lewin, Warren was initially expected to bolster the reserve side in the aftermath of the Munich air disaster. However, his performances were of such quality that he was offered a contract as a full professional and signed in November 1958, making his League debut the same month. At the end of the season his progress had been such that he was capped by England, scoring in the match against Italy. He was never part of Matt Busby's long-term plans, however, and in March 1962 he was sold to Bury for £40,000 and subsequently went back to playing non-League football.

1981 George Vose died in Wigan. Born in St Helens on 4th October 1911, he signed with United in September 1932 and made his debut in August 1953. A regular in the United side thereafter, he won a Second Division championship medal in 1935-36 as United went through a see-saw existence immediately prior to the Second World War. The outbreak of war cut across George's career and he guested for the likes of Chester, Manchester City, Stockport and Derby during the hostilities. He re-signed with United at the end of the war but soon after joined Runcorn, where he finished his career.

JUNE 21ST

1949 Stuart Pearson born in Hull. Stuart signed with Hull straight from school in 1966 and broke into the first team following the departure of Chris Chilton. After finishing top scorer for Hull in three consecutive seasons, he was sold to United for £200,000 in May 1974 and was top scorer as the side won the Second Division championship in his first season. He later helped the club to two FA Cup finals, scoring in the win against Liverpool in 1977, but a knee operation caused him to miss much of his final season at Old Trafford. A £220,000 deal took him to West Ham in 1982, where he collected his second FA Cup winners' medal in 1980, a further knee injury ending his career in 1982. After a brief spell spent playing rugby union for Sale, he turned to coaching and management.

JUNE 22ND

1948 Colin Waldron born in Bristol. Colin made his name with Burnley during a nine-year stay at Turf Moor and upon arrival at Old Trafford in October 1976 was confidently expected to help bolster the defence. Surprisingly, the move did not work out and after only four games he was loaned to Sunderland, later going to play in America. He finished his career with Rochdale and retired in 1980.

1995   Paul Ince completed his £7 million transfer to Inter Milan. The deal had been under discussion for a number of weeks, but up until now Paul had indicated he was more than happy to remain at Old Trafford.

JUNE 23RD

1995   Twenty-four hours after Paul Ince announced his departure to Inter Milan, Mark Hughes was on his way too, signing for Chelsea in a deal worth £1.5 million. Although Mark was over 31 years of age at the time of his transfer, there were many who felt he still had much to offer United. Certainly, his record at Chelsea would seem to prove the point, for he helped them win the FA Cup and Coca-Cola Cup.

1996   Old Trafford staged the European Championship quarter-final between Germany and Croatia, which the Germans won 2-1 thanks to a penalty from Klinsmann and a goal from Sammer.

JUNE 24TH

1950   It was reported that United favourite Charlie Mitten had signed a two-year deal with the Santa Fe club in Bogota in Columbia for a wage of £40 a week. Other key names from the British game were also lured by the promise of higher wages in Colombia than they could earn in England, including Neil Franklin (Stoke and England), George Mountford (Stoke) and Billy Higgins (Everton). They left behind them a maximum wage of £12 a week for the promise of a signing-on fee of £2,500, a salary of £2,500 per season, win bonuses of £35 a game and a further £1,500 on completion of their contracts in Bogota. Life in Colombia did not turn out as they expected, however, and Charlie Mitten returned home disillusioned to face a £250 fine by the FA and a six-month suspension. He later signed for Fulham.

1970   David May born in Oldham. David began his career with Blackburn Rovers, signing as a trainee in 1988, and soon displayed assured performances at the heart of their defence. A £1.4 million fee took him to Old Trafford in July 1994 as a ready-made replacement for Steve Bruce, and in addition to collecting two League title medals and an FA Cup winners' medal at club level he has gone on to feature in the England squad.

JUNE 25TH

1921   Tommy Arkesden died in Manchester. Born in Warwick in July 1878, Tommy had begun his career with Burton Wanderers in 1896 and joined Derby in 1898, partnering Steve Bloomer in the side that reached the 1899 FA Cup final. He returned to Burton in 1901, joining the newly formed Burton United, but then moved on to Manchester United in February 1903 after United had paid a fee of £150. He helped the club to promotion to the First Division in 1906 and after 70 League appearances left to join Gainsborough Trinity in 1907.

JUNE 26TH

1952   Gordon McQueen born in Kilbirnie in Ayrshire. After unsuccessful trials with Glasgow Rangers and Liverpool, Gordon, the son of former Accrington Stanley goalkeeper Tommy McQueen, signed with St Mirren in 1970 and quickly established himself as a commanding centre-half. In September 1972 Leeds paid £30,000 to take him to Elland Road as successor to Jack Charlton, and he subsequently won a League championship medal whilst at Leeds. United paid £495,000 for him in February 1978, shortly after buying Joe Jordan from the same club. Although he scored in the 1979 FA Cup final, United were beaten by Arsenal, but he collected more than adequate

CLOCKWISE FROM TOP LEFT: Cigarette card of George Wall; cigarette card of Sandy Turnbull; picture card of John Aston; picture card of John Smith

TOP LEFT: Cigarette card of Jack Silcock
TOP RIGHT: Cigarette card of Joe Spence
BOTTOM LEFT: Picture card of Bobby Charlton
BOTTOM RIGHT: Picture card of Willie Morgan
OPPOSITE PAGE (TOP): The programme issued at Old Trafford for the
closed-circuit screening of a league match from Highbury
OPPOSITE PAGE (BOTTOM): Picture card of Denis Law

Friday 3rd March 1967   Number 18   Price sixpence

Souvenir programme

A special edition of the official M.U.F.C. programme
to commemorate

THE FIRST FOOTBALL MATCH IN DIVISION ONE TO BE TELEVISED ON CLOSED-CIRCUIT T.V.

ARSENAL v MANCHESTER UTD.
KICK–OFF 7·30 p.m.

DIRECT FROM ARSENAL STADIUM

BY ARRANGEMENT WITH ARSENAL F.C. AND VIEWSPORT LTD.

DENIS LAW

STAR PLAYERS

MANCHESTER U.

Next Home Match
1st DIVISION
United v
NOTTS. FOREST
22 Feb. Kick-off 3.0 pm

Youth International
Match
ENGLAND v
GERMANY
Wednesday, 12 March
Kick-off 7-30 pm

R

L

Referee:
A. Bond, London
Kick-off 7-30 pm

FOOTBALL
GREEN
PLEASE

Linesmen:
F. Wain, Bakewell
Red Flag

F. P. Clarke, Coventry
Yellow Flag

L

R

FINNEY   FROGGATT   • SHINER   QUIXALL   WILKINSON

O'DONNELL   SWAN   KAY

JOHNSON   MARTIN

RYALLS

Team changes will be indicated by loudspeaker

Shirts Blue and White Stripes   SHEFFIELD WEDNESDAY   Knickers Black

Team changes will be indicated by loudspeaker

The inside of the programme for the FA Cup match against Sheffield
Wednesday, the first game after the Munich air disaster. The team
line-up for United was left blank

Jack Rowley scores his second goal of the 1948 FA Cup final against
Blackpool at Wembley

TOP: Nat Lofthouse crashes into Harry Gregg to put Bolton into the lead in the 1958 FA Cup final
BOTTOM: The 1956–57 team

The European Cup is paraded around Wembley after the 1968 final against Benfica

TOP: United line up shortly before the kick-off of the European Cup tie against Red Star Belgrade. This is the last photograph ever taken of the Busby Babes
BOTTOM: Matt Busby, Bill Foulkes and Bobby Charlton celebrate after the 1968 European Cup final

TOP: Tommy Docherty, manager
between 1972 and 1977

RIGHT: Charles Roberts

compensation in 1983 when Brighton were defeated after a replay. He was badly injured in January 1984, which effectively ended his Old Trafford career, and in August 1985 he went to play and coach in Hong Kong. He later became manager at Airdrieonians and coach at St Mirren.

1996   Old Trafford staged the European Championship semi-final between France and the Czech Republic, which finished goalless after extra time. The Czechs then won the penalty shoot-out 6-5 and would face Germany in the final at Wembley.

1998   David Beckham scored England's second goal in the 2-0 win over Columbia in the World Cup finals in France. It was the first match Beckham had started and the win confirmed that England would progress to the knockout stage of the tournament.

JUNE 27TH

1967   Denis Law was in considerable trouble during United's end-of-season tour of Australia, getting sent off for swearing at the referee in the 7-0 win over Western Australia in Perth. He was later fined about £20 for the offence.

JUNE 28TH

1933   Fred Goodwin born in Heywood. Spotted by United whilst playing for Cheshire Schools, he was signed in October 1953. The presence of Duncan Edwards and Eddie Colman limited his first-team opportunities prior to Munich, but when called upon thereafter he performed admirably and was part of the side that reached the 1958 FA Cup final. He was transferred to Leeds in 1960 for £10,000 and was a first-team regular until a triple leg fracture in the 1963-64 season brought his career at Elland Road to an end. After managerial stints in both England and America, he emigrated to the States.

1947   John Aston junior born in Manchester. John joined the groundstaff at United in July 1962, was made an apprentice the following year and was upgraded to full professional in July 1964. Although frequently overshadowed by the exploits of George Best, John Aston always gave United sterling effort, never better illustrated than by his performance in the 1968 European Cup success. He joined Luton for £30,000 in 1972 and after five years, during which he helped them into the First Division, he moved on to Mansfield Town. He finished his playing career with Blackburn Rovers.

1966   Jack Silcock died in Ashton-under-Lyme. Born in Wigan on 15th January 1898, he joined United in April 1916 as an amateur, becoming a professional the following year. He made his debut in 1919 against Derby and went on to make 449 appearances for the first team over the next 17 years, with three England caps the only honour he won whilst with the club. He joined Oldham in 1934 but less than a year later dropped into the non-League game. After retiring, he became a publican.

JUNE 29TH

1950   John Aston senior was a member of the England side that suffered its biggest ever upset, a 1-0 defeat by the United States in the World Cup match at Belo Horizonte in Brazil. Many years later, Alf Ramsey, who also took part in the match, was asked if he had played. 'Yes,' he replied, 'and I was the only bloody one who did!'

1982   Despite the presence of United stalwarts Bryan Robson, Ray Wilkins and Steve Coppell, there was more World Cup woe for England as they were held to a goalless draw with West Germany in Madrid.

JUNE 30TH

1963   Gary Pallister born in Ramsgate. Gary began his career with Middlesbrough in 1984 and was loaned to Darlington the following year, although a permanent move fell through after Darlington were unable to raise the £4,000. Upon return to Ayresome Park he claimed a first-team place and helped them to promotion in two successive seasons to reclaim their place in the First Division. In August 1989 a £2.3 million fee took him to United, and he has been almost ever-present in the heart of the defence since. He has won four League titles, three FA Cups, the League Cup and the European Cup-Winners' Cup, as well as over 20 caps for England. He was named PFA Player of the Year in 1992, in recognition of his consistent performances for United.

JULY 1ST

1971   Frank O'Farrell took over as manager of Manchester United, replacing Sir Matt Busby, who now relinquished all managerial positions and responsibilities and became a director of the club.

1986   Mark Hughes completed his sensational £2.5 million move to Spanish giants Barcelona, where he would link up with fellow British striker Gary Lineker.

JULY 2ND

1973   Denis Law signed for Manchester City following his release from United on a free transfer. It was his second spell at Maine Road, having previously signed for them in March 1960. He had joined United from Torino in August 1962 and spent 11 years at Old Trafford.

JULY 3RD

1966   England's World Cup warm-up continued with a 2-0 win over Denmark in Copenhagen. Although Bobby Charlton, who played in the previous two matches on the brief tour, was rested, John Connelly retained his place in the England side. Interestingly, Charlton did appear on the score sheet – Bobby's brother Jack, that is, who scored England's first, with George Eastham adding the second.

JULY 4TH

1977   United sacked manager Tommy Docherty for 'breach of contract', the charge relating to the revelation he was having an affair with the wife of coach Laurie Brown, Mary. 'I have been punished for falling in love. What I have done has got nothing at all to do with my track record as a manager,' was Docherty's comment at the time. That may well have been true, but it was certainly an embarrassing scenario for United, having both Docherty and Laurie Brown still at the club at the same time. One of them would have to leave. It was perhaps the wives of the directors who had demanded the club take action following Docherty's announcement two weeks previously that he was setting up home with Mrs Brown.

JULY 5TH

1891   James Hodge born in Stenhousemuir. James had made his name as a wing-half for Stenhousemuir at the time of his transfer to United in May 1910, but it was his subsequent switch to full-back in 1912 that made him a regular in the side. The First World War cut across his career at United and in December 1919 he was transferred to Millwall Athletic, later playing for Norwich City and Southend United before retiring in 1924. He died in Chorlton-cum-Hardy on 2nd September 1970. His brother John also had a spell on United's books, joining the club in June 1913 and making 30 appearances in the side.

JULY 6TH

1962   United offered a British record fee of £115,000 to Torino for Denis Law, although it was thought the deal would not go through for at least a month, as the Italian side had not yet appointed a finance council, without whom no deal could progress.

JULY 7TH

1947 John Sutcliffe died in Bradford. Born in Halifax on 14th April 1868, John had had only a brief career at United, making only 28 appearances in goal between May 1903 and January 1905, when he signed for Plymouth, but he was undoubtedly a great character and one of the finest goalkeepers of the era. He became a goalkeeper quite by accident: he was playing centre-forward for Bolton reserves in one game when, as the goalkeeper advanced to tackle him, John picked him up and threw him into the goal! After that Bolton converted him to goalkeeper and have seldom been better served. He helped them to the 1894 FA Cup final, where they lost 4-1 to Notts County. John also won five caps for England at football and one at rugby union; he is the last man to have represented England at full level at the two codes. He was already 35 years old when he joined United and past his best, but he managed to continue playing until he was 44 years of age, coaching at Southend United when his playing career ended.

1954 Mickey Thomas born in Mochdre, near Colwyn Bay. Mickey began his professional career with Wrexham in April 1972 and was already a Welsh international by the time of his transfer to United in November 1978 for £300,000. An instant favourite with the crowd, he was initially used as successor for Gordon Hill and appeared in the 1979 FA Cup final against Arsenal, although following the arrival of Ron Atkinson in 1981 he was sold to Everton in an exchange deal with John Gidman worth £450,000. Since then he has played for Brighton, Stoke, Chelsea, West Bromwich Albion, Derby, Shrewsbury, Leeds, Wrexham and two further spells with Stoke!

JULY 8TH

1991 United, Spurs and Arsenal all signed an exclusive deal with ITV to cover their home ties in European competition in the forthcoming season, United and Spurs in the European Cup-Winners' Cup and Arsenal in the European Cup.

JULY 9TH

1955 Steve Coppell born in Croxteth in Liverpool. Steve had signed with Tranmere as a professional in 1974 and was soon being tipped for greater honours. Indeed, Bill Shankly, then helping out at Tranmere, recommended him to Liverpool but was turned down, so in turn rang Tommy Docherty. United paid £60,000 to take him to Old Trafford in February 1975 and he lived up to his early promise. A member of the side that won the FA Cup in 1977 and reached the finals of 1976 and 1979, he broke into the England squad in 1977 and went on to win 42 caps. He retired from playing in October 1983, after sustaining a serious knee injury whilst playing for England, and was appointed manager of Crystal Palace, a position he held for nine years. After a brief spell as manager at Manchester City, he returned to Palace.

1969 Following incidents during the European Cup semi-final second leg against AC Milan, in which missiles were thrown at the Milan goalkeeper from sections of the crowd in the Stretford End, United faced a commission in Geneva and were ordered to erect fences behind both goals.

JULY 10TH

1956 Frank Stapleton born in Dublin. Frank had trials with United and Wolves before signing for Arsenal as an apprentice in 1972, upgrading to the professional ranks in September 1973. He won an FA Cup winners' medal with Arsenal against United in

1979 (when he scored one of their goals) as well as runners-up medals in the same competition in 1978 and 1980 and the European Cup-Winners' Cup in 1980. He was signed by United for £900,000 in August 1981, the fee being fixed by tribunal, and went on to collect a further two winners' medals in the FA Cup in 1983 and 1985, scoring in the former to become the first man to score for two different clubs in Wembley FA Cup finals. He left United for Ajax of Amsterdam in 1987, although injury meant his stay was a short one. He later played for Blackburn Rovers, Aldershot and Huddersfield Town, where he was player-coach, before taking up the role of player-manager with Bradford City.

JULY 11TH

1916   Reg Halton born in Buxton. Although Reg played only four games for United in his eight months with the club and his career seldom scaled the heights, he did feature in one remarkable game whilst guesting for Arsenal in 1945. A crowd of 54,640 turned out to watch Arsenal take on Moscow Dynamos during their tour, although the dense fog meant few would have seen the proceedings! Reg died in Derbyshire in March 1988.

JULY 12TH

1962   Manchester United signed Denis Law from Torino for a British record transfer fee of £115,000. In fact, Torino only received £75,000 of the money, with the remaining £40,000 being owed to Manchester City following Law's transfer the previous year. Matt Busby had long been an admirer of the goalscoring abilities of Law and moved quickly to prevent Law being sold by Torino to fellow Italian club Juventus. Law was soon to prove money well spent at Old Trafford.

JULY 13TH

1966   Old Trafford hosted its first match in the 1966 World Cup finals, being held in England, as Hungary took on Portugal. The Portuguese, who featured the likes of Eusebio, who was already familiar to United fans following his performances for Benfica, won 3-1.

JULY 14TH

1957   Arthur Albiston born in Edinburgh. Signed by United as an apprentice in July 1972, he was upgraded to the professional ranks in July 1974 and made his debut in October the same year. He went on to make over 360 League appearances for United and appeared in four FA Cup finals, collecting three winners' medals. In August 1988 he linked up again with Ron Atkinson at West Bromwich Albion and after a brief spell in Scotland wound down his career with Chester City. He also won 14 full caps for Scotland.

1977   Dave Sexton was announced as the new manager of Manchester United following the recent sacking of Tommy Docherty. Sexton had seemingly been heading to Arsenal but chose instead to take over at Old Trafford. This was the second time in his career Sexton had replaced Docherty, for in 1967 he had succeeded him at Chelsea. Sexton had previously been a player with West Ham, Brighton and Crystal Palace before turning to coaching, and had recently been at the helm at QPR.

JULY 15TH

1989   Former United player Laurie Cunningham, the second black player to have played for England, was killed in a car crash whilst returning home from a night club in Madrid. Cunningham had played for Leyton Orient, West Bromwich Albion, Manchester United and Real Madrid during his career, as well as collecting a winners' medal in the FA Cup whilst on loan to Wimbledon.

JULY 16TH

1971   An incident during the League match with Newcastle United in February had seen a knife thrown from the crowd on to the pitch, and the Football League had promised an inquiry into the matter. Today they announced their punishment: Old Trafford would be closed for the first two games of the 1971-72 season.

JULY 17TH

1932   Colin Webster born in Cardiff. He began his career with Cardiff City as a part-time professional but failed to make the grade and had been released on a free transfer when he was recommended to United by Dennis Viollet, signing at Old Trafford in May 1952. Severe competition for places in the forward line restricted Colin's opportunities for regular first-team action, although he did play in sufficient games in the 1955-56 season to qualify for a League championship medal. Thereafter he was used as a squad player, although influenza prevented him from travelling with the side to the ill-fated match with Red Star Belgrade in 1958. He was a regular in the team following Munich and played in the FA Cup final at the end of the season, and he then went on to add to his tally of Welsh caps in the World Cup (he won a total of four during his time at Old Trafford). In October 1958 he returned to Wales to play for Swansea Town, helping them win the 1961 Welsh Cup, and finished his League career with Newport County before moving into the non-League game.

JULY 18TH

1938   John Connelly born in St Helens. John began his professional career with Burnley in 1956 and developed into one of the best wingers in the game, helping the Turf Moor side to a League title in 1960 and an appearance in the 1962 FA Cup final. He was sold to United for £60,000 in 1964 and won a second championship medal in his first season at the club. A member of the England squad that won the World Cup in 1966, he was sold to Blackburn for £40,000 in September 1966 and finished his career with Bury, retiring in 1973.

JULY 19TH

1925   John Downie born in Lanark. In 1948 United paid a club record fee of £18,000 to bring John to Old Trafford from Bradford Park Avenue, where he began his League career. Initially bought to replace the outgoing Johnny Morris, John was a reliable goalscorer and won a League championship medal in 1952. In August 1953 he was sold to Luton for £10,000 and later played for Hull City before seemingly dropping out of League football. He returned in 1958 with Mansfield Town and then Darlington before returning to non-League football.

1947   Harry Erentz died in Dundee at the age of 72 years. Born in Dundee on September 17th 1875, Harry began his career with the local Dundee club before joining Oldham Athletic in 1896. After 12 months he was transferred to Newton Heath and won a medal in the Lancashire Senior Cup, the Heathens' first major trophy win. A month later he was transferred to Spurs, winning the Southern League championship in 1900 and the FA Cup the following year. A solid and reliable full-back, he was known as 'Tiger' because of the ferocity of his tackling and was a great favourite with the crowd. An injury led to him being released by Spurs in May 1904 and he was unable to secure another club until December of that year, when he joined Swindon Town. In March 1905, after only 16 appearances for the Wiltshire club, he broke a leg and was forced to retire.

JULY 20TH

1996   United completed the signing of Czech Republic star Karel Poborsky from Slavia Prague for £3.5 million. Karel had been one of the stars during the recent European Championships held in England, helping his country to the runners-up spot behind Germany.

JULY 21ST

1988   Frank Brett died in Chichester. Born in King's Norton on 10th March 1899, Frank arrived at Old Trafford in February 1921 having been spotted playing for Redditch. A fee of £300 was agreed, but it then transpired that he had earlier signed amateur forms with Aston Villa, a club United were unable to come to terms with over his transfer. The matter was subsequently put before the FA, who fined United ten guineas for having registered him before his transfer from Villa had come through. In August 1922 Frank returned to Villa but had little success, later moving on to Northampton Town and then Brighton and Hove Albion.

JULY 22ND

1976   United manager Tommy Docherty prepared to fly out to the United States to sign Alan Foggon. Foggon was currently playing for Hartford Bi-Centennials and after Docherty's 7,000-mile round trip signed for United for a fee of £40,000. However, after only three substitute appearances in the League he was sold to Sunderland for £25,000!

JULY 23RD

1941   Caesar Jenkyns died in Birmingham. Born in Builth on 24th August 1866, Caesar began his career with Small Heath St Andrews and arrived at Newton Heath via Walsall Swifts, Small Heath and Woolwich Arsenal. Already a Welsh international by the time he arrived at the club, he was made captain and proved an inspiring figure, although after only 47 appearances for the club he moved on to Walsall. He later played for Coventry and retired as a player in 1905. In 1934 he was the recipient of a unique cap, for he had contacted the Welsh FA to point out that although he had represented the country on a number of occasions, the Welsh FA had not at that time issued caps. The Welsh FA duly produced one for him and it was presented by William Bassett, chairman of West Bromwich Albion and England's winger when Caesar had been playing for Wales, at the Hawthorns.

JULY 24TH

1941   Tony Dunne born in Dublin. Tony began his career with Shelbourne and had already been capped by Eire when United paid £5,000 to bring him to Old Trafford in April 1960. He established himself as a regular in the side in 1961-62 and soon became one of the most consistent full-backs United have had during their history. Having collected an Irish Cup winners' medal in 1960, he added to his tally with United, winning an FA Cup winners' medal in 1963 and two League championship medals, and he was a member of the side that won the European Cup. After over 500 appearances for United he was given a free transfer in 1973. He joined Bolton and retired in 1979. He then served on the coaching staff for two years.

1958   Jim Leighton born in Johnstone in Renfrewshire. Jim will forever be known not for his exploits on the field but for the match he was forced to miss: after a hesitant performance in the 1990 FA Cup final against Crystal Palace he was dropped for the replay, allowing Les Sealey to pick up a winners' medal. Jim had begun his career with Aberdeen in 1977 and was signed by United in June 1988 for £450,000, by which time he was established as Scotland's first-choice goalkeeper. Despite having won numerous honours in Scotland and having helped Aberdeen to the European Cup-Winners' Cup, he was unable to add to his tally at United, and following his omission from the 1990 FA Cup final replay side he was unable to reclaim his position. He was sold to Dundee for £200,000 in February 1992, later playing for Hibernian.

JULY 25TH

1993   Bryan Robson got sent off for using foul and abusive language during the friendly with Arsenal at Ellis Park, Johannesburg, in front of a crowd of 70,000.

JULY 26TH

1966   Bobby Charlton scored both goals as England beat Portugal 2-1 in the World Cup semi-final at Wembley. Nobby Stiles also played a significant part in keeping Portuguese star Eusebio relatively quiet throughout the game.

JULY 27TH

1957   Garry Birtles born in Nottingham. After signing for Nottingham Forest in 1976, Garry proved a quality striker for the City Ground club, winning a host of domestic and European honours. A £1.25 million move to United in 1980 followed, but he failed to live up to expectations and suffered a loss of confidence, resulting in a cut-price return to Forest for £250,000 in September 1987. After five years he crossed the Trent Bridge to play for Notts County and later finished his career with Grimsby Town.

1961   Ten years after they had first shown an interest in him, United signed David Herd. He had first impressed with Stockport County in 1951 when he had played in the same side as his father, but whilst Matt Busby hesitated about signing him, Arsenal moved in. A casual call to Arsenal had revealed they would now be willing to part with him for £38,000, and Busby caught the next train down to London to obtain Herd's signature.

JULY 28TH

1969   Both Bobby Charlton and George Best played for the Rest of the United Kingdom in a match against Wales at Cardiff. The game, part of the celebrations to mark the investiture of Prince Charles as the Prince of Wales, was won 1-0 by the United Kingdom side.

JULY 29TH

1996   Manchester United missed out as Alan Shearer signed for Newcastle United for a fee of £15 million, a new world record. It is believed that Shearer was all set to sign for the Manchester club until the intervention of Blackburn Rovers' benefactor Jack Walker.

JULY 30TH

1872   Joseph Cassidy born in Dalziel in Lanarkshire. Signed by Newton Heath in March 1893 shortly before the club were due to play a series of Test matches, Joseph played his part in helping them overcome Small Heath. He returned to Scotland at the end of the season but came back to Newton Heath two years later in March 1895. A scorer of many vital goals, Joseph scored four in the match against Walsall that was subsequently expunged from the records. He was sold to Manchester City for £250 in 1900, but was later released to Middlesbrough for £75 a year. After finishing his career as player-coach with Workington in 1906, little more was heard from him until 1916 when it was reported that he had suffered a mental breakdown.

1874   Billy Meredith born in Chirk, just inside the Welsh border with Shropshire. He began
       working down the pits at the age of 12 and later combined this with playing for the
       local side, winning his first major honour in the game when he collected a Welsh FA
       Cup winners' medal in 1894 following a 2-0 victory over Westminster Rovers. (The
       same year, Chirk reached the semi-finals of the FA Amateur Cup but, as the dates of
       the semi-finals clashed, they were forced to withdraw from the latter competition.)
       That same year Meredith also made appearances for Northwich Victoria and Wrexham
       but soon attracted attention from further afield and signed with Manchester City as an
       amateur in November 1894. Two months later he packed in his job at the pit and
       signed professional forms with City, receiving a signing-on fee of £5 for the privilege.

       He stayed with City for the next 12 seasons and was quickly established as a
       prolific goalscoring winger, despite efforts by his manager to switch him to centre-
       forward. With Meredith supplying vital crosses and even more vital goals, Manchester
       City were transformed from a club constantly struggling at the wrong end of the
       Second Division into one frequently battling for honours at the right end of the First
       Division. They won the Second Division championship in both 1899 and 1903, the FA
       Cup in 1904 and nearly pulled off the double the same year, finishing League runners-
       up, three points behind Sheffield Wednesday.

       The following season they were widely expected to go one better, and they entered
       the final straight just behind Newcastle United and Everton. Two weeks before the end
       of the season they won 2-0 at Everton in something of a battle, then won 3-0 at
       Wolves, and then, on the final week of League action, took on FA Cup winners Aston
       Villa at Villa Park. This match also developed into an unpleasant spectacle, with Alec
       Leake and Sandy Turnbull trading punches during the game, which City lost 3-2. The
       punch-up alone ensured the game would attract the attentions of the FA, but when
       their deliberations were announced, they caused a major sensation – Billy Meredith
       had been suspended from football for 12 months for attempting to bribe an Aston Villa
       player to throw the match. Meredith protested his innocence and claimed he had been
       made a scapegoat. Later he was reported to the FA for attempting to claim his normal
       wages, even though he was under suspension from the club and had been asked to
       refrain from turning up at the ground.

       As a result, the FA set up another commission to investigate matters at City. This
       time they found evidence of a wholesale disregard for the rules relating to bonus
       payments and instructed City that all of the players would have to be sold. Meredith
       finally admitted that he had indeed offered a bribe and was lucky to have escaped
       without being given a life ban from the game. Manchester City, aware that Manchester
       United were eyeing Meredith, attempted to place a £600 fee on his head; Meredith
       refused to allow any club to pay it – his view was that he had cost City nothing when
       he signed and should therefore cost nothing when he left. In truth, a transfer fee was
       paid: £500 went directly to Meredith and another £100 was given to the FA to pay off
       his fine.

       Meredith stayed with Manchester United until the 1920-21 season, winning two
       League championship medals and another FA Cup winners' medal. His time at United
       was also surrounded in controversy, not least the subsequent FA and League enquiry
       into the match between United and Liverpool played on Good Friday 1915. Meredith
       stated he had no idea that the match had been 'squared' (the result agreed before kick-
       off); others on his own team felt sure he knew far more than he indicated. He was not
       implicated by the FA, but the episode soured his feelings towards the club. When
       football resumed after the First World War, Meredith made only sporadic appearances,
       further upset because United insisted on putting a transfer fee on his head. He was
       finally released on a free in August 1921 and returned to Manchester City as player-

coach. He made a further 28 League appearances for City as a player before retiring in 1924. Even then the Meredith story had a final twist to it, for in that last season City made their way to the FA Cup semi-final, largely inspired by the performances of the by-now 49-year-old Billy Meredith. At St Andrew's, Birmingham, the dream finally died, as Newcastle United won through to Wembley.

If Meredith's actions on the field ensured frequent battles with the FA, then off the field was little different. He was the guiding light behind the formation of the Players' Union and a move to bring the players out on strike in 1907. He won 48 caps for Wales (although Meredith claimed it was 50 and was indeed given a special honour in recognition of 50 caps, but this figure includes two unofficial Victory internationals) and is reckoned to have picked up 61 medals during his playing career, as well as chewing a toothpick during almost every game he played! After his football days were finished, he ran various public houses and appeared in films, usually with a football connection.

1963   Neil Webb born in Reading. Like his father Doug, Neil began his professional career with Reading and was then sold to Portsmouth in 1982 for £87,500. Having helped Portsmouth win the Third Division championship, his abilities in midfield became known to a wider audience and Brian Clough paid £250,000 to take him to Nottingham Forest in 1985. There he developed into one of the best midfielders in the country, helping his club to win the League Cup in 1989 and receiving international recognition with England. He was sold to United in July 1989 for a fee fixed by the tribunal at £1.5 million and it seemed his career could only get better. Unfortunately an injury sustained whilst on international duty was far more serious than first thought, and although he returned to the side in time to collect an FA Cup winners' medal in 1990, his real effectiveness had been blunted. He was sold back to Forest for £800,000 in November 1992. He later played on loan at Swindon before being released on a free transfer and subsequently signing for Grimsby.

1966   Both Bobby Charlton and Nobby Stiles help England to a 4-2 win over West Germany in the World Cup final at Wembley.

JULY 31ST

1952   Jack Picken died in Deveonport. Born in Ayrshire in 1880, Jack first appeared in the Football League with Bolton, whom he joined in 1899, and he was a regular in the side until breaking a leg in 1902. He joined Plymouth in May 1903, despite not having played for over six months, but soon showed that the enforced lay-off had done little to dampen his goalscoring exploits, returning 46 goals in 89 appearances. In May 1905 he joined United and was leading scorer in his first season with the club, although he subsequently lost his place when they won the championship in 1908 and the FA Cup in 1909. Compensation was received when he qualified for a medal in the 1911 championship-winning side, the same season he qualified for a benefit. In December of that year he joined Burnley and he finished his career with Bristol City.

1971   Halifax Town   A   Watney Cup 1st Round   1-2

AUGUST 1ST

1932   A Scott Duncan took over as manager of United for a salary reputed to be £800 per annum. Since the sacking of Herbert Bamlett in 1931, team selection had been the responsibility of secretary Walter Crickmer and chief scout Louis Rocca, and so Duncan's appointment was warmly greeted by both the players and fans alike. Duncan had been a former player with Dumbarton, Glasgow Rangers and Newcastle United and had also earned the distinction of being one of the very few players to have appeared for both Celtic and Rangers, guesting for the Celtic club during the First World War whilst signed to Rangers. He also turned out once for Manchester United as a guest during the war. After steering United to the Second Division championship in 1935-36 Duncan was given a five-year contract extension, but after United were relegated once again in 1936-37 he resigned 14 games into the 1937-38 season and took over at Southern League side Ipswich Town, later guiding them into the Football League. Following his departure from United, the club operated without a proper manager until after the Second World War and the appointment of Matt Busby.

1970   Reading   A   Watney Cup 1st Round   3-2

AUGUST 2ND

1872   Frank Barrett born in Dundee. Frank joined Newton Heath in September 1896 from Dundee having already won two caps for Scotland and soon established himself as the first choice goalkeeper. In four seasons with the club he made over 100 League appearances and then moved on to Brighton Tower, returning briefly to Manchester to play for City and finishing his career in Scotland. He died at the comparatively young age of 35 in 1907.

1954   Sammy McIlroy born in Belfast. Signed by United as an apprentice in August 1969 and upgraded to the professional ranks in 1971. He made his debut in November the same year and went on to give the club over ten years' service, making nearly 400 appearances for the first team and scoring 70 goals. He won a Second Division championship medal and appeared in three FA Cup finals for the club, collecting a winners' medal in 1977. He was sold to Stoke City for £350,000 in 1982, making over 100 appearances for the Potteries club before joining Manchester City on a free transfer in August 1985. He later played for Preston, taking his number of League appearances beyond the 600 mark and was awarded an MBE.

1957   Ashley Grimes born in Dublin. Ashley had failed a trial period with United in 1972, and when they signed him from Bohemians in March 1977 he cost £20,000. A versatile defender or midfielder Ashley struggled to hold down a regular place in the side and was sold to Coventry in 1983 for £200,000. A year later he joined Luton and, after a spell in Spain, he accepted a coaching position at Stoke.

AUGUST 3RD

1911   Billy Behan born in Dublin. Although Billy made only one appearance for United, in goal against Bury in March 1934, he gave the club over 50 years' service as chief scout in the Irish Republic. He was responsible for recommending Johnny Carey, Billy Whelan, Johnny Giles, Tony Dunne, Gerry Daly, Kevin Moran and Paul McGrath to the club and only retired in 1987. He died in November 1991.

1997   Chelsea   Wembley   FA Charity Shield   1-1
Chelsea won the FA Charity Shield 4-1 on penalties after the game had been drawn 1-1.

AUGUST 4TH

1987   Manchester City   A   Manchester International Tournament   3-1
Manchester hosted its own International Tournament with a four-team competition between City, United, PSV Eindhoven and Athletico Mineiro. This was to be the only City/United derby of the season as City had been relegated from the First Division at the end of the previous season. United won 3-1 and went on to beat PSV by a similar score the following day and so hold the trophy, presented by Sir Matt Busby, in perpetuity.

AUGUST 5TH

1970   Hull City   A   Watney Cup Semi-Final   1-1

[aet – won 4-3 on penalties]

Although the competition was a pre-season tournament, United and Hull City did create history, becoming the first British clubs to take part in a penalty shoot-out after their Watney Cup semi-final had ended all square at 1-1 after extra time. United won the shoot-out 4-3 to advance to the final, where they were to meet Derby County.

1974   George Best made his debut appearance for Dunstable Town in a friendly against Manchester United Reserves and was mobbed off the field after Dunstable won 3-2.

1987   PSV Eindhoven   A   Manchester International Tournament   3-1

1991   Defender Paul Parker joined United from Queens Park Rangers after United had paid a transfer fee of £2 million.

AUGUST 6TH

1912   Bert Whalley born in Ashton-under-Lyne. Bert joined United in May 1934 having previously played for Stalybridge Celtic and after a proposed move to Stockport County had fallen through on a technicality. He made his debut for United in November 1935 and went on to make 36 appearances for the first team before the war broke out. He guested for United (where he made nearly 200 war-time appearances), Oldham, Liverpool and Bolton during the war and returned to Old Trafford when League football resumed in 1946. After only three games he dropped into the reserve team, but an eye injury ended his playing career and he switched to coaching. In conjunction with Matt Busby and Jimmy Murphy, Bert was responsible for producing a string of fine young players for United during the 1950s, and although Busby and Murphy invariably got most of the credit, Bert's role cannot be understated. In 1958 Murphy helped Wales qualify for the World Cup and was required in Cardiff whilst United were travelling to Belgrade for a European Cup tie. Bert took Murphy's place on the trip and lost his life when the plane crashed at Munich. He had given United over 20 years of dedicated service at the time of his death.

AUGUST 7TH

1939   Charlie Roberts died in Manchester. One of the central figures in the development of Manchester United, he was born in Darlington on 6th April 1883 and began his professional career with Grimsby Town in 1903. A fee of £600 took him to Clayton in April 1904 and he soon became installed as captain within the team. He led the club to their greatest moments in the period prior to the First World War – two League championships and an FA Cup – and was an inspirational figure on the field for his team-mates. He was equally involved off the field too, helping found the Players' Union and remaining its chairman until 1921, and was instrumental in the numerous clashes between the union and the game's rulers. He joined Oldham as a player in 1913, retiring from playing during the war and being appointed manager in June 1921. He resigned in December 1922, claiming that nothing could replace the excitement of playing. He then became a wholesale tobacconist.

1972   George Best broke a hand in training (for Manchester United, despite his threats to leave the club and join one of the London clubs) and was therefore doubtful for Saturday's match.

1978   Real Madrid   H   Centenary Match   4-0

1993   Arsenal   Wembley FA Charity Shield   1-1

Both goals were scored in the first half, Wright for Arsenal and Mark Hughes for United, and so the game was settled on penalties. United won the shoot-out 5-4.

AUGUST 8TH

| 1959 | Bayern Munich | A | Friendly | 2-1 |
| 1970 | Derby County | A | Watney Cup Final | 1-4 |

1987   The Football League launched their centenary season with a match between a League side and a World XI, selected by Barcelona manager Terry Venables, at Wembley in front of 61,000 fans. The Football League XI ran out 3-0 winners with goals from Bryan Robson (two) and his United team-mate Norman Whiteside.

AUGUST 9TH

1933   Albert Quixall born in Sheffield. Signed by Sheffield Wednesday in May 1948 he was taken on as a professional in August 1950, making his League debut at the age of 17 and winning his first England cap three years later. In September 1958 he was sold to United for a then record fee of £45,000, his experience being vital to Old Trafford in the wake of the Munich disaster. In his six years at United he won an FA Cup winners' medal in 1963, but injury led to him being sold to Oldham for £8,500 in September 1964. He won a total of five caps for England and also collected Second Division championship medals with Sheffield Wednesday in 1952 and 1956.

1958   Gary Bailey born in Ipswich. Gary was living in Johannesburg when he was recommended to United in 1978 and quickly impressed, earning a contract and making his debut in November 1978 against Ipswich. A regular in goal thereafter, he won FA Cup winners' medals in 1983 and 1985 and broke into the England squad, although it was an injury sustained during an England training session in February 1986 that effectively ended his career. He was released by United in September 1987 and returned to South Africa to play for the Kaiser Chiefs.

| 1969 | Crystal Palace | A | First Division | 2-2 |

AUGUST 10TH

1909   Barely four months after winning the FA Cup for the first time in their history, United suspended the entire playing staff for refusing to resign from their trade union! The likes of Billy Meredith and John Bell had been instrumental in forming the Players Union in 1907, and as their influence had grown so had resentment and opposition from the game's rulers. The FA had decreed that the contracts signed by players with their clubs should have a clause disowning the union, and although many players had agreed to the clause, those at United did not. The club therefore took the unprecedented step of suspending all those who had refused to sign, an action which severely disrupted pre-season training. Captain Charlie Roberts had instructed the players to make their way to the Manchester Athletic Club in Fallowfield today (hired at the players' own expense) in order that training could be conducted. Although the players had had their summer pay withheld by the club for refusing to sign their contracts, they were all firmly behind the struggle for recognition for their union. Viewed as 'outcasts' they cheerfully agreed to pose for a photograph, Charlie Roberts chalking a defiant 'The Outcasts F.C.' on a board placed in front of the group. As publicity for the group spread, so did support, and players at other clubs began to side with their United counterparts. As the new season beckoned, there was the very real prospect that the League would have to be suspended as defiance against the FA was growing.

| 1968 | Everton | H | First Division | 2-1 |

1971   Roy Keane born in Cork. Spotted whilst playing for Cobh Ramblers by Nottingham Forest, he cost Forest £10,000 in June 1990 and quickly established himself as a competitive midfield player. An FA Cup final appearance at the end of his first season was followed by his first cap for the Republic of Ireland the same month. In July 1993 he was signed by United for a fee of £3.75 million and has since helped the club to three Premiership titles and two FA Cups. He suffered a serious injury midway through the 1997-98 season which sidelined him for many months.

| 1985 | Everton | Wembley | FA Charity Shield | 0-2 |
| 1997 | Tottenham Hotspur | A | FA Premier League | 2-0 |

AUGUST 11TH

| 1991 | Northern Ireland XI | H | Sir Matt Busby Testimonial | 1-1 |

Sir Matt Busby was granted a testimonial with 33,000 attending the game between the current United team and a Northern Ireland XI. The 1-1 draw yielded gate receipts of £250,000.

| 1996 | Newcastle United | Wembley | FA Charity Shield | 4-0 |

Despite the presence of Alan Shearer in the Newcastle side, Manchester United won as easily as the scoreline suggests thanks to goals from Eric Cantona, Nicky Butt, David Beckham and Roy Keane.

AUGUST 12TH

| 1967 | Tottenham Hotspur | H | FA Charity Shield | 3-3 |

The traditional curtain-raiser to the new football season, the FA Charity Shield, was played at Old Trafford between League champions Manchester United and FA Cup holders Spurs and ended in a 3-3 draw, with both clubs sharing the trophy for six months. One of Spurs' goals was scored by their goalkeeper Pat Jennings, whose long range punt found Alex Stepney stranded in the middle of his area. The ball bounced over his head and into the net! This game also saw Bobby Charlton booked for the only time in his career, although as it was for time-wasting and United were 3-2 behind at the time, it was a difficult decision to understand. The referee chose not to make reference of the booking in his match report.

| 1972 | Ipswich Town | H | First Division | 1-2 |

AUGUST 13TH

| 1969 | Everton | H | First Division | 0-2 |
| 1977 | Liverpool | Wembley | FA Charity Shield | 0-0 |

Although there were no goals and each side got to retain the shield for six months, the most controversial incident occurred when Emelyn Hughes pulled David McCreery down inside the penalty area. Although the lineman waved to indicate a penalty, the referee thought he was too far away from the incident to be certain it had been a penalty!

| 1989 | Manchester City | H | Mike Duxbury Testimonial | 0-2 |
| 1997 | Southampton | H | FA Premier League | 1-0 |

AUGUST 14TH

| 1965 | Liverpool | H | FA Charity Shield | 2-2 |

A crowd of 48,502 saw two evenly matched sides produce a thrilling curtain-raiser to the new season. Goals from George Best and David Herd were cancelled out by those from Yeats and Stevenson and each side retained the shield for six months.

1968	West Bromwich Albion	A	First Division	1-3
1971	Derby County	A	First Division	2-2
1979	United clinched the signing of midfielder Ray Wilkins for a club record fee of £850,000, linking the player once more with the manager who had signed him as a 15-year-old at Chelsea, Dave Sexton.			
1994	Blackburn Rovers	Wembley	FA Charity Shield	2-0

The FIFA-inspired refereeing clampdown resulted in seven players being booked in the FA Charity Shield between last season's double winners United, and the League runners-up Blackburn Rovers. Rovers had four men booked, United three in the 2-0 win for United. The respective managers, Kenny Dalglish of Rovers and Alex Ferguson of United, disagreed after the game over the impact the new rulings were likely to have – Dalglish felt that at the rate the game was going there would be no tackles at all, whilst Ferguson had no complaints about any of the bookings his side had picked up. In a break with tradition, Blackburn were led out on to the pitch by their benefactor Jack Walker rather than by the manager.

AUGUST 15TH

1905 Tommy Reid born in Motherwell. Tommy began his career with Clydebank in 1925 before a £1,000 deal took him to Liverpool in April 1926. Three years later he switched to Old Trafford and proved a worthwhile acquisition, scoring twice on his debut and going on to register a total of 67 goals in 101 appearances for the first team. In March 1933 he was loaned to Oldham, performing so well for the Latics that the supporters association donated the £400 required to make the move permanent. He later played for Barrow and then in the non-League game before dying in Liverpool in 1972.

1970	Leeds United	H	First Division	0-1
1972	Liverpool	A	First Division	0-2
1987	Southampton	A	First Division	2-2
1992	Sheffield United	A	FA Premier League	1-2
1993	Norwich City	A	FA Premier League	2-0

AUGUST 16TH

1969	Southampton	H	First Division	1-4
1975	Wolverhampton Wanderers	A	First Division	2-0
1980	Middlesbrough	H	First Division	3-0

1991 United and the rest of the First Division resigned from the First Division. The following day all these clubs signed founder member documents for the new Premier League, due to be introduced in season 1992-93. The First Division clubs also informed the current Second Division that they would not be members of the Premier League but would be offered three promotion places.

AUGUST 17TH

| 1963 | Everton | A | FA Charity Shield | 0-4 |

The League champions proved a little too powerful for the FA Cup holders as Everton won the FA Charity Shield 4-0 in front of a crowd of 54,840 at Goodison Park.

1968	Manchester City	A	First Division	0-0
1974	Orient	A	Second Division	2-0
1985	Aston Villa	H	First Division	4-0
1991	Notts County	H	First Division	2-0
1996	Wimbledon	A	FA Premier League	3-0

The BBC's 'Goal of the Season' competition was declared over following David Beckham's amazing lob over Sullivan in the Wimbledon goal – for David was inside his own half when he took the shot!

AUGUST 18TH

1924 Tommy Meehan died in London. Born in Manchester in 1896, he joined United from Rochdale in June 1917 although had to wait until the end of the First World War before making his League debut. He remained at United until December 1920 when Chelsea paid £3,300 to take him south. An England international, he died in St George's Hospital and a fund was set up to assist his widow and four children, raising £1,580.

1946   Tony Fitzpatrick born in Aberdeen. He joined United's groundstaff in September 1961 and rose through the ranks to full professional status in September 1963. Although he began his career as a half-back, it was a switch to full-back that led to an extended run in the team, although a succession of cartilage problems dogged his career. He had made 141 appearances for the first team when he was advised to retire in July 1973 at the age of only 26.

1951	West Bromwich Albion	A	First Division	3-3
1956	Birmingham City	H	First Division	2-2
1962	West Bromwich Albion	H	First Division	2-2
1971	Chelsea	A	First Division	3-2
1979	Southampton	A	First Division	1-1
1993	Sheffield United	H	FA Premier League	3-0

AUGUST 19TH

1912   As the new football season beckoned there was considerable transfer speculation within the media. United were known to have rejected offers of £1,200 from Blackburn Rovers for Enoch West and another of £1,500 from Manchester City for Charlie Roberts, but up until this date no one was aware that City were actually negotiating with United manager Ernest Mangnall with a view to installing him as their new manager! City had received a total of 107 applications for the position of secretary (the title of manager did not officially exist at this time, although the secretary was invariably responsible for picking the team) but had shortlisted only three, including Ernest Mangnall. As Mangnall had guided United to two Leage titles and an FA Cup win during his time at the club, it seemed a strange move to make, but perhaps the events of an emergency board meeting, held this evening, hid the true reasons. United announced they had been unable to make Mangnall change his mind about leaving, but one can only wonder how hard they tried. Certainly, the events of the next couple of years, which saw City rise towards the top of the table and United slump in the opposite direction, showed that the United board had badly erred in allowing Mangnall to leave. Although the First World War intervened and halted his work for a considerable time, he was largely responsible for getting the club through severe financial difficulties at the time and later instigated the building of their new ground at Maine Road. He left City in 1924 and died in September 1932. His importance to United, however, can never be understated, for following his departure it took over 40 years before they had anyone as influential in charge again.

1939	Manchester City	H	Jubilee Fund	1-1
1944	Manchester City	A	Friendly	2-2
1950	Fulham	H	First Division	1-0
1953	Chelsea	H	First Division	1-1

1958   Although United had finished the previous season in eighth place in the First Division, UEFA offered them a place in the European Cup as a token of respect, a move that was initially approved by the Football Association. They later had a change of mind and following pressure from both the FA and Football League, United withdrew from the competition, even though they had been drawn against Young Boys Berne in the qualifying round of the competition. This would give Young Boys a walkover into the next round, and they reached the semi-finals of the competition in this season.

1961	West Ham United	A	First Division	1-1
1967	Everton	A	First Division	1-3

1969	Everton	A	First Division	0-3
1970	Chelsea	H	First Division	0-0
1972	Everton	A	First Division	0-2
1975	Birmingham City	A	First Division	2-0

Strangest injury of the day – United goalkeeper Alex Stepney dislocated his jaw whilst shouting at a team-mate during the 2-0 win at Birmingham and was taken to hospital!

1978	Birmingham City	H	First Division	1-0
1980	Wolverhampton Wanderers	A	First Division	0-1
1987	Arsenal	H	First Division	0-0
1989	Arsenal	H	First Division	4-1

Manchester United unveiled a new signing – would-be chairman Michael Knighton, who bounced on to the pitch before the opening game of the season complete with United kit and went through a number of ball juggling exercises. More soberly dressed for the boardroom, it was revealed Knighton was offering £20 million to buy out Martin Edwards and provide a further £10 million for the modernisation of the Stretford End. Within two months, all of Knighton's balls had come crashing to the ground – he had no money of his own to buy the shares and none of the other millionaires he had approached were prepared to help with his package. He therefore withdrew from the deal, although he was given a seat on the United board to compensate him for his expenditure!

| 1992 | Everton | H | FA Premier League | 0-3 |
| 1995 | Aston Villa | A | FA Premier League | 1-3 |

Alex Ferguson came in for some considerable criticism following this opening day defeat, for instead of the likes of Paul Ince and Mark Hughes, both of whom had departed from other clubs, came a new reliance on youth. According to his critics, this defeat indicated he was wrong, although Alex would have the last laugh come the end of the season: United won the double for a second time!

AUGUST 20TH

| 1938 | Manchester City | A | Jubilee Fund | 1-2 |
| 1949 | Derby County | A | First Division | 1-0 |

On the same day, Stewart Houston was born in Dunoon in Argyle. After unsuccessful spells with Chelsea and Brentford, Stewart was signed by United for £55,000 in 1973 and became a mainstay of the defence over the next few seasons. A member of the side that won the Second Division in 1975, he appeared in the 1976 FA Cup final which United lost and seemed sure of a place in the following year's side which won. Unfortunately, two weeks before the final he suffered torn ankle ligaments and had to sit and watch Arthur Albiston take his place. Albiston offered Stewart his winners' medal at the end of the game, a gesture that was declined with gratitude. He was sold to Sheffield United in 1980 and later had spells coaching with Colchester and Plymouth before joining Arsenal's backroom staff as assistant manager. More recently he was manager at QPR.

1955	Birmingham City	A	First Division	2-2
1956	Preston North End	A	First Division	3-1
1960	Blackburn Rovers	H	First Division	1-3
1966	West Bromwich Albion	H	First Division	5-3
1971	Arsenal	H	First Division	3-1

As Old Trafford had been closed by the Football League following a knife throwing incident during a League match with Newcastle, United were forced to play this home match at Anfield. A crowd of 27,649 saw United win thanks to goals from Bobby Charlton, Alan Gowling and Brian Kidd.

| 1977 | Birmingham City | A | First Division | 4-1 |
| 1983 | Liverpool | Wembley | FA Charity Shield | 2-0 |

This was the first time in many a year that the FA Cup holders had beaten the League champions in the FA Charity Shield, but two goals from Bryan Robson were enough to give United victory over Liverpool. It was the Anfield club's first defeat in the shield since they had lost 1-0 to Leicester in 1971.

| 1985 | Ipswich Town | A | First Division | 1-0 |
| 1994 | Queens Park Rangers | H | FA Premier League | 2-0 |

AUGUST 21ST

1943	Manchester City	A	Friendly	2-2
1948	Derby County	H	First Division	1-2
1954	Portsmouth	H	First Division	1-3
1965	Sheffield Wednesday	H	First Division	1-0

Noel Cantwell was named as United's first ever substitute, although he was not used during the game, the honour of becoming the first substitute used going to Tony Fitzpatrick.

1968	Coventry City	H	First Division	1-0
1976	Birmingham City	H	First Division	2-2
1988	Manchester City	H	Kevin Moran Testimonial	5-2
1991	Aston Villa	A	First Division	1-0
1993	Newcastle United	H	FA Premier League	1-1
1996	Everton	H	FA Premier League	2-2

AUGUST 22ND

| 1942 | Manchester City | A | Friendly | 5-1 |
| 1951 | Middlesbrough | H | First Division | 4-2 |

Jack Rowley's blistering start to the season continued with a second consecutive hat-trick. He had scored three goals in the opening day draw with West Bromwich Albion and would go on to score 30 goals in the League in the championship season. United's other goal was scored by Stan Pearson.

1953	Liverpool	A	First Division	4-4
1959	West Bromwich Albion	A	First Division	2-3
1962	Everton	A	First Division	1-3
1964	West Bromwich Albion	H	First Division	2-2
1970	Arsenal	A	First Division	0-4
1979	West Bromwich Albion	H	First Division	2-0
1987	Watford	H	First Division	2-0
1989	Crystal Palace	A	First Division	1-1
1992	Ipswich Town	H	FA Premier League	1-1
1994	Nottingham Forest	A	FA Premier League	1-1

AUGUST 23RD

1913 Twelve months earlier Manchester United had allowed Ernest Mangnall to quit as manager and take up a similar post at Manchester City. Such an action was not the end of the comings and goings at Old Trafford either, with the more bizarre concerning the goings. In the space of 12 months, some of the most important cogs of the team that had won the League title in 1911 were sold off: Alex Bell joined Blackburn Rovers for £1,000, Harry Moger had moved on, and then came the biggest bombshell, with Charlie Roberts sold to Oldham Athletic for £1,500. Not for the first, nor for the last time there was more to the transfer than met the eye. United were in considerable financial difficulties and still trying to recover from the near £100,000 investment building Old Trafford had cost them. Against such a sum, £1,500 seems small change, but Roberts was also hankering after a second benefit match. It was customary during this age to give a benefit match, at which almost the entire gate receipts were handed over to the player, as a mark of so many years' service. But Roberts had already had a benefit match, which had realised over £900 for the player, and United felt he was being greedy in asking for another handout. Besides, in so doing they would have deprived a younger player of his benefit match. Selling Roberts therefore brought the club nearer to £2,500! Interestingly enough, Alex Bell was also sold after requesting a second benefit match, whilst other players at the club were known to be in dispute over theirs as well! Charlie Roberts galvanised the Oldham side just as he had done at United, and in 1914-15 led the club to second spot in the League, a tantalising one point behind Everton. When football stopped for the First World War, so did Charlie Roberts – only he gave up for good. He would later spend some 18 months in charge at Boundary Park, but nothing could ever replace the thrill of playing, and he quit in order to run a tobacconist's shop.

1947	Middlesbrough	A	First Division	2-2
1948	Blackpool	A	First Division	3-0
1950	Liverpool	A	First Division	1-2
1952	Chelsea	H	First Division	2-0
1954	Sheffield Wednesday	A	First Division	4-2
1958	Chelsea	H	First Division	5-2
1961	Chelsea	H	First Division	3-2
1966	Everton	A	First Division	2-1
1967	Leeds United	H	First Division	1-0
1969	Wolverhampton Wanderers	A	First Division	0-0
1971	West Bromwich Albion	H	First Division	3-1

This was the second 'home' match United were forced to play away from Old Trafford, with Stoke's Victoria Ground welcoming 23,146 fans for the clash with West Bromwich Albion. A brace of goals from George Best and a single strike from Alan Gowling secured victory for United.

1972	Leicester City	H	First Division	1-1
1975	Sheffield United	H	First Division	5-1
1978	Leeds United	A	First Division	3-2
1980	Birmingham City	A	First Division	0-0
1986	Arsenal	A	First Division	0-1
1993	Aston Villa	A	FA Premier League	2-1
1995	West Ham United	H	FA Premier League	2-1
1997	Leicester City	A	FA Premier League	0-0

AUGUST 24TH

1928 Tommy Docherty born in Glasgow. He began his playing career with Preston in 1949 and helped them to the 1954 FA Cup final before moving on to Arsenal in 1958. He was unfortunate to break his leg whilst playing for Arsenal against Preston and later moved to Chelsea, where he became senior coach. Later appointed manager, he took the club to the 1965 League Cup final which they won and 1967 FA Cup final which they lost. He then spent brief spells with Rotherham, QPR, Aston Villa and Porto before accepting the post of manager of Scotland. This was also shortlived for he then took over from Frank O'Farrell as manager at Old Trafford. After guiding the club to successive FA Cup finals he was sensationally sacked following the revelation that he was having an affair with the wife of Laurie Brown. He later managed Derby and

Preston before becoming a radio personality and regular on the after-dinner circuit.

| 1949 | Bolton Wanderers | H | First Division | 3-0 |

The moment every United fan had waited eight years for finally arrived with the visit of Bolton to Old Trafford, the first visitors since the Luftwaffe! A crowd of 41,748 saw Charlie Mitten score the first goal, and later strikes by Jack Rowley and an own goal completed United's win. There was still much work to be done to Old Trafford, but United's fans could not have cared less on this day – they were back home where they belonged.

1955	Tottenham Hotspur	H	First Division	2-2
1957	Leicester City	A	First Division	3-0
1960	Everton	A	First Division	0-4
1963	Sheffield Wednesday	A	First Division	3-3
1964	West Ham United	A	First Division	1-3
1965	Nottingham Forest	A	First Division	2-4
1968	Chelsea	H	First Division	0-4
1974	Millwall	H	Second Division	4-0
1976	Coventry City	A	First Division	2-0
1977	Coventry City	H	First Division	2-1
1985	Arsenal	A	First Division	2-1
1991	Everton	A	First Division	0-0
1992	Southampton	A	FA Premier League	1-0

AUGUST 25TH

1923	Bristol City	A	Second Division	2-1
1928	Leicester City	H	First Division	1-1
1934	Bradford City	H	Second Division	2-0
1945	Huddersfield Town	A	Football League North	2-3

Bill McKay made his last appearance for United. Born in West Benhar in Lanarkshire, he had joined United in March 1934 from Bolton and went on to make over 170 appearances in the League side at half-back. He arrived at a time when the club were desperately battling against relegation to the Third Division, with Bill and three other new acquisitions playing key roles in the ultimately successful fight. He then helped the club with the Second Division title in 1935-36 and during the war guested for Stockport County and Port Vale. He finished his playing career with Stalybridge Celtic in 1946.

1951	Newcastle United	H	First Division	2-1
1956	West Bromwich Albion	A	First Division	3-2
1962	Arsenal	A	First Division	3-1
1970	Burnley	A	First Division	2-0
1973	Arsenal	A	First Division	0-3
1979	Arsenal	A	First Division	0-0
1984	Watford	H	First Division	1-1
1986	West Ham United	H	First Division	2-3

| 1989 | | | | |

United paid a club record fee of £2 million for West Ham midfielder Paul Ince. The deal was no surprise, for Ince had already been photographed in a Manchester United kit before the deal came to light and alienated himself from the West Ham fans. He had been dropped from their side for a match against Bradford City and had watched from the stands, but had had to leave early owing to abuse from the fans.

| 1990 | Coventry City | H | First Division | 2-0 |
| 1996 | Blackburn Rovers | H | FA Premier League | 2-2 |

AUGUST 26TH

1922	Crystal Palace	H	Second Division	2-1
1933	Plymouth Argyle	A	Second Division	0-4
1939	Grimsby Town	H	First Division	4-0
1944	Everton	A	Football League North (First Championship)	2-1
1950	Bolton Wanderers	A	First Division	0-1

1951 Jeff Wealands born in Darlington. He began his career with Wolves in 1968 and after a brief spell on loan with Northampton joined his hometown club Darlington in 1970. After further service with Hull and Birmingham he was loaned to United in February 1983, the deal becoming permanent in August 1983 for a fee of £30,000. Jeff had already been pressed into service in United's goal whilst on loan, deputising for the injured Gary Bailey, but Jeff was to suffer his own injury problems with his back and after loan spells with Oldham and Preston joined non-League Altrincham in May 1985.

1953	West Bromwich Albion	H	First Division	1-3
1959	Chelsea	H	First Division	0-1
1961	Blackburn Rovers	H	First Division	6-1
1967	Leicester City	H	First Division	1-1
1972	Arsenal	H	First Division	0-0
1978	Ipswich Town	A	First Division	0-3
1985	West Ham United	H	First Division	2-0
1989	Derby County	A	First Division	0-2
1995	Wimbledon	H	FA Premier League	3-1

AUGUST 27TH

1921	Everton	A	First Division	0-5
1923	Southampton	H	Second Division	1-0
1927	Middlesbrough	H	First Division	3-0
1928	Aston Villa	A	First Division	0-0
1932	Stoke City	H	Second Division	0-2
1938	Middlesbrough	A	First Division	1-3
1947	Liverpool	H	First Division	2-0
1949	West Bromwich Albion	H	First Division	1-1
1952	Arsenal	A	First Division	1-2
1955	West Bromwich Albion	H	First Division	3-1

The growing success of the youth team, already dubbed the Busby Babes, was beginning to make its presence felt in the first team, and United today selected the youngest ever side to have represented the club at first-team level. The average age of the side was just 22 years and 106 days.

1958	Nottingham Forest	A	First Division	3-0
1966	Leeds United	A	First Division	1-3
1969	Newcastle United	H	First Division	0-0
1975	Coventry City	H	First Division	1-1
1977	Ipswich Town	H	First Division	0-0
1980	Coventry City	H	League Cup 2nd Round 1st Leg	0-1
1983	Queens Park Rangers	H	First Division	3-1
1988	Queens Park Rangers	H	First Division	0-0
1994	Tottenham Hotspur	A	FA Premier League	1-0
1997	Everton	A	FA Premier League	2-0

AUGUST 28TH

1920	Bolton Wanderers	H	First Division	2-3
1922	Sheffield Wednesday	A	Second Division	0-1
1926	Liverpool	A	First Division	2-4
1937	Newcastle United	H	Second Division	3-0
1943	Stockport County	H	Football League North (First Championship)	6-0
1948	Arsenal	A	First Division	1-0
1954	Blackpool	A	First Division	4-2
1957	Everton	H	First Division	3-0
1963	Ipswich Town	H	First Division	2-0
1965	Northampton Town	A	First Division	1-1
1968	Tottenham Hotspur	H	First Division	3-1
1971	Wolverhampton Wanderers	A	First Division	1-1
1974	Portsmouth	H	Second Division	2-1
1976	Derby County	A	First Division	0-0
1982	Birmingham City	H	First Division	3-0
1984	Southampton	A	First Division	0-0
1990	Leeds United	A	First Division	0-0
1991	Oldham Athletic	H	First Division	1-0
1993	Southampton	A	FA Premier League	3-1
1995	Blackburn Rovers	A	FA Premier League	2-1

Referee David Elleray booked seven players in a fiercely contested match between the top two sides of the previous season, but the most contentious moment came with the dismissal of Roy Keane, who was sent off for diving. Despite this setback United still managed to win thanks to goals from Lee Sharpe and David Beckham.

AUGUST 29TH

1908	Queens Park Rangers	Stamford Bridge		
		FA Charity Shield Replay		4-0

Whilst United had taken part in the first FA Charity Shield match reluctantly, citing a gruelling League season as the main reason, the summer break had recharged their batteries and they were much more enthusiastic about the replay. A crowd of some 60,000 (although the figure is sometimes quoted as 40,000 in some sources) packed into Stamford Bridge, despite the attraction of the Olympic Games taking place a few miles up the road at White City, and saw United take control right from the start. It was an exceptional performance from United, with Jimmy Turnbull helping himself to a hat-trick and George Wall completing the scoring. Indeed, United's victory also helped establish the FA Charity Shield as the perfect curtain-raiser for a new season.

1921	West Bromwich Albion	H	First Division	2-3
1925	West Ham United	A	First Division	0-1
1927	Sheffield Wednesday	A	First Division	2-0
1931	Bradford Park Avenue	A	Second Division	1-3
1932	Charlton Athletic	A	Second Division	1-0
1936	Wolverhampton Wanderers	H	First Division	1-1
1942	Everton	A	Football League North (First Championship)	2-2
1951	Middlesbrough	A	First Division	4-1
1953	Newcastle United	H	First Division	1-1
1956	Preston North End	H	First Division	3-2

On the same day, Viv Anderson was born in Nottingham. He began his professional career with Nottingham Forest in 1974 and helped the club to the First Division title in 1978, the European Cup in 1979 and 1980 and League Cup honours in 1979 and

1980. He then signed with Arsenal in 1984 where he won a further League Cup winners' medal and was signed by Manchester United in July 1987 for £250,000. Although he failed to add to his medal tally, he was a more than capable squad member and was given a free transfer in January 1991 upon which he joined Sheffield Wednesday. After a spell in charge as player-manager at Barnsley he linked up with Bryan Robson at Middlesbrough.

1959	Newcastle United	H	First Division	3-2
1962	Everton	H	First Division	0-1
1964	Leicester City	A	First Division	2-2
1970	West Ham United	H	First Division	1-1
1973	Stoke City	H	First Division	1-0
1979	Tottenham Hotspur	A	League Cup 2nd Round 1st Leg	1-2
1981	Coventry City	A	First Division	1-2
1983	Nottingham Forest	H	First Division	1-2
1987	Charlton Athletic	A	First Division	3-1
1992	Nottingham Forest	A	FA Premier League	2-0

AUGUST 30TH

| 1919 | Derby County | A | First Division | 1-1 |

After a break of four years, League football resumed once again. The fixtures were exactly the same as those of the 1915-16 season, had it taken place, but the line-ups were considerably different. Some of those who had been on United's books had been injured or lost their lives during the Great War; others had retired, West was banned and Meredith was in dispute with the club. Only four players from the pre-war era were still in the line-up, and it was one of these, Woodcock, who opened the scoring for United, only to see Derby later equalise.

1920	Arsenal	A	First Division	0-2
1924	Leicester City	H	Second Division	1-0
1926	Sheffield Wednesday	A	First Division	2-2
1930	Aston Villa	H	First Division	3-4
1933	Nottingham Forest	H	Second Division	0-1
1937	Coventry City	A	Second Division	0-1
1939	Chelsea	A	First Division	1-1
1941	New Brighton	H	Football League Northern Section (First Championship)	13-1

The opening day of the season saw United register one of their biggest ever wins, although as it was in a war-time competition the score does not officially count. The goals were scored by Jack Rowley, who grabbed seven, John Smith (three), Billy Bryant (two) and Charlie Mitten. Owing to crowd restrictions the attendance was only 2,000.

1947	Charlton Athletic	H	First Division	6-2
1950	Liverpool	H	First Division	1-0
1952	Manchester City	A	First Division	1-2

League champions United may have started the match against their local rivals as favourites, but form seldom counts for much in the Manchester battles. So it proved at Maine Road where Roy Clarke gave the home side the lead after being put through by Ivor Broadis, with Broadis later adding the second himself. Although John Downie pulled one back with a quarter of an hour left on the clock and set up a furious final charge by United, City held on to register their first derby win since 1937.

| 1958 | Blackpool | A | First Division | 1-2 |
| 1961 | Chelsea | A | First Division | 0-2 |

1969	Sunderland	H	First Division	3-1
1972	Chelsea	H	First Division	0-0
1975	Stoke City	A	First Division	1-0
1977	Arsenal	A	League Cup 2nd Round	2-3
1978	Stockport County	A	League Cup 2nd Round	3-2

Although Stockport County were drawn at home, the match was switched to Old Trafford and a crowd of 41,761 saw goals from Sammy McIlroy, Jimmy Greenhoff and Joe Jordan help United to a 3-2 victory.

1980	Sunderland	H	First Division	1-1
1986	Charlton Athletic	H	First Division	0-1
1989	Norwich City	H	First Division	0-2
1997	Coventry City	H	FA Premier League	3-0

AUGUST 31ST

1909　The dispute between the Football Association and the Players' Union had grown over the previous few weeks to such an extent there was now a real threat that the Football League season, due to start the following day, would have to be postponed. Whilst it was the Manchester United players who had been the most resolute throughout the dispute, support for their actions had grown and players from Newcastle, Sunderland, Middlesbrough, Liverpool and Everton had soon joined with their Manchester counterparts. This forced the FA to the bargaining table and an agreement was hammered out at the eleventh hour: the players had the right to join the Union and the FA would recognise it, only if the Union in turn dropped plans to affiliate with the General Federation of Trade Unions. It has to be said that Charles Roberts was suspended by his club and therefore not admitted to the meeting, even though he had been one of the main instigators in the rebellion. One could therefore question whether it would have taken the Players' Union, which did later affiliate with the TUC, the 50 years or so it took to win rights over pay and transfers had Charlie Roberts been present. As it was, the agreement meant the League season could take place as arranged.

1929	Newcastle United	A	First Division	1-4
1935	Plymouth Argyle	A	Second Division	1-3
1938	Bolton Wanderers	H	First Division	2-2
1940	Rochdale	A	North Regional League	3-1
1946	Grimsby Town	H	First Division	2-1

The Football League resumed action for the first time since the Second World War with exactly the same fixtures as had been drawn up for the abandoned 1939-40 season. Then, United had beaten Grimsby 4-0; this time around the game was much closer, and a crowd of 41,025 were present at Maine Road (Old Trafford was still closed owing to bomb damage) to see the game. Much had changed in the intervening seven years, with only three of the United players who had taken part in the 1939 clash playing today.

1949	Bolton Wanderers	A	First Division	2-1
1955	Tottenham Hotspur	A	First Division	2-1
1957	Manchester City	H	First Division	4-1
1960	Everton	H	First Division	4-0
1963	Everton	H	First Division	5-1
1966	Everton	H	First Division	3-0
1968	Sheffield Wednesday	A	First Division	4-5
1971	Everton	A	First Division	0-1
1974	Cardiff City	A	Second Division	1-0

1981	Nottingham Forest	H	First Division	0-0
1985	Nottingham Forest	A	First Division	3-1
1987	Chelsea	H	First Division	3-1
1991	Leeds United	H	First Division	1-1
1994	Wimbledon	H	FA Premier League	3-0

SEPTEMBER 1ST

| 1896 | Gainsborough Trinity | H | Second Division | 2-0 |

On the same day, Ray Bennion was born in Wrexham. He joined United in April 1921 and went on to make over 300 appearances for the first team as well as ten caps for Wales. He turned down United's terms for the 1932-33 season and moved on to Burnley, remaining as a player for one season before joining their coaching staff. He held the position for the next 30 years until ill-health forced him to relinquish his position as head trainer, although he remained on the staff. He died in Burnley on 12th March 1968.

| 1900 | Glossop | A | Second Division | 0-1 |

Newton Heath gave a debut to Alf Schofield. He began his career with Everton in 1895, making his debut the following year and joined the Heathens in August 1900, where he was to replace Billy Bryant. He remained with the club until 1907 (by which time it had become Manchester United), his place on the wing having effectively been taken over by Billy Meredith.

1906	Bristol City	A	First Division	2-1
1909	Bradford City	H	First Division	1-0
1910	Woolwich Arsenal	A	First Division	2-1
1917	Blackburn Rovers	A	Lancashire Section Principal Tournament	5-0
1919	Sheffield Wednesday	H	First Division	0-0
1923	Bristol City	H	Second Division	2-1
1924	Stockport County	A	Second Division	1-2
1928	Manchester City	A	First Division	2-2
1934	Sheffield United	A	Second Division	2-3
1945	Huddersfield Town	H	Football League North	2-3
1948	Blackpool	H	First Division	3-4
1951	Bolton Wanderers	A	First Division	0-1
1954	Sheffield Wednesday	H	First Division	2-0
1956	Portsmouth	H	First Division	3-0

| 1959 | Mike Duxbury born in Accrington. He joined United in May 1975, signing |

professional forms in October 1976. He made his debut in September 1980 and went on to make 343 first-team appearances, including the cup finals of 1983 and 1985. A knee injury in 1988-89 restricted his first-team opportunities and he was given a free transfer in 1990, joining Blackburn. He later joined Bradford City.

1962	Birmingham City	H	First Division	2-0
1965	Nottingham Forest	H	First Division	0-0
1973	Queens Park Rangers	H	First Division	2-1
1976	Tranmere Rovers	H	League Cup 2nd Round	5-0
1979	Middlesbrough	H	First Division	2-1
1982	Nottingham Forest	A	First Division	3-0
1984	Ipswich Town	A	First Division	1-1
1990	Sunderland	A	First Division	1-2
1993	West Ham United	H	FA Premier League	3-0

SEPTEMBER 2ND

| 1893 | Burnley | H | First Division | 3-2 |

Throughout their opening season in the Football League it had been obvious that the North Road ground in Monsall was totally unsuitable. The pitch was one of the worst in the League, prone to becoming a mud-bath at one end whilst remaining rock hard at the other, and the players had to change half a mile away at the Three Crowns public house. It was obvious that somewhere else had to be found, and the club finally settled on Bank Street in Clayton, a move of some three miles across the city. A crowd of 10,000 gathered to watch the Heathens in their new surroundings and were rewarded by a 3-2 win over Burnley, with Farman netting a hat-trick. Unfortunately, however, the fans also found Bank Street's pitch to be little better than the one they had just left, and a chemical works alongside the ground ensured toxic fumes headed in their direction whenever there was a breeze!

1899	Gainsborough Trinity	H	Second Division	2-2
1905	Bristol City	H	Second Division	5-1
1907	Aston Villa	A	First Division	4-1
1911	Manchester City	A	First Division	0-0
1912	Woolwich Arsenal	A	First Division	0-0
1914	Oldham Athletic	H	First Division	1-3
1916	Port Vale	H	Lancashire Section Principal Tournament	2-2

1918 John James Bentley died at the age of 58. Born in Turton in 1860 he had begun his career as a player, earning county caps until injury forced his retirement in 1884 and he switched to administration. He became secretary of Bolton Wanderers and held the post until 1897, and also served as president of the Football League from 1893, following the retirement of founder William McGregor, until 1910. His involvement with United had begun in 1902 when John Henry Davies had taken over the club and installed J.J. Bentley as chairman, a post he held until 1908. He was instrumental in luring Ernest Mangnall to the club as secretary/manager and when Mangnall switched to Manchester City, Bentley took over this role, stepping down in 1914 when poor results had caused him stress and ill-health. He continued as secretary, however, until 1916. He was also a referee and journalist and, along with William McGregor and John McKenna, was largely responsible for establishing football as the major sporting pastime. His importance to United is equally vital.

| 1922 | Crystal Palace | A | Second Division | 3-2 |
| 1925 | Aston Villa | H | First Division | 3-0 |

On the same day, Ernie Taylor was born in Sunderland. Ernie had a brief stay with United, but as he was the first player signed by acting manager Jimmy Murphy in the aftermath of the Munich air disaster, his place in United's history is assured. He began his professional career with Newcastle United in 1942 and helped them win the FA Cup in 1951. Two years later he returned to Wembley, this time with Blackpool, and helped them beat Bolton 4-3. He was signed by United in February 1958 and given permission to play in the FA Cup tie against Sheffield Wednesday, even though he was ineligible, and subsequently helped United reach Wembley where they lost to Bolton. After ten months at United he was sold to Sunderland for £7,000, having done a remarkable job in raising the spirit at Old Trafford. He retired as a player in 1962 and took to coaching and died in Birkenhead on 9th April 1985.

| 1929 | Leicester City | A | First Division | 1-4 |

United full-back Charlie Moore was sent off for retaliation during the game, although even the Leicester officials felt he had been hard done by. Eventually, so did the FA, who took into account his exemplary record over the previous 11 years of his career and giving him only a caution instead of a ban.

1931	Southampton	H	Second Division	2-3
1933	Lincoln City	H	Second Division	1-1
1936	Huddersfield Town	A	First Division	1-3
1939	Charlton Athletic	A	First Division	0-2

The day after United had lost to Charlton, the announcement was made that Britain was at war with Germany and that all sports had been halted. Although it was initially hoped that this would be temporary, a further two days later the League Management Committee announced the cancellation of the season and that the results of the games played thus far would be expunged from the records. There was to be no proper League football until 1946, and Old Trafford would have to wait some time longer.

1944	Everton	H	Football League North (First Championship)	1-3
1950	Blackpool	H	First Division	1-0
1953	West Bromwich Albion	A	First Division	0-2
1959	Chelsea	A	First Division	6-3
1961	Blackpool	A	First Division	3-2
1964	West Ham United	H	First Division	3-1
1967	West Ham United	A	First Division	3-1
1970	Everton	H	First Division	2-0
1972	West Ham United	A	First Division	2-2
1975	Manchester City	A	Mike Summerbee Testimonial	4-3
1978	Everton	H	First Division	1-1
1980	Coventry City	A	League Cup 2nd Round 2nd Leg	0-2
1992	Crystal Palace	H	FA Premier League	1-0

SEPTEMBER 3RD

1892	Blackburn Rovers	A	First Division	3-4

This day saw the very first Football League fixture fulfilled by Newton Heath. The club had previously been members of the Football Alliance and during the summer of 1892, the Football League had decided to expand, increasing the number of First Division clubs by two from 14 to 16 and adding a Second Division, in effect the Football Alliance. Newton Heath had been fortunate enough to be instantly elected to the First Division and their first match pitted them against probably the most famous club in the land: winners of the FA Cup on five occasions and a team packed with internationals. A crowd of 8,000 braved torrential rain to witness the game, with Blackburn proving far too experienced for the Heathens, being 3-0 ahead at half-time. The Heathens showed a little more fight in the second half, with Bob Donaldson scoring Newton Heath's very first League goal, but having pulled the game back to 3-2 down they allowed Blackburn to regain control, making the score 4-2 until shortly before the end when Farman added a third goal for Newton Heath.

1898	Gainsborough Trinity	A	Second Division	2-0
1904	Port Vale	A	Second Division	2-2
1906	Derby County	A	First Division	2-2
1910	Blackburn Rovers	H	First Division	3-2

1914 Jimmy Delaney born in Lanark. Delaney is in the record books for his cup-winning exploits – he won a Scottish Cup winners' medal with Celtic in 1937, an FA Cup winners' medal with Manchester United in 1948 and an Irish Cup winners' medal with Derry City in 1954. He missed out on a clean sweep when Shamrock Rovers were beaten by Cork Celtic in the FA of Ireland Cup final in 1956. He was with United from February 1946 to November 1950 and died in Lanarkshire on 26th September 1989.

1921	Everton	H	First Division	2-1

On the same day, John Aston senior was born in Manchester. John signed with United as an amateur in 1938 and was upgraded to the professional ranks in December 1939, although owing to the war he was unable to make his debut until 1946. Thereafter he made nearly 300 appearances for the first team and appeared in both the 1948 FA Cup and 1952 championship winning teams. He retired in 1954 and promptly became junior coach, later serving the club as chief scout from 1970 until 1972. His son, also John, also played for United.

1923	Southampton	A	Second Division	0-0
1927	Birmingham	A	First Division	0-0
1930	Middlesbrough	A	First Division	1-3
1932	Southampton	A	Second Division	2-4
1934	Bolton Wanderers	A	Second Division	1-3

1935 Stan Crowther born in Bilston in Staffordshire. Although Stan made only 13 first-team appearances for United during his brief spell at the club, he had played against them in the 1957 FA Cup final for Villa and was transferred to United immediately after Munich. Indeed, he was signed a little over an hour before the first match, against Sheffield Wednesday, and played an integral part in helping United reach the 1958 final, even though he had already played in that season's competition for Villa. He later played for Chelsea and Brighton before drifting into non-League circles.

1938	Birmingham City	H	First Division	4-1
1947	Liverpool	A	First Division	2-2
1949	Manchester City	H	First Division	2-1

Old Trafford played host to a Manchester derby for the first time since before the Second World War. With both the previous season's meetings having finished goalless another close encounter was promised, and so it proved. Jimmy Munro gave City the lead shortly after half an hour, catching Jack Crompton unawares with a snap shot from outside the area, and City might have added to their lead soon after the break when Andy Black headed on to the crossbar. Although City continued to dominate, United kept battling away and got their reward when Stan Pearson scored a hotly disputed goal. Stan put United into the lead soon after and as City pressed for an equaliser tempers began to fray, with Henry Cockburn of United and Billy Linacre of City receiving their marching orders two minutes from time. A crowd of 47,760 watched all the action.

1952	Arsenal	H	First Division	0-0
1955	Manchester City	A	First Division	0-1
1958	Nottingham Forest	H	First Division	1-1
1960	Tottenham Hotspur	A	First Division	1-4
1963	Ipswich Town	A	First Division	7-2
1966	Newcastle United	H	First Division	3-2
1969	Middlesbrough	H	League Cup 2nd Round	1-0
1977	Derby County	A	First Division	1-0
1983	Stoke City	A	First Division	1-0
1988	Liverpool	A	First Division	0-1
1991	Wimbledon	A	First Division	2-1

SEPTEMBER 4TH

1897	Lincoln City	H	Second Division	5-0
1905	Blackpool	H	Second Division	2-1
1909	Bury	H	First Division	2-0
1915	Oldham Athletic	A	Lancashire Section Principal Tournament	2-3
1920	Bolton Wanderers	A	First Division	1-1
1922	Sheffield Wednesday	H	Second Division	1-0

1926	Leeds United	H	First Division	2-2
1935	Charlton Athletic	H	Second Division	3-0

What was to be United's championship and promotion winning season had started with a 3-1 reverse at Plymouth and it was therefore vital the club got quickly into winning ways if a concentrated push for promotion was to be made. The opening home game of the season therefore saw a crowd of 21,211 at Old Trafford for the visit of Charlton, the reigning Third Division South champions. Goals from Bamford, Cape and Chester secured the points for United, although at the end of the season Charlton would also be promoted as runners-up.

1937	Luton Town	A	Second Division	0-1
1943	Stockport County	A	Football League North (First Championship)	3-3
1946	Chelsea	A	First Division	3-0
1948	Huddersfield Town	H	First Division	4-1
1950	Aston Villa	A	First Division	3-1
1954	Charlton Athletic	H	First Division	3-1
1957	Everton	A	First Division	3-3
1965	Stoke City	H	First Division	1-1
1971	Ipswich Town	H	First Division	1-0
1976	Tottenham Hotspur	H	First Division	2-3
1982	West Bromwich Albion	A	First Division	1-3
1985	Newcastle United	H	First Division	3-0
1990	Luton Town	A	First Division	1-0

Steve Bruce became the first First Division player to be sent off for a 'professional foul' when he was dismissed during the 1-0 win at Luton.

1996	Derby County	A	FA Premier League	1-1

SEPTEMBER 5TH

1896	Burton Swifts	A	Second Division	5-3
1903	Bristol City	H	Second Division	2-2
1908	Preston North End	A	First Division	3-0
1914	Manchester City	H	First Division	0-0
1925	Arsenal	H	First Division	0-1
1931	Swansea Town	H	Second Division	2-1
1936	Derby County	A	First Division	4-5

Although United were the reigning Second Division champions, they were finding life in the First Division considerably tougher, with only one point gained from the opening three games. This was despite a hat-trick from Tommy Bamford, his fourth goal of the season. He scored only ten more during the rest of the season but still finished United's top goalscorer, one of the chief reasons why they were due to make an immediate return to the Second Division.

1942	Everton	H	Football League North (First Championship)	2-1
1951	Charlton Athletic	H	First Division	3-2
1953	Manchester City	A	First Division	0-2
1956	Chelsea	A	First Division	2-1
1959	Birmingham City	A	First Division	1-1
1960	West Ham United	A	First Division	1-2
1962	Bolton Wanderers	A	First Division	0-3
1964	Fulham	A	First Division	1-2
1970	Liverpool	A	First Division	1-1
1973	Leicester City	A	First Division	0-1
1979	Tottenham Hotspur	H	League Cup 2nd Round 2nd Leg	3-1

This was the first season that home and away legs had been introduced to the second round of the League Cup, although it was still some time before seeding was introduced to prevent First Division sides from clashing so early on in the competition. Although Spurs had won the first leg 2-1 at White Hart Lane, a 3-1 victory at Old Trafford saw United through 4-3 on aggregate. Spurs' Paul Miller scored the decisive goal – an own goal!

1981	Ipswich Town	H	First Division	1-2
1984	Chelsea	H	First Division	1-1
1987	Coventry City	A	First Division	0-0

SEPTEMBER 6TH

| 1890 | Darwen | H | Football Alliance | 4-2 |
| 1902 | Gainsborough Trinity | A | Second Division | 1-0 |

Following the end of the 1901-02 season Newton Heath had effectively reformed itself, with a new board of directors, a new name and a new kit. This was the first League match the club played as Manchester United, with Charlie Richards netting the only goal of the game some five minutes from time. According to press reports, that was about all Charlie did throughout the match, but his place in United's history is assured regardless.

1909	Notts County	H	First Division	2-1
1913	Sheffield Wednesday	A	First Division	3-1
1919	Derby County	H	First Division	0-2
1920	Arsenal	H	First Division	1-1
1924	Stoke City	A	Second Division	0-0
1930	Chelsea	A	First Division	2-6
1933	Nottingham Forest	A	Second Division	1-1
1941	New Brighton	A	Football League Northern Section (First Championship)	3-3
1947	Arsenal	A	First Division	1-2
1952	Portsmouth	A	First Division	0-2
1958	Blackburn Rovers	H	First Division	6-1

Old Trafford's biggest crowd of the season was rewarded with one of the biggest wins of the season. A crowd of 65,187 saw goals from Bobby Charlton (two), Dennis Viollet (two), Albert Scanlon and Colin Webster bury Blackburn.

1967	Sunderland	A	First Division	1-1
1969	Leeds United	A	First Division	2-2
1972	Oxford United	A	League Cup 2nd Round	2-2
1975	Tottenham Hotspur	H	First Division	3-2
1980	Tottenham Hotspur	A	First Division	0-0
1983	Arsenal	A	First Division	3-2
1986	Leicester City	A	First Division	1-1
1992	Leeds United	H	FA Premier League	2-0

SEPTEMBER 7TH

1895	Crewe Alexandra	H	Second Division	5-0
1896	Walsall	H	Second Division	2-0
1901	Gainsborough Trinity	H	Second Division	3-0
1903	Burnley	A	Second Division	0-2
1907	Liverpool	H	First Division	4-0
1908	Bury	H	First Division	2-1
1912	Manchester City	H	First Division	0-1

Ernest Mangnall had just announced his intention to leave Manchester United in favour of their neighbours and rivals City and so this was his last match in charge. It was also staged as a benefit match for the great Billy Meredith, now aged some 38 years but still showing the same enthusiasm for the game as he had as an 18-year-old. A crowd of 40,000 would eventually provide a benefit of some £2,000, but that was to be all Billy won on the day. The only goal was scored by City's George Wynan, and his goal was significant for allowing City to leave Old Trafford with both points for the first time since the ground had opened in 1910.

1918	Oldham Athletic	H	Lancashire Section Principal Tournament	1-4
1921	West Bromwich Albion	A	First Division	0-0
1927	Sheffield Wednesday	H	First Division	1-1
1929	Blackburn Rovers	H	First Division	1-0
1931	Stoke City	A	Second Division	0-3
1932	Charlton Athletic	H	Second Division	1-1
1938	Liverpool	A	First Division	0-1
1940	Bury	H	North Regional League	0-0
1946	Charlton Athletic	A	First Division	3-1
1949	Liverpool	A	First Division	1-1
1955	Everton	H	First Division	2-1
1957	Leeds United	H	First Division	5-0

United's unbeaten start to the season continued with a 5-0 demolition of Leeds at Old Trafford. A crowd of 50,842 saw United get back on the winning trail following their draw at Everton thanks to goals from Johnny Berry (two), Tommy Taylor (two) and Dennis Viollet.

1963	Birmingham City	A	First Division	1-1
1966	Stoke City	A	First Division	0-3
1968	West Ham United	H	First Division	1-1
1971	Ipswich Town	A	League Cup 2nd Round	3-1
1974	Nottingham Forest	H	Second Division	2-2
1985	Oxford United	H	First Division	3-0
1991	Norwich City	H	First Division	3-0
1996	Leeds United	A	FA Premier League	4-0

SEPTEMBER 8TH

| 1894 | Burton Wanderers | A | Second Division | 0-1 |

James Peters made his League debut for Newton Heath. Signed from Heywood Central in June 1894 he formed an effective left wing partnership with inside-forward Dick Smith, although James was allowed to sign for New Brompton in 1896. He later played for Sheppey United. The Heathens also gave a debut to Dick Smith, who would go on to spend two spells at Newton Heath. He was originally signed in June 1894 from Heywood Central and remained with the club until January 1898. After playing for Halliwell Rovers and Wigan County he returned to Newton Heath in February 1900 and remained with the club for almost a year before joining Bolton. He finished his playing career with Wigan United.

1900	Middlesbrough	H	Second Division	4-0
1906	Notts County	H	First Division	0-0
1913	Sunderland	H	First Division	3-1
1917	Blackburn Rovers	H	Lancashire Section Principal Tournament	6-1
1919	Sheffield Wednesday	A	First Division	3-1
1923	Bury	A	Second Division	0-2
1924	Barnsley	H	Second Division	1-0

1928	Leeds United	A	First Division	2-3
1934	Barnsley	H	Second Division	4-1
1937	Coventry City	H	Second Division	2-2
1945	Chesterfield	H	Football League North	0-2
1947	Burnley	A	First Division	0-0
1948	Wolverhampton Wanderers	A	First Division	2-3
1951	Stoke City	H	First Division	4-0
1954	Tottenham Hotspur	A	First Division	2-0
1956	Newcastle United	A	First Division	1-1
1958	West Ham United	A	First Division	2-3
1962	Leyton Orient	A	First Division	0-1
1964	Everton	A	First Division	3-3
1965	Newcastle United	A	First Division	2-1
1973	Ipswich Town	A	First Division	1-2
1979	Aston Villa	A	First Division	3-0
1982	Everton	H	First Division	2-1
1984	Newcastle United	H	First Division	5-0
1990	Queens Park Rangers	H	First Division	3-1

SEPTEMBER 9TH

1893	West Bromwich Albion	A	First Division	1-3
1899	Bolton Wanderers	A	Second Division	1-2
1905	Grimsby Town	A	Second Division	1-0
1907	Middlesbrough	H	First Division	2-1
1911	Everton	H	First Division	2-1
1916	Oldham Athletic	A	Lancashire Section Principal Tournament	2-0
1922	Wolverhampton Wanderers	A	Second Division	1-0
1925	Aston Villa	A	First Division	2-2
1933	Bolton Wanderers	H	Second Division	1-5

United were still without a win and had picked up only two points from their opening four games in the season, one of the worst in their history and which was to end with the club almost relegated to the Third Division. Local rivals Bolton, who were already pushing for promotion, were in no mood to ease the pressure, inflicting United's biggest home defeat of the season.

1935	Bradford City	H	Second Division	3-1
1936	Huddersfield Town	H	First Division	3-1
1944	Stockport County	H	Football League North (First Championship)	3-4
1950	Tottenham Hotspur	A	First Division	0-1
1953	Middlesbrough	H	First Division	2-2
1957	Blackpool	A	First Division	4-1
1959	Leeds United	H	First Division	6-0
1961	Tottenham Hotspur	H	First Division	1-0
1967	Burnley	H	First Division	2-2
1970	Aldershot	A	League Cup 2nd Round	3-1
1972	Coventry City	H	First Division	0-1
1978	Queens Park Rangers	A	First Division	1-1
1989	Everton	A	First Division	2-3
1995	Everton	A	FA Premier League	3-2

SEPTEMBER 10TH

1892	Burnley	H	First Division	1-1

Andrew Mitchell made his debut for Newton Heath. Signed by the club from Airdrieonians the same month, Andrew proved a reliable and consistent performer for the Heathens, making 49 consecutive appearances in the first team. When the club lost their First Division status following the 1894 Test matches he left the club, signing for Burton Swifts. This was also the first ever Football League match played at North Road, Monsall, the Heathens' ground at the time. They remained there until 1893, when they moved to Clayton.

1898	Manchester City	H	Second Division	3-0
1904	Bristol City	H	Second Division	4-1
1910	Nottingham Forest	A	First Division	1-2
1921	Chelsea	A	First Division	0-0
1927	Newcastle United	H	First Division	1-7

Manchester United have only twice conceded as many as seven goals at home in the Football League and on both occasions it was Newcastle who inflicted the damage! This was the first occasion, with a Joe Spence goal little more than a consolation effort. A crowd of 50,217 witnessed the destruction at Old Trafford.

1930	Huddersfield Town	H	First Division	0-6
1932	Tottenham Hotspur	A	Second Division	1-6
1938	Grimsby Town	A	First Division	0-1
1949	Chelsea	A	First Division	1-1
1952	Derby County	A	First Division	3-2
1955	Sheffield United	A	First Division	0-1
1960	Aston Villa	H	First Division	1-1
1966	Tottenham Hotspur	A	First Division	1-2
1975	Brentford	H	League Cup 2nd Round	2-1
1977	Manchester City	A	First Division	1-3
1983	Luton Town	H	First Division	2-0
1988	Middlesbrough	H	First Division	1-0

SEPTEMBER 11TH

1897	Burton Swifts	A	Second Division	4-0
1909	Tottenham Hotspur	A	First Division	2-2
1915	Everton	H	Lancashire Section Principal Tournament	2-4
1920	Chelsea	H	First Division	3-1
1926	Newcastle United	A	First Division	2-4
1929	Leicester City	H	First Division	2-1
1935	Charlton Athletic	A	Second Division	0-0
1937	Barnsley	H	Second Division	4-1

Barnsley suffered two misfortunes during the game, losing goalkeeper Binns, who broke two of his fingers, and then Ives with broken ribs. A hat-trick from Tommy Bamford in the second half ensured both points for United, with Barnsley's effort a late consolation from former United player Hine from the penalty spot.

1943	Everton	H	Football League North (First Championship)	4-1
1946	Liverpool	H	First Division	5-0
1948	Manchester City	A	First Division	0-0
1954	Bolton Wanderers	A	First Division	1-1
1963	Blackpool	H	First Division	3-0
1965	Burnley	A	First Division	0-3
1971	Crystal Palace	A	First Division	3-1
1974	Charlton Athletic	H	League Cup 2nd Round	5-1
1976	Newcastle United	A	First Division	2-2

1982	Ipswich Town	H	First Division	3-1
1993	Chelsea	A	FA Premier League	0-1
1994	Leeds United	A	FA Premier League	1-2
1996	Juventus	A	European Cup Group C	0-1

This could well have been a case of a missed opportunity for United, for Juventus were struggling to qualify from the group stage of the competition and not only needed a win but for other results in other groups to go their way. United, having already qualified for the next stage, perhaps had their minds elsewhere, for although they created chances to have eliminated the Italians, scorned every one. As it turned out, Juventus got the win they needed and the right combination of results elsewhere to take their place in the knockout stage.

SEPTEMBER 12TH

1891	Burton Swifts	A	Football Alliance	2-3
1896	Lincoln City	H	Second Division	3-1
1903	Port Vale	A	Second Division	0-1
1908	Middlesbrough	H	First Division	6-3
1914	Bolton Wanderers	A	First Division	0-3
1925	Manchester City	A	First Division	1-1
1931	Tottenham Hotspur	H	Second Division	1-1
1934	Bolton Wanderers	H	Second Division	0-3
1936	Manchester City	H	First Division	3-2
1942	Chester	H	Football League North (First Championship)	0-2
1945	Middlesbrough	A	Football League North	1-2
1951	Charlton Athletic	A	First Division	2-2
1953	Bolton Wanderers	A	First Division	0-0
1956	RSC Anderlecht	A	European Cup Preliminary Round 1st Leg	2-0

When Chelsea had finished champions in 1954-55, they had been invited to enter the newly created European Champions Cup by UEFA. Although they were keen to do so, they were persuaded by the Football League not to take part, leaving Hibernian as Britain's only representatives. When United won the League the following year, the Football League again tried to dissuade the club from entering, but Matt Busby was determined to prove his side against the best of Europe and refused to withdraw. Eventually the Football League relented, and so United's great European adventures began. Goals from Viollet and Taylor gave them a 2-0 lead to take back to Manchester for the second leg.

1959	Tottenham Hotspur	H	First Division	1-5
1962	Bolton Wanderers	H	First Division	3-0
1964	Nottingham Forest	H	First Division	3-0
1970	Coventry City	H	First Division	2-0
1972	Oxford United	H	League Cup 2nd Round Replay	3-1
1973	Leicester City	H	First Division	1-2
1981	Aston Villa	A	First Division	1-1
1987	Newcastle United	H	First Division	2-2
1992	Everton	A	FA Premier League	2-0
1995	Rotor Volgograd	A	UEFA Cup 1st Round 1st Leg	0-0

SEPTEMBER 13TH

| 1890 | Grimsby Town | A | Football Alliance | 1-3 |
| 1902 | Burton United | H | Second Division | 1-0 |

The first chance home fans had to see the new Manchester United in action came in this Second Division clash at Clayton. A small number of improvements had also been made to the ground, including the provision of a roof on one stand. A crowd of 15,000 gathered at Bank Street, and the only goal of the game was scored by Daniel Hurst.

1913	Bolton Wanderers	H	.	First Division	0-1
1919	Preston North End	A		First Division	3-2
1924	Coventry City	H		Second Division	5-1
1930	Newcastle United	H		First Division	4-7
1937	Bury	A		Second Division	2-1
1941	Stockport County	A		Football League Northern Section (First Championship)	5-1
1947	Sheffield United	H		First Division	0-1
1950	Aston Villa	H		First Division	0-0
1952	Bolton Wanderers	H		First Division	1-0

1957 Mal Donaghy born in Belfast. Mal signed for Luton in 1978 and enjoyed a ten-year career at Kenilworth Road before his surprising switch to Old Trafford for £650,000 in 1988, a big fee for a player over 30 years of age. It proved money well spent, however, for he brought stability to the United defence when it was most needed. He spent a brief spell on loan to Luton before signing for Chelsea in 1992 for £100,000.

1958	Newcastle United	A	First Division	1-1

1968 Frank Barson, the former Burnley, Aston Villa, Manchester United, Watford, Hartlepools and Wigan Borough player died. Frank is remembered, most especially by referees, as the player who served more suspensions than any other in the history of the game – statisticians stopped counting at 12! His year at Watford was particularly revealing for it included nine months during which he was suspended! That said, Barson was an accomplished player, as one England cap (against Wales in 1920) and an FA Cup winners' medal with Aston Villa in 1920 testify.

1969	Liverpool	H	First Division	1-0
1975	Queens Park Rangers	A	First Division	0-1
1980	Leicester City	H	First Division	5-0
1986	Southampton	H	First Division	5-1
1997	West Ham United	H	FA Premier League	2-1

SEPTEMBER 14TH

1895	Loughborough Town	A	Second Division	3-3
1901	Middlesbrough	A	Second Division	0-5
1907	Middlesbrough	A	First Division	1-2
1912	West Bromwich Albion	A	First Division	2-1
1918	Oldham Athletic	A	Lancashire Section Principal Tournament	2-0

1923 Henry Cockburn born in Ashton-under-Lyme. He joined United in August 1944 and made his debut in August 1946, going on to make 275 appearances for the first team. He was part of the side that won the 1948 FA Cup and 1952 League championship, and also won 13 caps for England as part of the half-back line-up that included Billy Wright and Neil Franklin. After losing his place at United to Duncan Edwards, he moved to Bury and later had a spell at Peterborough United and other non-League clubs.

1929	Middlesbrough	A	First Division	3-2
1935	Newcastle United	A	Second Division	2-0
1940	Oldham Athletic	A	North Regional League	1-2
1946	Middlesbrough	H	First Division	1-0
1955	Everton	A	First Division	2-4

1956 Ray Wilkins born in Hillingdon in Middlesex. Known by his nickname of 'Butch',

Ray was signed by Chelsea straight from school and was their youngest ever captain when appointed at the age of 18. In 1979 former Chelsea manager Dave Sexton, by this time occupying the hot seat at Old Trafford, paid £825,000 to take him to United. The highlight of his United career was the 1983 FA Cup final, in which he won a winners' medal, and his performances in midfield alongside Bryan Robson were also repeated with England. In July 1984 he was sold to AC Milan for £1.5 million, where he remained for three years before spending a brief spell with Paris St Germain. He returned to Britain with Glasgow Rangers and then went south of the border to play for QPR in 1989. After five years at Loftus Road he joined Crystal Palace but returned six months later as player-manager. He resigned this position in September 1996 and after brief spells playing for Wycombe Wanderers, Hibernian, Millwall and Leyton Orient was appointed manager at Fulham.

1957	Bolton Wanderers	A	First Division	0-4
1960	West Ham United	H	First Division	6-1
1963	West Bromwich Albion	H	First Division	1-0

George Best made his United debut in the 1-0 home win over West Bromwich Albion, David Sadler scoring the only goal. A crowd of 50,453 saw the start of a great if erratic career.

| 1966 | Blackpool | A | League Cup 2nd Round | 1-5 |

Although United had entered the very first League Cup competition in 1960-61, they were then conspicuous by their absence for a further six years. Their return was hardly an auspicious start either, going down 5-1 at Blackpool with David Herd scoring their goal.

1968	Burnley	A	First Division	0-1
1974	West Bromwich Albion	A	Second Division	1-1
1977	St Etienne	A	European Cup-Winners' Cup 1st Round 1st Leg	1-1

There was trouble between Manchester United and St Etienne fans before, during and after the European Cup-Winners' Cup tie in the Geoffrey-Guichard Stadium in St Etienne, resulting in a reserve match having to be abandoned and dozens of arrests. Although the match, when finally played, ended in a 1-1 draw, there was a real fear that United could be thrown out of Europe as a result of the trouble.

1983	Dukla Prague	H	European Cup-Winners' Cup 1st Round 1st Leg	1-1
1985	Manchester City	A	First Division	3-0
1991	Southampton	A	First Division	1-0
1994	IFK Gothenburg	H	European Cup Group A	4-2
1996	Nottingham Forest	H	FA Premier League	4-1

SEPTEMBER 15TH

1894	Crewe Alexandra	H	Second Division	6-1
1900	Burnley	A	Second Division	0-1
1906	Sheffield United	A	First Division	2-0
1917	Rochdale	A	Lancashire Section Principal Tournament	0-3
1923	Bury	H	Second Division	0-1
1926	Arsenal	H	First Division	2-2
1928	Liverpool	H	First Division	2-2
1930	Huddersfield Town	A	First Division	0-3

Jack Mellor made his debut for United. Signed by United from Witton Albion in May 1929, he became first-choice full-back following the retirement of Charlie Moore and remained there for the next three seasons, although his final three and a half seasons were spent mainly on reserve team duty. He left United for Cardiff in January 1937, retiring from the game in May 1938.

1934	Port Vale	A	Second Division	2-3
1945	Chesterfield	A	Football League North	1-1
1948	Wolverhampton Wanderers H		First Division	2-0
1951	Manchester City	A	First Division	2-1
1954	Tottenham Hotspur	H	First Division	2-1
1956	Sheffield Wednesday	H	First Division	4-1

1958 Chris Turner born in Sheffield. He began his career with Sheffield Wednesday in 1976 and had a brief spell on loan to Lincoln before signing for Sunderland for £80,000 in July 1979. In August 1985 United paid £275,000 to bring him to Old Trafford, initially as reserve to Gary Bailey. When Gary's career was brought to an end by injury Chris took over as first choice, but the subsequent emergence of Gary Walsh meant a return to the reserves, and the arrival of Jim Leighton pushed Chris even further down the list. He returned to Sheffield Wednesday for £175,000 in September 1988 and later played for Leyton Orient.

1962	Manchester City	H	First Division	2-3
1965	Newcastle United	H	First Division	1-1
1973	West Ham United	H	First Division	3-1
1976	Ajax (Amsterdam)	A	UEFA Cup 1st Round 1st Leg	0-1
1979	Derby County	H	First Division	1-0
1982	Valencia	H	UEFA Cup 1st Round 1st Leg	0-0
1984	Coventry City	A	First Division	3-0
1993	Kispest Honved	A	European Cup 1st Round 1st Leg	3-2

United's return to the European Cup for the first time in 25 years got off to an excellent start with Roy Keane netting twice and Eric Cantona once before they allowed the Hungarians back into the match late in the game.

SEPTEMBER 16TH

1893	Sheffield Wednesday	A	First Division	1-0
1899	Loughborough Town	H	Second Division	4-0
1905	Glossop	A	Second Division	2-1
1911	West Bromwich Albion	A	First Division	0-1
1916	Preston North End	H	Lancashire Section Principal Tournament	2-1

On the same day, Allenby Chilton was born in South Hylton in County Durham. Allenby joined United in November 1938 and made his debut in the aborted 1939-40 season. After guesting for many clubs during the war (in which he was twice injured, at Caen and during the Normandy D-Day landings) he returned to Old Trafford to make over 400 appearances for the first team over the next ten years. He played in the sides that won the 1948 FA Cup and 1952 League title and left United in March 1955 to become player-manager at Grimsby. After retiring as a player in 1956 he remained manager until 1959, and later had spells in charge at Wigan Athletic and Hartlepools United.

1922	Wolverhampton Wanderers H		Second Division	1-0
1925	Leicester City	H	First Division	3-2
1931	Stoke City	H	Second Division	1-1
1933	Brentford	A	Second Division	4-3
1944	Stockport County	A	Football League North (First Championship)	4-4
1950	Charlton Athletic	H	First Division	3-0
1953	Middlesbrough	A	First Division	4-1

1957 David McCreery born in Belfast. Recommended to United as a 15-year-old, David joined the club as a professional in October 1974 and made his debut in August 1975. Although he appeared in two FA Cup finals for United, on both occasions he was a substitute, a situation that seemed to sum up his career at United, for in addition to starting 57 first-team games he was introduced midway through the action on a further 52 occasions. He was sold to QPR for £200,000 in August 1979 and later played in the United States before returning to England and moving into coaching.

1959	Leeds United	A	First Division	2-2
1961	Cardiff City	A	First Division	2-1
1963	Blackpool	A	First Division	0-1
1964	Everton	H	First Division	2-1
1967	Sheffield Wednesday	A	First Division	1-1
1972	Wolverhampton Wanderers	A	First Division	0-2
1974	Millwall	A	Second Division	1-0
1978	Nottingham Forest	H	First Division	1-1
1986	Watford	A	First Division	0-1
1989	Millwall	H	First Division	5-1
1990	Liverpool	A	First Division	0-4
1992	Torpedo Moscow	H	UEFA Cup 1st Round 1st Leg	0-0
1995	Bolton Wanderers	H	FA Premier League	3-0

SEPTEMBER 17TH

1892	Burnley	A	First Division	1-4
1898	Glossop	A	Second Division	2-1
1904	Bolton Wanderers	H	Second Division	1-2
1910	Manchester City	H	First Division	2-1
1921	Chelsea	H	First Division	0-0
1927	Huddersfield Town	A	First Division	2-4
1932	Grimsby Town	H	Second Division	1-1
1938	Stoke City	A	First Division	1-1
1949	Stoke City	H	First Division	2-2
1955	Preston North End	H	First Division	3-2
1958	West Ham United	H	First Division	4-1
1960	Leicester City	A	First Division	1-3
1966	Manchester City	H	First Division	1-0

After a four-year break, the Manchester derby was resumed for League points with this clash at Old Trafford. In what was to become United's last League championship season for 26 years, a crowd of 62,085 saw Denis Law score the only goal of the game.

1969	Sheffield Wednesday	A	First Division	3-1
1977	Chelsea	H	First Division	0-1
1980	Widzew Lodz	H	UEFA Cup 1st Round 1st Leg	1-1
1983	Southampton	A	First Division	0-3
1988	Luton Town	A	First Division	2-0
1994	Liverpool	H	FA Premier League	2-0
1997	Kosice	A	UEFA Champions League	3-0

SEPTEMBER 18TH

1897	Luton Town	H	Second Division	1-2
1909	Preston North End	H	First Division	1-1
1915	Bolton Wanderers	A	Lancashire Section Principal Tournament	5-3
1920	Chelsea	A	First Division	2-1
1926	Burnley	H	First Division	3-1
1935	Hull City	H	Second Division	2-0
1937	Stockport County	A	Second Division	0-1

1942   Alex Stepney born in Mitcham in Surrey. Signed by Millwall as an amateur from Tooting and Mitcham, he spent three seasons at Millwall before a £50,000 fee took him to Chelsea. Four months later he was on the move again as Matt Busby paid £55,000, then a record for a goalkeeper, to take him to Old Trafford. At the end of his first season with the club he won a championship medal, and in May 1968 appeared at Wembley twice within a week, collecting his one and only England cap on the 22nd and a European Cup winners' medal with United on the 29th. He was still firmly established as United's first choice goalkeeper the following decade when he won a Second Division championship medal and appeared in successive FA Cup finals, in 1976 (runners-up) and 1977 (winners). He left United in February 1979 and played for a spell in America, returning briefly to Altrincham as player-coach before finishing his playing career back in America.

1943	Everton	A	Football League North (First Championship)	1-6
1946	Chelsea	H	First Division	1-1
1948	Sheffield United	A	First Division	2-2
1954	Huddersfield Town	H	First Division	1-1
1957	Blackpool	H	First Division	1-2
1961	Aston Villa	A	First Division	1-1
1965	Chelsea	H	First Division	4-1
1968	Waterford	A	European Cup 1st Round 1st Leg	3-1

United's defence of the trophy won so convincingly at Wembley the previous May began in Ireland, where Denis Law grabbed a hat-trick to confirm United's victory.

1971	West Ham United	H	First Division	4-2
1976	Middlesbrough	H	First Division	2-0
1982	Southampton	A	First Division	1-0
1985	Everton	H	Screen Sport Super Cup Group B	2-4
1991	Athinaikos	A	European Cup-Winners' Cup 1st Round 1st Leg	0-0

SEPTEMBER 19TH

1891	Bootle	H	Football Alliance	4-0
1896	Grimsby Town	A	Second Division	0-2
1903	Glossop	A	Second Division	5-0
1908	Manchester City	A	First Division	2-1
1914	Blackburn Rovers	H	First Division	2-0
1925	Liverpool	A	First Division	0-5

Prior to the start of the season the offside rule had been changed; whereas it had previously required three defenders, including the goalkeeper, to be between the attacker and the goal, it now required only two. As teams struggled to adjust to the new ruling there was an abundance of results which almost defied belief, including this 5-0 reverse for United at Liverpool. Ultimately, perhaps Arsenal best worked out how to counter the change, with the introduction of the stopper centre-half, but in the meantime the fans were treated to an avalanche of goals at almost every League ground.

1927	Blackburn Rovers	A	First Division	0-3
1931	Nottingham Forest	A	Second Division	1-2
1936	Sheffield Wednesday	H	First Division	1-1
1942	Chester	A	Football League North (First Championship)	2-2
1953	Preston North End	H	First Division	1-0
1959	Manchester City	A	First Division	0-3
1964	Stoke City	A	First Division	2-1
1970	Ipswich Town	A	First Division	0-4

1977 Manchester United were thrown out of the European Cup-Winners' Cup by UEFA following unruly behaviour by their fans at St Etienne. United announced they would appeal and sent Sir Matt Busby to Switzerland to present their case.

1981	Swansea City	H	First Division	1-0
1984	Raba Vasas ETO Gyor	H	UEFA Cup 1st Round 1st Leg	3-0
1987	Everton	A	First Division	1-2
1990	Pecsi Munkas	H	European Cup-Winners' Cup 1st Round 1st Leg	2-0
1992	Tottenham Hotspur	A	FA Premier League	1-1
1993	Arsenal	H	FA Premier League	1-0

SEPTEMBER 20TH

1890	Nottingham Forest	H	Football Alliance	1-1
1902	Bristol City	A	Second Division	1-3
1913	Chelsea	A	First Division	2-0
1919	Preston North End	H	First Division	5-1
1924	Oldham Athletic	A	Second Division	3-0
1930	Sheffield Wednesday	A	First Division	0-3

1933 Dennis Viollet born in Manchester. Dennis was signed by United straight from school, signing professional forms in September 1950 and making his debut three years later. He eventually went on to form a lethal partnership with Tommy Taylor and helped the club win successive League championships in 1956 and 1957. He survived the Munich air crash and recovered sufficiently to take his place in the 1958 FA Cup final side, although he missed the 1957 Cup final through injury. In 1959-60 he scored 32 League goals in 36 appearances, United's record haul by an individual in one season. In January 1962 he was surprisingly sold to Stoke City for £25,000, winning a Second Division championship medal in 1963 and a League Cup runners-up medal in 1964. After a brief spell in America he became player-coach at Linfield, collecting another medal as Linfield won the 1970 Irish Cup. Despite all the goals he scored during his career (including 178 for United in 291 appearances), he won only two caps for England. He later coached in America.

1935 David Pegg born in Doncaster. David joined United straight from school and was an integral part of the Youth side that won the FA Youth Cup in 1953 and 1954. He broke into the first team in 1955-56 and went on to win successive League title medals as well as a runners-up medal in the 1957 FA Cup final, the same year he made his debut for England. A loss of form in 1957-58 saw his place in the side being taken by Albert Scanlon, but David travelled with the squad to the ill-fated European Cup tie with Red Star Belgrade and lost his life in the crash at Munich.

1941	Stockport County	H	Football League Northern Section	
			(First Championship)	7-1
1945	Stoke City	A	Football League North	2-1
1947	Manchester City	A	First Division	0-0
1952	Aston Villa	A	First Division	3-3
1958	Tottenham Hotspur	H	First Division	2-2
1967	Hibernian (Malta)	H	European Cup 1st Round 1st Leg	4-0
1969	Arsenal	A	First Division	2-2
1975	Ipswich Town	H	First Division	1-0
1980	Leeds United	A	First Division	0-0
1989	Portsmouth	A	Littlewoods Cup 2nd Round 1st Leg	3-2
1995	York City	H	Coca-Cola Cup 2nd Round 1st Leg	0-3
1997	Bolton Wanderers	A	FA Premier League	0-0

1889 Sunderland Albion H Football Alliance 4-1
This was Newton Heath's first match in the Football Alliance, a collection of teams organised in much the same way as the Football League, which also commenced this season. Ultimately the Football Alliance would be amalgamated into the League and become the Second Division. The Heathens' goals were scored by Wilson (two), J. Doughty and Stewart, with a crowd estimated at 3,000 in attendance.

1895 Burton Swifts H Second Division 5-0
1896 Walsall A Second Division 3-2
1901 Bristol City H Second Division 1-0
1902 George McLachlan born in Glasgow. George began his League career with Cardiff City in November 1925 and was a member of the side that beat Arsenal in the 1927 FA Cup final, so taking the trophy out of England for the first and only time. Two years later he joined United and remained with the club for four years, making over 100 appearances and captaining the side in 1931-32. He left United to become player-manager at Chester and later returned to Scotland to manage at Queen of the South.

1907 Sheffield United H First Division 2-1
1911 Jack Warner born in Tonypandy. Jack was first spotted by United whilst playing for Swansea Town and gave an impressive performance against United in a League match between the sides in 1938. Two months later he was sold to United and looked set for a long and illustrious career, but no sooner had he broken into the side than the Second World War started and League football was suspended. Although he resumed his career in 1946 his best years were already gone and in 1951 he moved on to Oldham to become player-coach, later becoming player-manager at Rochdale. He was 42 years of age when he retired from playing and had won two caps for Wales. He did create one record whilst at United: he is the oldest player to have appeared for United since the war, a feat he achieved on 22nd April 1950.

1912 Everton H First Division 2-0
On the same day, George Mutch was born in Aberdeen. He was signed by United for the ridiculously low fee of £800 in May 1934 from Abroath and was soon introduced into the side, making his debut in August 1934. After three quiet games Mutch got on the score sheet with a vengeance, scoring a hat-trick. He was leading scorer in the Second Division championship winning side of 1935-36 and was sold to Preston in September 1937 for £5,000, winning an FA Cup winners' medal at the end of his first season at Deepdale. Indeed, it was he who had been heavily challenged in the last minute of extra time to earn the penalty against Huddersfield, and after receiving treatment took it himself. His shot crashed on to the underside of the bar and into the net for a dramatic winner. The onset of the Second World War robbed him of a large part of his career and in 1946 he signed for Bury, later playing for Southport before retiring.

1918 Blackburn Rovers H Lancashire Section Principal Tournament 1-0
1929 Liverpool H First Division 1-2
1935 Tottenham Hotspur H Second Division 0-0
Hubert Redwood made his debut for United. Born in St Helens in 1913, he joined United from Shardley Albion as an amateur in 1933 and was promoted to the professional ranks three months later. He went on to make 96 appearances for the United first team before the outbreak of the Second World War, during which he quested for New Brighton. He contracted tuberculosis whilst serving in the Army and died in St Helens in October 1943.

1940 Oldham Athletic H North Regional League 2-3
1946 Stoke City A First Division 2-3

1957	Arsenal	H	First Division	4-2
1963	Arsenal	A	First Division	1-2
1968	Newcastle United	H	First Division	3-1
1974	Bristol Rovers	H	Second Division	2-0
1985	West Bromwich Albion	A	First Division	5-1
1986	Everton	A	First Division	1-3
1991	Luton Town	H	First Division	5-0
1994	Port Vale	A	Coca-Cola Cup 2nd Round 1st Leg	2-1
1996	Aston Villa	A	FA Premier League	0-0

SEPTEMBER 22ND

1894	Leicester Fosse	A	Second Division	3-2
1900	Port Vale	H	Second Division	4-0
1906	Bolton Wanderers	H	First Division	1-2
1917	Rochdale	H	Lancashire Section Principal Tournament	1-1
1923	South Shields	A	Second Division	0-1
1928	West Ham United	A	First Division	1-3
1934	Norwich City	H	Second Division	5-0
1945	Barnsley	A	Football League North	2-2
1951	Tottenham Hotspur	A	First Division	0-2

The White Hart Lane clash between United and the side they would replace as League champions drew a crowd of 70,882, the biggest crowd to watch United all season. Unfortunately United were on the wrong end of a 2-0 scoreline but would regain ample revenge later in the season.

1956	Manchester City	H	First Division	2-0
1962	Burnley	H	First Division	2-5
1965	HJK Helsinki	A	European Cup Preliminary Round 1st Leg	3-2
1973	Leeds United	A	First Division	0-0
1976	Sunderland	H	League Cup 3rd Round	2-2
1979	Wolverhampton Wanderers	A	First Division	1-3
1981	Middlesbrough	A	First Division	2-0
1984	Liverpool	H	First Division	1-1
1990	Southampton	H	First Division	3-2
1993	Stoke City	A	Coca-Cola Cup 2nd Round 1st Leg	1-2

United were later accused of fielding a weakened side in the Coca-Cola Cup clash, but a glance at the team sheet should have been enough to refute this argument. As it was Stoke took the game far more seriously than United and won 2-1 thanks to two goals from Mark Stein, United's goal coming from Dion Dublin. United, however, had their minds on the European Cup.

SEPTEMBER 23RD

1889	Bootle	A	Football Alliance	1-4
1893	Nottingham Forest	H	First Division	1-1

1895 Fred Hopkin born in Dewsbury in Yorkshire. Although signed by Darlington before the First World War, Fred made a number of guest appearances for both Spurs and United during the war and when League football resumed in 1919 had switched to Old Trafford. He was the regular outside-left for two years and made 74 appearances for the first team before moving to Anfield, where he later won two championship medals. He later had a second spell with Darlington and then became a coach and died in Darlington in March 1970.

1899	Burton Swifts	A	Second Division	0-0

1905	Stockport County	H	Second Division	3-1
1907	Manchester City	H	Lancashire Senior Cup 1st Round	3-0
1911	Sunderland	H	First Division	2-2
1916	Burnley	A	Lancashire Section Principal Tournament	1-7
1922	Coventry City	A	Second Division	0-2
1933	Burnley	H	Second Division	5-2
1944	Bury	H	Football League North (First Championship)	2-2
1950	Middlesbrough	A	First Division	2-1
1961	Manchester City	H	First Division	3-2

Nobby Stiles seldom got on the score sheet twice in one day, but this was one occasion he must have wished he had not, for one of his goals was an own goal past Harry Gregg! He had earlier found the right net to give United the lead soon after the start, and Dennis Viollet had doubled the advantage on 14 minutes. Then came Nobby's own goal and a strike by Bobby Kennedy which levelled the scores, sending City's fans in the 55,993 crowd in raptures. Fate, however, had not yet finished with this match, and the second own goal of the day, this time from Ewing, gave United the victory.

| 1964 | Djurgaarden | A | Inter-Cities Fairs Cup 1st Round 1st Leg | 1-1 |

On the same day, Clayton Blackmore was born in Neath. After impressing at both rugby and football, Clayton decided to concentrate on football and signed with United straight from school. He made his debut in May 1984 and began to break into the United side on a regular basis in 1985-86, although he had already been capped for Wales before he'd made even three League appearances for the club. He won a medal in the 1990 FA Cup final win over Crystal Palace, appearing as a substitute in the first match but not the replay, and also collected another winners' medal in the European Cup-Winners' Cup the following season. Although he won a Premiership title with United in 1993 his appearances for the side became less frequent and following a free transfer in 1994 he joined Middlesbrough, linking up again with Bryan Robson.

1967	Tottenham Hotspur	H	First Division	3-1
1969	Wrexham	H	League Cup 3rd Round	2-0
1972	Derby County	H	First Division	3-0
1978	Arsenal	A	First Division	1-1
1987	Hull City	H	Littlewoods Cup 2nd Round 1st Leg	5-0
1989	Manchester City	A	First Division	1-5
1992	Brighton & Hove Albion	A	Coca-Cola Cup 2nd Round 1st Leg	1-1
1995	Sheffield Wednesday	A	FA Premier League	0-0

SEPTEMBER 24TH

1892	Everton	A	First Division	0-6
1898	Walsall	H	Second Division	1-0
1904	Glossop	A	Second Division	2-1
1910	Everton	A	First Division	1-0
1921	Preston North End	A	First Division	2-3
1927	Tottenham Hotspur	H	First Division	3-0
1932	Oldham Athletic	A	Second Division	1-1
1938	Chelsea	H	First Division	5-1
1949	Burnley	A	First Division	0-1
1952	Newcastle United	H	FA Charity Shield	4-2

This match probably represented the swansong for Matt Busby's first great United side, for some of the old faces who had taken the club to the FA Cup in 1948 and the League title in 1952 were already beginning to disappear, their places taken by rather more fresh-faced young men. Only three of the side that helped beat Newcastle would still be in United's side the next time they lifted the FA Charity Shield (Wood, Berry and Byrne), and goals from Rowley (two), Downie and Byrne ensured the 1952 vintage signed off in the best manner.

| 1955 | Burnley | A | First Division | 0-0 |
| 1960 | Wolverhampton Wanderers | H | First Division | 1-3 |

1962 Mike Phelan born in Nelson. Signed by Burnley straight from school and made his debut in 1981, helping them win the Third Division championship in 1981-82, but by the end of the 1984-85 season they were relegated into the Fourth Division. He was signed by Norwich in May 1985, helping them win the Second Division championship in his first season and in July 1989 he was transferred to United for £750,000. Whilst at United he won winners' medals in the FA Cup, European Cup-Winners' Cup and League Cup. He was released on a free transfer in May 1994.

1966	Burnley	H	First Division	4-1
1975	Derby County	A	First Division	1-2
1977	Leeds United	A	First Division	1-1
1983	Liverpool	H	First Division	1-0
1985	Crystal Palace	A	Milk Cup 2nd Round 1st Leg	1-0
1986	Port Vale	H	Littlewoods Cup 2nd Round 1st Leg	2-0
1988	West Ham United	H	First Division	2-0
1994	Ipswich Town	A	FA Premier League	2-3
1997	Chelsea	H	FA Premier League	2-2

SEPTEMBER 25TH

1897	Blackpool	A	Second Division	1-0
1909	Notts County	A	First Division	2-3
1911	Swindon Town		Stamford Bridge	
			FA Charity Shield	8-4

By virtue of their League championship win at the end of the 1910-11 season, United were again invited to compete for the FA Charity Shield against the Southern League champions, who this time around happened to be Swindon Town. A meagre crowd of 8,000, paying receipts of £229, gathered at Stamford Bridge, but both teams served up a football feast that would have done justice to a crowd ten times as big. Swindon took an early lead, but Turnbull soon equalised and then Harold Halse set about demolishing them almost single-handedly, scoring a hat-trick before half-time, although two additional Swindon goals gave them hope that they might rescue the game. United began pulling away again in the second half, with Halse getting yet another hat-trick and George Wall scoring almost on full-time. From the kick-off Swindon raced downfield and added one final goal in a truly remarkable game to leave the final score at 8-4. Harold Halse's six-goal tally is one of the finest single goalscoring achievements in United's history; to have done so in a match as important as the FA Charity Shield makes it even more of a feat. It was reported later that after each goal he scored, Harold turned to the Swindon goalkeeper and said, 'I'll be back in a minute!'

1915	Manchester City	H	Lancashire Section Principal Tournament	1-1
1920	Tottenham Hotspur	H	First Division	0-1
1926	Cardiff City	A	First Division	2-0
1937	Southampton	H	Second Division	1-2
1943	Blackburn Rovers	H	Football League North (First Championship)	2-1
1948	Aston Villa	H	First Division	3-1
1954	Manchester City	A	First Division	2-3
1957	Shamrock Rovers	A	European Cup Preliminary Round 1st Leg	6-0

| 1963 | Willem II Tilburg | A | European Cup-Winners' Cup 1st Round 1st Leg | 1-1 |

David Herd had an eventful game in United's European Cup-Winners' Cup debut, scoring their goal in the match against the German side and later getting sent off.

| 1965 | Arsenal | A | First Division | 2-4 |
| 1968 | Estudiantes | A | World Club Championship 1st Leg | 0-1 |

Victory over Benfica in the European Cup final the previous season gave United a two-legged tie against Estudiantes of Argentina in the World Club Championship. If there was joy at having qualified, there was also trepidation, for Celtic's experiences the previous season did not bode well, added to which there was still resentment in the Argentine side over the manner of their elimination from the World Cup in 1966 against England – the stage was set for an explosion. Right from the start Estudiantes used every trick in the book to halt their opponents: Denis Law had his hair pulled, Bobby Charlton needed stitches in a shin wound and Nobby Stiles was headbutted in the face. To their credit United showed no sign of retaliation, although Stiles was sent off with ten minutes to go for showing dissent at a linesman's decision. That Estudiantes' tactics also won them the only goal of the night was lost in the media coverage of the game afterwards, and there were those who feared the worst for the return fixture.

1971	Liverpool	A	First Division	2-2
1974	Bolton Wanderers	H	Second Division	3-0
1976	Manchester City	A	First Division	3-1
1982	Arsenal	H	First Division	0-0
1991	Cambridge United	H	Rumbelows Cup 2nd Round 1st Leg	3-0
1993	Swindon Town	H	FA Premier League	4-2
1996	Rapid Vienna	H	European Cup Group C	2-0

SEPTEMBER 26TH

1891	Birmingham St George's	A	Football Alliance	3-1
1896	Newcastle United	H	Second Division	4-0
1900	Manchester City	H	Friendly	0-0
1903	Bradford City	H	Second Division	3-1

Dick Pegg registered the first hat-trick by a United player in a League match in this game against Bradford City. A crowd of 30,000 were in attendance at Clayton.

1908	Liverpool	H	First Division	3-2
1914	Notts County	A	First Division	2-4
1925	Burnley	H	First Division	6-1

1926 An FA Investigating Committee, under the direction of Frederick Wall, met at the Grand Hotel in Manchester to begin an inquiry into the affairs of Manchester United. At this point there was little indication of what had prompted the investigation, who was under suspicion or what they were under suspicion of; everyone had to wait for an announcement which was duly made on October 7th.

1931	Chesterfield	H	Second Division	3-1
1936	Preston North End	A	First Division	1-3
1942	Blackburn Rovers	A	Football League North (First Championship)	2-4
1951	Hapoel	H	Friendly	6-0

Hapoel of Tel Aviv in Israel were the first team from outside Europe to visit Old Trafford, although a late-afternoon kick-off and the relatively unknown nature of the opposition attracted only 12,000 fans to Old Trafford.

| 1953 | Tottenham Hotspur | A | First Division | 1-1 |
| 1956 | RSC Anderlecht | H | European Cup Preliminary Round 2nd Leg | 10-0 |

With floodlights still to be installed at Old Trafford, United turned once again to their neighbours Manchester City for assistance in staging the European Cup second-leg match. A crowd of 40,000 saw United in scintillating form, 5-0 ahead at half-time and a further five goals being added in the second half. Denis Viollett led the charge, scoring four, with Tommy Taylor adding a hat-trick, Bill Whelan two and Johnny Berry one to complete a 12-0 aggregate victory.

1959	Preston North End	A	First Division	0-4
1964	Tottenham Hotspur	H	First Division	4-1
1970	Blackpool	H	First Division	1-1

1977 The Appeal Committee of UEFA readmitted United into the European Cup-Winners' Cup but the club were fined £7,500 and ordered to play their return leg with St Etienne 300 km from Manchester.

1979	Norwich City	A	League Cup 3rd Round	1-4
1981	Arsenal	A	First Division	0-0
1984	Burnley	H	Milk Cup 2nd Round 1st Leg	4-0
1987	Tottenham Hotspur	H	First Division	1-0
1990	Halifax Town	A	Rumbelows Cup 2nd Round 1st Leg	3-1
1992	Queens Park Rangers	H	FA Premier League	0-0
1995	Rotor Volgograd	H	UEFA Cup 1st Round 2nd Leg	2-2

With barely a minute to go in the UEFA Cup tie between United and Rotor Volgograd, United trailed 2-1 on the night and on aggregate. When they forced a last-minute corner, Peter Schmeichel threw caution to the wind and ran upfield to join the attack. He scored United's equaliser with a header, but the final whistle blew soon after and United went out on away goals.

SEPTEMBER 27TH

1890	Stoke	A	Football Alliance	1-2
1902	Glossop	H	Second Division	1-1
1913	Oldham Athletic	H	First Division	4-1
1919	Middlesbrough	A	First Division	1-1

Johnny Morris born in Radcliffe. He signed amateur forms with United in August 1939, subsequently becoming a professional in 1941, although owing to the Second World War he had to wait until October 1946 before making his League debut. A member of the side that won the FA Cup in 1948, he had a disagreement with Matt Busby after being left out of the side in 1949 and handed in a transfer request, subsequently being sold to Derby in March 1949 for a then record fee of £24,500. He later played for Leicester City before going into non-League football.

1924	Sheffield Wednesday	H	Second Division	2-0
1930	Grimsby Town	H	First Division	0-2

1932 Geoff Bent born in Salford. Geoff signed with United as an amateur in May 1949 and was upgraded to the professional ranks in April 1951. He made his debut in 1954 but was seldom more than cover for others in the United side. Indeed, in February 1958 a knock sustained by Roger Byrne in the League match at Highbury prompted Matt Busby to take Geoff to Belgrade in case Byrne failed a fitness test. Byrne duly passed it and played against Red Star, making Geoff's trip unnecessary. He was subsequently killed when the plane crashed at Munich.

1941	Everton	H	Football League Northern Section (First Championship)	2-3
1947	Preston North End	A	First Division	1-2
1952	Sunderland	H	First Division	0-1
1958	Manchester City	A	First Division	1-1
1967	Hibernian (Malta)	A	European Cup 1st Round 2nd Leg	0-0

1969	West Ham United	H	First Division	5-2
1975	Manchester City	A	First Division	2-2
1980	Manchester City	H	First Division	2-2
1983	Dukla Prague	A	European Cup-Winners' Cup 1st Round 2nd Leg	2-2

United had been held at home in the first leg 1-1 and faced a tough game in Czechoslovakia for the second leg. Goals from Bryan Robson and Frank Stapleton enabled them to draw 2-2 in Prague and progress into the next round on away goals, the first time United had had to rely on the system to go through.

1997	Leeds United	A	FA Premier League	0-1

SEPTEMBER 28TH

1889	Crewe Alexandra	A	Football Alliance	2-2
1895	Crewe Alexandra	A	Second Division	2-0
1901	Blackpool	A	Second Division	4-2

1903 Manager James West (officially he was the club's secretary with authority to select the team) resigned from the club. His letter to the board stated: 'I am not unmindful that my name may be associated with the failure of several of the newer members of the club to sustain the high reputations they had previously gained in first-class football; and solely with a view to relieving the executive of the club from embarrassment I have decided to place the resignation of the secretaryship in the hands of the members of the board.'

1907	Chelsea	H	First Division	4-1
1912	Sheffield Wednesday	A	First Division	3-3
1918	Blackburn Rovers	A	Lancashire Section Principal Tournament	1-1
1929	West Ham United	A	First Division	1-2
1935	Southampton	A	Second Division	1-2
1940	Manchester City	A	North Regional League	1-3
1946	Arsenal	H	First Division	5-2

On the same day that United were beating Arsenal in a League match, Johnny Carey was capped by Northern Ireland in the match against England in Belfast. After the game he travelled down to Dublin, where two days later he was capped by Eire, again against England, the most celebrated example of a player having dual nationality. In May 1947 he also played for the Rest of Europe against Great Britain.

1957	Wolverhampton Wanderers	A	First Division	1-3
1963	Leicester City	H	First Division	3-1

1968 Russell Beardsmore born in Wigan. Russell was first spotted by United whilst playing for Wigan Schoolboys and signed as an apprentice in June 1985. Upgraded to the professional ranks in October 1986, he made his debut for the first team in October 1988, but over the next five years he found first-team opportunities severely restricted, making almost half of his appearances after coming off the substitutes' bench. After a loan spell with Blackburn in 1991, he was released on a free transfer in June 1993 and joined Bournemouth.

1974	Norwich City	A	Second Division	0-2
1985	Southampton	H	First Division	1-0
1986	Chelsea	H	First Division	0-1
1988	Rotherham United	A	Littlewoods Cup 2nd Round 1st Leg	1-0
1991	Tottenham Hotspur	A	First Division	2-1
1994	Galatasary	A	European Cup Group A	0-0

SEPTEMBER 29TH

1900	Leicester Fosse	A	Second Division	0-1

1906	Derby County	H	First Division	1-1
1917	Manchester City	A	Lancashire Section Principal Tournament	1-3
1923	South Shields	H	Second Division	1-1
1928	Newcastle United	H	First Division	5-0
1934	Swansea Town	H	Second Division	3-1
1945	Barnsley	H	Football League North	1-1
1951	Preston North End	H	First Division	1-2
1956	Arsenal	A	First Division	2-1

1957   Les Sealey born in London. He began his professional career with Coventry City in 1976 and moved on to Luton in 1983. A member of the side that finished runners-up in the League Cup in 1989, he initially joined United on loan in December 1989 and again in March 1990, the loan due to expire at the end of the season. United had won through to the FA Cup final and Les was expected to provide cover for first choice Jim Leighton, but Jim's nervous performance in the first match prompted Alex Ferguson to drop him for the replay and bring Les in. Les's performance not only helped United lift the cup but was also responsible for gaining the goalkeeper a one-year contract. At the end of that term he helped United win the European Cup-Winners' Cup. He then joined Aston Villa but was unable to claim a regular place and had loan spells with Coventry and Birmingham City before returning to United for a second spell. Although he made only two appearances this time round, they came in the FA Cup quarter-final and League Cup final, the latter against Aston Villa which Villa won 3-1. He was released on a free transfer in 1993 and has since played for Blackpool, West Ham, Leyton Orient and West Ham for a second time.

1962	Sheffield Wednesday	A	First Division	0-1
1973	Liverpool	H	First Division	0-0
1976	Ajax (Amsterdam)	H	UEFA Cup 1st Round 2nd Leg	2-0

United managed to overcome a 1-0 deficit from the first leg thanks to goals from Lou Macari and Sammy McIlroy at Old Trafford.

1979	Stoke City	H	First Division	4-0
1982	Valencia	A	UEFA Cup 1st Round 2nd Leg	1-2
1984	West Bromwich Albion	A	First Division	2-1
1990	Nottingham Forest	H	First Division	0-1
1992	Torpedo Moscow	A	UEFA Cup 1st Round 2nd Leg	0-0

[lost 4-3 on pens]

Mark Hughes was sent off during the second goalless draw with Torpedo Moscow and it was left to penalties to decide which club would progress into the next round. Torpedo scored four to United's three to move into the second round.

1993	Kispest Honved	H	European Cup 1st Round 2nd Leg	2-1
1996	Tottenham Hotspur	H	FA Premier League	2-0

SEPTEMBER 30TH

1893	Darwen	A	First Division	0-1
1899	Sheffield Wednesday	A	Second Division	1-2

1903   Ernest Mangnall was appointed as successor to James West. Born in Bolton, he was a goalkeeper who played for Lancashire County before concentrating on the administrative side of the game, becoming a director of Bolton Wanderers and later being appointed secretary of the club. He left Bolton in 1900 in order to take up the post of secretary of Burnley and had thereafter been recommended to United by J.J. Bentley. Aside from establishing United as a major force during his time with the club (they would go on to win the League title and FA Cup for the first time under his stewardship), he is best remembered for his ability in the transfer market; when 17

Manchester City players were suspended by the Football Association in 1907, he swooped to take four of their better players, including Billy Meredith, to United! When he left United in 1912 he took over a similar position with Manchester City!

1905	Blackpool	A	Second Division	1-0
1911	Blackburn Rovers	A	First Division	2-2
1916	Blackpool	A	Lancashire Section Principal Tournament	2-2
1922	Coventry City	H	Second Division	2-1
1933	Oldham Athletic	A	Second Division	0-2
1939	Manchester City	H	Friendly	2-3
1944	Bury	A	Football League North (First Championship)	2-4
1950	Wolverhampton Wanderers	A	First Division	0-0
1961	Wolverhampton Wanderers	H	First Division	0-2
1964	Chelsea	A	First Division	2-0
1967	Manchester City	A	First Division	2-1
1972	Sheffield United	A	First Division	0-1
1978	Manchester City	H	First Division	1-0
1981	Leeds United	H	First Division	1-0

OCTOBER 1ST

1892	West Bromwich Albion	A	First Division	0-0
1898	Burton Swifts	A	Second Division	1-5
1910	Sheffield Wednesday	H	First Division	3-2
1921	Preston North End	H	First Division	1-1
1927	Leicester City	A	First Division	0-1
1932	Preston North End	H	Second Division	0-0

1936 Duncan Edwards born in Dudley. He joined Manchester United straight from school and made his debut in 1952, even before he had signed professional forms with the club. He signed as a professional in October 1953, by which time he was an established team member and one of the most gifted youngsters of his age. He became England's youngest ever cap when selected to play against Scotland, having moved through the ranks of schoolboy, youth and Under-23 level. Despite a relatively short career, Duncan was capped 18 times by England and won two League championship medals and a runners-up medal in the FA Cup. Severely injured in the Munich air disaster, he lived for almost two weeks before losing his gallant battle for life. A permanent memorial to Duncan Edwards can be seen in Dudley, where the church has a stained glass window depicting Duncan and his achievements.

1938	Preston North End	A	First Division	1-1
1949	Sunderland	H	First Division	1-3
1955	Luton Town	H	First Division	3-1
1960	Bolton Wanderers	A	First Division	1-1
1966	Nottingham Forest	A	First Division	1-4
1977	Liverpool	H	First Division	2-0
1980	Widzew Lodz	A	UEFA Cup 1st Round 2nd Leg	0-0

With the first leg at Old Trafford having finished in a 1-1 draw, United were eliminated from the competition on away goals counting double.

1983	Norwich City	A	First Division	3-3
1988	Tottenham Hotspur	A	First Division	2-2
1994	Everton	H	FA Premier League	2-0
1995	Liverpool	H	FA Premier League	2-2

Eric Cantona returned after his eight-month suspension and made it a sensational comeback, laying on the first United goal for Nicky Butt and later scoring the equaliser from the penalty spot after Ryan Giggs had been brought down. Although he was obviously short of match practice, all his old tricks and flicks were in evidence.

| 1997 | Juventus | H | UEFA Champions League | 3-2 |

OCTOBER 2ND

1897	Leicester Fosse	H	Second Division	2-0
1909	Newcastle United	H	First Division	1-1
1915	Stoke City	A	Lancashire Section Principal Tournament	0-0
1920	Tottenham Hotspur	A	First Division	1-4
1926	Aston Villa	H	First Division	2-1
1937	Sheffield United	H	Second Division	0-1
1943	Blackburn Rovers	A	Football League North (First Championship)	1-2

1944 Willie Morgan born in Sauchie near Alloa. He began his professional career with Burnley in October 1961, eventually taking over the role vacated by John Connelly's transfer to Old Trafford in the 1963-64 season and was signed by United for £100,000 in August 1968. Initially used as a winger, he later dropped into midfield, all the time giving the club excellent service which was rewarded by 20 caps for Scotland to go with the one he had already won at Burnley. A disagreement with manager Tommy Docherty prompted a move to Burnley in June 1975 and he later played for Bolton and in the United States before retiring in 1982. In November 1978 his clash with Tommy Docherty reached the High Court, with a libel case Docherty brought against both Willie and Granada TV collapsing after he admitted to lying on oath.

1948	Sunderland	A	First Division	1-2
1954	Wolverhampton Wanderers	A	First Division	2-4
1957	Shamrock Rovers	H	European Cup Preliminary Round 2nd Leg	3-2

Having already won the away leg 6-0 United were never in any danger of allowing Shamrock Rovers back into the game, but if the fans were expecting a goal avalanche they were to be disappointed, for two goals from Dennis Viollet and a single strike from David Pegg gave United the narrowest of wins.

1963	Chelsea	A	First Division	1-1
1968	Waterford	H	European Cup 1st Round 2nd Leg	7-1
1971	Sheffield United	H	First Division	2-0
1976	Leeds United	A	First Division	2-0
1982	Luton Town	A	First Division	1-1
1991	Athinaikos	H	European Cup-Winners' Cup 1st Round 2nd Leg	2-0
1993	Sheffield Wednesday	A	FA Premier League	3-2

OCTOBER 3RD

| 1891 | Ardwick | H | FA Cup 1st Qualifying Round | 5-1 |

The first competitive Manchester derby took place between Newton Heath and Ardwick (forerunners to the current Manchester City club) at Monsall. The importance of the game, despite the fact that neither side had yet attained Football League status, can be judged by the fact that local MP Sir James Ferguson kicked the game off! Despite the flattering nature of the scoreline, Ardwick battled gamely throughout and had an opportunity to take the lead when awarded a penalty. Slater fisted the ball away and the Heathens immediately broke away to take the lead through Sneddon. The second half was all one-way traffic as Newton Heath pressed continuously at the visitors' goal, finally winning 5-1.

1896	Manchester City	A	Second Division	0-0
1903	Woolwich Arsenal	A	Second Division	0-4
1908	Bury	A	First Division	2-2

1914	Sunderland	H	First Division	3-0
1925	Leeds United	A	First Division	0-2
1931	Burnley	A	Second Division	0-2
1936	Arsenal	H	First Division	2-0
1942	Blackburn Rovers	H	Football League North (First Championship)	5-2
1953	Burnley	H	First Division	1-2
1959	Leicester City	H	First Division	4-1
1970	Wolverhampton Wanderers	A	First Division	2-3
1972	Bristol Rovers	A	League Cup 3rd Round	1-1
1981	Wolverhampton Wanderers	H	First Division	5-0

Shortly before the kick-off United revealed their latest signing Bryan Robson, for whom they had paid West Bromwich Albion a then-record £1.5 million. The actual signing took place on the pitch.

1983	Port Vale	A	Milk Cup 2nd Round 1st Leg	1-0
1984	Raba Vasas ETO Gyor	A	UEFA Cup 1st Round 2nd Leg	2-2
1987	Luton Town	A	First Division	1-1
1989	Portsmouth	H	Littlewoods Cup 2nd Round 2nd Leg	0-0
1990	Pecsi Munkas	A	European Cup-Winners' Cup 1st Round 2nd Leg	1-0
1992	Middlesbrough	A	FA Premier League	1-1
1995	York City	A	Coca-Cola Cup 2nd Round 2nd Leg	3-1

United had put out a weakened side for the first leg at Old Trafford and had slipped to one of their most humiliating defeats of all time, allowing the Second Division side (equal to the old Third Division) to register a 3-0 lead. Alex Ferguson brought back many of the big guns for the second leg at Bootham Crescent, but Scott Jordan's first-half strike for York proved decisive. Although United scored three, with Paul Scholes grabbing two and Terry Cooke one, York ended up with a 4-3 aggregate victory that must have seemed impossible when the draw had first been made.

OCTOBER 4TH

| 1890 | Higher Walton | A | FA Cup 1st Qualifying Round | 2-0 |

Although Higher Walton were drawn at home in the FA Cup tie, they agreed to switch the match to Newton Heath's North Road ground in order to take their share in higher receipts. As it turned out a crowd of 3,000 were in attendance to see Farman and Evans score the goals that took the Heathens into the next round.

1902	Chesterfield	H	Second Division	2-1
1913	Tottenham Hotspur	H	First Division	3-1
1919	Middlesbrough	H	First Division	1-1
1924	Clapton Orient	A	Second Division	1-0
1930	Manchester City	A	First Division	1-4
1941	Everton	A	Football League Northern Section (First Championship)	3-1
1947	Stoke City	H	First Division	1-1
1952	Wolverhampton Wanderers	A	First Division	2-6
1958	Wolverhampton Wanderers	A	First Division	0-4

United were already without the services of Bobby Charlton, Harry Gregg and Wilf McGuinness, all of whom were in Belfast playing in the Northern Ireland v England international. The Football League also wanted to experiment with playing League football on a Saturday evening, rather than the afternoon, and chose this match for their experiment. It was probably one United didn't wish to see repeated, for they slumped to a 4-0 defeat at the hands of the League champions.

| 1969 | Derby County | A | First Division | 0-2 |

1975	Leicester City	H	First Division	0-0
1976	Sunderland	A	League Cup 3rd Round Replay	2-2 [aet]
1978	Watford	H	League Cup 3rd Round	1-2
1980	Nottingham Forest	A	First Division	2-1
1986	Nottingham Forest	A	First Division	1-1

1993 Former Scotland, United and Coventry defender Jim Holton died behind the wheel of his car, apparently from a heart attack, at the age of 42.

| 1997 | Crystal Palace | H | FA Premier League | 2-0 |

OCTOBER 5TH

1895	Manchester City	H	Second Division	1-1
1901	Stockport County	H	Second Division	3-3
1907	Nottingham Forest	A	First Division	4-0
1912	Blackburn Rovers	H	First Division	1-1
1918	Manchester City	H	Lancashire Section Principal Tournament	0-2
1929	Manchester City	H	First Division	1-3

1934 Ronnie Cope born in Crewe. Ronnie was signed by United as an amateur in June 1950 and as a professional in October 1951. Although he made his debut for the club in 1956, he did not get a chance to break into the first team on a regular basis until after the Munich air disaster, for he had been third choice at the club at the time. He did go on to make over 100 appearances for United, appearing in the 1958 FA Cup final and joined Luton in 1961. He later moved into non-League circles as a player and then manager and coach.

| 1935 | Port Vale | A | Second Division | 3-0 |
| 1940 | Manchester City | H | North Regional League | 0-2 |

David Gaskell born in Orrell in Lancashire. David was spotted by United whilst playing for Lancashire Schoolboys and signed professional forms in October 1957, although he had already made his first-team debut for the club under the most unusual of circumstances. He had gone along to watch United play Manchester City in the FA Charity Shield at Maine Road in October 1956 when midway through the action United goalkeeper Ray Wood suffered a hip injury and had to retire from the match. As the game was not considered a first-class competitive game, United were able to bring on a substitute and so selected the barely 16-year-old David, who did well in the 1-0 win. His League debut was not pleasant, for Spurs' Bobby Smith scored a first-half hat-trick against him! Although he was invariably in direct competition with Ray Wood and Harry Gregg for the number one jersey, he still managed to make over 100 appearances for the first team and won a winners' medal in the 1963 FA Cup final before moving on to Wrexham in 1969.

| 1946 | Preston North End | H | First Division | 1-1 |
| 1957 | Aston Villa | H | First Division | 4-1 |

Aston Villa's Peter McParland expected a hostile atmosphere to greet him in the first meeting between the two sides since the FA Cup final clash the previous May when McParland had clattered into Ray Wood and forced him to leave the field injured. As it was Villa received a sporting welcome from the United fans.

1963	Bolton Wanderers	A	First Division	1-0
1968	Arsenal	H	First Division	0-0
1974	Fulham	A	Second Division	2-1
1977	St Etienne	H	European Cup-Winners' Cup 1st Round 2nd Leg	2-0

Following crowd trouble at the first leg match, United were forced to play the second leg at least 300 km away from Old Trafford and thus met St Etienne at Home Park, Plymouth. A crowd of 31,634 saw the game in Plymouth, whilst nearly 30,000 watched at Old Trafford via close circuit television.

| 1985 | Luton Town | A | First Division | 1-1 |

United began the season in blistering form, registering 10 straight wins and with a chance of equalling Spurs' 1960-61 record of 11 from the start of the season. They fell one short of the record held at Kenilworth Road, but this was a temporary blip as they recorded another three wins and a draw for a 15-match unbeaten run. Interestingly enough, Spurs' first defeat in their season was at Sheffield Wednesday, the very same club that had inflicted United's first defeat in 1985-86.

| 1994 | Port Vale | H | Coca-Cola Cup 2nd Round 2nd Leg | 2-0 |

United came in for some considerable criticism for fielding weakened sides in both legs of the Coca-Cola Cup ties with Port Vale, although the Football League decided to take no financial action against the club for so doing. Instead, it was recommended that clubs competing in European competitions should be exempt from the Coca-Cola Cup until the third round.

OCTOBER 6TH

1894	Darwen	A	Second Division	1-1
1900	New Brighton	H	Second Division	1-0
1906	Stoke City	A	First Division	2-1
1917	Manchester City	H	Lancashire Section Principal Tournament	1-1
1923	Oldham Athletic	A	Second Division	2-3

Both of United's goals were own goals scored by Oldham full-back Sam Wynne. The same player also netted two of Oldham's goals, hitting a free-kick and a penalty! Wynne later entered the record books when he became the first man to die during a first-class match.

1928	Burnley	A	First Division	4-3
1934	Burnley	A	Second Division	2-1
1945	Everton	H	Football League North	0-0
1948	Arsenal	A	FA Charity Shield	3-4
1951	Derby County	H	First Division	2-1
1956	Charlton Athletic	H	First Division	4-2

Bobby Charlton made his debut for United against appropriately named opponents and scored two goals into the bargain. United's other goals were scored by Berry and Whelan.

1962	Blackpool	A	First Division	2-2
1964	Burnley	A	First Division	0-0
1965	HJK Helsinki	H	European Cup Preliminary Round 2nd Leg	6-0
1971	Burnley	H	League Cup 3rd Round	1-1
1973	Wolverhampton Wanderers	A	First Division	1-2

Alex Stepney missed a golden opportunity to move ahead in the ranks of United's top goalscorer for the season when he missed a penalty in this League match. It proved decisive as well, as United slipped to a home defeat by Wolves.

1976	Sunderland	H	League Cup 3rd Round 2nd Replay	1-0
1979	Brighton & Hove Albion	H	First Division	2-0
1982	AFC Bournemouth	H	Milk Cup 2nd Round 1st Leg	2-0
1984	Aston Villa	A	First Division	0-3
1991	Liverpool	H	First Division	0-0
1993	Stoke City	H	Coca-Cola Cup 2nd Round 2nd Leg	2-0

OCTOBER 7TH

| 1893 | Derby County | A | First Division | 0-2 |
| 1899 | Lincoln City | H | Second Division | 1-0 |

1905	Bradford City	H	Second Division	0-0
1911	Sheffield Wednesday	H	First Division	3-1

1912 Tom Manley born in Northwich. Signed by United as an amateur from Northwich Victoria in 1930, he was upgraded to the professional ranks in May 1931. He made his debut in December the same year and over the next eight years played at full-back, half-back and forward. In July 1939 he joined Brentford, but following the outbreak of the Second World War returned to United to guest for them for the duration, returning to Griffin Park at the end of the war. He retired in May 1952 and became a publican, although he had a brief spell managing Northwich Victoria.

1916	Liverpool	H	Lancashire Section Principal Tournament	0-0

1920 Jack Rowley born in Wolverhampton. Originally discovered by Wolves, he was released to Bournemouth in 1937 without having made a first-team appearance for Wolves, although a tally of ten goals in his first 11 games at Dean Court soon had bigger clubs showing an interest. He joined United for £3,000 in October 1937 and had established himself as a regular in the side when the Second World War broke out. During the war he guested for a number of clubs, usually dependent upon where he was stationed (he was top goalscorer for Spurs when they won the League South title in 1944), returning to United's League side when the war ended. He scored twice in the 1948 FA Cup final as United beat Blackpool 4-2 and hit the net 30 times in the championship winning season of 1951-52, a record haul in a season for United until Dennis Violett scored 32 in 1959-60. In 1955 he accepted an offer from Plymouth Argyle to take over as player-manager, retiring from playing in 1957 and remaining as manager at Home Park until 1960. He then served Oldham, Wrexham, Bradford Park Avenue and Oldham again as manager, and also had a brief spell coaching Ajax in Amsterdam. His brother Arthur was an equally renowned goalscorer and holds the League record of 433 goals in a career.

1922	Port Vale	H	Second Division	1-2

1926 The FA Investigating Committee, headed by Frederick Wall, made the following short announcement: 'For improper conduct in his position as Secretary-Manager of the Manchester United Football Club, the Football Association have suspended Mr J.A. Chapman from taking part in football or football management during the present season.' There has never been any further announcement from the FA, nor from the club itself, as to what had caused such an action. Indeed, not even the press and media of the day offered even any speculation as to what had happened. Instead, John Chapman quietly packed his bags and left the club! In his place United made Clarence Hilditch player-manager, the only player-manager in the club's history. Whilst the club could have been thrown into turmoil over the situation, Hilditch did a remarkable job in ensuring morale remained high and United remained in the First Division until a permanent replacement could be found.

1929	Sheffield United	A	First Division	1-3
1931	Manchester City	H	Lancashire Senior Cup 1st Round	2-3
1933	Preston North End	H	Second Division	1-0
1944	Chester	A	Football League North (First Championship)	0-2
1950	Sheffield Wednesday	H	First Division	3-1
1961	West Bromwich Albion	A	First Division	1-1
1967	Arsenal	H	First Division	1-0
1970	Portsmouth	H	League Cup 3rd Round	1-0
1972	West Bromwich Albion	A	First Division	2-2
1978	Middlesbrough	H	First Division	3-2
1981	Tottenham Hotspur	A	League Cup 2nd Round 1st Leg	0-1
1986	Port Vale	A	Littlewoods Cup 2nd Round 2nd Leg	5-2
1987	Hull City	A	Littlewoods Cup 2nd Round 2nd Leg	1-0

1992 Brighton & Hove Albion   H   Coca-Cola Cup 2nd Round 2nd Leg   1-0
1995 Eric Cantona's appearance for the reserves, only his second match of any kind since the
      completion of his eight-month suspension, was sufficient to attract a crowd of 21,502
      to Old Trafford to watch the reserves take on their Leeds United counterparts.

OCTOBER 8TH

1892	West Bromwich Albion	H	First Division	2-4
1898	Port Vale	H	Second Division	2-1
1904	Bradford City	A	Second Division	1-1
1910	Bristol City	A	First Division	1-0
1921	Tottenham Hotspur	A	First Division	2-2
1927	Everton	A	First Division	2-5

Everton would go on to win the League championship at the end of the season, but the main story of the 1927-28 season was the goalscoring form of Dixie Dean, who crashed in 60 goals, a record which beat the previous best of 59 set by George Camsell just a year earlier. Dean grabbed all five of Everton's goals in this game in front of a crowd of over 40,000.

1932	Burnley	A	Second Division	3-2
1938	Charlton Athletic	H	First Division	0-2
1949	Charlton Athletic	H	First Division	3-2
1955	Wolverhampton Wanderers	H	First Division	4-3
1958	Preston North End	H	First Division	0-2
1966	Blackpool	A	First Division	2-1
1969	Southampton	A	First Division	3-0
1973	Middlesbrough	H	League Cup 2nd Round	0-1
1975	Aston Villa	A	League Cup 3rd Round	2-1
1977	Middlesbrough	A	First Division	1-2
1980	Aston Villa	H	First Division	3-3
1994	Sheffield Wednesday	A	FA Premier League	0-1

OCTOBER 9TH

1897	Newcastle United	A	Second Division	0-2
1909	Liverpool	A	First Division	2-3
1915	Burnley	H	Lancashire Section Principal Tournament	3-7
1920	Oldham Athletic	H	First Division	4-1
1926	Bolton Wanderers	A	First Division	0-4

With manager John Chapman having been suspended from football for the rest of the current season, United were forced to turn to player Clarence Hilditch to take temporary charge until either the suspension was lifted or a replacement could be found. In the event, Chapman never returned and Herbert Bamlett arrived at the end of the season to take over, but it still meant Clarence had a difficult job in trying to raise the spirits at the club for some six or seven months.

1943	Chester	H	Football League North (First Championship)	3-1
1948	Charlton Athletic	H	First Division	1-1
1954	Cardiff City	H	First Division	5-2
1965	Liverpool	H	First Division	2-0
1968	Tottenham Hotspur	A	First Division	2-2
1971	Huddersfield Town	A	First Division	3-0
1974	Manchester City	H	League Cup 3rd Round	1-0
1982	Stoke City	H	First Division	1-0
1984	Burnley	A	Milk Cup 2nd Round 2nd Leg	3-0

| 1985 | Crystal Palace | H | Milk Cup 2nd Round 2nd Leg | 1-0 |
| 1991 | Cambridge United | A | Rumbelows Cup 2nd Round 2nd Leg | 1-1 |

OCTOBER 10TH

1608 The *Manchester Lete Roll* contained the resolution, 'That whereas there has been heretofore great disorder in our towne of Manchester, and the inhabitants thereof greatly wronged and charged with makinge and amendinge of their glasse windowes broken yearelye and spoyled by a companye of lewd and dis-ordered psons using that unlawfull exercise of playinge with the ffote-ball in ye streets of ye sd towne breaking many men's windowes and glasse at their plesures and other great enormyties. Therefore we of this jurye doe order that no manner of psons hereafter shall play or use footeball in any street within the said towne of Manchester, subpoend to evyeone that shall use the same for evye time.'

1891	Ardwick	H	Football Alliance	3-1
1896	Small Heath	H	Second Division	1-1
1903	Barnsley	H	Second Division	4-0

Harry Moger made his debut for United. Born in Southampton in September 1879 he began his career at Southampton but found first-team opportunities limited by the presence of international goalkeeper John Robinson and transferred to United in May 1903. After a hesitant start he became first choice goalkeeper and won medals for two League championships and the FA Cup, although was never capped at international level. The introduction of Hugh Edmonds forced Harry out of the side and he announced his retirement in June 1912.

1908	Sheffield United	H	First Division	2-1
1914	Sheffield Wednesday	A	First Division	0-1
1925	Newcastle United	H	First Division	2-1
1931	Preston North End	H	Second Division	3-2

1935 Albert Scanlon born in Manchester. Albert joined United straight from school and became a professional in December 1952, making his debut in November 1954. Although he was not a regular in the side, he was an important squad member and travelled with the side to the ill-fated match with Red Star Belgrade, surviving the crash and then recovering enough from head and leg injuries to resume his battle for a place in the side. In 1960 he was sold to Newcastle United for £18,000 but was unable to settle and was later sold on to Lincoln for £2,000 in 1962. He later played for Mansfield before moving into the non-League game.

1936	Brentford	A	First Division	0-4
1942	Liverpool	H	Football League North (First Championship)	3-4
1953	Sunderland	H	First Division	1-0
1959	Arsenal	H	First Division	4-2
1964	Sunderland	H	First Division	1-0
1970	Crystal Palace	H	First Division	0-1
1979	West Bromwich Albion	A	First Division	0-2
1981	Manchester City	A	First Division	0-0
1987	Sheffield Wednesday	A	First Division	4-2
1990	Halifax Town	H	Rumbelows Cup 2nd Round 2nd Leg	2-1

OCTOBER 11TH

1890	Bootle	A	Football Alliance	0-5
1902	Stockport County	A	Second Division	1-2
1913	Burnley	A	First Division	2-1
1919	Manchester City	A	First Division	3-3

| 1924 | Crystal Palace | H | Second Division | 1-0 |
| 1930 | West Ham United | A | First Division | 1-5 |

1937 Bobby Charlton born in Ashington. As befitted a relative of the famous Milburn footballing family, Bobby Charlton was a schoolboy prodigy, representing England at schoolboy and youth levels before signing professional forms with Manchester United in 1954. An integral part of the famed Busby Babes, he effectively came to the fore after surviving the Munich crash of 1958, winning the first of his many England caps the same year. At domestic level he won two League championship medals, a winners' medal in the FA Cup and, perhaps most importantly, led the side to victory in the 1968 European Cup final against Benfica, scoring two of the goals in the 4-1 victory. The importance of this victory to United in general and Busby in particular was revealed in the immediate aftermath: Busby reserved his longest and most heart-felt hug for Charlton. Two years previously Charlton had been a member of the England team that won the World Cup at Wembley, the same year he was declared Footballer of the Year. He finished his playing career as player-manager of Preston North End, but found he was perhaps not cut out for management. He won a then record 106 caps for England, scoring a record 49 goals (which has yet to be beaten), and as well as collecting a CBE he was made a knight in 1994. He currently combines running a travel agency with serving Manchester United as a director.

1941	Chester	A	Football League Northern Section	
			(First Championship)	7-0
1947	Grimsby Town	H	First Division	3-4
1952	Stoke City	H	First Division	0-2
1958	Arsenal	H	First Division	1-1
1969	Ipswich Town	H	First Division	2-1
1972	Bristol Rovers	H	League Cup 3rd Round Replay	1-2
1975	Leeds United	A	First Division	2-1
1980	Arsenal	H	First Division	0-0
1986	Sheffield Wednesday	H	First Division	3-1

OCTOBER 12TH

1895	Liverpool	A	Second Division	1-7
1901	Burton United	A	Second Division	0-0
1907	Newcastle United	A	First Division	6-1

United gave a League debut to George Stacey. Born in Rotherham in 1887, he was signed by Sheffield Wednesday in 1902 but did not make the grade with them, moving on to Thornhill United and then Barnsley in August 1905. In April 1907 United paid £200 to bring him to Clayton as understudy to Herbert Burgess. He got his chance at regular football when he switched to right-back, taking over from Dick Holden, winning a championship medal at the end of his first season at the club. The following year he collected an FA Cup winners' medal and then a second League championship medal in 1911. The following year he was selected for an England trial, although he did not win a cap. After guesting for Rotherham County during the war he was released by United when League football resumed in 1919. This was a tremendous result for United, for although they ended the season as champions, Newcastle were the reigning title holders themselves and had gone through the entire previous season without a single home defeat!

| 1912 | Derby County | A | First Division | 1-2 |

1917 Jimmy Hanlon born in Manchester. Signed by United to amateur forms in 1934, he was upgraded to the professional ranks in November 1935 and made his debut almost exactly three years later. During the war he served with the Durham Light Infantry and spent three years as a POW after being captured in Crete. He returned to United at the end of the war, although he was not a regular in the side and left to join Bury in 1948. He had made 70 appearances for United, scoring 22 goals during his time with the club.

1918	Manchester City	A	Lancashire Section Principal Tournament	0-0
1929	Grimsby Town	H	First Division	2-5
1935	Fulham	H	Second Division	1-0
1940	Burnley	A	North Regional League	1-0
1946	Sheffield United	A	First Division	2-2
1949	Manchester City	H	Lancashire Senior Cup 1st Round	2-1
1957	Nottingham Forest	A	First Division	2-1
1968	Liverpool	A	First Division	0-2
1974	Notts County	H	Second Division	1-0
1985	Queens Park Rangers	H	First Division	2-0
1988	Rotherham United	H	Littlewoods Cup 2nd Round 2nd Leg	5-0
1996	Liverpool	H	FA Premier League	1-0

OCTOBER 13TH

| 1894 | Woolwich Arsenal | H | Second Division | 3-3 |

This was the first of what would be one of the most compelling fixtures of the football calendar, although Newton Heath and the then Woolwich Arsenal first locked horns in the Second Division. A crowd of 4,000 were at Clayton to see the 3-3 draw, the Heathens' goals coming from Clarkin and a brace from Donaldson.

1900	Gainsborough Trinity	A	Second Division	1-0
1906	Blackburn Rovers	H	First Division	1-1
1917	Everton	A	Lancashire Section Principal Tournament	0-3
1923	Oldham Athletic	H	Second Division	2-0
1928	Cardiff City	H	First Division	1-1
1934	Oldham Athletic	H	Second Division	4-0
1945	Everton	A	Football League North	0-3
1951	Aston Villa	A	First Division	5-2
1956	Sunderland	A	First Division	3-1

United were still unbeaten from the start of the season, having now won ten and drawn two of their opening 12 games. Goals from Billy Whelan, Dennis Viollet and an own goal at Roker Park in front of a crowd of 49,487 ensured maximum points.

1962	Blackburn Rovers	H	First Division	0-3
1973	Derby County	H	First Division	0-1
1979	Bristol City	A	First Division	1-1
1984	West Ham United	H	First Division	5-1

OCTOBER 14TH

| 1893 | West Bromwich Albion | H | First Division | 4-1 |

The match report that appeared in the *Birmingham Gazette* was strongly critical of the style of play of Newton Heath, claiming that a number of Heathens, including George Perrins, had been guilty of dirty play. Newton Heath took objection to the offending article and sued the paper for damages, hoping to win at least £200. Although the jury at Manchester Assizes found in their favour, they awarded damages of the least valuable coin of the realm, one farthing. Both sides had to pay their own costs, which were believed to amount to some £145 (the equivalent of some £6,000 today), money Newton Heath could ill-afford.

| 1899 | Small Heath | A | Second Division | 0-1 |

1905	West Bromwich Albion	A	Second Division	0-1
1911	Bury	A	First Division	1-0
1916	Stockport County	A	Lancashire Section Principal Tournament	0-1
1922	Port Vale	A	Second Division	0-1
1933	Bradford Park Avenue	A	Second Division	1-6
1944	Chester	H	Football League North (First Championship)	1-0
1950	Arsenal	A	First Division	0-3
1961	Birmingham City	H	First Division	0-2
1967	Sheffield United	A	First Division	3-0
1969	Burnley	A	League Cup 4th Round	0-0
1972	Birmingham City	H	First Division	1-0
1978	Aston Villa	A	First Division	2-2
1989	Sheffield Wednesday	H	First Division	0-0
1995	Manchester City	H	FA Premier League	1-0
1997	Ipswich Town	A	Coca-Cola Cup 3rd Round	0-2

There was no doubting manager Alex Ferguson's priorities for the season: the retention of the Premiership title and the lifting of the European Cup, with the Coca-Cola Cup quite a way down the list, especially as when the competition started this season there was not a guaranteed place in Europe for the winners. Ferguson used the opportunity to rest key players for the League struggles that lay ahead, but at the end of the game, it wouldn't have mattered to Ipswich whether United had put out a youth or veteran side; they had claimed a notable scalp by winning 2-0.

OCTOBER 15TH

| 1892 | Wolverhampton Wanderers | H | First Division | 10-1 |

What is still Manchester United's record League score was actually achieved by Newton Heath in their very first season in the Football League. Although the Heathens struggled throughout much of their inaugural season, winning only six of their 30 matches, this 10-1 mauling was very much a record book performance, for the game also saw Bob Donaldson score the very first League hat-trick achieved by a Heathen. Stewart also grabbed a hat-trick, whilst Newton's other goals were scored by Carson, Farman, Hendry and Hood.

1898	Small Heath	A	Second Division	1-4
1904	Lincoln City	H	Second Division	2-0
1910	Newcastle United	H	First Division	2-0
1921	Tottenham Hotspur	H	First Division	2-1
1927	Cardiff City	H	First Division	2-2
1932	Bradford Park Avenue	H	Second Division	2-1
1938	Blackpool	H	First Division	0-0
1949	Aston Villa	A	First Division	4-0
1955	Aston Villa	A	First Division	4-4
1960	Burnley	A	First Division	3-5
1963	Willem II Tilburg	H	European Cup-Winners' Cup 1st Round 2nd Leg	6-1
1966	Chelsea	H	First Division	1-1

1971 Andy Cole born in Nottingham. Signed as a trainee by Arsenal, Andy made only one substitute appearance for the Highbury club before being loaned to Fulham and then Bristol City. His performances for City prompted a permanent transfer for £500,000 in March 1992, and after scoring 12 goals in 29 games he was then sold on to Newcastle United for £1.75 million. At St James Park they structured the team around his strengths and were rewarded when he scored 41 goals in the 1993-94 season, including 34 in the League. In January 1995 he was sensationally sold to Manchester

United for £7 million, the fee being made up by £6 million in cash and Keith Gillespie moving in the opposite direction. He took a while to settle at Old Trafford, but slowly but surely he started grabbing the goals he was bought to get. He helped the club win the Premiership in 1996 and 1997 and FA Cup in 1996 and has also appeared for England. He was named PFA Young Player of the Year in 1994.

1974	Portsmouth	A	Second Division	0-0
1977	Newcastle United	H	First Division	3-2
1983	West Bromwich Albion	H	First Division	3-0
1994	West Ham United	H	FA Premier League	1-0

OCTOBER 16TH

1897	Manchester City	H	Second Division	1-1
1909	Aston Villa	H	First Division	2-0
1915	Preston North End	A	Lancashire Section Principal Tournament	0-0
1920	Oldham Athletic	A	First Division	2-2
1926	Bury	A	First Division	3-0
1937	Blackburn Rovers	A	Second Division	1-1
1943	Chester	A	Football League North (First Championship)	4-5
1948	Stoke City	A	First Division	1-2
1954	Chelsea	A	First Division	6-5
1965	Tottenham Hotspur	A	First Division	1-5

One half of a remarkable pair of League meetings with Spurs during the season, for in the return United were destined to exact perfect revenge by winning 5-1! This match is also historic for United for it saw the first substitution, John Fitzpatrick replacing Denis Law.

| 1968 | Estudiantes | H | World Club Championship 2nd Leg | 1-1 |

Estudiantes employed much the same tactics in the second leg as they had in the first, using any means fair or foul to stop United. Already one goal ahead from the first leg, they added a second after six minutes thanks to Veron, after which their tackling became even more ferocious. Ten minutes from the end, George Best, the victim of some of the more robust challenges, finally lost patience and snapped, resulting in his dismissal along with Medina. Willie Morgan equalised on the night with three minutes to go and then, just on the stroke of full-time, Brian Kidd netted for what everybody assumed was the winner. The referee disallowed the goal, claiming to have already blown for time before the ball entered the net, and if there was a feeling of disappointment there was also relief, for few among the 63,500 in the crowd or ten left on the field relished a third match against such opposition as Estudiantes.

1971	Derby County	H	First Division	1-0
1976	West Bromwich Albion	A	First Division	0-4
1982	Liverpool	A	First Division	0-0
1991	Ryan Giggs became the youngest player to represent Wales when he appeared as a substitute in the match against West Germany at the age of 17 years and 321 days.			
1993	Tottenham Hotspur	H	FA Premier League	2-1
1996	Fenerbahce	A	European Cup Group C	2-0

OCTOBER 17TH

1891	Grimsby Town	A	Football Alliance	2-2
1896	Blackpool	A	Second Division	2-4
1903	Lincoln City	A	Second Division	0-0
1908	Aston Villa	A	First Division	1-3
1914	West Bromwich Albion	H	First Division	0-0

| 1925 | Tottenham Hotspur | H | First Division | 0-0 |

1930 The 1930-31 season was a disaster from beginning to end for United as they finished the season bottom of the First Division and suffered relegation to the Second Division. Midway through it had become apparent to the Supporters Club that the present management and board did not possess the ability to keep United in the top flight, and so they issued leaflets in September calling for a new manager, an improved scouting system in order to recruit more home-grown players, some new signings to lift the spirits of the current team, five shareholders to be co-opted on to the board, and additional funds raised via a new share scheme. Not only did the board ignore the leaflets, but they refused to meet with the Supporters Club as well, claiming they were an unofficial body and therefore not recognised by the club. This may well have been so, but background information that had formed the backbone of their demands had been supplied by some of the players and others in a position to know the turmoil that was threatening to wreck the club. The Supporters Club issued an ultimatum to the board that there would be a mass protest if the board did not react, the protest taking the form of a boycott of the game against Arsenal. As there was no response from the board, a public meeting was held at Hulme Town Hall by some 3,000 the night prior to the game. Charles Roberts, a former United player and now a nominee of the Supporters Club, spoke out against the boycott, arguing that it would affect the players, against whom the Supporters Club had no gripe. Although the main argument was with the board, with a motion of no confidence being passed, the boycott was to go ahead.

1931	Barnsley	A	Second Division	0-0
1936	Portsmouth	A	First Division	1-2
1942	Liverpool	A	Football League North (First Championship)	1-2

1948 Francis Burns born in Lanarkshire. Signed by United as an amateur in June 1964, he became a professional in October the following year. He made his debut in September 1967 and was a regular for much of the season, although he missed out on the European Cup final to Shay Brennan after being injured in the semi-final against Real Madrid. He remained with United until 1972 when he joined Southampton for £60,000, but after only one season moved on to Preston. He finished his playing career with Shamrock Rovers in 1981.

| 1953 | Wolverhampton Wanderers | A | First Division | 1-3 |
| 1956 | Borussia Dortmund | H | European Cup 1st Round 1st Leg | 3-2 |

A crowd of 75,598 were attracted to Maine Road to see United take on the West German champions in the European Cup first round, United's record attendance for a home European match. They were not disappointed either, for goals from David Pegg and two from Dennis Viollet gave United a slender victory to take into the second leg.

1959	Wolverhampton Wanderers	A	First Division	2-3
1964	Wolverhampton Wanderers	A	First Division	4-2
1970	Leeds United	A	First Division	2-2
1981	Birmingham City	H	First Division	1-1
1987	Norwich City	H	First Division	2-1

OCTOBER 18TH

| 1890 | Grimsby Town | H | Football Alliance | 3-1 |

1900 Tom Smith born in Whitburn in County Durham. He began his career with South Shields in May 1919 but was transferred to Leicester City six months later. Four years later he joined United and soon formed an effective wing partnership with Joe Spence, helping the club to promotion from the Second Division in 1924-25. He remained at United until June 1927 when he joined Northampton Town for £250, and three years later he moved on again, this time to Norwich City. He finished his playing career back home with Whitburn FC and died prematurely on 21st February 1934.

1913	Preston North End	H	First Division	3-0
1919	Manchester City	H	First Division	1-0
1924	Southampton	A	Second Division	2-0
1930	Arsenal	H	First Division	1-2

Despite the call for a boycott the previous evening, a crowd of 23,000 attended the Arsenal match, United's highest gate of the season, although a figure nearer 50,000 had been expected. The board did at least take the threat seriously enough, with extra police being in attendance in the event of any trouble. Whether the boycott was a success or not we will never know, but at the end of the season United were relegated. The Supporters Club's worst fears had been realised.

1941	Chester	H	Football League Northern Section (First Championship)	8-1
1947	Sunderland	A	First Division	0-1
1952	Preston North End	A	First Division	5-0
1958	Everton	A	First Division	2-3
1969	Nottingham Forest	H	First Division	1-1
1971	Burnley	A	League Cup 3rd Round Replay	1-0
1975	Arsenal	H	First Division	3-1
1980	Ipswich Town	A	First Division	1-1
1986	Luton Town	H	First Division	1-0
1992	Liverpool	H	FA Premier League	2-2
1997	Derby County	A	FA Premier League	2-2

OCTOBER 19TH

1889	Walsall Town Swifts	A	Football Alliance	0-4
1892	Everton	H	First Division	3-4
1895	Newcastle United	H	Second Division	2-1
1901	Glossop	A	Second Division	0-0
1907	Blackburn Rovers	A	First Division	5-1
1912	Tottenham Hotspur	H	First Division	2-0
1918	Everton	H	Lancashire Section Principal Tournament	1-1
1929	Portsmouth	A	First Division	0-3
1935	Sheffield United	H	Second Division	3-1
1940	Preston North End	H	North Regional League	4-1
1946	Blackpool	A	First Division	1-3
1957	Portsmouth	H	First Division	0-3
1960	Exeter City	A	League Cup 1st Round	1-1

United made their debut in the Football League Cup in its inaugural season, although it was hardly an auspicious start as they were held to a 1-1 draw at St James' Park in front of a crowd of 14,494. Alex Dawson had the honour of scoring United's first goal in the competition, which came 12 minutes from time and enabled United to force a replay.

1963	Nottingham Forest	A	First Division	2-1
1968	Southampton	H	First Division	1-2
1974	Blackpool	A	Second Division	3-0
1977	FC Porto	A	European Cup-Winners' Cup 2nd Round 1st Leg	0-4

United slumped to one of their biggest defeats in European competition with a 4-0 defeat in Porto. Having survived being thrown out of the competition in the previous round, hopes were high that the club could make real progress in the competition, but this result gave little hope for the second leg.

1983	Spartak Varna	A	European Cup-Winners' Cup 2nd Round 1st Leg	2-1
1985	Liverpool	H	First Division	1-1
1991	Arsenal	H	First Division	1-1
1994	Barcelona	H	European Cup Group A	2-2

This was one of the most exciting European games ever played at Old Trafford, with a television audience estimated at 80 million also following the action live. Mark Hughes gave United the lead after 18 minutes with a header but they were pegged back before the break when Romario equalised. Soon after the interval Bakero put Barcelona ahead with a shot past Schmeichel, the signal for an almost non-stop onslought on the Barcelona goal as United searched for the equaliser. It finally came shortly before the end of the game, Lee Sharpe back-heeling the ball home to tie the score.

OCTOBER 20TH

1894	Burton Swifts	A	Second Division	2-1
1900	Walsall	H	Second Division	1-1
1906	Sunderland	A	First Division	1-4
1917	Everton	H	Lancashire Section Principal Tournament	0-0
1923	Stockport County	H	Second Division	3-0
1928	Birmingham	H	First Division	1-0
1934	Newcastle United	A	Second Division	1-0
1945	Bolton Wanderers	A	Football League North	1-1
1951	Sunderland	H	First Division	0-1
1956	Everton	H	First Division	2-5

This was United's first defeat at home since March 1955, a run of 31 League games. The last team to have won at Old Trafford in the League had been Everton who won 2-1 on 19th March 1955!

| 1969 | Burnley | H | League Cup 4th Round Replay | 1-0 |
| 1973 | Birmingham City | H | First Division | 1-0 |

United's goal was scored from the penalty spot by goalkeeper Alex Stepney, appointed chief penalty-taker by manager Tommy Docherty at the start of the season. This was the second penalty Alex had converted and actually made him United's joint top goalscorer at this stage in the season!

1976	Juventus	H	UEFA Cup 2nd Round 1st Leg	1-0
1979	Ipswich Town	H	First Division	1-0
1984	Tottenham Hotspur	H	First Division	1-0
1990	Arsenal	H	First Division	0-1

Twenty-one Manchester United and Arsenal players were involved in a touchline brawl during the League meeting at Old Trafford won by the visitors. Only Arsenal goalkeeper David Seaman was not involved.

| 1993 | Galatasaray | H | European Cup 2nd Round 1st Leg | 3-3 |
| 1996 | Newcastle United | A | FA Premier League | 0-5 |

OCTOBER 21ST

1893	Burnley	A	First Division	1-4
1896	Gainsborough Trinity	A	Second Division	0-2
1899	New Brighton Tower	H	Second Division	2-1
1905	Leicester City	H	Second Division	3-2
1911	Middlesbrough	H	First Division	3-4
1916	Bury	H	Lancashire Section Principal Tournament	3-1
1922	Fulham	H	Second Division	1-1

1933	Bury	A	Second Division	1-2
1939	Manchester City	H	War Regional League, Western Division	0-4

The Football League had been abandoned after three games had been completed and for the next six weeks there was much confusion as to whether football itself would be suspended or whether regional competitions would be organised. Eventually a series of regional Leagues were organised, although they were an extremely haphazard collection of fixtures. This was the first of the war-time fixtures United played, a local derby with Manchester City, although warnings of possible air-raids kept the attendance down to 7,000.

1944	Tranmere Rovers	H	Football League North (First Championship)	6-1
1950	Portsmouth	H	First Division	0-0
1961	Arsenal	A	First Division	1-5

1967 Paul Ince born in Ilford in Essex. Signed by West Ham as a professional in July 1985, he soon established himself as a commander in the midfield for the Hammers and was soon the subject of numerous transfer enquiries. At the end of the 1988-89 season he announced his wish to leave Upton Park, although the circumstances surrounding his subsequent arrival at Old Trafford in September 1989 ensured a hostile reception whenever he has returned to West Ham. At United he was the driving force behind victories in the 1990 and 1994 FA Cup finals, the European Cup-Winners' Cup in 1991 and League Cup in 1992, as well as the championship years of 1993 and 1994. He was allowed to join Inter Milan in 1995 but later returned home with Liverpool in 1997.

1972	Newcastle United	A	First Division	1-2
1978	Bristol City	H	First Division	1-3
1981	Middlesbrough	H	First Division	1-0
1989	Coventry City	A	First Division	4-1
1995	Chelsea	A	FA Premier League	4-1

OCTOBER 22ND

1892	Sheffield Wednesday	A	First Division	0-1
1898	Loughborough Town	H	Second Division	6-1
1900	Manchester City	A	Lancashire Senior Cup 2nd Round	0-2
1904	Leicester Fosse	A	Second Division	3-0
1910	Tottenham Hotspur	A	First Division	2-2
1921	Manchester City	A	First Division	1-4
1927	Derby County	H	First Division	5-0
1932	Millwall	H	Second Division	7-1

This was United's biggest League win of the season, with Tommy Reid scoring a hat-trick, James Brown two and individual goals from Stanley Gallimore and Joe Spence. Despite this win United could finish the season no higher than sixth in the Second Division when a concerted effort towards promotion had been expected.

1938	Derby County	A	First Division	1-5
1949	Wolverhampton Wanderers	H	First Division	3-0
1955	Huddersfield Town	H	First Division	3-0
1957	Aston Villa	H	FA Charity Shield	4-0

United's sixth appearance in the FA Charity Shield saw them register their biggest winning margin since the successes of 1911 and 1908. A crowd of 27,923 saw United ensure the shield remained at Old Trafford for the second consecutive season with goals from Johnny Berry and a Tommy Taylor hat-trick.

1960	Newcastle United	H	First Division	3-2
1977	West Bromwich Albion	A	First Division	0-4
1980	Stoke City	A	First Division	2-1

1983	Sunderland	A	First Division	1-0
1988	Wimbledon	A	First Division	1-1
1996	Swindon Town	H	Coca-Cola Cup 3rd Round	2-1
1997	Feyenoord	H	UEFA Champions League	2-1

OCTOBER 23RD

1897	Small Heath	A	Second Division	1-2
1909	Sheffield United	A	First Division	1-0

Jimmy Turnball of Manchester United was ordered off for the second week running. After getting his marching orders in last week's home match with Aston Villa, he was sent off today against Sheffield United at Bramall Lane. Manchester United won both games, 2-0 against Villa and 1-0 today.

1912 Jack Hall born in Failsworth in Lancashire. Signed by United in September 1932 from local football, he broke into the first team in 1933 but had to wait until 1935-36 before he was considered the first-choice goalkeeper. At the end of the season Jack surprised everyone by rejecting United's terms and joining Spurs, even though United had won promotion to the First Division and Spurs were languishing in the Second! He was not retained by Spurs at the end of the Second World War and slipped into non-League football.

1915	Stockport County	H	Lancashire Section Principal Tournament	3-0
1920	Preston North End	H	First Division	1-0

United gave a debut to goalkeeper Alf Steward. Born in Manchester, Alf was first spotted by United whilst keeping goal for Stalybridge Celtic and signed with the club as an amateur in 1919. A dispute with his employers who disagreed with him leaving early on a Saturday in order to play football led to him resigning and signing as a professional with United in January 1920. By 1923-24 he had established himself as a regular in the first team and went on to make 326 appearances for the club. In 1932 he became player-manager with Manchester North End, guiding them to the final of a local cup competition where they drew with Altrincham. By the time the replay took place the following season, Alf was player-manager with Altrincham, who then won the final! In 1938 he became manager of Torquay United, although he resigned in 1940 in order to work in a munitions factory in Birmingham.

1926	Birmingham	H	First Division	0-1
1937	Sheffield Wednesday	H	Second Division	1-0
1943	Liverpool	A	Football League North (First Championship)	4-3
1948	Burnley	H	First Division	1-1
1954	Newcastle United	H	First Division	2-2
1965	Fulham	A	First Division	4-1
1971	Newcastle United	A	First Division	1-0
1976	Norwich City	H	First Division	2-2
1982	Manchester City	H	First Division	2-2
1990	Wrexham	H	European Cup-Winners' Cup 2nd Round 1st Leg	3-0

UEFA announced that they were unable to amend their rules and so Wrexham had to set off from Wrexham 24 hours before their tie. The journey on the M56 normally takes 40 minutes!

1991	Athletico Madrid	A	European Cup-Winners' Cup 2nd Round 1st Leg	0-3
1993	Everton	A	FA Premier League	1-0
1994	Blackburn Rovers	A	FA Premier League	4-2

OCTOBER 24TH

1891	Heywood	H	FA Cup 2nd Qualifying Round	walk over

Heywood scratched from the competition giving Newton Heathen an automatic bye into the next round, but the match was played as a friendly which the Heathens won 3-2.

1896	Burton Wanderers	H	Second Division	3-0
1903	Stockport County	H	Second Division	3-1
1908	Nottingham Forest	H	First Division	2-2

Making his debut for United in this match was Oscar Linkson. He had been spotted by United whilst playing for a touring team, The Pirates, and came to Old Trafford in July 1908. After making 59 appearances for the first team he was released to sign for Shelbourne in August 1913 and made a number of guest appearances for QPR during the First World War. He was killed in action in France in December 1916.

1914	Everton	A	First Division	2-4
1925	Cardiff City	A	First Division	2-0
1931	Notts County	H	Second Division	3-3
1936	Chelsea	H	First Division	0-0
1942	Stockport County	A	Football League North (First Championship)	4-1
1953	Aston Villa	H	First Division	1-0
1956	Manchester City	A	FA Charity Shield	1-0

Although both City and United had made numerous appearances in the FA Charity Shield during its long history, this was the first time they had met to directly contest the trophy. And whilst it may have been traditional for the League champions to host the game with their FA Cup winning opponents, the fact that Old Trafford had yet to install floodlights led to a switch to Maine Road. A crowd of 30,495 saw an enthralling contest, dominated by the story of the goalkeepers. City's Bert Trautmann had been the man of the match in City's FA Cup final win but had broken his neck midway through the game and was therefore unable to play in this meeting. After 40 minutes Ray Wood in the United goal was injured and had to leave the field, and although substitutes had yet to be introduced into League football, the fact that this was not classified as a competitive game allowed United to put 16-year-old reserve David Gaskell into goal. He kept a clean sheet too, and Dennis Viollet's 75th minute strike was enough to win the game.

1959	Sheffield Wednesday	H	First Division	3-1
1960	Nottingham Forest	H	First Division	2-1
1962	Tottenham Hotspur	A	First Division	2-6
1964	Aston Villa	H	First Division	7-0
1970	West Bromwich Albion	H	First Division	2-1
1973	Manchester City	H	Tony Dunne Testimonial	1-2
1981	Liverpool	A	First Division	2-1
1984	PSV Eindhoven	A	UEFA Cup 2nd Round 1st Leg	0-0
1992	Blackburn Rovers	A	FA Premier League	0-0

OCTOBER 25TH

| 1890 | Bootle Reserves | A | FA Cup 2nd Qualifying Round | 0-1 |

Newton Heath fielded a reserve side for the FA Cup tie with Bootle Reserves and were promptly knocked out of the competition 1-0!

1898 John Grimwood born in Marsden near South Shields. Signed by United in May 1919, he made his debut in the derby match with City in October that year, deputising for Clarence Hilditch who was on international duty. Grimwood did well enough to subsequently become a permanent fixture in United's half-back line, making over 200 appearances for the first team during his time with the club. He left in June 1927 for Aldershot Town but was signed by Blackpool weeks later for £2,750, staying a year with the Seasiders before going into non-League football.

1902	Woolwich Arsenal	A	Second Division	1-0
1905	Gainsborough Trinity	A	Second Division	2-2
1913	Newcastle United	A	First Division	1-0
1919	Sheffield United	A	First Division	2-2
1924	Wolverhampton Wanderers	A	Second Division	0-0
1930	Portsmouth	A	First Division	1-4

1932 Harry Gregg born in County Derry. After impressing in the Irish League, Harry was signed by Doncaster Rovers for £2,000 in 1952. Over the next five years he earned rave reviews for his heroics in goal and was then signed by United for a record fee of £25,000 in December 1957. Two months later Harry was one of the heroes of the Munich air crash, returning time after time into the burning fuselage to carry survivors to safety. He played in the 1958 FA Cup final, in which he collected his only honour from his time at United, a runners-up medal, but the general consensus was that he deserved much more, especially after having been bundled into the goal by Nat Lofthouse for Bolton's second goal. That same year he was part of the Northern Ireland side that reached the World Cup quarter-finals and was voted best goalkeeper of the tournament. After a series of niggling injuries he moved to Stoke in 1966 but played only twice before turning to management. He also spent a brief spell as specialist goalkeeping coach at Old Trafford from 1978 to 1981.

1937 Wilf McGuinness born in Manchester. Although Wilf will forever be remembered as the man who took over from Sir Matt Busby at the helm of the club, he had begun his association with the club in January 1953, signing amateur forms as a player. He was upgraded to the professional ranks in November 1954 and made his first-team debut in October 1955 and won a League championship medal the same season. He was injured at the time of the Munich air crash and the 1958 FA Cup final, but a broken leg sustained in a reserve match in December 1959 brought his playing career to an end. He then moved into coaching, graduating through the ranks to take over as chief coach in June 1969 and manager in 1970. He lost his job in December 1970 but remained at United as reserve team coach until taking up a managerial position in Greece in 1971. He finished his career with Bury, spending 11 years at Gigg Lane.

1941	Stoke City	A	Football League Northern Section (First Championship)	1-1
1947	Aston Villa	H	First Division	2-0
1952	Burnley	H	First Division	1-3

On the same day, Tommy O'Neil was born in St Helens. Signed by United as an apprentice in August 1968, he signed professional forms in November 1969 and made his debut in May 1971. Given an extended run at full-back by manager Frank O'Farrell, he lost his place following the arrival of new manager Tommy Docherty and Tommy's preference for Tony Young. After a loan period with Blackpool he was sold to Southport, later playing for Tranmere and Halifax before moving into the non-League game.

1958	West Bromwich Albion	H	First Division	1-2
1967	Coventry City	H	First Division	4-0
1969	West Bromwich Albion	A	First Division	1-2
1975	West Ham United	A	First Division	1-2
1980	Everton	H	First Division	2-0
1987	West Ham United	A	First Division	1-1
1989	Tottenham Hotspur	H	Littlewoods Cup 3rd Round	0-3
1997	Barnsley	H	FA Premier League	7-0

Andy Cole scored his first hat-trick of the season in this seven-goal rout of Barnsley, with the other goals coming from Ryan Giggs (two), Paul Scholes and Karel Poborsky.

OCTOBER 26TH

1889	Birmingham St George's	A	Football Alliance	1-5
1895	Newcastle United	A	Second Division	1-2
1901	Doncaster Rovers	H	Second Division	6-0
1907	Bolton Wanderers	H	First Division	2-1
1912	Middlesbrough	A	First Division	2-3
1918	Everton	A	Lancashire Section Principal Tournament	2-6
1929	Arsenal	H	First Division	1-0
1935	Bradford Park Avenue	A	Second Division	0-1
1940	Preston North End	A	North Regional League	1-3
1946	Sunderland	H	First Division	0-3

1952 Arthur Graham born in Castlemilk in Glasgow. Arthur began his career with Aberdeen in 1970 and after only four League matches helped them win the Scottish Cup against Celtic. He was transferred to Leeds United for £125,000 in 1977, after having added a Scottish League Cup winners' medal to his collection. A cut-price fee of £45,000 took him to Old Trafford in August 1983, where he provided short-term cover following the retirement of Steve Coppell. The arrival of Jesper Olsen in 1984 restricted his first-team opportunities and he joined Bradford City in June 1985.

1957	West Bromwich Albion	A	First Division	3-4
1960	Exeter City	H	League Cup 1st Round Replay	4-1

This was the first League Cup tie staged at Old Trafford, although a crowd of only 15,662 meant the fans were not yet impressed that the competition would amount to very much. United's goals were scored by Johnny Giles, Mark Pearson and Albert Quixall, whose two goals included one from the penalty spot.

1963	West Ham United	H	First Division	0-1
1968	Queens Park Rangers	A	First Division	3-2
1974	Southampton	H	Second Division	1-0
1982	AFC Bournemouth	A	Milk Cup 2nd Round 2nd Leg	2-2
1983	Port Vale	H	Milk Cup 2nd Round 2nd Leg	2-0
1985	Chelsea	A	First Division	2-1
1986	Manchester City	A	First Division	1-1
1988	Norwich City	H	First Division	1-2
1991	Sheffield Wednesday	A	First Division	2-3
1994	Newcastle United	A	Coca-Cola Cup 3rd Round	0-2
1996	Southampton	A	FA Premier League	3-6

OCTOBER 27TH

1894	Leicester Fosse	H	Second Division	2-2
1900	Burton Swifts	A	Second Division	1-3
1906	Birmingham	H	First Division	2-1
1917	Port Vale	H	Lancashire Section Principal Tournament	3-3
1923	Stockport County	A	Second Division	2-3
1928	Huddersfield Town	A	First Division	2-1
1934	West Ham United	H	Second Division	3-1
1945	Bolton Wanderers	H	Football League North	2-1
1951	Wolverhampton Wanderers	A	First Division	2-0
1956	Blackpool	A	First Division	2-2
1962	West Ham United	H	First Division	3-1
1964	Djurgaarden	H	Inter-Cities Fairs Cup 1st Round 2nd Leg	6-1

Old Trafford hosted its first Inter-Cities Fairs Cup with the visit of Djurgaarden, with a crowd of 38,437 seeing goals from George Best, a Denis Law hat-trick and a brace from Bobby Charlton complete a 7-2 aggregate victory. This was the second of what would be 11 matches in the competition this season.

1971	Stoke City	H	League Cup 4th Round	1-1
1973	Burnley	A	First Division	0-0
1976	Newcastle United	H	League Cup 4th Round	7-2

United registered their biggest win in the League Cup with a 7-2 win over the side that were runners-up the previous season! United's goals came from Gordon Hill, who scored a hat-trick, Jimmy Nicholl, Stewart Houston, Steve Coppell and Stuart Pearson with a crowd of 52,002 in attendance.

1979	Everton	A	First Division	0-0
1984	Everton	A	First Division	0-5
1987	Crystal Palace	H	Littlewoods Cup 3rd Round	2-1
1990	Manchester City	A	First Division	3-3

With City having won the previous Manchester derby 5-1, United were out for revenge, but after only half an hour things had gone from bad to worse as David White hit the home side two goals ahead. That at last galvanised United into action and Mark Hughes reduced the deficit before half-time, but City started the second half as though they intended putting matters beyond doubt. White was unfortunate not to complete his hat-trick, but City did add a third through Colin Hendry. That was the way the score remained until ten minutes from the end, when Brian McClair rescued a game that was seemingly lost with two goals within a minute.

| 1993 | Leicester City | H | Coca-Cola Cup 3rd Round | 5-1 |

OCTOBER 28TH

1893	Wolverhampton Wanderers	A	First Division	0-2
1899	South Shore	A	FA Cup 3rd Qualifying Round	1-3
1905	Hull City	A	Second Division	1-0
1911	Notts County	A	First Division	1-0
1916	Stoke City	A	Lancashire Section Principal Tournament	0-3
1922	Fulham	A	Second Division	0-0
1933	Hull City	H	Second Division	4-1
1939	Chester	A	War Regional League, Western Division	4-0

On the same day, Mark Pearson was born in Ridgeway in Derbyshire. Signed by United straight from school, he made his debut in the aftermath of the Munich air disaster, but a succession of injuries meant he struggled to maintain a regular place in the side. He was sold to Sheffield Wednesday for £20,000 in October 1963 where he suffered two broken legs before finishing his career with Fulham and then Halifax.

1944	Tranmere Rovers	A	Football League North (First Championship)	4-2
1950	Everton	A	First Division	4-1
1961	Bolton Wanderers	H	First Division	0-3
1963	Blackburn Rovers	H	First Division	2-2
1967	Nottingham Forest	A	First Division	1-3
1970	Chelsea	H	League Cup 4th Round	2-1
1972	Tottenham Hotspur	H	First Division	1-4
1978	Wolverhampton Wanderers	A	First Division	4-2
1981	Tottenham Hotspur	H	League Cup 2nd Round 2nd Leg	0-1
1989	Southampton	H	First Division	2-1
1992	Aston Villa	A	Coca-Cola Cup 3rd Round	0-1
1995	Middlesbrough	H	FA Premier League	2-0

OCTOBER 29TH

1892	Nottingham Forest	A	First Division	1-1

Newton Heath had found the First Division extremely tough going in the opening two months of the season, registering only one victory (although that win, 10-1 over founder members Wolves, remains the club's record score!) and three draws in their opening ten games. By comparison, Nottingham Forest, who had also been promoted into the First Division from the Football Alliance at the end of the previous season, had consolidated relatively well and would finish the season in mid-table safety. The Heathens would be relegated.

1898	Manchester City	A	Friendly	1-2
1904	Barnsley	H	Second Division	4-0
1910	Middlesbrough	H	First Division	1-2
1921	Manchester City	H	First Division	3-1
1927	West Ham United	A	First Division	2-1
1932	Port Vale	A	Second Division	3-3
1938	Sunderland	H	First Division	0-1
1949	Portsmouth	A	First Division	0-0
1955	Cardiff City	A	First Division	1-0
1960	Arsenal	A	First Division	1-2
1966	Arsenal	H	First Division	1-0
1977	Aston Villa	A	First Division	1-2
1983	Wolverhampton Wanderers	H	First Division	3-0
1985	West Ham United	H	Milk Cup 3rd Round	1-0
1986	Southampton	H	Littlewoods Cup 3rd Round	0-0

Old Trafford had first installed floodlights in 1957, which, following the style in vogue at the time, had been placed on pylons around the ground. The completion of cantilever roofs all around the ground had prompted a change in the lighting system, with the lights now being placed on gantries all around the roof. These were turned on for the first time in this Littlewoods Cup tie, although the action was hardly as illuminating!

1994	Newcastle United	H	FA Premier League	2-0

OCTOBER 30TH

1886	Fleetwood Rangers	A	FA Cup 1st Round	2-2

This was the first FA Cup tie Newton Heath ever played, although unlike later years it was not a glorious end that awaited them. At the end of the 90 minutes with the score tied at 2-2, Jack Doughty having scored both, the referee instructed both sides that extra time would be played. Newton Heath did not agree with the decision and walked off the field, with the result that the referee awarded the tie to Fleetwood. As strange as it may seem, such occurrences were commonplace in the last century in the competition, even though it had been operating for some 15 years. The incident obviously upset Newton Heath because they did not enter the FA Cup again until 1889!

1897	Walsall	H	Second Division	6-0
1909	Woolwich Arsenal	H	First Division	1-0
1915	Liverpool	A	Lancashire Section Principal Tournament	2-0
1920	Preston North End	A	First Division	0-0
1926	West Ham United	A	First Division	0-4
1937	Fulham	A	Second Division	0-1
1943	Liverpool	H	Football League North (First Championship)	1-0
1948	Preston North End	A	First Division	6-1
1954	Everton	A	First Division	2-4

1965	Blackpool	A	First Division	2-1
1971	Leeds United	H	First Division	0-1
1976	Ipswich Town	H	First Division	0-1
1982	West Ham United	A	First Division	1-3
1984	Everton	H	Milk Cup 3rd Round	1-2
1988	Everton	A	First Division	1-1
1991	Portsmouth	H	Rumbelows Cup 3rd Round	3-1
1993	Queens Park Rangers	H	FA Premier League	2-1
1996	Fenerbahce	H	European Cup Group C	0-1

United lost at home for the first time in European competition, a record that had stretched over 40 years and 52 games. Despite this defeat, and another at home later in the competition, United still qualified for the knockout stage of the European Cup.

OCTOBER 31ST

1891	Burton Swifts	H	Football Alliance	3-1
1908	Sunderland	A	First Division	1-6
1914	Chelsea	H	First Division	2-2
1925	Huddersfield Town	H	First Division	1-1
1931	Plymouth Argyle	A	Second Division	1-3
1936	Stoke City	A	First Division	0-3
1942	Stockport County	H	Football League North (First Championship)	3-1
1953	Huddersfield Town	A	First Division	0-0
1959	Blackburn Rovers	A	First Division	1-1
1964	Liverpool	A	First Division	2-0

1965   Dennis Irwin born in Cork. After beginning his career with Leeds United, Dennis was allowed to leave on a free transfer in 1986 and joined Oldham where his stylish performances won many admirers. Two semi-final clashes against United in the FA Cup in 1990 alerted Alex Ferguson to Dennis's abilities and during the summer he paid £625,000 to bring him to Old Trafford. Since then he has won winners' medals in the FA Cup in 1994 and 1996, the League Cup in 1992, the European Cup-Winners' Cup in 1991 and four Premiership titles, as well as approaching 50 caps for the Republic of Ireland.

1970	Newcastle United	A	First Division	0-1
1981	Notts County	H	First Division	2-1
1987	Nottingham Forest	H	First Division	2-2
1990	Liverpool	H	Rumbelows Cup 3rd Round	3-1
1992	Wimbledon	H	FA Premier League	0-1

NOVEMBER 1ST

1890	Crewe Alexandra	H	Football Alliance	6-3
1902	Accrington Stanley	H	FA Cup 3rd Qualifying Round	7-0

1903   John Moody born in Heeley in Sheffield. After unsuccessful spells with Arsenal and Bradford, John made his reputation at Doncaster Rovers, where his safe goalkeeping earned him a transfer to United in February 1932. An ever-present during the 1932-33 season, he was surprisingly released at the end of the term and joined Chesterfield.

1913	Liverpool	H	First Division	3-0

United gave a debut to Wilf Woodcock. Wilf was born in Ashton-under-Lyme in 1892 and joined United from Stalybridge Celtic in May 1912, remaining with the club until May 1920. Unfortunately he lost a considerable part of his career to the First World War. The United board refused to grant him a benefit match, on the basis that although he had been registered as a player for eight seasons, he had only played three seasons of League football. He promptly handed in a transfer request and was sold to Manchester City, later playing for Stockport County and Wigan Borough.

1919	Sheffield United	H	First Division	3-0

1921	John Chapman assumed the role of manager of Manchester United, replacing John Robson who had resigned owing to ill-health. Chapman joined United from Scottish club Airdrieonians where he had spent 15 seasons and he took over a United side struggling at the wrong end of the table. His appointment brought no immediate change in their fortunes either, and at the end of the season they were relegated into the Second Division. It took Chapman three seasons to get them back into the top flight. Whether he could have made United a force to be reckoned with again was never fully tested, for he left the club in October 1926 under mysterious circumstances.

1924	Fulham	H	Second Division	2-0
1930	Birmingham	H	First Division	2-0

1936	Eddie Colman born in Salford. Signed by United as an amateur in 1952, he was upgraded to the professional ranks in November 1953, making his debut in November 1955. In just three seasons in the first team he won two League championship medals and appeared in the 1957 FA Cup final and had become a crowd favourite. He would surely have gone on to win many further domestic honours and international recognition had he not lost his life in the Munich air disaster at the age of 21 years old.

1941	Stoke City	H	Football League Northern Section (First Championship)	3-0
1947	Wolverhampton Wanderers	A	First Division	6-2
1952	Tottenham Hotspur	A	First Division	2-1
1958	Leeds United	A	First Division	2-1

1963	Mark Hughes born in Wrexham. Signed by United as a professional in June 1980, Mark soon developed a reputation as a feared striker, even though he had begun his career as a midfielder! First introduced to the side in 1983, he won an FA Cup winners' medal in 1985 and was sensationally sold to Barcelona for £2.5 million in July 1986. The move was not a success and he was subsequently loaned to Bayern Munich before a £1.5 million return home to Old Trafford. His second spell with the club paid dividends for all concerned, for he collected further FA Cup medals in 1990 and 1994, Premiership medals in 1993 and 1994, a League Cup medal in 1992 and scored both goals in the European Cup-Winners' Cup final victory over Barcelona in 1991. He was allowed to join Chelsea for £1.5 million in 1995, a move which many believe was too early for him to have left Old Trafford. Indeed, his medal collection grew, with a further FA Cup medal in 1997 and a League Cup medal in 1998, and the promise of more to come.

1969	Stoke City	H	First Division	1-1
1975	Norwich City	H	First Division	1-0
1980	Crystal Palace	A	First Division	0-1
1986	Coventry City	H	First Division	1-1
1997	Sheffield Wednesday	H	FA Premier League	6-1

NOVEMBER 2ND

1895	Liverpool	H	Second Division	5-2

In addition to the five goals that counted, Newton Heath had a further four goals disallowed. Three of the Heathens' goals were scored by winger James Peters, the first time a winger had registered a hat-trick since 1893. The other two goals were scored by Clarkin and Dick Smith.

1907	Birmingham	A	First Division	4-3

1912	Notts County	H	First Division	2-1
1918	Rochdale	H	Lancashire Section Principal Tournament	3-1
1929	Aston Villa	A	First Division	0-1
1935	Leicester City	H	Second Division	0-1
1940	Burnley	H	North Regional League	4-1
1946	Aston Villa	A	First Division	0-0
1957	Burnley	H	First Division	1-0
1960	Bradford City	A	League Cup 2nd Round	1-2
1963	Wolverhampton Wanderers	A	First Division	0-2
1968	Leeds United	H	First Division	0-0

1971 Revealing that death threats had been made against George Best, United withdrew the player from Northern Ireland's squad to play Spain in Belfast on November 10th.

1974	Oxford United	H	Second Division	4-0
1977	FC Porto	H	European Cup-Winners' Cup 2nd Round 2nd Leg	5-2

United were 4-0 down from the first leg in Porto and had little real chance of overcoming the deficit. They came mightily close, winning 5-2 on the night but losing 6-5 on aggregate, with their goals coming from Steve Coppell (two), Jimmy Nicholl and two own goals from Murca!

1983	Spartak Varna	H	European Cup-Winners' Cup 2nd Round 2nd Leg	2-0
1984	Arsenal	H	First Division	4-2
1985	Coventry City	H	First Division	2-0
1988	Wimbledon	A	Littlewoods Cup 3rd Round	1-2
1991	Sheffield United	H	First Division	2-0
1994	Barcelona	A	European Cup Group A	0-4
1996	Chelsea	H	FA Premier League	1-2

NOVEMBER 3RD

1894	Manchester City	A	Second Division	5-2

The very first League meeting between Manchester City and United's forerunners Newton Heath took place at Hyde Road in front of a crowd of 14,000. City had only recently changed their name from Ardwick, a team Newton Heath had met on a number of occasions previously, including the FA Cup and local cup competitions. By the time of their first League meeting, Newton Heath were already established as the premier club within the city, thanks to their two seasons in the First Division, even if they had battled against relegation on both occasions. When they met in November, both teams had nine points in the bag and a close contest was predicted. City were giving a home debut to new signing Billy Meredith, and he would mark the occasion by scoring both City's goals. Unfortunately for him, Richard Smith of Newton Heath went better, scoring four times to write himself into the record books; his four goals in a Manchester League derby has yet to be equalled. The Heathens' other goal was scored by Sharples in the closing minutes. It is, of course, interesting to compare the records of the two main goalscorers, Meredith and Smith. The former, singled out for special praise in both the local and national press for his performance on the day, would go on to play an integral part in the histories of both clubs, whilst for the latter this was about as good as it got, for he left the club in 1900 having failed to maintain the momentum established here.

1906	Everton	A	First Division	0-3
1917	Port Vale	A	Lancashire Section Principal Tournament	2-2
1923	Leicester City	A	Second Division	2-2
1928	Bolton Wanderers	H	First Division	1-1
1934	Blackpool	A	Second Division	2-1

1945	Preston North End	H	Football League North	6-1
1951	Huddersfield Town	H	First Division	1-1
1956	Wolverhampton Wanderers	H	First Division	3-0
1962	Ipswich Town	A	First Division	5-3
1973	Chelsea	H	First Division	2-2
1976	Juventus	A	UEFA Cup 2nd Round 2nd Leg	0-3
1979	Southampton	H	First Division	1-0
1990	Crystal Palace	H	First Division	2-0
1993	Galatasaray	A	European Cup 2nd Round 2nd Leg	0-0

Quite possibly the most hostile atmosphere United have ever had to play a match in took place in Turkey. The players had been jostled when they had arrived in the city, and banners with the message 'Welcome to Hell' had greeted them. United needed to win, having drawn the first leg 3-3 at Old Trafford, but a defensive display from the Turks kept them at bay and United went out on away goals. There was more trouble to follow too, with Eric Cantona being sent off after the final whistle had blown and then he and Bryan Robson were struck by police as they made their way back to the dressing-room.

NOVEMBER 4TH

1893	Darwen	H	First Division	0-1
1899	Woolwich Arsenal	H	Second Division	2-0
1905	Lincoln City	H	Second Division	2-1
1911	Tottenham Hotspur	H	First Division	1-2

Both United and Spurs spent much of the season flirting with relegation, only making themselves mathematically safe in the closing weeks. For United the fall from grace couldn't have been greater, for they had been League champions the previous season! Ultimately, it was the realisation that the great United side of the previous decade was on the wane that prompted Ernest Mangnall to move on to Manchester City at the end of the season.

1916	Southport Central	H	Lancashire Section Principal Tournament	1-0
1922	Clapton Orient	H	Second Division	0-0
1933	Fulham	A	Second Division	2-0
1944	Liverpool	A	Football League North (First Championship)	2-3
1950	Burnley	H	First Division	1-1
1961	Sheffield Wednesday	A	First Division	1-3
1967	Stoke City	H	First Division	1-0
1972	Leicester City	A	First Division	2-2
1978	Southampton	H	First Division	1-1
1986	Southampton	A	Littlewoods Cup 3rd Round Replay	1-4

United crashed out of the Littlewoods Cup in what was to be Ron Atkinson's last game in charge. Almost as soon as the final whistle sounded speculation about his job began to mount, for United were now out of two competitions as they were too far behind in the League to make any real headway.

1989	Charlton Athletic	A	First Division	0-2
1995	Arsenal	A	FA Premier League	0-1

NOVEMBER 5TH

1892	Blackburn Rovers	H	First Division	4-4
1898	Grimsby Town	H	Second Division	3-2
1904	West Bromwich Albion	A	Second Division	2-0
1910	Preston North End	A	First Division	2-0

1921	Middlesbrough	H	First Division	3-5
1927	Portsmouth	H	First Division	2-0
1932	Notts County	H	Second Division	2-0
1938	Aston Villa	A	First Division	2-0
1949	Huddersfield Town	H	First Division	6-0

Sonny Feehan made his debut for United, deputising for Jack Crompton. As such he was the first Irishman to keep goal for United since the Second World War, although the former car salesman and Gaelic footballer was never able to force a regular place in the side. He had a bright start however, keeping a clean sheet in the six-goal hammering of Huddersfield.

1955	Arsenal	H	First Division	1-1
1960	Sheffield Wednesday	H	First Division	0-0
1966	Chelsea	A	First Division	3-1
1977	Arsenal	H	First Division	1-2
1983	Aston Villa	H	First Division	1-2
1988	Aston Villa	H	First Division	1-1
1997	Feyenoord	A	UEFA Champions League	3-1

United produced a highly polished performance to virtually guarantee their qualification for the knockout stage of the European Cup, for their record now read four straight wins out of four. A home crowd of 45,000 made for a hostile atmosphere, but the most United had to fear was some wayward tackling by the Feyenoord defenders; Dennis Irwin was put out of the game by one such tackle. A hat-trick from Andy Cole, confirming his newly found confidence, was undoubtedly the United highlight.

NOVEMBER 6TH

| 1897 | Lincoln City | A | Second Division | 0-1 |

1904 Jimmy Hanson born in Manchester. After impressing as a schoolboy Jimmy was signed by United in May 1924 and scored on his debut against Hull in November the same year. After scoring 52 goals in 147 appearances for United his career was brought to an abrupt end following a broken fibia, although he was retained by the club until the end of the 1930-31 season in the hope he might recover. He then became a monumental mason in Manchester.

1909	Bolton Wanderers	A	First Division	3-2
1915	Bury	H	Lancashire Section Principal Tournament	1-1
1920	Sheffield United	H	First Division	2-1
1926	Sheffield Wednesday	H	First Division	0-0
1937	Plymouth Argyle	H	Second Division	0-0

1940 Johnny Giles born in Dublin. Although he is best remembered for his career at Leeds United, Johnny joined Manchester United in July 1956 as an amateur and was upgraded to the professional ranks in November 1957. He made 114 appearances for United, winning an FA Cup winners' medal in 1963 before a £37,500 switch to Elland Road. His last appearance for Leeds was in another cup final, this time the European Cup final in 1975. He then became player-manager of West Bromwich Albion, later coaching in the States and Canada before returning for a second spell at the Hawthorns.

1943	Manchester City	A	Football League North (First Championship)	2-2
1948	Everton	H	First Division	2-0
1954	Preston North End	H	First Division	2-1
1965	Blackburn Rovers	H	First Division	2-2

Harry Gregg achieved the unwanted distinction of becoming the first United goalkeeper to be sent off in this 2-2 draw with Blackburn Rovers.

1971	Manchester City	A	First Division	3-3
1976	Aston Villa	A	First Division	2-3
1982	Brighton & Hove Albion	A	First Division	0-1
1985	Norwich City	H	Screen Sport Super Cup Group B	1-1

1986   Ron Atkinson and his assistant Mick Brown were sacked by Manchester United. Although Atkinson had won two FA Cups during his time at Old Trafford, the inability to sustain a title challenge effectively cost him his job. United had started the 1985-86 season with a 15-match unbeaten run and were seemingly on their way to the title until faltering in the final two months. They began this season in much the same form, fourth from bottom and out of the Littlewoods Cup and with no European matches to provide further finance. On the same day he sacked Atkinson and Brown, chairman Martin Edwards flew to Aberdeen to persuade Alex Ferguson that he was the man they wanted to take over at United. The discussions didn't take long, for in the late afternoon Edwards was able to announce Alex Ferguson's impending arrival at Old Trafford.

1991	Athletico Madrid	H	European Cup-Winners' Cup 2nd Round 2nd Leg	1-1
1994	Aston Villa	A	FA Premier League	2-1

NOVEMBER 7TH

1891	Crewe Alexandra	A	Football Alliance	2-0
1896	Grimsby Town	H	Second Division	4-3
1903	Bolton Wanderers	H	Second Division	0-0
1908	Chelsea	H	First Division	0-1
1914	Bradford City	A	First Division	2-4
1925	Everton	A	First Division	3-1
1931	Leeds United	H	Second Division	2-5
1936	Charlton Athletic	H	First Division	0-0
1953	Arsenal	H	First Division	2-2
1959	Fulham	H	First Division	3-3
1964	Sheffield Wednesday	H	First Division	1-0
1970	Stoke City	H	First Division	2-2
1981	Sunderland	A	First Division	5-1
1984	PSV Eindhoven	H	UEFA Cup 2nd Round 2nd Leg	1-0 [aet]

United left it late, very late, before finally overcoming their Dutch opponents in the second round UEFA Cup match, Gordon Strachan scoring in extra time to win the tie 1-0 on aggregate.

1990	Wrexham	A	European Cup-Winners' Cup 2nd Round 2nd Leg	2-0
1992	Aston Villa	A	FA Premier League	0-1
1993	Manchester City	A	FA Premier League	3-2

Four days after their European Cup exit at the hands of Galatasary, United were determined to get back on the winning trail, but for 45 minutes one could have been forgiven for thinking that their minds were still in Turkey. City took a two-goal lead in the first half, with Niall Quinn in particular causing many problems for the United defence and scoring twice in the space of ten minutes. Whatever was said at half-time obviously worked, for Eric Cantona put the disappointments of midweek behind him and began to galvanise the United side. First he shot low past Coton to put United back in the game with 52 minutes on the clock. With a little over ten minutes to go he levelled the scores, shooting right-footed from Ryan Giggs's centre. Finally, with three minutes to go and City holding on for a draw, Roy Keane completed the comeback and fired in from close range.

NOVEMBER 8TH

1890	Walsall Town Swifts	A	Football Alliance	1-2
1902	Lincoln City	A	Second Division	3-1
1913	Aston Villa	A	First Division	1-3
1919	Burnley	A	First Division	1-2
1924	Portsmouth	A	Second Division	1-1
1930	Leicester City	A	First Division	4-5
1941	Tranmere Rovers	H	Football League Northern Section (First Championship)	6-1
1947	Huddersfield Town	H	First Division	4-4

Jack Rowley scored all four of United's goals in the League clash with Huddersfield but the game still ended in a draw! A crowd of 59,772 saw the action.

1952	Sheffield Wednesday	H	First Division	1-1
1958	Burnley	H	First Division	1-3
1967	Leeds United	A	First Division	0-1
1969	Coventry City	A	First Division	2-1
1971	Stoke City	A	League Cup 4th Round Replay	0-0 [aet]
1975	Liverpool	A	First Division	1-3

George Best was officially released by Manchester United and was therefore free to sign for any club in any country as the FIFA ban was automatically lifted.

1980	Coventry City	H	First Division	0-0
1983	Colchester United	A	Milk Cup 3rd Round	2-0
1986	Oxford United	A	First Division	0-2
1993	In the aftermath of United's away goals defeat by Galatasaray in the European Cup, Eric Cantona was reported to have made bribery allegations against the referee, and today UEFA announced they would be contacting the player with regard to these.			

NOVEMBER 9TH

1889	Long Eaton Rovers	H	Football Alliance	3-0
1895	Woolwich Arsenal	A	Second Division	1-2
1901	West Bromwich Albion	H	Second Division	1-2
1907	Everton	H	First Division	4-3
1912	Sunderland	A	First Division	1-3
1918	Rochdale	A	Lancashire Section Principal Tournament	0-1
1929	Derby County	H	First Division	3-2
1935	Swansea Town	A	Second Division	1-2
1940	Everton	A	North Regional League	2-5
1946	Derby County	H	First Division	4-1
1957	Preston North End	A	First Division	1-1
1963	Tottenham Hotspur	H	First Division	4-1
1968	Sunderland	A	First Division	1-1
1974	Bristol City	A	Second Division	0-1
1985	Sheffield Wednesday	A	First Division	0-1

This was United's first defeat of the season, having previously won 13 and drawn the other two of their opening 15 matches. The match against United attracted a crowd of 48,105 to Hillsborough and a goal from Lee Chapman ended United's winning run and began a run of a different kind: six League and cup games without a victory. Earlier in the season United had failed by one game to match Spurs' winning start to the season, which had been set in 1960-61. That season Spurs had also suffered their first defeat of the season at Hillsborough!

1997	Arsenal	A	FA Premier League	2-3

NOVEMBER 10TH

1894	Rotherham Town	H	Second Division	3-2
1900	Woolwich Arsenal	A	Second Division	1-2
1906	Woolwich Arsenal	H	First Division	1-0
1913	Manchester City	A	Lancashire Senior Cup Semi-Final	1-1
1917	Bolton Wanderers	H	Lancashire Section Principal Tournament	1-3
1923	Leicester City	H	Second Division	3-0
1928	Sheffield Wednesday	A	First Division	1-2
1934	Bury	H	Second Division	1-0
1945	Preston North End	A	Football League North	2-2
1951	Chelsea	A	First Division	2-4
1956	Bolton Wanderers	A	First Division	0-2
1962	Liverpool	H	First Division	3-3
1970	Manchester City	H	Bill Foulkes Testimonial	0-3
1973	Tottenham Hotspur	A	First Division	1-2
1976	Sunderland	H	First Division	3-3

After an hour's play United brought on Jonathan Clark for Colin Waldron, his only first-team appearance in a United shirt. He was later sold to Derby County for £50,000, despite his lack of first-team experience!

1979	Manchester City	A	First Division	0-2
1982	Bradford City	A	Milk Cup 3rd Round	0-0
1984	Leicester City	A	First Division	3-2

1986 United were in conflict with their midfield player Remi Moses after it was revealed the club were refusing to pay a £7,000 bill for a medical clinic in Amsterdam, claiming the player had gone there without their permission.

1990	Derby County	A	First Division	0-0
1994	Manchester City	H	FA Premier League	5-0

United gained the perfect revenge for their 5-1 defeat in 1989 with a 5-0 hammering of local rivals City at Old Trafford. Andrei Kanchelskis became the first United player to register a hat-trick in the Premier League, his final goal coming two minutes from time. United's other goals were scored by Eric Cantona and Mark Hughes.

NOVEMBER 11TH

1893	Wolverhampton Wanderers	H	First Division	1-0
1899	Barnsley	A	Second Division	0-0
1905	Chesterfield	A	Second Division	0-1
1911	Preston North End	H	First Division	0-0
1916	Blackburn Rovers	A	Lancashire Section Principal Tournament	2-1
1922	Clapton Orient	A	Second Division	1-1
1933	Southampton	H	Second Division	1-0
1939	Crewe Alexandra	H	War Regional League, Western Division	5-1
1942	Manchester City	H	Football League North (First Championship)	2-1
1944	Liverpool	H	Football League North (First Championship)	2-5
1950	Chelsea	A	First Division	0-1
1961	Leicester City	H	First Division	2-2
1964	Borussia Dortmund	A	Inter-Cities Fairs Cup 2nd Round 1st Leg	6-1

Bobby Charlton scored the only European hat-trick of his career in this 6-1 annihilation of Borussia Dortmund. David Herd, Denis Law and George Best scored United's other goals in one of their best performances away from home in European competition.

1967	Liverpool	A	First Division	2-1

1972	Liverpool	H	First Division	2-0
1978	Birmingham City	A	First Division	1-5
1993	Eric Cantona was cleared by UEFA for making bribery allegations against the referee in the recent European Cup tie against Galatasaray.			

NOVEMBER 12TH

1881	West Gorton	H	Friendly	3-0
1892	Notts County	H	First Division	1-3
1898	Barnsley	H	Second Division	0-0
1904	Burnley	H	Second Division	1-0
1910	Notts County	H	First Division	0-0
1921	Middlesbrough	A	First Division	0-2
1927	Sunderland	A	First Division	1-4
1932	Bury	A	Second Division	2-2
1938	Wolverhampton Wanderers	H	First Division	1-3
1949	Everton	A	First Division	0-0
1955	Bolton Wanderers	A	First Division	1-3
1960	Birmingham City	A	First Division	1-3
1966	Sheffield Wednesday	H	First Division	2-0
1969	Derby County	A	League Cup 5th Round	0-0
1975	Manchester City	A	League Cup 4th Round	0-4

City inflicted a devastating defeat on United, winning as easily as the scoreline suggests, but of far greater concern was the injury sustained by Colin Bell, which would keep him out for a season and a half and eventually force his retirement.

1977	Nottingham Forest	A	First Division	1-2
1980	Wolverhampton Wanderers	H	First Division	0-0
1983	Leicester City	A	First Division	1-1
1988	Derby County	A	First Division	2-2
1989	Nottingham Forest	H	First Division	1-0

1990 The FA fined both Manchester United and Arsenal £50,000 for bringing the game into disrepute following the 21-man brawl on 20th October. In addition, United had one point and Arsenal two points deducted (the additional point taken from Arsenal was punishment for having previously been found guilty of a similar charge last year during a match with Norwich).

1993 More fines for United to contend with as UEFA fined them £2,500 for incorrect conduct during their recent European Cup tie with Galatasaray. This was a direct result of three bookings collected during the game and Eric Cantona's dismissal after the final whistle. Eric was also banned for four European games. Galatasaray did not escape unpunished either, for they were fined £7,000 for the fireworks let off by their fans and £2,500 for inadequate security arrangements at the stadium.

NOVEMBER 13TH

| 1897 | Newcastle United | H | Second Division | 0-1 |

Bob Donaldson made his last appearance for Newton Heath. He had joined the Heathens from Blackburn Rovers in May 1892 and scored on his debut for the club against . . . Blackburn! He went on to make 155 appearances for the first team, scoring 66 goals, the last two coming in the recent 6-0 win over Walsall. He also scored the Heathens' first League goal and the first League hat-trick. He left Newton Heath in December 1897 and joined Luton and then Glossop North End.

| 1902 | Oswaldtwistle Rovers | H | FA Cup 4th Qualifying Round | 3-2 |
| 1909 | Chelsea | H | First Division | 2-0 |

1915	Rochdale	H	Lancashire Section Principal Tournament	2-0
1920	Sheffield United	A	First Division	0-0
1926	Leicester City	A	First Division	3-2
1937	Chesterfield	A	Second Division	7-1

After a faltering start to the season United hit top form with a 7-1 demolition of Chesterfield. Although Stan Pearson made his debut he did not get on the score sheet, United's goals coming from Tommy Bamford (four), Harry Baird, Billy Bryant and Tom Manley.

1943	Manchester City	H	Football League North (First Championship)	3-0
1948	Chelsea	A	First Division	1-1
1954	Sheffield United	A	First Division	0-3
1965	Leicester City	A	First Division	5-0
1968	RSC Anderlecht	H	European Cup 2nd Round 1st Leg	3-0
1971	Tottenham Hotspur	H	First Division	3-1
1974	Burnley	H	League Cup 4th Round	3-2
1982	Tottenham Hotspur	H	First Division	1-0

NOVEMBER 14TH

1891	South Shore	A	FA Cup 3rd Qualifying Round	2-0
1908	Blackburn Rovers	A	First Division	3-1
1914	Burnley	H	First Division	0-2
1925	Birmingham	H	First Division	3-1
1931	Oldham Athletic	A	Second Division	5-1
1936	Grimsby Town	A	First Division	2-6
1942	Manchester City	A	Football League North (First Championship)	5-0
1953	Cardiff City	A	First Division	6-1
1959	Bolton Wanderers	A	First Division	1-1

1960 Remi Moses born in Manchester. Although he had played for Manchester Schoolboys, Remi began his professional career with West Bromwich Albion, signing professional forms in November 1978. When Ron Atkinson was appointed manager at Old Trafford he returned to the Hawthorns to sign two of his star midfield players, landing Bryan Robson and Remi Moses in a joint deal of over £2 million, with Remi being valued at around £600,000. His time at Old Trafford was beset by misfortune of one kind or another: a sending-off in a League match against Arsenal in 1983 meant he subsequently missed the FA Cup final victory over Brighton, and injury robbed him of a place in the victorious 1985 side. A succession of further injuries forced him to retire in June 1988 at the age of only 27 years.

| 1964 | Blackpool | A | First Division | 2-1 |
| 1970 | Nottingham Forest | A | First Division | 2-1 |

1989 Former Manchester United coach and assistant manager Jimmy Murphy died aged 89. A right-half with West Bromwich Albion before the Second World War, he became coach at Old Trafford at the cessation of hostilities, a post he held for ten years. Elevated to the position of assistant manager in 1955 he was also manager of Wales between 1957 and 1963, a position that perhaps saved his life; he was on World Cup duty with Wales against Israel when the Munich air disaster took place. (In fact, Wales had already been eliminated from the competition but, following political boycotts, Israel qualified from their group without having played a single game, a situation FIFA were not prepared to allow. They therefore conducted a draw of group runners-up to provide opposition for Israel – and Wales came out of the hat.) He took temporary control of Manchester United whilst Matt Busby was recovering from his injuries and led a patched-up Manchester United to Wembley for the 1958 FA Cup final, the same year taking Wales to Sweden for the World Cup finals. He retired as assistant manager of Manchester United in 1971.

NOVEMBER 15TH

| 1890 | Ardwick | H | Friendly | 4-1 |

1895 Neil McBain born in Campbeltown. Although Neil spent only just over one year at United, he is assured of his place in the history books for becoming the oldest player to have appeared in the Football League; in 1947, at the age of 51 years and four months, he was forced to select himself as emergency goalkeeper for New Brighton, where he was manager, conceding three goals as Hartlepools United won 3-0. Neil's United career had begun in November 1921 shortly after his £6,250 transfer from Ayr United. He requested a transfer in January 1923 and was sold to Everton, later playing for St Johnstone, Liverpool and Watford before moving into management. His last position was back at Ayr United in 1963. He died on 13th May 1974.

| 1902 | Small Heath | H | Second Division | 0-1 |
| 1913 | Middlesbrough | H | First Division | 0-1 |

Dick Duckworth made his last appearance for United. He had joined the club in October 1903 and went on to make 250 first-team appearances prior to today's game. Unfortunately he suffered a serious knee injury in December 1913 which ended his playing career although he was retained by the club until 1915. He won two League championship and an FA Cup winners' medal whilst at United and later became a publican.

1919	Burnley	H	First Division	0-1
1924	Hull City	H	Second Division	2-0
1930	Blackpool	H	First Division	0-0
1941	Tranmere Rovers	A	Football League Northern Section (First Championship)	1-1
1947	Derby County	A	First Division	1-1
1952	Cardiff City	A	First Division	2-1
1958	Bolton Wanderers	A	First Division	3-6
1967	FK Sarajevo	A	European Cup 2nd Round 1st Leg	0-0
1969	Manchester City	A	First Division	0-4
1971	Stoke City	A	League Cup 4th Round 2nd Replay	1-2
1975	Aston Villa	H	First Division	2-0
1980	Middlesbrough	A	First Division	1-1
1986	Norwich City	A	First Division	0-0
1987	Liverpool	H	First Division	1-1

NOVEMBER 16TH

| 1895 | Lincoln City | H | Second Division | 5-5 |

One of the highest scoring League matches Newton Heath ever played in resulted in a 5-5 draw at home to Lincoln City, one of only three draws the Heathens recorded in the League. Every one of their 30 League matches that season saw at least two goals being scored in aggregate, but Newton Heath's woeful away form left them adrift of the sides competing for the test matches series.

1901	Woolwich Arsenal	A	Second Division	0-2
1907	Sunderland	A	First Division	2-1
1912	Aston Villa	A	First Division	2-4
1918	Preston North End	A	Lancashire Section Principal Tournament	2-4
1929	Sheffield Wednesday	A	First Division	2-7

United were still in free fall from the start of the season, with only ten points secured from their opening 15 games, and this turned out to be their heaviest defeat of the season. This proved to be something of a turning point, however, for United were unbeaten in their following eight games and still managed to avoid relegation at the end of the season.

1935	West Ham United	H	Second Division	2-3
1940	Everton	H	North Regional League	0-0
1946	Everton	A	First Division	2-2
1957	Sheffield Wednesday	H	First Division	2-1
1963	Aston Villa	A	First Division	0-4
1968	Ipswich Town	H	First Division	0-0
1974	Aston Villa	H	Second Division	2-1

On the same day, Paul Scholes was born in Salford. Paul joined United as a trainee and made his debut in a Coca-Cola Cup tie in September 1994, scoring twice. He was a fringe player in the 1995-96 season but won a medal as the side won the Premiership title, and also collected a winners' medal in the FA Cup final when he replaced Andy Cole. The summer arrival of many foreign imports threatened his chances of a regular place, but his ability to play in midfield or up front proved beneficial and he has since gone on to become not only a regular for United but a vital member of the England squad. He added a further Premiership medal in 1997.

1985	Tottenham Hotspur	H	First Division	0-0
1991	Manchester City	A	First Division	0-0
1996	Arsenal	H	FA Premier League	1-0

NOVEMBER 17TH

1894	Grimsby Town	A	Second Division	1-2
1906	Sheffield Wednesday	A	First Division	2-5
1917	Bolton Wanderers	A	Lancashire Section Principal Tournament	2-4
1923	Coventry City	A	Second Division	1-1
1928	Derby County	H	First Division	0-1
1934	Hull City	A	Second Division	2-3
1945	Leeds United	A	Football League North	3-3
1951	Portsmouth	H	First Division	1-3

This was the last home defeat United were to suffer in a season that culminated in them being crowned champions. Indeed, after this defeat United were beaten only twice more all season, these defeats coming in consecutive games at the end of March and the beginning of April, a run of 16 games without defeat which set up the title.

1956	Leeds United	H	First Division	3-2
1962	Wolverhampton Wanderers	A	First Division	3-2
1965	ASK Vorwaerts	A	European Cup 1st Round 1st Leg	2-0

Despite securing an away win United were largely unimpressive against the East German side, scoring only in the last ten minutes after almost constant pressure from the home side. United's goals were scored by Denis Law and John Connelly.

1973	Newcastle United	A	First Division	2-3
1979	Crystal Palace	H	First Division	1-1
1984	Luton Town	H	First Division	2-0
1990	Sheffield United	H	First Division	2-0

NOVEMBER 18TH

1905	Port Vale	H	Second Division	3-0
1911	Liverpool	A	First Division	2-3
1916	Manchester City	H	Lancashire Section Principal Tournament	2-1
1922	Bury	A	Second Division	2-2

1933	Blackpool	A	Second Division	1-3
1939	Liverpool	A	War Regional League, Western Division	0-1
1944	Manchester City	H	Football League North (First Championship)	3-2
1950	Stoke City	H	First Division	0-0
1961	Ipswich Town	A	First Division	1-4

1963 Peter Schmeichel born in Gladsaxe in Denmark. Although United had won the FA Cup and European Cup-Winners' Cups in successive seasons, Alex Ferguson had already begun searching for a new goalkeeper, one of world-class ability who would turn his team into title challengers. He found him in Peter, paying a cut-price £500,000 to bring him to Old Trafford from Brondby. Since then Peter has been first choice at United and has helped the club win four League titles and two FA Cups. A Danish international he helped his country win the European Championship in 1992.

1967	Southampton	H	First Division	3-2
1970	Crystal Palace	H	League Cup 5th Round	4-2
1972	Manchester City	A	First Division	0-3
1978	Ipswich Town	H	First Division	2-0
1987	Bury	A	Littlewoods Cup 4th Round	2-1

Although United were drawn away in the Littlewoods Cup tie against Bury, the match was switched to Old Trafford where a crowd of 33,519 saw goals from Norman Whiteside and Brian McClair take United into the quarter-finals.

1989	Luton Town	A	First Division	3-1
1995	Southampton	H	FA Premier League	4-1

NOVEMBER 19TH

1892	Aston Villa	H	First Division	2-0
1898	New Brighton Tower	A	Second Division	3-0
1904	Grimsby Town	A	Second Division	1-0
1910	Oldham Athletic	A	First Division	3-1
1921	Aston Villa	A	First Division	1-3
1927	Aston Villa	H	First Division	5-1

United ended the season having scored 51 goals at Old Trafford, with five of them coming in this clash with Aston Villa. The scorers were Teddy Partridge (two), Billy Johnston, Frank McPherson and Joe Spence.

1932	Fulham	H	Second Division	4-3
1938	Everton	A	First Division	0-3
1949	Middlesbrough	H	First Division	2-0
1955	Chelsea	H	First Division	3-0
1960	West Bromwich Albion	H	First Division	3-0
1966	Southampton	A	First Division	2-1
1969	Derby County	H	League Cup 5th Round Replay	1-0
1977	Norwich City	H	First Division	1-0
1983	Watford	H	First Division	4-1
1988	Southampton	H	First Division	2-2
1991	Red Star Belgrade	H	European Super Cup	1-0

With the former Yugoslavian state tearing itself apart in civil war, UEFA decided that the traditional two-legged Super Cup (played between the winners of the European Cup and European Cup-Winners' Cup) should be changed to a single match at Old Trafford. United won 1-0 thanks to a goal from Brian McClair, although Steve Bruce also missed a penalty.

1994	Crystal Palace	H	FA Premier League	3-0

NOVEMBER 20TH

1897	Leicester Fosse	A	Second Division	1-1
1909	Blackburn Rovers	A	First Division	2-3
1915	Blackpool	A	Lancashire Section Principal Tournament	1-5
1920	Manchester City	H	First Division	1-1
1926	Everton	H	First Division	2-1
1937	Aston Villa	H	Second Division	3-1
1943	Tranmere Rovers	H	Football League North (First Championship)	6-3
1948	Birmingham City	H	First Division	3-0
1954	Arsenal	H	First Division	2-1
1957	Dukla Prague	H	European Cup 1st Round 1st Leg	3-0

A sell-out crowd of 60,000 saw United obtain a commanding first leg win in the European Cup tie against Dukla Prague. Goals from Colin Webster (his only European goal for United), Tommy Taylor and David Pegg ensured the victory against the Czechoslovakian side.

1965	Sheffield United	H	First Division	3-1
1971	Leicester City	H	First Division	3-2
1976	Leicester City	A	First Division	1-1
1982	Aston Villa	A	First Division	1-2
1993	Wimbledon	H	FA Premier League	3-1
1996	Juventus	H	European Cup Group C	0-1

Having gone 40 years without a home defeat in European competition, United now slipped to their second consecutive loss at Old Trafford. A penalty from Del Piero shortly before half-time settled the match in front of 53,529 fans. It left United needing victory in their final group match to ensure progress into the knockout stage of the competition.

NOVEMBER 21ST

1891	Lincoln City	H	Football Alliance	10-1

Newton Heath recorded their highest ever win in the Football Alliance with this 10-1 demolition of Lincoln. At the end of the season the Heathens finished in second place in the Alliance and, as the Football League was going to be extended with two extra clubs in the First Division and the creation of a Second Division, their placing was sufficient to earn them an immediate place in the upper echelon.

1903	Preston North End	H	Second Division	0-2
1908	Bradford City	H	First Division	2-0
1914	Tottenham Hotspur	A	First Division	0-2
1925	Bury	A	First Division	3-1
1931	Bury	H	Second Division	1-2
1936	Liverpool	H	First Division	2-5
1942	Tranmere Rovers	A	Football League North (First Championship)	5-0
1953	Blackpool	H	First Division	4-1
1956	Borussia Dortmund	A	European Cup 1st Round 2nd Leg	0-0

Having already won the first leg in Manchester 6-0 United rarely looked threatened and contented themselves with doing just enough to ensure a goalless draw and immediate progress into the next round.

1959	Luton Town	H	First Division	4-1
1964	Blackburn Rovers	H	First Division	3-0
1970	Southampton	A	First Division	0-1
1978	Everton	A	First Division	0-3
1981	Tottenham Hotspur	A	First Division	1-3

| 1987 | Wimbledon | A | First Division | 1-2 |
| 1992 | Oldham Athletic | H | FA Premier League | 3-0 |

NOVEMBER 22ND

| 1890 | Nottingham Forest | A | Football Alliance | 2-8 |
| 1902 | Leicester Fosse | A | Second Division | 1-1 |

The train carrying the United team to Leicester was delayed owing to a derailment at Nottingham, and the team had to change on the train whilst en route. The kick-off was delayed considerably, so much so that there was no half-time, the teams changing around straight away, and the game was eventually completed in semi-darkness.

1913	Sheffield United	A	First Division	0-2
1919	Oldham Athletic	A	First Division	3-0
1924	Blackpool	A	Second Division	1-1
1930	Sheffield United	A	First Division	1-3
1941	Liverpool	A	Football League Northern Section (First Championship)	1-1
1947	Everton	H	First Division	2-2
1952	Newcastle United	H	First Division	2-2
1958	Luton Town	H	First Division	2-1
1969	Tottenham Hotspur	H	First Division	3-1
1975	Arsenal	A	First Division	1-3
1980	Brighton & Hove Albion	A	First Division	4-1
1986	Queens Park Rangers	H	First Division	1-0
1995	Coventry City	A	FA Premier League	4-0

United took the opportunity of closing the gap on League leaders Newcastle with a 4-0 hammering of Coventry at Highfield Road. United's goals were scored by Dennis Irwin, Brian McClair (two) and David Beckham. This was proof of United's goalscoring prowess, for they had won their previous League match 4-0 with goals from three different players!

| 1997 | Wimbledon | A | FA Premier League | 5-2 |

NOVEMBER 23RD

1895	Notts County	A	Second Division	2-0
1901	Barnsley	H	Second Division	1-0
1907	Woolwich Arsenal	H	First Division	4-2

Sandy Turnbull scored all four of United's goals as they beat Woolwich Arsenal. Sandy ended the season as United's top goalscorer with 25 League strikes to his credit in his first season for the club.

1912	Liverpool	H	First Division	3-1
1918	Preston North End	H	Lancashire Section Principal Tournament	1-2
1929	Burnley	H	First Division	1-0
1935	Norwich City	A	Second Division	5-3
1940	Liverpool	A	North Regional League	2-2
1946	Huddersfield Town	H	First Division	5-2
1957	Newcastle United	A	First Division	2-1
1963	Liverpool	H	First Division	0-1
1968	Stoke City	A	First Division	0-0
1974	Hull City	A	Second Division	0-2
1985	Leicester City	A	First Division	0-3
1988	Sheffield Wednesday	H	First Division	1-1
1991	West Ham United	H	First Division	2-1

1994	IFK Gothenburg	A	European Cup Group A	1-3

Defeat in Gothenburg effectively ended United's interest in the European Cup for another season, despite Barcelona's shock defeat against Galatasaray. United had failed to win any of their last four European matches, and to make matters worse Paul Ince was sent off late in the game.

1996	Middlesbrough	A	FA Premier League	2-2

NOVEMBER 24TH

1894	Darwen	H	Second Division	1-1
1900	Stockport County	A	Second Division	0-1
1906	Bury	H	First Division	2-4
1913	Manchester City	H	Lancashire Senior Cup Semi-Final Replay	2-0
1917	Preston North End	H	Lancashire Section Principal Tournament	2-1
1928	Sunderland	A	First Division	1-5

United were in the middle of a run of 16 games without a win as they headed towards the lower reaches of the table. Only a late rally saved them from almost-certain relegation at the end of the season.

1934	Nottingham Forest	H	Second Division	3-2
1945	Leeds United	H	Football League North	6-1
1951	Liverpool	A	First Division	0-0

One of the earliest references to the the Busby Babes accompanied United's introduction of 18-year-old Jackie Blanchflower and 21-year-old Roger Byrne, both of whom slotted into United's defence exceptionally well.

1956	Tottenham Hotspur	A	First Division	2-2
1962	Aston Villa	H	First Division	2-2
1973	Norwich City	H	First Division	0-0
1979	Norwich City	H	First Division	5-0
1982	Bradford City	H	Milk Cup 3rd Round Replay	4-1
1984	Sunderland	A	First Division	2-3

Both United's Mark Hughes and David Hodgson received their marching orders in a hard-fought League meeting at Roker Park. Mark had scored United's first goal, with the other coming from Bryan Robson.

1993	Ipswich Town	H	FA Premier League	0-0

NOVEMBER 25TH

1893	Sheffield United	A	First Division	1-3
1899	Luton Town	A	Second Division	1-0
1905	Barnsley	A	Second Division	3-0
1911	Aston Villa	H	First Division	3-1

Enoch West scored twice as United got back into winning ways with a 3-1 victory over Aston Villa. United's other goal was scored by Charlie Roberts.

1916	Everton	A	Lancashire Section Principal Tournament	2-3
1922	Bury	H	Second Division	0-1
1933	Bradford City	H	Second Division	2-1
1939	Port Vale	H	War Regional League, Western Division	8-1

When the Football League was abandoned in September it was not certain whether football itself would survive the war. Eventually a number of regional Leagues were organised and this was United's biggest victory in the Western Division for that season. Billy Wrigglesworth scored five of United's goals, with the others coming from Asquith, Pearson and Williams.

1944	Manchester City	A	Football League North (First Championship)	0-4

1950	West Bromwich Albion	A	First Division	1-0
1961	Burnley	H	First Division	1-4
1967	Chelsea	A	First Division	1-1
1972	Southampton	H	First Division	2-1
1978	Chelsea	A	First Division	1-0
1989	Chelsea	H	First Division	0-0
1990	Chelsea	H	First Division	2-3

NOVEMBER 26TH

1892	Accrington	A	First Division	2-2
1898	Lincoln City	H	Second Division	1-0
1910	Liverpool	A	First Division	2-3

1913 Billy Bryant born in Shildon. He began his career with Wolves in 1931 but made his name with Wrexham before signing for United in October 1934. He was first choice outside-right until the outbreak of the war and remained with United until November 1945, when he joined Bradford City, helping them to an appearance in the 1945 League North Cup final. He died in County Durham in 1975.

1921	Aston Villa	H	First Division	1-0
1927	Burnley	A	First Division	0-4
1932	Chesterfield	A	Second Division	1-1
1938	Huddersfield Town	H	First Division	1-1
1949	Blackpool	A	First Division	3-3
1955	Blackpool	A	First Division	0-0
1960	Cardiff City	A	First Division	0-3
1966	Sunderland	H	First Division	5-0
1977	Queens Park Rangers	A	First Division	2-2
1985	Liverpool	A	Milk Cup 4th Round	1-2
1994	Arsenal	A	FA Premier League	0-0

United had a player dismissed at Highbury for the second consecutive season; following Eric Cantona's sending off in the meeting the previous season, Mark Hughes was sent off for the fifth time in his United career.

1996	Leicester City	A	Coca-Cola Cup 4th Round	0-2

NOVEMBER 27TH

1897	Grimsby Town	H	Second Division	2-1
1909	Nottingham Forest	H	First Division	2-6
1915	Southport Central	H	Lancashire Section Principal Tournament	0-0
1920	Manchester City	A	First Division	0-3
1926	Blackburn Rovers	A	First Division	1-2
1937	Norwich City	A	Second Division	3-2
1943	Tranmere Rovers	A	Football League North (First Championship)	1-0
1948	Middlesbrough	A	First Division	4-1
1954	West Bromwich Albion	A	First Division	0-2
1968	RSC Anderlecht	A	European Cup 2nd Round 2nd Leg	1-3

United had a real scare in Brussels against the Belgian champions Anderlecht, almost throwing away a 3-0 lead from the first leg. In the end a goal from Carlos Satori gave them a slender 4-3 aggregate victory and a passport into the next round against Rapid Vienna.

1971	Southampton	A	First Division	5-2

George Best scored a hat-trick as United overcame stiff opposition from Southampton at The Dell, with further goals being added by Brian Kidd and Sammy McIlroy. After

70 minutes George left the field with a leg injury but to a standing ovation as he was replaced by John Aston. This win enabled United to open up a three-point lead at the top of the table over local rivals Manchester City, having suffered only two defeats so far in the season.

1976	West Ham United	H	First Division	0-2
1982	Norwich City	H	First Division	3-0
1983	West Ham United	A	First Division	1-1
1988	Newcastle United	A	First Division	0-0
1993	Coventry City	A	FA Premier League	1-0
1995	Nottingham Forest	A	FA Premier League	1-1
1997	Kosice	H	UEFA Champions League	3-0

NOVEMBER 28TH

1891	Walsall Town Swifts	A	Football Alliance	4-1
1896	Small Heath	A	Second Division	0-1
1908	Sheffield Wednesday	H	First Division	3-1
1914	Newcastle United	H	First Division	1-0
1925	Blackburn Rovers	H	First Division	2-0
1931	Port Vale	A	Second Division	2-1
1936	Leeds United	A	First Division	1-2

Making his debut for United was Walter Winterbottom. Born in Oldham in 1914, Walter joined United from Mossley FC and seemed assured of a successful career as a player, but a back injury sustained in season 1937-38 brought his career to an abrupt end. He guested for Chelsea during the war and following demobilisation became Director of Coaching for the FA in 1946, holding the post until 1962. This position was that of manager in all but name, although he did not enjoy the same kind of freedom enjoyed by his successor Alf Ramsey. He was awarded a CBE in 1963 and was knighted in 1978 for his services to football.

1942	Tranmere Rovers	H	Football League North (First Championship)	5-1
1953	Portsmouth	A	First Division	1-1
1959	Everton	A	First Division	1-2
1964	Arsenal	A	First Division	3-2
1970	Huddersfield Town	H	First Division	1-1
1981	Brighton & Hove Albion	H	First Division	2-0
1984	Dundee United	H	UEFA Cup 3rd Round 1st Leg	2-2
1990	Arsenal	A	Rumbelows Cup 4th Round	6-2

Apart from a brief spell during which Arsenal's Alan Smith scored twice, United totally dominated this game in front of Arsenal's own supporters. Goals from Clayton Blackmore, Mark Hughes, Danny Wallace and a hat-trick from Lee Sharpe inflicted one of Arnseal's heaviest home defeats in many a year as United headed towards the quarter-final of the one domestic competition they had yet to win.

| 1992 | Arsenal | A | FA Premier League | 1-0 |

NOVEMBER 29TH

| 1890 | Sunderland Albion | H | Football Alliance | 1-5 |

Newton Heath played with only ten men throughout this match.

1899	Manchester City	H	Friendly	0-1
1902	Southport Central	H	FA Cup 5th Qualifying Round	4-1
1913	Derby County	H	First Division	3-3
1924	Derby County	H	Second Division	1-1
1930	Sunderland	H	First Division	1-1

1941	Liverpool	H	Football League Northern Section	
			(First Championship)	2-2
1947	Chelsea	A	First Division	4-0

1949 Steve James born in Coseley near Wolverhampton. Signed as a professional in December 1966, Steve was introduced to the first team in October 1968 as a replacement for Bill Foulkes, although he was later replaced by Ian Ure. After breaking back into the side he was then displaced by Jim Holton, although by the time he left for York City in 1976 he had made 160 appearances for United's first team. He later finished his playing career in non-League football.

1952	West Bromwich Albion	A	First Division	1-3
1958	Birmingham City	A	First Division	4-0
1967	FK Sarajevo	H	European Cup 2nd Round 2nd Leg	2-1
1969	Burnley	A	First Division	1-1

1972 George Best failed to turn up for training all week and, after he had been dropped from the team, was rumoured to have put in a transfer request at Manchester United.

1973 Ryan Giggs born in Cardiff. He is one of the most exciting talents in the game today and is already being compared with another former Manchester United great – George Best. He won his first cap for Wales at the age of 17 years 321 days to become their youngest player and was PFA Young Player of the Year in both 1992 and 1993. Introduced into the United first team in 1991, he has since won four Premiership medals, two FA Cup and one League Cup winners' medals.

| 1975 | Newcastle United | H | First Division | 1-0 |

1978 Viv Anderson, who later joined Manchester United, became the first black player to be capped by England when he was selected for the international against Czechoslovakia at Wembley.

| 1980 | Southampton | H | First Division | 1-1 |
| 1986 | Wimbledon | A | First Division | 0-1 |

NOVEMBER 30TH

1889	Sheffield Wednesday	A	Football Alliance	1-3
1895	Woolwich Arsenal	H	Second Division	5-1
1901	Leicester Fosse	A	Second Division	2-3
1907	Sheffield Wednesday	A	First Division	0-2
1912	Bolton Wanderers	A	First Division	1-2
1918	Bolton Wanderers	A	Lancashire Section Principal Tournament	1-3
1929	Sunderland	A	First Division	4-2

1934 Alex Bell died in Chorlton-cum-Hardy. Born in Cape Town in South Africa in 1882, Alex joined United in 1903 for £700 from Ayr Parkhouse. Originally signed as a centre-forward, he was soon converted to half-back and gave the club excellent service for the next ten years in this position, winning two League titles and an FA Cup during his time with the club. He joined Blackburn for £1,000 in 1913 and helped them to the League title in his first season, and after retiring as a player he joined Coventry as trainer in July 1922. He subsequently moved to Manchester City in the same capacity and held the position until his death.

1935	Doncaster Rovers	H	Second Division	0-0
1940	Liverpool	H	North Regional League	2-0
1946	Wolverhampton Wanderers	A	First Division	2-3
1957	Tottenham Hotspur	H	First Division	3-4

United suffered their first home defeat to a team from the capital for the first time since 1938 when Charlton Athletic had won at Old Trafford.

| 1963 | Sheffield United | A | First Division | 2-1 |
| 1966 | Leicester City | A | First Division | 2-1 |

1968	Wolverhampton Wanderers	H	First Division	2-0

1972 Dutch club Feyenoord were rumoured to be interested in Manchester United's want-away star George Best.

1974	Sunderland	H	Second Division	3-2
1983	Oxford United	A	Milk Cup 4th Round	1-1
1985	Watford	H	First Division	1-1
1991	Crystal Palace	A	First Division	3-1
1993	Everton	A	Coca-Cola Cup 4th Round	2-0
1996	Leicester City	H	FA Premier League	3-1
1997	Blackburn Rovers	H	FA Premier League	4-0

DECEMBER 1ST

1894	Crewe Alexandra	A	Second Division	2-0
1900	Small Heath	H	Second Division	0-1
1906	Manchester City	A	First Division	0-3

The very first Manchester derby in the First Division took place at Hyde Road in front of a crowd of some 40,000. Despite the fact that City had been decimated by the recent suspensions handed out to 17 players, they still proved too strong for their opponents from across the city and went on to win 3-0.

1917	Preston North End	A	Lancashire Section Principal Tournament	0-0
1923	Leeds United	A	Second Division	0-0
1928	Blackburn Rovers	H	First Division	1-4
1934	Brentford	A	Second Division	1-3
1945	Burnley	H	Football League North	3-3
1951	Blackpool	H	First Division	3-1
1956	Luton Town	H	First Division	3-1
1962	Sheffield United	A	First Division	1-1
1965	ASK Vorwaerts	H	European Cup 1st Round 2nd Leg	3-1

United completed a 5-1 aggregate win over Vorwaerts with a 3-1 win at Old Trafford. David Herd scored all three of their goals in front of a crowd of 30,082.

1976	Everton	H	League Cup 5th Round	0-3
1979	Tottenham Hotspur	A	First Division	2-1
1982	Southampton	H	Milk Cup 4th Round	2-0
1984	Norwich City	H	First Division	2-0
1990	Everton	A	First Division	1-0

DECEMBER 2ND

1893	Everton	H	First Division	0-3
1899	Port Vale	H	Second Division	3-0
1905	Clapton Orient	H	Second Division	4-0
1911	Newcastle United	A	First Division	3-2
1916	Rochdale	H	Lancashire Section Principal Tournament	1-1
1922	Rotherham United	H	Second Division	3-0
1925	Manchester City	A	Lancashire Senior Cup 3rd Round	2-3
1933	Port Vale	A	Second Division	3-2
1939	Tranmere Rovers	A	War Regional League, Western Division	4-2
1944	Crewe Alexandra	A	Football League North (First Championship)	4-1
1950	Newcastle United	H	First Division	1-2
1961	Everton	A	First Division	1-5

United had now gone ten matches without a win, a run that had brought only two points and had sent them tumbling down the table. This result equalled their worst of the season, a 5-1 reverse at Highbury the previous month.

| 1964 | Borussia Dortmund | H | Inter-Cities Fairs Cup 2nd Round 2nd Leg | 4-0 |

Following on from a 6-1 win away in the first leg, United completed their rout with a 4-0 home win and a final aggregate score of 10-1. Their goals in the second leg were scored by John Connelly, Denis Law and two from Bobby Charlton. Despite the European nature of the competition, their next opponents would be Everton!

1967	West Bromwich Albion	H	First Division	2-1
1972	Norwich City	A	First Division	2-0
1995	Chelsea	H	FA Premier League	1-1

DECEMBER 3RD

1892	Bolton Wanderers	A	First Division	1-4
1898	Woolwich Arsenal	A	Second Division	1-5
1904	Doncaster Rovers	A	Second Division	1-0
1910	Bury	H	First Division	3-2
1921	Bradford City	A	First Division	1-2
1927	Bury	H	First Division	0-1
1932	Bradford City	H	Second Division	0-1
1938	Portsmouth	A	First Division	0-0
1949	Newcastle United	H	First Division	1-1
1955	Sunderland	H	First Division	2-1
1960	Preston North End	H	First Division	1-0
1963	Tottenham Hotspur	A	European Cup-Winners' Cup 2nd Round 1st Leg	0-2

Spurs had been exempt from the first round of the competition as holders, so the pairing of both English representatives in the competition raised more than a few eyebrows! Goals at White Hart Lane from Dave Mackay and Terry Dyson seemingly gave Spurs a good advantage to take into the second leg at Old Trafford.

| 1966 | Aston Villa | A | First Division | 1-2 |
| 1969 | Manchester City | A | League Cup Semi-Final 1st Leg | 1-2 |

United and City had met in the FA Cup semi-final back in 1926 but this was the first time they had met at the same stage of the League Cup. The match at Maine Road was a tight affair, as one would expect between such great rivals, and the game was not without controversy. Colin Bell had fired City into the lead only for Bobby Charlton to equalise on 66 minutes. As the game entered its final two minutes, Francis Lee fell over Ian Ure's leg in the penalty area. The referee pointed for a penalty, a decision that was greeted with disbelief by both United's players and fans, and whilst the fans could voice their displeasure to their heart's content, the players could not. That didn't stop George Best trying, for which he was subsequently banned for four weeks! Lee converted the penalty to give City a slight edge for the second leg.

1977	Wolverhampton Wanderers	H	First Division	3-1
1983	Everton	H	First Division	0-1
1988	Charlton Athletic	H	First Division	3-0
1989	Arsenal	A	First Division	0-1
1994	Norwich City	H	FA Premier League	1-0

DECEMBER 4TH

1909	Sunderland	A	First Division	0-3
1915	Oldham Athletic	H	Lancashire Section Principal Tournament	2-0
1920	Bradford Park Avenue	H	First Division	5-1
1926	Huddersfield Town	H	First Division	0-0
1937	Swansea Town	H	Second Division	5-1

Jack Rowley became United's youngest ever hat-trick hero in a League match with four against Swansea. He was just 17 years and 58 days old at the time. United's other goal was scored by Billy Bryant.

1943	Wrexham	A	Football League North (First Championship)	4-1
1948	Newcastle United	H	First Division	1-1
1954	Leicester City	H	First Division	3-1
1957	Dukla Prague	A	European Cup 1st Round 2nd Leg	0-1

1959 Paul McGrath born in Ealing in London. Paul and his family moved to Ireland whilst he was a youngster and he began his career with St Patrick's Athletic. A £30,000 transfer took him to United in October 1982 and he quickly became established as an integral part of the United defence, solid and reliable. He won an FA Cup winners' medal in 1985 but continuing problems with his knees prompted fears that he would be unable to withstand the rigours of First Division football and he was sold to Aston Villa for £450,000 in August 1989. There he defied all and sundry with his consistent performances, winning the 1993 PFA Player of the Year Award and helping Villa to two League Cup trophy wins. In October 1996 he was sold to Derby County for £100,000.

1965	West Ham United	H	First Division	0-0
1971	Nottingham Forest	H	First Division	3-2

1972 George Best left Manchester without the permission of his club and was spotted later that evening in a London nightclub.

1974	Middlesbrough	A	League Cup 5th Round	0-0
1982	Watford	A	First Division	1-0
1985	Everton	A	Screen Sport Super Cup Group B	0-1
1991	Oldham Athletic	H	Rumbelows Cup 4th Round	2-0
1993	Norwich City	H	FA Premier League	2-2
1996	Rapid Vienna	A	European Cup Group C	2-0

DECEMBER 5TH

1891	Blackpool	H	FA Cup 4th Qualifying Round	3-4
1908	Everton	A	First Division	2-3
1914	Middlesbrough	A	First Division	1-1
1925	Sunderland	A	First Division	1-2
1931	Millwall	H	Second Division	2-0
1936	Birmingham City	H	First Division	1-2
1942	Wrexham	H	Football League North (First Championship)	6-1
1953	Sheffield United	H	First Division	2-2
1959	Blackpool	H	First Division	3-1

1961 Alan Davies born in Manchester. Alan signed professional forms with United in December 1978 and made his debut in May 1981. He got his big chance in May 1983 when injuries threatened United's run-in to the season and performed well, especially in the two cup finals against Brighton. With international recognition for Wales following soon after, a great career seemed in prospect, but sadly he broke an ankle in a pre-season friendly. Although he returned in April 1984 (and scored) he was not the player he had been and was sold to Newcastle for £30,000 in 1985. A broken leg spoilt his time with the club and he was sold on to Swansea in 1987. He rediscovered something approaching his earlier form and earned an international recall. He moved to Bradford City in 1989 but returned to Swansea a year later. On 4th February 1992 he took his own life at the age of 30 years.

1964	Leeds United	H	First Division	0-1
1970	Tottenham Hotspur	A	First Division	2-2

1972 George Best was officially put on the transfer list by Manchester United. Only Brian

Clough of Derby County expressed any immediate interest in purchasing him.

| 1981 | Southampton | A | First Division | 2-3 |
| 1987 | Queens Park Rangers | A | First Division | 2-0 |

DECEMBER 6TH

| 1893 | Sunderland | A | First Division | 1-4 |

1899 Tom Jones born in Penycae near Wrexham. Having previously failed a trial with Everton, Tom was signed by United in May 1924 from Oswestry Town but didn't effectively break into the first team until the 1927-28 season, although during the summer he was injured whilst playing tennis and took a considerable time to recover full fitness. Indeed, it wasn't until 1933-34 that he was a regular in the side once again. By the time he left United in 1937 he had made exactly 200 appearances for the first team, although he had been unable to get on the score sheet. He did however win four caps for Wales.

1902	Burnley	A	Second Division	2-0
1913	Manchester City	A	First Division	2-0
1919	Aston Villa	A	First Division	0-2
1924	South Shields	A	Second Division	2-1
1930	Blackburn Rovers	A	First Division	1-4
1941	Wrexham	H	Football League Northern Section (First Championship)	10-3
1947	Blackpool	H	First Division	1-1
1952	Middlesbrough	H	First Division	3-2
1958	Leicester City	H	First Division	4-1
1969	Chelsea	H	First Division	0-2
1975	Middlesbrough	A	First Division	0-0
1980	Norwich City	A	First Division	2-2
1992	Manchester City	H	FA Premier League	2-1

Old Trafford hosted the first ever Premier League clash between the two Manchester rivals and it was United who gained the upper hand, Paul Ince giving them the lead after 20 minutes. Mark Hughes added to the score after the break which seemed to galvanise City into action, but they had to wait for some time before Niall Quinn reduced the deficit. The last 15 minutes of the match saw City press hard for the equaliser but United's defence held firm.

| 1997 | Liverpool | A | FA Premier League | 3-1 |

DECEMBER 7TH

1889	Bootle	H	Football Alliance	3-0
1895	Manchester City	A	Second Division	1-2
1901	Preston North End	A	Second Division	1-5
1907	Bristol City	H	First Division	2-1
1912	Sheffield United	H	First Division	4-0
1918	Bolton Wanderers	H	Lancashire Section Principal Tournament	1-0
1929	Bolton Wanderers	H	First Division	1-1
1935	Blackpool	A	Second Division	1-4

1939 Ian Ure born in Ayr. Signed by Dundee in August 1958, he helped the club win the Scottish League championship in 1962 and progress in the European Cup the following season, all of which attracted the interest of bigger clubs. He was sold to Arsenal for £62,500 in August 1963, although a succession of injuries restricted his first-team appearances. He did manage to appear in successive League Cup finals, although Arsenal lost both, to Leeds and Swindon respectively. He was then sold to

United for £80,000 in August 1969 as an eventual replacement for Bill Foulkes, although Ian was eventually unable to get past Paul Edwards in the first team. He was sold to St Mirren in August 1972 and later coached in Iceland.

1940	Blackburn Rovers	A	North Regional League	5-5
1946	Brentford	H	First Division	4-1
1957	Birmingham City	A	First Division	3-3
1963	Stoke City	H	First Division	5-2
1968	Leicester City	A	First Division	1-2
1974	Sheffield Wednesday	A	Second Division	4-4
1983	Oxford United	H	Milk Cup 4th Round Replay	1-1 [aet]
1985	Ipswich Town	H	First Division	1-0
1986	Tottenham Hotspur	H	First Division	3-3
1991	Coventry City	H	First Division	4-0

The draws for both domestic cup competitions, the FA Cup and the Rumbelows Cup, were drawn on the same day. At lunchtime, in the latter competition United were drawn away at Leeds United. In the evening the same two clubs were paired at the same venue in the FA Cup!

| 1993 | Sheffield United | A | FA Premier League | 3-0 |
| 1994 | Galatasaray | H | European Cup Group A | 4-0 |

Despite a winning end to their European group matches, United were eliminated from the competition as a result of Barcelona gaining a point in their match with Gothenburg.

DECEMBER 8TH

| 1894 | Burton Swifts | H | Second Division | 5-1 |

1897 Arthur Lochhead born in Busby in Lanarkshire. Signed by United from Hearts in July 1921 and quickly became a popular feature of the forward line, scoring 50 goals in his 153 appearances for the club. He was surprisingly transferred to Leicester City for £3,300 in October 1925, the move not being well received by United's fans. He went on to give Leicester sterling service, subsequently becoming manager in 1934, although he later became a school teacher.

1900	Grimsby Town	A	Second Division	0-2
1906	Middlesbrough	H	First Division	3-1
1917	Blackpool	H	Lancashire Section Principal Tournament	1-0
1923	Leeds United	H	Second Division	3-1
1928	Arsenal	A	First Division	1-3
1934	Fulham	H	Second Division	1-0
1945	Burnley	A	Football League North	2-2
1951	Arsenal	A	First Division	3-1
1956	Aston Villa	A	First Division	3-1
1962	Nottingham Forest	H	First Division	5-1

1963 Brian McClair born in Airdrie. After a 14-month spell as an apprentice with Aston Villa, Brian returned to Scotland, signing for Motherwell and later transferring to Celtic for £75,000 in 1983. His record at Celtic Park was exceptional: 99 goals in 145 League appearances attracted interest from numerous clubs, and he finally signed for United in July 1987 for £850,000. He continued his rich vein of goalscoring at United, becoming the first United player to notch as many as 20 goals in a season since George Best. He helped the club win four League titles, two FA Cups, the European Cup-Winners' Cup and the League Cup, although in recent times he was more of a squad member than a permanent fixture in the side. He was released at the end of the 1997-98 season.

| 1973 | Southampton | H | First Division | 0-0 |

1979	Leeds United	H	First Division	1-1
1984	Nottingham Forest	A	First Division	2-3
1990	Leeds United	H	First Division	1-1
1996	West Ham United	A	FA Premier League	2-2

DECEMBER 9TH

1893	Bolton Wanderers	A	First Division	0-2
1905	Burnley	A	Second Division	3-1
1911	Sheffield United	H	First Division	1-0
1916	Bolton Wanderers	A	Lancashire Section Principal Tournament	1-5
1922	Rotherham United	A	Second Division	1-1
1933	Notts County	H	Second Division	1-2
1939	Stockport County	A	War Regional League, Western Division	7-4
1944	Crewe Alexandra	H	Football League North (First Championship)	2-0
1950	Huddersfield Town	A	First Division	3-2

1953 Alex Downie died in Manchester. Born in Dunoon in 1876, he joined United in October 1902 from Swindon Town and over the next seven years made nearly 200 appearances for the first team. He was unfortunate not to have played enough games in the 1907-08 championship season to have qualified for a medal and also missed out in the FA Cup winning side the following year. He left United in October 1909 and joined Oldham, later playing for Crewe.

1961	Fulham	H	First Division	3-0
1967	Newcastle United	A	First Division	2-2
1972	Stoke City	H	First Division	0-2
1978	Derby County	A	First Division	3-1
1989	Crystal Palace	H	First Division	1-2
1995	Sheffield Wednesday	H	FA Premier League	2-2

DECEMBER 10TH

1892	Bolton Wanderers	H	First Division	1-0
1898	Blackpool	H	Second Division	3-1
1904	Gainsborough Trinity	H	Second Division	3-1
1910	Sheffield United	A	First Division	0-2
1921	Bradford City	H	First Division	1-1
1927	Sheffied United	A	First Division	1-2
1932	West Ham United	A	Second Division	1-3
1938	Arsenal	H	First Division	1-0
1949	Fulham	A	First Division	0-1
1955	Portsmouth	A	First Division	2-3
1960	Fulham	A	First Division	4-4
1963	Tottenham Hotspur	H	European Cup-Winners' Cup 2nd Round 2nd Leg	4-1

United overcame a two-goal deficit against Spurs to move into the quarter-finals of the European Cup-Winners' Cup, but not before a night of high drama. Spurs lost Dave Mackay with a broken leg after only eight minutes, and although their ten men battled bravely for the rest of the match, United were not to be denied. Two goals apiece from Bobby Charlton and David Herd saw United home 4-3 on aggregate.

1966	Liverpool	H	First Division	2-2
1977	West Ham United	A	First Division	1-2
1983	Ipswich Town	A	First Division	2-0
1988	Coventry City	A	First Division	0-2
1994	Queens Park Rangers	A	FA Premier League	3-2

1997   Juventus   A   UEFA Champions League   0-1

With United having already qualified for the knockout stage of the European Cup they had little at stake other than pride in the clash with Italian giants Juventus in Turin. However, the way results had fallen, they did have an opportunity of removing a major obstacle from their path to the trophy had they won, for Juventus's own qualification was not nearly so clear cut. Not only did they have to win, they also had to hope for a series of results in other groups also falling their way. Juventus got their win in the end and also scraped into the next stage.

DECEMBER 11TH

1897	Walsall	A	Second Division	1-1
1915	Everton	A	Lancashire Section Principal Tournament	0-2
1920	Bradford Park Avenue	A	First Division	4-2
1926	Sunderland	A	First Division	0-6
1929	Manchester City	A	Lancashire Senior Cup Semi-Final	1-3
1937	Bradford Park Avenue	A	Second Division	0-4
1943	Wrexham	H	Football League North (First Championship)	5-0
1948	Portsmouth	A	First Division	2-2
1954	Burnley	A	First Division	4-2
1965	Sunderland	A	First Division	3-2
1971	Stoke City	A	First Division	1-1

1972   George Best was wanted by Manchester City! Malcolm Allison claimed Best would be made more than welcome at Maine Road, although club chairman Eric Alexander said City had no intention of bidding for Best and that Allison was 'talking out of turn'.

| 1982 | Notts County | H | First Division | 4-0 |
| 1985 | Norwich City | A | Screen Sport Super Cup Group B | 1-1 |

United's last match in the Screen Sport Super Cup confirmed their elimination from the competition without having won a single game, collecting only two points from two draws. Their goal in this match was scored by Colin Gibson.

| 1993 | Newcastle United | A | FA Premier League | 1-1 |

DECEMBER 12TH

1891	Sheffield Wednesday	A	Football Alliance	4-2
1896	West Manchester	H	FA Cup 3rd Qualifying Round	7-0
1903	Small Heath	H	FA Cup Intermediate Round	1-1
1908	Leicester Fosse	H	First Division	4-2
1914	Sheffield United	H	First Division	1-2
1925	Sheffield United	H	First Division	1-2
1931	Bradford City	A	Second Division	3-4
1936	Middlesbrough	A	First Division	2-3
1942	Wrexham	A	Football League North (First Championship)	5-2
1953	Chelsea	A	First Division	1-3
1959	Nottingham Forest	A	First Division	5-1

While the first team were beating Forest 5-1 thanks to a hat-trick from Dennis Viollet and additional goals from Alex Dawson and Albert Scanlon, Wilf McGuinness broke his leg whilst playing for the reserves against Stoke City at Old Trafford. The break was sufficiently bad enough to end his career at the age of just 22 years, although Wilf did make an ill-fated attempt at a comeback. He was later found a position on the coaching staff and would ultimately go on to manage the club, although replacing Sir Matt Busby was a difficult job and he was later sacked, returning to trainer-coach with the reserves.

1964	West Bromwich Albion	A	First Division	1-1
1970	Manchester City	H	First Division	1-4
1984	Dundee United	A	UEFA Cup 3rd Round 2nd Leg	3-2

Manchester United had been held to a 2-2 draw at Old Trafford in the first leg and few gave much for their chances in the return at Tannadice, but goals from Mark Hughes, Arnold Muhren and an own goal from McGinnis enabled them to progress into the fourth round with a 5-4 aggregate win. Meanwhile Old Trafford hosted a European Cup-Winners' Cup match; Celtic had beaten Rapid Vienna 3-0 in a second-round second-leg tie at Parkhead to go through 4-3 on aggregate, but following crowd trouble at that game UEFA ordered the match replayed at Old Trafford. This time Celtic lost 1-0 to go out of the competition, although there was further trouble for Celtic when one of their fans attacked the Austrians' goalkeeper at the final whistle.

| 1987 | Oxford United | H | First Division | 3-1 |
| 1992 | Norwich City | H | FA Premier League | 1-0 |

DECEMBER 13TH

| 1890 | Small Heath | H | Football Alliance | 3-1 |
| 1902 | Burton United | H | FA Cup Intermediate Round | 1-1 |

This was United's fourth match in the competition so far, even though they had still to reach the first round! After beating Accrington Stanley, Oswaldtwistle Rovers and Southport Central, United had to face Burton and nearly suffered a shock, a goal from Billy Griffiths ensuring a replay which would also be played at Clayton.

1913	Bradford City	H	First Division	1-1
1919	Aston Villa	H	First Division	1-2
1924	Bradford City	H	Second Division	3-0
1930	Derby County	H	First Division	2-1
1941	Wrexham	A	Football League Northern Section (First Championship)	4-3
1947	Blackburn Rovers	A	First Division	1-1
1952	Liverpool	A	First Division	2-1
1958	Preston North End	A	First Division	4-3

United scored four goals for the third consecutive match; having beaten Birmingham 4-0 and Leicester 4-1 they now beat Preston 4-3 at Deepdale. United were to lose only three more games all season on their way to finishing as runners-up in the League behind Wolves.

1969	Liverpool	A	First Division	4-1
1975	Sheffield United	A	First Division	4-1
1980	Stoke City	H	First Division	2-2
1986	Aston Villa	A	First Division	3-3

DECEMBER 14TH

1895	Notts County	H	Second Division	3-0
1901	Lincoln City	H	FA Cup Intermediate Round	1-2
1907	Notts County	A	First Division	1-1
1912	Newcastle United	A	First Division	3-1

Enoch West scored all three of United's goals in the win at St James' Park. He would finish the season as top goalscorer with 21 goals to his credit.

1918	Port Vale	A	Lancashire Section Principal Tournament	1-3
1929	Everton	A	First Division	0-0
1935	Nottingham Forest	H	Second Division	5-0

United bounced back from a 4-1 defeat at Blackpool by beating strugglers Nottingham

Forest 5-0 at Old Trafford. United's goals were scored by Tommy Bamford (two), Tom Manley, George Mutch and Jack Rowley, and at the end of the season United finished as Second Division champions.

1940	Rochdale	H	North Regional League	3-4
1946	Blackburn Rovers	A	First Division	1-2
1957	Chelsea	H	First Division	0-1
1963	Sheffield Wednesday	H	First Division	3-1
1968	Liverpool	H	First Division	1-0

1972 George Best announced he was to return to training with Manchester United and was presumably off the transfer list according to United chairman Louis Edwards.

| 1974 | Orient | H | Second Division | 0-0 |
| 1985 | Aston Villa | A | First Division | 3-1 |

DECEMBER 15TH

| 1894 | Notts County | A | Second Division | 1-1 |

1898 Joe Spence born in Throckley in Northumberland. After starring in schools and army football he was signed by United in March 1919 and made his League debut in August the same year. Joe remained at Old Trafford for 14 years and made a then record 481 appearances in the League side. He was regularly top scorer and was awarded two caps by England. In May 1933 he was released and joined Chesterfield, with whom he won his only major honour at club level: a Third Division North championship medal. He retired as a player in 1938 but retained his links with Chesterfield, scouting for them after the Second World War. He died on 31st December 1966.

1900	Lincoln City	H	Second Division	4-1
1906	Preston North End	A	First Division	0-2
1917	Blackpool	A	Lancashire Section Principal Tournament	3-2
1923	Port Vale	A	Second Division	1-0
1928	Everton	H	First Division	1-1
1934	Bradford Park Avenue	A	Second Division	2-1
1945	Sunderland	H	Football League North	2-1
1951	West Bromwich Albion	H	First Division	5-1

On the same day, Joe Jordan was born in Carluke. Joe was playing in Scottish football for Morton when he was recommended to Leeds United, joining them for £15,000 in October 1970. Whilst at Leeds he won a League championship medal and appeared in two European finals before a £350,000 move to Old Trafford in January 1978. An instant crowd favourite, he made 125 appearances for United before a cut-price move to Italy and AC Milan for £250,000 in July 1981. After also playing for Verona he returned to England and played for Southampton and Bristol City before going into management.

1956	Birmingham City	A	First Division	1-3
1962	West Bromwich Albion	A	First Division	0-3
1965	Everton	H	First Division	3-0
1973	Coventry City	H	First Division	2-3
1979	Coventry City	A	First Division	2-1
1984	Queens Park Rangers	H	First Division	3-0
1990	Coventry City	A	First Division	2-2
1991	Chelsea	A	First Division	3-1
1997	Aston Villa	H	FA Premier League	1-0

DECEMBER 16TH

| 1893 | Aston Villa | H | First Division | 1-3 |

1899	Middlesbrough	H	Second Division	2-1
1903	Small Heath	A	FA Cup Intermediate Round Replay	1-1
1911	Oldham Athletic	A	First Division	2-2
1922	Stockport County	H	Second Division	1-0
1933	Swansea Town	A	Second Division	1-2

1936 Maurice Setters born in Honiton in Devon. Maurice was first spotted by Exeter City as a schoolboy and signed professional forms with the club in January 1954. A year later West Bromwich Albion paid £3,000 to take him to the Hawthorns, and his performances at half-back soon attracted glowing reports and interest from other clubs. In January 1960 he was signed by United for a fee of £30,000 and over the next four years more than repaid that fee, helping the club to the FA Cup in 1963. The emergence of Nobby Stiles threatened to restrict his first-team opportunities and he was sold to Stoke City in November 1964 for £30,000, later playing for Coventry and Charlton before moving into management. He was Jack Charlton's assistant with the Republic of Ireland from 1986.

1944	Wrexham	H	Football League North (First Championship)	1-0
1950	Fulham	A	First Division	2-2
1961	West Ham United	H	First Division	1-2
1964	Birmingham City	H	First Division	1-1
1967	Everton	H	First Division	3-1
1970	Aston Villa	H	League Cup Semi-Final 1st Leg	1-1

United were confidently expected to build up a healthy lead in the semi-final first leg against Third Division Aston Villa, especially as Villa's expected promotion charge had not taken place. As it was, Villa took the game to United and took the lead through Andy Lochhead four minutes before the half-time break, although Brian Kidd equalised soon after from Carlo Satori's cross. Despite all their efforts, United could not find a way through in the second half, leaving the tie delicately poised for the second leg.

1972	Crystal Palace	A	First Division	0-5
1978	Tottenham Hotspur	H	First Division	2-0
1983	Tottenham Hotspur	H	First Division	4-2

This was the first match to be televised live from Old Trafford: a Friday night clash with Spurs that would normally be played in front of a sell-out crowd of over 50,000 but which only attracted an attendance of 33,616. Both Arthur Graham and Kevin Moran scored twice to set up United's 4-2 victory.

| 1989 | Tottenham Hotspur | H | First Division | 0-1 |

DECEMBER 17TH

1892	Wolverhampton Wanderers	A	First Division	0-2
1898	Leicester Fosse	A	Second Division	0-1
1902	Burton United	H	FA Cup Intermediate Round Replay	3-1
1904	Burton United	A	Second Division	3-2
1910	Aston Villa	H	First Division	2-0
1921	Liverpool	A	First Division	1-2
1927	Arsenal	H	First Division	4-1
1932	Lincoln City	H	Second Division	4-1
1938	Brentford	A	First Division	5-2
1949	Derby County	H	First Division	0-1
1955	Birmingham City	H	First Division	2-1
1960	Blackburn Rovers	A	First Division	2-1
1966	West Bromwich Albion	A	First Division	4-3

| 1969 | Manchester City | H | League Cup Semi-Final 2nd Leg | 2-2 |

This was one of five clashes with City in the same season, the two League meetings being joined by pairings in the League Cup and FA Cup. City had already won the first leg 2-1 and were confident that they could hold their rivals sufficiently to progress on to Wembley. A crowd of 63,418 crammed into Old Trafford to see the latest instalment and saw a tentative start as both sides struggled to impose their authority. City settled first and took the lead through Ian Bowyer, reacting first after Neil Young's shot had been parried. Paul Edwards equalised six minutes later and then took the ball away from Francis Lee just as the City player was about to shoot. Denis Law then pulled United level on aggregate on the hour to set up a frantic final half-hour, but the winning goal came not from a rampant United but by City. Francis Lee shaped to take an indirect free-kick which whistled towards the goal; Alex Stepney should have left it but instead attempted a catch and dropped the ball almost in front of Mike Summerbee, who could not miss. United surged forwards for the remaining seven minutes but could not breach the City defence and so slipped out of the cup. They would gain their revenge in the FA Cup, but losing at the semi-final stage hurt.

1977	Nottingham Forest	H	First Division	0-4
1988	Arsenal	A	First Division	1-2
1994	Nottingham Forest	H	FA Premier League	1-2
1995	Liverpool	A	FA Premier League	0-2

DECEMBER 18TH

1909	Middlesbrough	A	First Division	2-1
1915	Bolton Wanderers	H	Lancashire Section Principal Tournament	1-0
1920	Newcastle United	H	First Division	2-0
1921	Jack Crompton born in Newton Heath. After a brief spell as an amateur, Jack

Crompton signed for United in January 1945 and eventually succeeded Jack Breedon as United's goalkeeper. A member of the side that won the FA Cup in 1948, he then vied with Reg Allen and Ray Wood for the first-team position until 1956, when he retired. He had a brief spell as coach at Luton before returning to United to assist Jimmy Murphy in the aftermath of Munich. In 1962 he accepted an offer to become manager of Luton but changed his mind and remained at Old Trafford. He left in 1971 to become manager of Barrow and after spells at Bury and Preston returned to United for a third spell in 1974. He left in 1981 following the arrival of Ron Atkinson.

1926	West Bromwich Albion	H	First Division	3-0
1943	Bolton Wanderers	H	Football League North (First Championship)	3-1
1948	Derby County	A	First Division	3-1
1954	Portsmouth	A	First Division	0-0
1965	Tottenham Hotspur	H	First Division	5-1
1971	Ipswich Town	A	First Division	0-0
1974	Middlesbrough	H	League Cup 5th Round Replay	3-0
1976	Arsenal	A	First Division	1-3
1982	Swansea City	A	First Division	0-0
1996	Sheffield Wednesday	A	FA Premier League	1-1

DECEMBER 19TH

1891	Ardwick	A	Football Alliance	2-2
1896	Notts County	A	Second Division	0-3
1903	Gainsborough Trinity	H	Second Division	4-2
1908	Woolwich Arsenal	A	First Division	1-0
1914	Aston Villa	A	First Division	3-3

1925	West Bromwich Albion	A	First Division	1-5
1931	Bristol City	H	Second Division	0-1
1936	West Bromwich Albion	H	First Division	2-2
1942	Bolton Wanderers	A	Football League North (First Championship)	2-0
1953	Liverpool	H	First Division	5-1
1959	West Bromwich Albion	H	First Division	2-3
1970	Arsenal	H	First Division	1-3

1972 United announced they had sacked manager Frank O'Farrell, assistant manager Malcolm Musgrove and chief scout John Aston, and that George Best would not be playing for the club again as they had placed him on the transfer list. What they did not know was that George Best had decided he wouldn't be playing for anyone again, having just written a letter to the club announcing his retirement!

| 1983 | Oxford United | A | Milk Cup 4th Round 2nd Replay | 1-2 [aet] |

Oxford may have been on their way to winning the Second Division championship, but United should have been able to overcome their challenge in the Milk Cup tie. Instead the tie went to three games before Oxford won in extra time.

1987	Portsmouth	A	First Division	2-1
1992	Chelsea	A	FA Premier League	1-1
1993	Aston Villa	H	FA Premier League	3-1

DECEMBER 20TH

1902	Port Vale	A	Second Division	1-1
1913	Blackburn Rovers	A	First Division	1-0
1919	Newcastle United	H	First Division	2-1
1924	Port Vale	A	Second Division	1-2
1930	Leeds United	A	First Division	0-5

United's 21 away games would eventually bring them only one win (at Sunderland) and two draws, but far more alarming was a porous defence which leaked in 78 goals in those games. As well as the five against Leeds, they conceded five at West Ham, Leicester and Blackpool, six at Chelsea and Derby and seven at Aston Villa. They also conceded 37 goals at home, and not surprisingly finished the season at the foot of the table.

1941	Manchester City	A	Football League Northern Section (First Championship)	1-2
1947	Middlesbrough	H	First Division	2-1
1952	Chelsea	A	First Division	3-2
1958	Chelsea	A	First Division	3-2

Bobby Charlton scored in his sixth consecutive game as United won at Stamford Bridge 3-2. United's other goals were scored by Fred Goodwin and an own goal.

1975	Wolverhampton Wanderers	H	First Division	1-0
1980	Arsenal	A	First Division	1-2
1986	Leicester City	H	First Division	2-0

DECEMBER 21ST

1895	Darwen	A	Second Division	0-3
1901	Port Vale	H	Second Division	1-0
1903	Small Heath	N	FA Cup Intermediate Round 2nd Replay	1-1
1907	Manchester City	H	First Division	3-1

Sandy Turnbull had an eventful day playing against his former club, scoring twice to set up the victory and then getting sent off. He thus became the first United player to be dismissed in the local derby.

1912	Oldham Athletic	H	First Division	0-0
1918	Port Vale	H	Lancashire Section Principal Tournament	5-1
1929	Leeds United	H	First Division	3-1
1940	Bury	A	North Regional League	1-4
1957	Leicester City	H	First Division	4-0
1963	Everton	A	First Division	0-4
1968	Southampton	A	First Division	0-2
1974	York City	A	Second Division	1-0

United's relegation into the Second Division at the end of the 1973-74 season was initially viewed as a disaster, with nothing less than an immediate return to the First Division being acceptable. As United ran away with the title, there were several benefits, not least the attendances at Old Trafford, which actually improved. Everywhere they went United were a major attraction, with 15,567 cramming into Bootham Crescent to see Stuart Pearson score the only goal of the game.

1985	Arsenal	H	First Division	0-1
1996	Sunderland	H	FA Premier League	5-0
1997	Newcastle United	A	FA Premier League	1-0

DECEMBER 22ND

1894	Lincoln City	H	Second Division	3-0
1900	Chesterfield	A	Second Division	1-2
1906	Newcastle United	H	First Division	1-3
1917	Burnley	A	Lancashire Section Principal Tournament	5-0
1923	Port Vale	H	Second Division	5-0
1928	Portsmouth	A	First Division	0-3
1934	Plymouth Argyle	H	Second Division	3-1
1945	Sunderland	A	Football League North	2-4
1951	Newcastle United	A	First Division	2-2

1956   United had been due to face West Bromwich Albion at Old Trafford in the League, but owing to dense fog the train carrying the visitors did not ferry them to the ground until 4 p.m., almost two hours after the game had been scheduled to kick off. By the time Albion arrived at the ground, the game had been called off and the crowd had all gone home! The match was finally played at the end of the season, by which time United had been crowned as champions.

1969   Mark Robins born in Ashton-under-Lyme. Signed by United straight from school as a trainee in July 1986 and upgraded to the professional ranks in September 1986, he was an exceptional goal-taker and a useful man to have on the bench. This was ably demonstrated in the FA Cup semi-final replay in 1990 when he netted the winner to take United to Wembley, and he collected a winners' medal after appearing as a substitute against Crystal Palace. His desire for more regular football prompted a transfer request in January 1992, later joining Norwich City for £800,000 in the summer of that year. Whilst his career has seldom hit the heights promised in 1990, he remains a deadly predator around the penalty area, and in January 1995 he joined Leicester City for £1 million.

1973	Liverpool	A	First Division	0-2
1978	Bolton Wanderers	A	First Division	0-3
1979	Nottingham Forest	H	First Division	3-0
1984	Ipswich Town	H	First Division	3-0
1990	Wimbledon	A	First Division	3-1

DECEMBER 23RD

1884   Ernie Payne born in Worcester. Ernie made only 11 appearances for Manchester United, usually when Billy Meredith was on international duty, but he is assured a place in sports record books, for he was also an exceptional cyclist. He was a member of the Worcester St John's Cycling Club and won a gold medal at the 1908 Olympics held at White City in London in the Cycling Team Pursuit along with Ben Jones, Clarrie Kingsbury and Leon Meredith, the first time the competition had been featured in the Olympics. Ernie died in Worcester on 10th September 1961.

1893	Preston North End	A	First Division	0-2
1899	Chesterfield	A	Second Division	1-2
1905	Burton United	A	Second Division	2-0
1911	Bolton Wanderers	H	First Division	2-0
1916	Oldham Athletic	H	Lancashire Section Principal Tournament	3-2
1922	Stockport County	A	Second Division	0-1
1933	Millwall	H	Second Division	1-1
1939	Wrexham	H	War Regional League, Western Division	5-1
1944	Wrexham	A	Football League North (First Championship)	1-2
1950	Bolton Wanderers	H	First Division	2-3

1962   Terry Gibson born in Walthamstow. Signed by Spurs in 1979, he was unable to break into the first team on a regular basis and was sold to Coventry for £100,000 in August 1983. There he blossomed into an exceptional goalscorer, averaging a goal every other game, and his televised hat-trick against Liverpool in December 1983 prompted speculation he could be on the move to a bigger club, a deal that finally came off for £600,000 in January 1986 when he arrived at Old Trafford. Competition for places at United was just as tough as it had been at Spurs and Terry struggled to hold down a place, scoring only one goal before a £200,000 move to Wimbledon in August 1987. He won an FA Cup winners' medal in 1988 and was released on a free transfer in 1993.

1967	Leicester City	A	First Division	2-2
1970	Aston Villa	A	League Cup Semi-Final 2nd Leg	1-2

Since the League Cup had switched to a single match final at Wembley, two Third Division sides had beaten First Division opposition to win the cup: QPR in 1967 and Swindon in 1969. Now, two years on, many thought it might be Villa's turn to upset the form book, and a crowd of 58,667 packed into Villa Park to see the Third Division side overcome a United team that boasted some of the biggest names in football: Charlton, Best, Law and Crerand were all on duty. Despite Brian Kidd's goal for United, Villa managed to score twice to make it to the final where they would face Spurs.

1972	Leeds United	H	First Division	1-1
1975	Everton	A	First Division	1-1
1989	Liverpool	A	First Division	0-0

DECEMBER 24TH

1869   Matthew Gillespie born in Strathclyde. He joined Newton Heath in November 1896 having previously played for Strathclyde, Leith Athletic and Lincoln City and scored a hat-trick in his first game for the club, a friendly against Fairfield. He went on to give the Heathens four seasons of service, scoring 21 goals in his 89 outings.

1892	Sheffield Wednesday	H	First Division	1-5
1894	Port Vale	A	Second Division	5-2
1898	Darwen	H	Second Division	9-0
1904	Liverpool	H	Second Division	3-1

1910	Sunderland	A	First Division	2-1
1921	Liverpool	H	First Division	0-0
1927	Liverpool	A	First Division	0-2
1932	Swansea Town	A	Second Division	1-2
1938	Middlesbrough	H	First Division	1-1
1949	West Bromwich Albion	A	First Division	2-1

1952 Tony Young born in Urmston. Signed by United straight from school, he was made a professional in December 1969 and broke into the side on a regular basis in season 1971-72 in midfield, although he was later used as a full-back. He won a Second Division championship medal in 1975 and joined Charlton in January 1976, subsequently playing for York before drifting into non-League football with Bangor.

1955	West Bromwich Albion	A	First Division	4-1
1960	Chelsea	A	First Division	2-1
1995	Leeds United	A	FA Premier League	1-3

DECEMBER 25TH

1893	Ardwick	H	Friendly	2-1
1895	Manchester City	A	Friendly	1-3
1896	Manchester City	H	Second Division	2-1
1897	Manchester City	A	Second Division	1-0
1901	Lincoln City	A	Second Division	0-2
1902	Manchester City	H	Second Division	1-1
1903	Chesterfield	H	Second Division	3-1
1905	Chelsea	H	Second Division	0-0
1906	Liverpool	H	First Division	0-0
1907	Bury	H	First Division	2-1
1908	Newcastle United	A	First Division	1-2
1909	Sheffield Wednesday	H	First Division	0-3
1911	Bradford City	H	First Division	0-1
1912	Chelsea	A	First Division	4-1
1913	Everton	H	First Division	0-1
1915	Manchester City	A	Lancashire Section Principal Tournament	1-2
1917	Manchester City	A	Friendly	2-0
1918	Manchester City	A	Friendly	1-2
1920	Aston Villa	A	First Division	4-3
1922	West Ham United	H	Second Division	1-2
1923	Barnsley	H	Second Division	1-2
1924	Middlesbrough	A	Second Division	1-1
1925	Bolton Wanderers	H	First Division	2-1
1926	Tottenham Hotspur	A	First Division	1-1
1928	Sheffield United	H	First Division	1-1
1929	Birmingham	H	First Division	0-0

After only 15 minutes of play United forward Jimmy Hanson broke his fibia. It was an injury which ended his career, although he was kept on United's books until the end of the season in 1930-31.

1930	Bolton Wanderers	A	First Division	1-3
1931	Wolverhampton Wanderers	H	Second Division	3-2
1933	Grimsby Town	H	Second Division	1-3
1934	Notts County	H	Second Division	2-1
1936	Bolton Wanderers	H	First Division	1-0
1939	Manchester City	A	Friendly	1-1

1940	Stockport County	A	North Regional League	3-1
1941	Manchester City	H	Football League Northern Section (First Championship)	2-2
1942	Bolton Wanderers	H	Football League North (First Championship)	4-0
1943	Bolton Wanderers	A	Football League North (First Championship)	3-1
1945	Sheffield United	A	Football League North	0-1
1946	Bolton Wanderers	A	First Division	2-2
1947	Portsmouth	H	First Division	3-2
1948	Liverpool	H	First Division	0-0
1950	Sunderland	A	First Division	1-2
1951	Fulham	H	First Division	3-2
1952	Blackpool	A	First Division	0-0
1953	Sheffield Wednesday	H	First Division	5-2

United gave their fans a Christmas Day present to remember, with Tommy Taylor scoring a hat-trick and additional goals from Jackie Blanchflower and Dennis Viollet in front of a crowd of 27,123.

| 1957 | Luton Town | H | First Division | 3-0 |

The very last Christmas Day fixture United played saw them win 3-0 at home to Luton thanks to goals from Bobby Charlton, Duncan Edwards and Tommy Taylor in front of a crowd of 39,444. After the game both United and Luton travelled down on the same train in order to play the return match at Kenilworth Road on Boxing Day!

DECEMBER 26TH

1891	Small Heath	H	Football Alliance	3-3
1892	Preston North End	A	First Division	1-2
1894	Walsall	A	Second Division	2-1
1896	Blackpool	H	Second Division	2-0
1898	Manchester City	A	Second Division	0-4
1899	Grimsby Town	A	Second Division	7-0

Newton Heath registered their biggest ever away win in the Football League with goals from William Bryant (two), Joe Cassidy (two), William Jackson, Robert Parkinson and an own goal. Two of the goalscorers, Bryant and Parkinson, were suspended and placed on the transfer list by the club in March 1900, never to play another game for the Heathens.

1900	Blackpool	H	Second Division	4-0
1902	Blackpool	H	Second Division	2-2
1903	Burton United	A	Second Division	2-2
1904	Chesterfield	H	Second Division	3-0
1906	Aston Villa	A	First Division	0-2
1908	Newcastle United	H	First Division	1-0
1910	Woolwich Arsenal	H	First Division	5-0
1911	Bradford City	A	First Division	1-0
1912	Chelsea	H	First Division	4-2
1913	Everton	A	First Division	0-5
1914	Liverpool	A	First Division	1-1
1916	Manchester City	H	Friendly	1-0
1919	Liverpool	H	First Division	0-0
1921	Burnley	H	First Division	0-1
1922	West Ham United	A	Second Division	2-0
1923	Barnsley	A	Second Division	0-1
1924	Middlesbrough	H	Second Division	2-0

1927	Blackburn Rovers	H	First Division	1-1
1928	Sheffield United	A	First Division	1-6
1929	Birmingham	A	First Division	1-0
1930	Bolton Wanderers	H	First Division	1-1
1931	Wolverhampton Wanderers	A	Second Division	0-7

This defeat equalled United's heaviest ever League defeats, having previously been suffered against Blackburn Rovers in 1926 and against Aston Villa the previous year.

1932	Plymouth Argyle	A	Second Division	3-2
1933	Grimsby Town	A	Second Division	3-7
1934	Notts County	A	Second Division	0-1
1935	Barnsley	H	Second Division	1-1
1936	Wolverhampton Wanderers	A	First Division	1-3
1938	Leicester City	H	First Division	3-0
1939	Manchester City	H	Friendly	3-1
1942	Chester	H	Football League North (Second Championship)	3-0
1944	Sheffield United	A	Football League North (Second Championship)	4-3
1945	Sheffield United	H	Football League North	2-3
1946	Bolton Wanderers	H	First Division	1-0
1948	Liverpool	A	First Division	2-0
1949	Arsenal	H	First Division	2-0
1950	Sunderland	H	First Division	3-5
1951	Fulham	A	First Division	3-3
1952	Blackpool	H	First Division	2-1
1953	Sheffield Wednesday	A	First Division	1-0
1955	Charlton Athletic	H	First Division	5-1
1956	Cardiff City	H	First Division	3-1
1957	Luton Town	A	First Division	2-2
1958	Aston Villa	H	First Division	2-1
1959	Burnley	H	First Division	1-2
1960	Chelsea	H	First Division	6-0
1961	Nottingham Forest	H	First Division	6-3
1962	Fulham	A	First Division	1-0
1963	Burnley	A	First Division	1-6
1964	Sheffield United	A	First Division	1-0
1966	Sheffield United	A	First Division	1-2
1967	Wolverhampton Wanderers	H	First Division	4-0
1968	Arsenal	A	First Division	0-3
1969	Wolverhampton Wanderers	H	First Division	0-0
1970	Derby County	A	First Division	4-4
1972	Derby County	A	First Division	1-3
1973	Sheffield United	H	First Division	1-2
1974	West Bromwich Albion	H	Second Division	2-1
1977	Everton	A	First Division	6-2

Goals from Lou Macari (two), Steve Coppell, Jimmy Greenhoff, Gordon Hill and Sammy McIlroy enabled United to register one of the best away performances in many a year in this win at Goodison Park.

1978	Liverpool	H	First Division	0-3
1979	Liverpool	A	First Division	0-2
1980	Liverpool	H	First Division	0-0
1983	Coventry City	A	First Division	1-1
1984	Stoke City	A	First Division	1-2

1985	Everton	A	First Division	1-3
1986	Liverpool	A	First Division	1-0
1987	Newcastle United	A	First Division	0-1
1988	Nottingham Forest	H	First Division	2-0
1989	Aston Villa	A	First Division	0-3
1990	Norwich City	H	First Division	3-0
1991	Oldham Athletic	A	First Division	6-3

Both Brian McClair and Dennis Irwin scored twice, the latter player against his previous club, in the 6-3 win at Boundary Park. United's other goals were scored by Andrei Kanchelskis and Ryan Giggs.

1992	Sheffield Wednesday	A	FA Premier League	3-3
1993	Blackburn Rovers	H	FA Premier League	1-1
1994	Chelsea	A	FA Premier League	3-2
1996	Nottingham Forest	A	FA Premier League	4-0
1997	Everton	H	FA Premier League	2-0

DECEMBER 27TH

1890	Bootle	H	Football Alliance	2-1
1897	Gainsborough Trinity	A	Second Division	1-2
1902	Barnsley	H	Second Division	2-1
1909	Sheffield Wednesday	A	First Division	1-4
1910	Bradford City	A	First Division	0-1
1913	Sheffield Wednesday	H	First Division	2-1

1915 The *Athletic News*, which had been instrumental in bringing the Football Association's attentions to the events surrounding the League match between United and Liverpool on April 2nd 1915, carried the result of the investigation. A total of eight players were handed life bans from the game after being held guilty of fixing the result, a 2-0 win for United. (They were not found guilty since the investigation was not carried out in a court of law, although the FA's investigators were prominent lawyers. The players, however, were refused access to legal representation.) The players named were Sandy Turnbull, Enoch West and Arthur Whalley from United and Jackie Sheldon (a former United player), Tommy Miller, Tom Fairfoul and Bob Purcell from Liverpool. Another player from Chester was also implicated. Of the United players named, only West had actually played in the game and it was he who continued to protest his innocence of any wrongdoing, instigating a libel action against the *Athletic News*, which he lost, and appealing to have the ban lifted, which he also lost. According to the FA, the reason why the game had been fixed was so that the players could earn quick money by betting on the score ending as a 2-0 win to United. With League football about to be suspended owing to the First World War and their livelihoods soon to disappear, perhaps the chance of easy money seemed too good a chance to miss. The win, which was allowed to stand, enabled United to lift themselves out of a relegation spot. The other players, innocent or not, made no comment, and at the end of the war their bans were lifted in recognition of their efforts during the war (Turnbull lost his life in France in 1917). West, however, did not have his ban lifted until 1945, perhaps to spite his efforts to get the ban overturned. By then, of course, he was too old to play and too bitter towards the game he had once graced.

| 1919 | Newcastle United | A | First Division | 1-2 |
| 1920 | Aston Villa | H | First Division | 1-3 |

The record crowd for a League clash at Old Trafford was established when 70,504 spectators turned out for the holiday clash with Aston Villa, even though both clubs were occupying mid-table positions in the League. One or two sources claim the gate was nearer 72,000, although this has since been downgraded. What all sources agree on, however, is the result: a 3-1 win for the visitors, with Harrison scoring United's only goal.

1921	Burnley	A	First Division	2-4
1924	Leicester City	A	Second Division	0-3
1926	Tottenham Hotspur	H	First Division	2-1
1930	Aston Villa	A	First Division	0-7

This equalled United's record defeat which had been set against Blackburn Rovers in 1926. In 1931 the record was again equalled with a 7-0 reverse against Wolverhampton Wanderers.

1937	Nottingham Forest	H	Second Division	4-3
1938	Leicester City	A	First Division	1-1
1941	Bolton Wanderers	H	Football League Northern Section (Second Championship)	3-1
1943	Halifax Town	H	Football League North (Second Championship)	6-2
1947	Portsmouth	A	First Division	3-1
1949	Arsenal	A	First Division	0-0
1954	Aston Villa	H	First Division	0-1
1955	Charlton Athletic	A	First Division	0-3
1958	Aston Villa	A	First Division	2-0
1965	West Bromwich Albion	H	First Division	1-1
1966	Sheffield United	H	First Division	2-0
1969	Sunderland	A	First Division	1-1
1971	Coventry City	H	First Division	2-2
1975	Burnley	H	First Division	2-1
1976	Everton	H	First Division	4-0
1977	Leicester City	H	First Division	3-1
1980	West Bromwich Albion	A	First Division	1-3
1982	Sunderland	H	First Division	0-0
1983	Notts County	H	First Division	3-3

Nine Notts County players were booked in the League meeting at Old Trafford, seven of them in one go when they refused to retreat the required ten yards at a free-kick!

1986	Norwich City	H	First Division	0-1
1995	Newcastle United	H	FA Premier League	2-0

Manchester United reduced the gap between them and Newcastle to seven points with this 2-0 win at Old Trafford. Goals from Andy Cole and Roy Keane secured the points in a passionate game, with Eric Cantona the man of the match.

DECEMBER 28TH

1889	Darwen	A	Football Alliance	1-4
1896	Leicester Fosse	A	Second Division	0-1
1907	Preston North End	A	First Division	0-0
1912	Manchester City	A	First Division	2-0

1914 John Robson was appointed manager of United, the first such man with the title. Whilst Ernest Mangnall is widely regarded as United's first manager, his actual title was that of secretary, as was those of his successors, T.J. Wallworth and J.J. Bentley. With the arrival of Robson, Bentley concentrated on secretarial duties, allowing Robson a free hand on all team matters. Of course, the First World War, then in full swing, would lead to the suspension of League football in 1915, and in 1916 Bentley resigned as secretary, with Robson assuming his responsibilities as well during the difficult war years. John Robson remained as manager until October 1921, when he resigned owing to ill-health, but he remained at United in the position of assistant manager to John Chapman.

1918	Blackpool	A	Lancashire Section Principal Tournament	2-2
1920	Corinthians	H	Friendly	Score unknown

Barely one day after registering their highest League attendance figure at Old Trafford, United played a friendly against the leading amateur side of the day, the Corinthians. Despite fielding their entire first team, only 3,000 fans turned out to see the game.

1925	Leicester City	A	First Division	3-1
1926	Arsenal	A	First Division	0-1
1929	Newcastle United	H	First Division	5-0
1935	Plymouth Argyle	H	Second Division	3-2
1936	Bolton Wanderers	A	First Division	4-0
1937	Nottingham Forest	A	Second Division	3-2
1940	Blackburn Rovers	H	North Regional League	9-0
1946	Grimsby Town	A	First Division	0-0
1954	Aston Villa	A	First Division	1-2
1957	Manchester City	A	First Division	2-2
1959	Burnley	A	First Division	4-1
1963	Burnley	H	First Division	5-1
1964	Sheffield United	H	First Division	1-1
1974	Oldham Athletic	A	Second Division	0-1
1982	Coventry City	A	First Division	0-3
1987	Everton	H	First Division	2-1
1992	Coventry City	H	FA Premier League	5-0
1994	Leicester City	H	FA Premier League	1-1
1996	Leeds United	H	FA Premier League	1-0

DECEMBER 29TH

1894	Lincoln City	A	Second Division	0-3
1900	Glossop	H	Second Division	3-0
1906	Bristol City	H	First Division	0-0

1907 Jack Breedon born near Barnsley. He joined United in 1935 and remained with the club until October 1945, but only managed to appear in 39 League games. He had begun his career with Barnsley in 1928 and joined United from Sheffield Wednesday. After leaving the club he joined Burnley and a year later became manager of Halifax, later briefly serving Bradford Park Avenue in the same capacity. He then scouted for Leeds.

1917	Burnley	H	Lancashire Section Principal Tournament	1-0
1923	Bradford City	A	Second Division	0-0
1928	Leicester City	A	First Division	1-2
1934	Bradford City	A	Second Division	0-2
1945	Middlesbrough	H	Football League North	4-1
1951	Bolton Wanderers	H	First Division	1-0
1956	Portsmouth	A	First Division	3-1

1970 With United lying in 18th place in the First Division and having recently been dumped out of the League Cup at the semi-final stage by Third Division Aston Villa, there had been mounting speculation as to the fate of manager Wilf McGuinness. The board had recently given him a vote of confidence, but last night had informed him that he was to be relieved of his position of manager, with Sir Matt Busby returning to the role in order to restore some morale to the side and McGuinness reverting to reserve-team trainer.

1973	Ipswich Town	H	First Division	2-0
1979	Arsenal	H	First Division	3-0
1984	Chelsea	A	First Division	3-1
1990	Aston Villa	H	First Division	1-1
1991	Leeds United	A	First Division	1-1
1993	Oldham Athletic	A	FA Premier League	5-2
1997	Coventry City	A	FA Premier League	2-3

DECEMBER 30TH

1899	Gainsborough Trinity	A	Second Division	1-0
1905	Bristol City	A	Second Division	1-1
1911	Manchester City	H	First Division	0-0
1916	Preston North End	A	Lancashire Section Principal Tournament	2-3
1922	Hull City	A	Second Division	1-2

1929 Tommy McNulty born in Salford. Signed by United as an amateur in May 1945, he was upgraded to the professional ranks in June 1947. Initially introduced to the side as a full-back partner to Roger Byrne, he won a championship medal in 1951-52, but the emerging talents of Bill Foulkes halted his progress and he was sold to Liverpool for £7,000 in February 1954. He remained at Liverpool for four years before moving into non-League football.

1933	Plymouth Argyle	H	Second Division	0-3
1944	Oldham Athletic	A	Football League North (Second Championship)	4-3
1967	Wolverhampton Wanderers	A	First Division	3-2

1972 Tommy Docherty was appointed manager of United, although he was still officially manager of the Scottish national side. Although his career as a club manager (with Chelsea, Aston Villa, QPR, Rotherham and Porto) had been a mixture of highs and lows, he was undoubtedly the man United wanted after the sacking of Frank O'Farrell. Docherty's assistant would be former United player Pat Crerand.

1978	West Bromwich Albion	H	First Division	3-5
1989	Wimbledon	A	First Division	2-2
1995	Queens Park Rangers	H	FA Premier League	2-1

DECEMBER 31ST

1892	Derby County	H	First Division	7-1
1898	Gainsborough Trinity	H	Second Division	6-1
1904	Port Vale	H	Second Division	6-1

1908 James Brown born in Kilmarnock. Although he had played junior football in Scotland he was not signed by any club and at the age of 17 emigrated to America. He represented the USA in the 1930 World Cup as they reached the semi-final stage, where he scored their consolation goal in the 6-1 defeat by Argentina. He was signed by United whilst aboard the liner Caledonia in September 1932 and spent two years at the club before moving on to Brentford in May 1934. He later played for Spurs, Guildford City and Clydebank before returning to the States in 1948.

1910	Blackburn Rovers	A	First Division	0-1
1921	Newcastle United	A	First Division	0-3
1927	Middlesbrough	A	First Division	2-1
1932	Stoke City	A	Second Division	0-0

1933 Jeff Whitefoot born in Cheadle in Cheshire. Signed by United straight from school in 1950, he signed professional forms in January 1951, by which time he had already made his League debut. Indeed, his appearance against Portsmouth in April 1950 made him United's youngest post-war player at the age of only 16 years and 105 days. He became a regular in the side by 1953-54 at right half-back and won a League championship medal in 1955-56 but eventually lost his place to Eddie Colman. In November 1957 he was on the verge of signing for Nottingham Forest when a late offer from Grimsby came along and he signed for the Mariners, later switching to Forest in July 1958 and helping them win the FA Cup in 1959. He spent ten years at Forest before injury forced him to retire in 1968.

| 1938 | Birmingham City | A | First Division | 3-3 |

1941   Alex Ferguson born in Scotland. Alex spent his playing career with St Mirren and Glasgow Rangers and began his managerial career with East Stirling. He returned to St Mirren and guided them to the Scottish First Division championship before taking over at Aberdeen in 1978. He enabled Aberdeen to break the stranglehold of Glasgow giants Rangers and Celtic, taking Aberdeen to three Scottish League titles, the Scottish Cup four times and the League Cup once, as well as success in the European Cup-Winners' Cup. After rejecting numerous offers he accepted an invitation to take over from Ron Atkinson at United in 1986, and after a tentative start, during which there was considerable speculation about his future, turned United into the team of the 1990s. He has won four League titles, the FA Cup three times, the League Cup once and the European Cup-Winners' Cup in 1991. However, the one trophy he desires more than any other, the European Cup, continues to elude him.

1949	Manchester City	A	First Division	2-1
1955	Manchester City	H	First Division	2-1
1960	Manchester City	H	First Division	5-1

On the same day, Steve Bruce was born in Northumberland. After failing trials with five clubs Steve began his professional career with Gillingham in 1978. He was sold to Norwich for £135,000 in 1984 and helped them win the Milk Cup in his first season. In December 1987 he cost United £825,000 and subsequently formed a solid partnership with Gary Pallister at the heart of the United defence. By the time he was given a free transfer in 1996 he had helped the club win three Premiership titles, the League Cup, two FA Cups, the European Cup-Winners' Cup and three Charity Shields, although the closest he came to international honours was a single appearance for the England B team. He subsequently joined Birmingham City.

1966	Leeds United	H	First Division	0-0
1977	Coventry City	A	First Division	0-3
1983	Stoke City	H	First Division	1-0
1994	Southampton	A	FA Premier League	2-2